Your Career: How to Make It Happen

Levitt

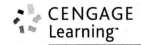 CENGAGE
Learning™

Australia • Brazil • Japan • Korea • Mexico • Singapore • Spain • United Kingdom • United States

Your Career: How to Make It Happen

Levitt

Executive Editors:
Michele Baird

Maureen Staudt

Michael Stranz

Project Development Manager:
Linda deStefano

Senior Marketing Coordinators:
Sara Mercurio

Lindsay Shapiro

Production/Manufacturing Manager:
Donna M. Brown

PreMedia Services Supervisor:
Rebecca A. Walker

Rights & Permissions Specialist:
Kalina Hintz

Cover Image:
Getty Images*

* Unless otherwise noted, all cover images used
by Custom Solutions, a part of Cengage Learning,
have been supplied courtesy of Getty Images with
the exception of the Earthview cover image, which
has been supplied by the National Aeronautics
and Space Administration (NASA).

ISBN-13: 978-0-324-57207-0

ISBN-10: 0-324-57207-7

Cengage Learning
5191 Natorp Boulevard
Mason, Ohio 45040
USA

Cengage Learning is a leading provider of customized learning solutions with
office locations around the globe, including Singapore, the United Kingdom,
Australia, Mexico, Brazil, and Japan. Locate your local office at:
international.cengage.com/region

Cengage Learning products are represented in Canada by Nelson Education, Ltd.

For your lifelong learning solutions, visit **custom.cengage.com**

Visit our corporate website at **cengage.com**

Printed in the United States of America

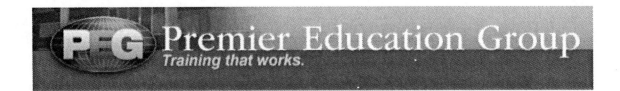

Congratulations on your decision and commitment to excellence in your chosen career.

As a partner in your success, be assured that our organization will make every effort to assist you in achieving your goals.

Success always requires a decision.

I urge you to focus on the information and skills within this text. This text has been designed to help your transition into a great career.

The next step is the culmination of all of your hard work.

"Soar high in all your future endeavors."

Gary Camp

CEO – Premier Education Group

table of *Contents*

APPENDICES

career action *Assignments*

PART 1   PLANNING YOUR CAREER

PART 2   YOUR JOB SEARCH

PART 3   CAREER SEARCH DOCUMENTS

PART 4 YOUR INTERVIEW

PART 5   AFTER YOUR INTERVIEW

personal best *Features*

Dear Reader:

Welcome to *Your Career: How to Make It Happen*—The Career Power Kit!

Typically, 97 percent of the students in my classes secure jobs using the techniques in this text—before they finish the course! This text is your career power kit. It contains all the tools you need to assess, plan, and succeed in achieving your job search and career goals.

Get the Competitive Advantage

Did you know that people who develop sound job search and career planning skills are **80 percent more successful** in landing jobs than those who don't develop these skills? *Your Career: How to Make It Happen* provides the career management/job search tools that give you this huge competitive edge!

Learn How to Make Your Career Happen

This text provides the most thorough, practical career management and job search advice and guidelines available on the topic today. These guidelines offer big career dividends for you—jobs, promotions, and career success! *Your Career: How to Make It Happen* shows you how to:

- Develop proactive success attitudes.
- Increase your self-motivation and confidence-building skills.
- Identify and focus on your job strengths and match them to the best possible job and career targets.
- Organize your job search and identify the best potential employers.
- Develop a strong career network.
- Prepare resumes and cover letters that get positive results.
- Prepare professional electronic resumes and cover letters.
- Develop a career portfolio that demonstrates your job readiness.
- Get interviews and interview skillfully.
- Negotiate for a fair salary and benefits package.
- Use the Internet to increase your career knowledge and employment potential.
- Take charge of your career by monitoring workplace trends and succeeding in the changing workplace.
- Change jobs or careers successfully and seek a promotion professionally.

The success of these tools and guidelines keeps *Your Career: How to Make It Happen* in high demand. This sixth edition clearly reflects the needs of the twenty-first-century workplace.

Take charge of your career with these practical tools. Use them to gain a competitive advantage and achieve your full career potential.

Sincerely,

Julie Levitt

Julie Levitt

This text provides the necessary job and career management tools to help you reach your full career potential. You will develop essential career success skills and gain a competitive advantage in the workplace through class activities, direct practice in the business community, and Internet activities.

KEY FEATURES OF THIS TEXT

The key features of *Your Career: How to Make It Happen* are listed below. The graphic icons you see here are also used throughout the text to signal types of reader activities.

Career Action—Your Competitive Edge: Career Action assignments represent a major objective of the textbook title—the *How to Make It Happen* part. You are the one who ultimately makes your career happen, and the hands-on assignments in each chapter guide you clearly and explicitly in the right direction. These assignments take you into the business community to learn about employers and jobs in your field, provide important practice in meeting and interacting with business people, and focus on the activities necessary to achieve your immediate and future career goals. Some of these assignments include the following:

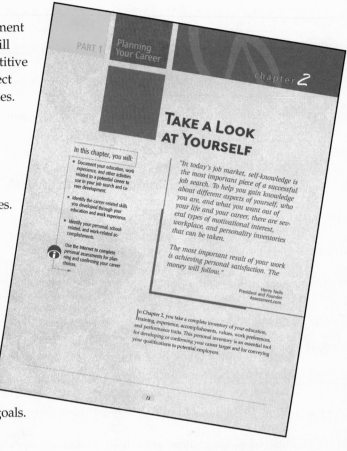

- Effective job search organization
- Development of essential career Internet skills, such as networking electronically and finding information on careers, jobs, and employers
- Preparation of winning resumes, cover letters, and career portfolios
- Actual career networking to develop contacts and access information
- Interview practice

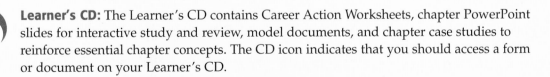

CAREER ACTION 1-4

Improve Assertiveness

Directions: Review the techniques for developing assertiveness just discussed. Select at least two activities for practicing assertiveness—exercises provided in the chapter or others more pertinent to your needs. Access your Learner's CD to write out a plan for improving your assertiveness skills through the exercises you have chosen, and follow through with your plan.

File your assertiveness improvement plan in your Career Management Files Binder.

Learner's CD: The Learner's CD contains Career Action Worksheets, chapter PowerPoint slides for interactive study and review, model documents, and chapter case studies to reinforce essential chapter concepts. The CD icon indicates that you should access a form or document on your Learner's CD.

Instructor's Resource CD: This CD offers a complete and customizable set of instructor resources, including teaching suggestions, chapter tests, chapter PowerPoint slides, case studies with solutions, teaching masters, and more.

Personal Best Features: Each chapter contains an important "Personal Best" feature that highlights a strategic application or a key contemporary issue. These features focus on career management and communication skills that will help you achieve your personal best.

Internet Assignments: *Your Career: How to Make It Happen* emphasizes the important role the Internet plays in successful job search/career planning by integrating guided Internet assignments throughout. This icon signals that an assignment involves use of the Internet.

Success Tips: More than 100 easy Success Tips highlight the key steps you can take to achieve full job satisfaction and career potential.

Employer Quotes: Quotes from leading employers and career experts introduce each chapter and highlight important concepts from the employer's perspective.

Career Management Files Binder: A pivotal career management component of the textbook is the ongoing development of your own set of career management and reference documents. As you complete key Career Action assignments, you will be directed to save those considered the most essential as references throughout your lifetime career. The binder icon indicates that you should file the completed assignment in your Career Management Files Binder.

Your Career Advantage Companion Web Site: The *Your Career: How to Make It Happen* Web site provides convenient access to over 100 of the most timely, value-added career and job information links. These links are organized by category as well as by chapter. You can also find useful career-boosting articles at this site. For easy access to this career resource, go to http://levitt.swlearning.com.

PERSONALBEST

Maintaining Work and Life Balance

Balancing the demands of your work and personal lives can sometimes feel like a juggling act. As you identify career goals that are important to you, consider how they affect:

▲ **Your values.** What do you consider important in your life—family, personal interests, work, education, community service, spiritual development, and so on?

▲ **Your priorities.** Based on your values, which daily tasks are the most important to you? Which are the least important?

▲ **Your physical health.** With a fit body, you are better able to deal with emotional stress and physical strain.

▲ **Your stress level.** Are your goals achievable? Be realistic about what you can accomplish in one day.

---

7. **Make a public commitment.** If appropriate, share your goals with someone who encourages you to go the extra mile. This will increase your sense of responsibility and provide motivation.

8. **Be realistic about limitations.** Don't set a short-term goal to get a job requiring more education. Set separate goals to get the education, take an interim job, and then reach the ultimate goal.

9. **Use positive self-talk and affirmation statements.** Do this every day! Write down your statements, post them prominently, and review them regularly.

Success Tip

Write down your goals and you'll increase their achievement by 80 percent! Focus on how achieving your goals will benefit you and others.

10. **Use positive visualization.** This boosts goal achievement.

11. **Practice.** Practice new skills regularly. Get additional information, training, coaching, and feedback on your progress.

12. **Evaluate and revise goals as necessary.** Evaluate your progress. Experiment with new methods if you're not getting the results you want, and, if necessary, revise your goals.

13. **Persevere.** Stay the course until you succeed!

14. **Reward yourself.** Rewards are motivators. As you make progress toward your goals, do something nice for yourself.

15. **Record progress on your goals.** As simplistic as it may seem, a long series of check marks on a calendar can motivate you by providing a sense of accomplishment. Don't let missing an occasional daily goal deter you, however. Keep focusing on the ultimate goal.

"When we set goals, the magic begins: The switch turns on, the current starts to flow, and the power to accomplish becomes a reality."
Wynn Davis
The Best of Success

...take regular positive action (no matter how small) and make progress toward goals, you create real evidence of achievement. This increases confidence and creativity and boosts your momentum. Action fuels more action! Deliberately plan and regularly work toward your goals to maximize your success.

Say you have a long-term goal of specializing in a career field. You can take momentum-building intermediate actions, as follows:

▲ Research to learn exactly what skills you need to qualify in the specialty. Contact specialists in your area to learn what skills they require.

▲ Take courses to help you develop these skills. As you complete each course, you will be a step closer to your final goal.

▲ Get help in arranging an internship or a work-study program with a firm noted in your target specialty area.

▲ Work in an entry-level position for a firm noted in your targeted specialty area. Then get additional training or education to qualify for the specialty.

Complete Career Action 1-3

Develop Assertive Abilities

Assertive behavior is:

▲ Standing up for your rights.
▲ Expressing yourself honestly, courteously, and comfortably.
▲ Observing and respecting the rights of others.

Assertive behavior promotes equality and a healthy balance in human relationships. Assertion is based on respect in all situations—especially the right to be treated with human rights. Every person has the right to be listened to and taken seriously, to say yes or no with conviction, to express his or her opinion, and to ask for what he or she wants.

7

Organize • Engage • Achieve

***Your Career: How to Make It Happen* WebTutor™:** The WebTutor is an optional online component for *Your Career: How to Make It Happen*. It includes PowerPoint presentations, Career Action Worksheets, chapter summaries and checklists, quizzes, and online discussion topics. Visit Cengage Learning's WebTutor site at academic.cengage.com/webtutor.

WHO CAN USE THIS BOOK?

This text is written for anyone seeking employment, a promotion, or a career change. This includes students (career and technical, college, and university level) and individuals currently working in or reentering the workforce. This book is appropriate for traditional students; adults who are reentering postsecondary systems to gain additional training; and those who are planning a new job, promotion, or career.

WHAT BENEFITS WILL YOU GAIN FROM THIS BOOK?

The authoring team conducts active, ongoing job seeking and career development research. They refine and enhance the instructional materials as required to meet the changing needs of the job market. This text reflects more than 20 years of professional expertise in career management. You will develop all the tools you need to manage your career successfully and gain the following benefits:

- **The right job and the right career moves:** This text will prepare you to land the right job or promotion and succeed in your career through practice and development of proven career management techniques.

- **Competitive advantage:** You will learn and apply strategies that will give you the winning advantage when competing in today's job market.

- **Convenient career management skills/tools:** You will develop efficient job search and career management skills and tools that will help you achieve current and future career goals.

You will also gain an important competitive and timesaving edge with these career management tools:

- **Career Management Files Binder.** As you complete the activities in this text, you will compile a set of documents and information you can use for future career activities. Your Career Management Files Binder will consist of personal data; content for resumes, cover letters, and applications; reference lists; and summaries of your qualifications, education, training, and more. You can use this base of information any time you seek a promotion, consider a new job, or pursue a new career.

- **Career Portfolio.** You will prepare a master set of documents and other items that provide evidence of your skills, abilities, achievements, experience, and other job qualifications. This Career Portfolio is designed to demonstrate and document your employability.

- **Interview Marketing Kit.** This professional-looking binder or case contains selected items from your Career Portfolio for each job interview. You will tailor the contents of your Interview Marketing Kit for each interview by choosing items that match the specific needs of individual employers. This targeted evidence of your qualifications will greatly enhance your interview effectiveness.

WHAT SKILLS WILL YOU DEVELOP?

This text offers a unique combination of knowledge and practical applications designed to build skills for your job search and career development. You will learn how to:

- Assess your occupational qualifications.
- Identify and confirm the best job and career choices.
- Use the Internet to increase your job search and career management success.
- Stay informed about job market trends and workplace issues.
- Organize your job search to find the best possible job in the least possible time.
- Research prospective employers and your career field.
- Succeed in the application process (application, resume, and cover letter).
- Look for a job.
- Get interviews and succeed in them.
- Follow up an interview successfully.
- Adjust quickly and achieve peak success in a new position.
- Apply techniques on the job that result in maximum career advancement.
- Evaluate the pros and cons of changing jobs or careers or relocating and how to plan for such changes.
- Deal effectively with being laid off, downsized, or terminated.

YOU WILL LEARN BY DOING

You can gain an 80 to 100 percent advantage over your competition by using this text. Through the practice assignments, you develop the essential job search and career planning skills that give you this competitive advantage. The goal of this text is to help you attain the most suitable job possible and to develop your career successfully. You won't just read about succeeding in a job search; you will practice the skills in your business community through class and Career Action assignments.

Some of these assignments include researching your career field and target job, submitting resumes and cover letters for evaluation, taking practice interviews in actual offices, and more.

THE INTERNET WILL BE YOUR CAREER PARTNER

Using the Internet is a must for a successful job search and for career management in the twenty-first century. This is why *Your Career: How to Make It Happen* incorporates exercises to build your Internet skills. Job applicants who use the Internet for employer and industry research and for professional electronic communication with employers outdistance those applicants who don't use this important tool. You will be counted among the Internet-savvy applicants when you complete this text.

The *Your Career: How to Make It Happen* Web site serves as your central Internet career resource. The site provides convenient, direct links to invaluable career information. You will also find useful articles and directions for preparing Web resumes. For easy access to this career resource, go to http://levitt.swlearning.com.

YOU ARE PART OF THE SCRIPT

Consider this book to be a partial script. You, the principal player in the development of your own career, will fill in the blanks. You will be carefully coached and directed through exercises that will help you identify, confirm, and realize your job and career goals. Good communication skills are vital to achieving career success. For this reason, you will be given ample guidance, practice, and real applications in developing winning resumes and cover letters and in developing verbal and nonverbal skills required to attain and succeed in job interviews.

HOW TO GET THE MOST FROM THIS BOOK

Before reading a chapter, review the learning objectives listed on the first page of the chapter to see exactly what you will learn. An overall summary is presented in the first paragraphs of each chapter to clarify the content.

The assignments are designed to focus on your personal job and career goals, not on generalized theories. Reading alone will not give you the practice you need to develop these skills adequately. You will be an active doer, taking charge of your own career success by following the guided steps necessary to ensure it. To get the best results, read each chapter and study and complete all the assignments. The path is clearly laid out for you to reach your job and career goals.

EVALUATION

To help you assess your understanding of the principles of each chapter and identify any areas you need to review, three levels of evaluation are provided with the curriculum for *Your Career: How to Make It Happen:*

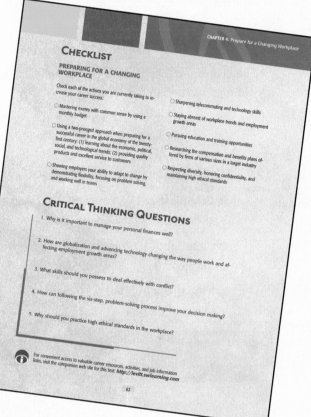

- ■ **Critical Thinking Questions** are included at the end of each chapter. The purpose of these questions is to prompt your consideration of how the key concepts of the chapter apply directly to you and your career goals.

- ■ **Chapter Tests** are provided on the Instructor's Resource CD. Your instructor may use these tests to evaluate your mastery of the key concepts of each chapter.

- ■ **Case Studies** are provided on the Learner's CD. They are designed to give you practice in applying the essential career concepts of each chapter.

DEVELOP LIFETIME CAREER SKILLS AND INFORMATION

Each chapter of this book contains Career Actions, special assignments designed to help you develop skills and compile information necessary for getting the job you want, succeeding in it, and advancing your career. Many of these assignments make use of corresponding perforated worksheets found at the end of the chapters. You can write your answers on these forms, or you can access the forms on the Learner's CD and complete them using your computer. Some assignments are to be prepared using separate paper. If possible, use the forms on your Learner's CD for easier completion of assignments. See additional details regarding the Learner's CD on the next page.

The information you assemble by completing the Career Action assignments is essential for developing your resumes, cover letters, employment applications, networking lists, and so on, throughout your life. You will file your completed Career Actions in your Career Management Files Binder, creating a convenient collection of information you can quickly access and update any time you pursue a job or career goal. You will be making a smart investment in your lifetime career success as you create your personal base of career information.

Content of the Learner's CD

The Learner's CD provides greater convenience and added value. The components are summarized below:

- **Career Action assignments** that contain forms are available on the Learner's CD, and content can be keyed into the forms instead of handwritten on the Career Action Worksheets in the textbook. These Career Action forms are provided in both formats, however, for students who do not have ready access to computers.

- **Complete set of PowerPoint slides** reviews the key points of all chapters. These slides increase knowledge retention and serve as a convenient study guide.

- **Case Studies** and Case Study Questions are included for each chapter. They are designed to reinforce key chapter topics through application-focused exercises.

- **Model Documents** are provided, including selected model resumes, cover letters, and other career development resource materials.

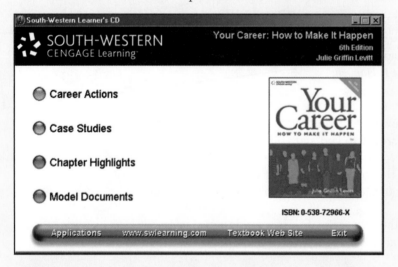

Back Up Your Career Action Assignment Content

Because so much of the information you gain and so many of the documents you create while using the text will be useful throughout your career, you should back up your work. In this way, you will have convenient access to your basic resume, cover letter, networking information, and more. By backing up all files throughout the course on your personal storage media, you will create a kind of electronic "Career to Go." This media will contain all your essential career data, which you can easily update or revise any time you seek a promotion or a job or career change. Use the following procedures to back up your work:

- **Career Action Forms.** Selected Career Action forms, which you can retrieve and complete electronically, are provided on the Learner's CD. Permanently save your completed Career Action forms onto your hard drive or network drive, and then back them up on a personal CD.

- **Job Search Documents.** Also back up all other job search document files (cover and other job search letters, resumes, reference sheets, and so on) that you create throughout the course onto a personal CD.

- **Storage of Backup Media.** Store all your backup media in your Career Management Files Binder. Also save your completed resumes and cover letters and the other career management documents you create in your Career Action assignments onto a personal CD.

A FINAL WORD OF ADVICE AND ENCOURAGEMENT

National studies verify that job seekers who are persistent, informed of current job market trends, and organized in their approach are at least 80 percent more successful in attaining their career goals than those without this training. The tools necessary to succeed in your job search and career development are conveniently organized in this book. Apply these tools to maximize your career potential and the quality of your working life.

It's YOUR CAREER—make it happen with the winning success tools presented in this text!

ACKNOWLEDGMENTS

This book reflects the influence of many people skilled in career management education. Foremost in this category is the thorough and professional writing and subject-matter guidance provided by:

Mr. Richard Rapp, Associate Vice President for Student Affairs and Director of the Career Center, Boise State University. Mr. Rapp contributed significantly to Chapters 8 and 20 and advised on the entire text. Mr. Rapp has personally assisted over 20,000 people in finding appropriate career employment. He also serves in leadership roles in local and national career planning and placement organizations.

Shelley Metzger, Ph.D., Associate Director, Boise State University Career Center. With her expertise in career counseling and education, Shelley greatly enhanced the curriculum with her contributions to the chapter tests, WebTutor quizzes, case studies, model resumes, and teaching activities.

In addition, the following people deserve recognition for their contributions to this curriculum.

Lynne Whaley, textbook author and resume/career expert, researched and wrote many of the resumes and job search letters, developing excellent market-driven content. **Mary Seroski,** computer technology expert, network specialist, and programmer with The Network Group, provided important research assistance with computer technology and electronic resume topics and developed the set of motivational slides. **Ben Botti,** University of California at Davis, assisted with research and development of content regarding Web resume technology.

Grateful acknowledgment is made to **Dr. and Mrs. Richard Griffin,** the sources of inspiration and experience upon which Chapter 1 of this text is based.

Importantly, I wish to recognize **Dr. Monte Levitt,** who provided artwork and the personal support so essential to developing this comprehensive curriculum. Thank you, Monte, I am profoundly grateful.

I am also grateful to the following reviewers and instructors who offered valuable suggestions and support:

D. Ross Thomson, Ph.D.
Bryant & Stratton College
Albany, NY

Robert R. Rizzo
Brown Mackie College
Akron, OH

Darien V. Hartman
Boise State University
Boise, ID

ABOUT THE AUTHOR

Photographed by Sims Studios, Inc.

Julie Griffin Levitt is a corporate trainer and consultant, lecturer, and author of numerous educational and training publications. She teaches and consults throughout the United States and in Canada in the areas of career planning and job search skills, office occupations, written and oral communications, supervision, and personal motivation. Her home base is Boise, Idaho. She has taught job-seeking and career planning skills at the secondary and postsecondary levels.

REACH YOUR FULL CAREER POTENTIAL

In this chapter, you will:

Set up a Career Management Files System.

- Identify the forces that are rapidly changing the nature of today's workplace.

- Use affirmation statements and positive self-talk to help achieve your goals.

- Identify techniques for successfully setting and achieving your goals.

- Improve your assertive behavior and apply it in your job search.

Access the Internet and complete a proactive success action plan.

"A sense of purpose generates action and movement in the direction of dreams and goals, while wishes generate only half-hearted intentions. Think about it. Purpose says, 'I will do this.' Wish says, 'If only I could.'

Life is not a spectator sport. Set your sights on what you want in your career and then make it happen. Now, what are you waiting for?"

Joan C. Borgatti, R.N., M.Ed.
Editorial Director
NursingSpectrum.com

Chapter 1 provides guidelines to help you strengthen career-boosting skills, attitudes, and strategies that persuade employers to hire and promote. You will learn and apply nine strategies to give you the competitive edge in achieving career success and reaching your full potential.

The Changing Workplace

The forces of technology and globalization are rapidly changing the nature of work. Savvy job seekers know that they need to prepare for these predicted workplace developments:

▲ Technology will continue to advance and will affect how, when, and where business is done; the pace of work; and how people communicate.

▲ The global economy will continue to result in some jobs being outsourced to other countries and will lead to more mergers and management changes. Resourcefulness, adaptability, and efficiency will be essential for workers to succeed.

▲ International time zone differences will demand flexible hours and possibly extra hours to communicate and conduct business.

▲ A complex and diverse workforce will require workers to be flexible, respect differences, and work together to increase productivity.

▲ Workers can expect to change jobs about 10 times! Managing one's career is a must.

▲ Small businesses will prosper, and home-based businesses and services will multiply. Entrepreneurial skills and attitudes will be important.

▲ The fastest-growing occupations are in computers; preventive health care; and other health and human services, such as registered nursing, social work, teaching, police work, and security.

▲ Most of the fastest-growing occupations will require specific post-secondary education, on-the-job training, or a bachelor's degree. Education and training will be critical.

To gain a competitive edge, today's job seekers must know about changes like these and demonstrate a positive attitude that shows they are ready, willing, and able to take on these challenges.

Get the Competitive Edge With Nine Success Strategies

Successful leaders in all fields, from business to entertainment, consistently use the nine success strategies discussed in this chapter to achieve their career goals. These strategies focus on positive attitudes and ac-

tions. Throughout the world, Olympic sports psychologists coach competitors to achieve maximum performance by learning and applying these strategies. Renowned motivational experts—such as Anthony Robbins, Brian Tracy, Denis Waitley, and Stephen Covey—teach these strategies to help business leaders, politicians, and performers reach their peak potential.

Use Nine Success Strategies

Review and use the nine strategies that follow to help achieve your full career potential. They profoundly affect career success at every step.

1. Positive Thinking and Behavior

2. Visualization

3. Positive Self-Talk

4. Affirmation Statements

5. Dynamic Goal Setting

6. Positive Action

7. Assertive Behavior

8. Self-Esteem Builders

9. Proactive Habits

These nine success strategies and behaviors are major career enhancers that help transform goals into realities. Pay close attention to any that are new ideas for you. They provide wide-ranging benefits; you can use them to:

▲ Create and sustain your inner drive.

▲ Increase your confidence.

▲ Generate mental and physical energy.

▲ Guide you toward goals.

▲ Help you project competence, enthusiasm, and presence.

▲ Improve your performance.

It's shocking but true: The most qualified person is not always the one who gets the job or promotion. The person hired is the one the employer perceives to be the most qualified. Your experience, skills, resumes, and more—your entire job search package—are greatly enhanced when you practice these key success strategies.

Success Tip

The winning job candidate is perceived to be the most qualified. Use the nine success strategies to project your competence.

Set Up Your Career Management Files Binder

To help you prepare for job search and career success, *Your Career: How to Make It Happen* guides you through the development of your own Career Management Files. Your Career Management Files will include career development and job search documents (self-assessments, records of experience and skills developed, resumes, cover letters, job search organizational aids, and more) that you can use throughout your career each time you seek a promotion, a new job, or a career change. Career Action 1-1 is the first step in organizing this essential career information.

Complete Career Action 1-1

Improve Performance Through Positive Thinking and Behavior

Positive thinking is making a conscious effort to think with an optimistic attitude and anticipate posi-

tive outcomes. Positive behavior means purposely acting with energy and enthusiasm. When you think and behave positively, you guide your mind toward your goals and generate matching mental and physical energy.

Positive thinking and behavior are often deciding factors in landing a top job—your first job, a promotion, a change of jobs—whatever career step you are targeting. That's because the subconscious is literal; it accepts what you regard as fact.

The function of your subconscious is to support your thoughts and behaviors by triggering matching physiological responses. Research has proved that positive thinking and behavior have a powerful impact on personal performance, confidence, and even health. This chapter explains how you can learn to use the power of autosuggestion to enhance your performance and career development.

Positive thinking causes the brain to generate matching positive chemical and physical responses, such as increased mental alertness and physical energy, improved respiration and circulation, and increased beneficial endorphins. Thinking positively actually boosts your ability to perform and to project enthusiasm, energy, competence, and confidence—the qualities interviewers look for when they hire and promote candidates.

CAREER ACTION 1-1

Set Up Your Career Management Files System

Directions: In Appendix B, Career Management Tool 1: Career Management Files, follow the instructions to set up your own Career Management Files Binder. In this binder, store completed Career Action assignments specified throughout the book. When you have completed all of these assignments, you will have a valuable collection of career-related information that you can use throughout your life. Your completed binder will include records of your education and work experience, summaries of job- and career-related values and skills, resumes, cover letters, and more.

Negative thinking causes the brain to stimulate matching negative chemical and physical responses, such as increased blood pressure, reduced mental alertness, increased anxiety, decreased physical energy, and fight or flight reactions. These responses decrease energy, creativity, and performance and simultaneously erode self-confidence.

Follow these steps to form the habit of positive thinking and to boost your success:

1. **Deliberately motivate yourself every day.** Think of yourself as successful, and expect positive outcomes for everything you attempt.

2. **Project energy and enthusiasm.** Employers hire people who project positive energy and enthusiasm. Develop the habit of speaking, moving, and acting with these qualities.

3. **Practice this positive expectation mind-set until it becomes a habit.** Applicants who project enthusiasm and positive behavior generate a positive chemistry that rubs off. Hiring decisions are influenced largely by this positive energy. The habit will help you reach your peak potential.

4. **Dwell on past successes.** Focusing on past successes to remind yourself of your abilities will help you attain your goals. For example, no one is ever born knowing how to ride a bicycle or use a computer software program. Through training, practice, and trial and error, you master new abilities. During the trial-and-error phases of development, remind yourself of past successes; look at mistakes as part of the natural learning curve. Continue until you achieve the result you want, and remind yourself that you have succeeded in the past and can do so again. You fail only when you quit trying!

> *"No pessimist ever discovered the secrets of the stars, or sailed to an uncharted land, or opened a new heaven to the human spirit."*
>
> Helen Keller

Success Tip

Interviewers say that projecting enthusiasm and positive behaviors generates a positive chemistry that is a big hiring advantage.

Use Visualization to Your Advantage

Positive visualization is purposely forming a mental picture of your successful performance and recalling the image frequently. Visualization improves performance because the positive picture triggers your subconscious to generate matching positive physiological responses that increase performance.

Athletic champions and successful people throughout the world use positive visualization to boost their performance and achieve goals. The act of visualizing the successful performance of any skill or activity in detail actually increases learning and skill development. This is because visualization serves as a form of mental practice or rehearsal that strengthens performance. Have you used it personally or in a group to help improve performance? This is definitely a technique you should apply in all your career activities.

Apply the following visualization techniques to boost your success in job searches and interviews and in attaining your goals:

1. **Relax.** Sit in a chair, close your eyes, breathe deeply, and clear your mind.

2. **Draw a mental picture or create a mental video that shows you succeeding in your goal.** To project a positive and competent image, visualize yourself doing just that—walking and speaking with confidence, maintaining good posture, and performing optimally.

3. **Make the picture detailed and visualize success.** Do not permit any negative visions or thoughts (fear, failure, anxiety, or errors). See yourself as having already achieved your goal.

4. **Incorporate pictures, words, actions, and senses.** Mentally practice exactly what you plan to say or do. This mental rehearsal strengthens your actual performance.

5. **Dwell on the image; be able to recall it instantly.** Repeat the visual picture as often as possible before the actual event.

Success Tip

Visualize your positive performance. Your brain then triggers positive responses that enhance performance.

Practice Positive Self-Talk

Positive self-talk means purposely giving yourself positive reinforcement, motivation, and recognition—just as you would do for a friend. Congratulate yourself when you do well, and remind yourself of your abilities, accomplishments, strengths, and skills. Keep a to-do list, check off accomplishments, and review your progress periodically.

Make Self-Talk Work for You. What you habitually say to yourself has a profound impact on your self-image, your self-esteem, and your performance and success. Remember, your subconscious triggers physiological responses that match the pictures and thoughts you have of yourself to make them happen. Make this work *for* you by keeping your self-talk positive. For example:

▲ I did a good job on that report.

▲ I can do this.

Stop Negative Self-Talk. You may be quick to nag yourself because you want to be perfect. However, negative self-talk is damaging because the subconscious believes what you say about yourself. If you catch yourself using negative self-talk, stop and rephrase. Eliminate the negative words. Focus instead on the best course of action you can take, and *do it.*

Make positive communication a habit. Focus on the positive in goal statements, self-talk, and all communications. Compare the following phrases, and notice how the positive words convey confidence, commitment, and enthusiasm.

Negative	Positive
I'll try	I will
I should do	I will do
I must	I want to/I choose to

Figure 1-1: You project your positive self-image.

Focus With Affirmation Statements

Affirmation statements are positive self-statements or reminders to help achieve goals. They are positive messages with a punch, "mental bumper stickers" to motivate your subconscious to work for you. The following guidelines explain how to use this powerful mental reminder technique:

1. **Make the statements personal.** Use *I,* your name, or *you.*

2. **Keep affirmations short!** If you can't remember them, how can you use them?

3. **Phrase them positively.** The mind accepts as truth the words you give it. Use positive words only. Leave out negative words. For example:

    ▲ **Negative:** I will not be nervous during my interview.

    ▲ **Positive:** I will be calm and self-assured during my interview.

4. **Include a positive emotion.** A phrase that triggers a positive emotion strengthens the affirmation. For example: "My goal is *valuable* and it *excites* me."

5. **Phrase affirmations as fact.** Phrase a goal as though it is happening or has happened (even if you haven't achieved it yet). Your subconscious believes mental messages and works to make them reality.

   ▲ I am making good progress on my goal.

   ▲ I am strengthening my speaking abilities.

6. **Say your affirmations at least once a day.** Repetition enhances self-confidence, acts as a reminder, and stimulates your subconscious to help you achieve your goal.

> Complete Career Action 1-2

Success Tip

Use positive self-talk and affirmation statements to trigger matching positive physical responses that enhance performance.

Get Ahead With Dynamic Goal Setting

Career goal setting involves recording clear objectives and the actions required to achieve them. The main reason people don't achieve goals is that they don't set any to begin with. Use the following steps to focus your efforts and maximize your goal achievement. You can also use this process to set team or group goals.

1. **Define your goals clearly in writing.** Writing down your goals increases your likelihood of achieving them by 80 percent! It increases your sense of commitment, clarifies required steps in the achievement process, and helps you remember important details.

2. **Identify and focus on the benefits (to you and others) of achieving goals.** This is a strong motivator.

3. **Define the purpose of your goals.** Link your goals to a practical, specific purpose. To boost your own motivation, base your goals on inspiration, not just logic.

4. **Identify your supportive forces.** Examples of supportive forces include instructors, books, training, people who encourage you to persevere, skilled coaches or mentors, and printed and online research materials.

5. **Develop an action plan, set deadlines, and act.** Establish subgoals. Divide each main goal into logical, progressive steps. Set deadlines for completing each step, and complete the steps on time.

6. **Establish priorities.** Take action in order of priority.

CAREER ACTION 1-2

Practice Positive Self-Talk and Affirmation Statements

 Directions: Access your Learner's CD or use a separate sheet of paper to write your responses.

1. Recall a goal you have been striving to achieve and on which you are making progress. Then write a positive statement about your progress.

2. Describe one or more of your work skills or abilities that fit the requirements of the job you are or will be seeking. Write complete sentences.

3. Write an affirmation statement to use as a reminder to help you achieve an important career goal.

File your affirmation statements in your Career Management Files Binder.

7. **Make a public commitment.** If appropriate, share your goals with someone who encourages you to go the extra mile. This will increase your sense of responsibility and provide motivation.

8. **Be realistic about limitations.** Don't set a short-term goal to get a job requiring more education. Set separate goals to get the education, take an interim job, and then reach the ultimate goal.

9. **Use positive self-talk and affirmation statements.** Do this every day! Write down your statements, post them prominently, and review them regularly.

Success Tip

Write down your goals and you'll increase their achievement by 80 percent! Focus on how achieving your goals will benefit you and others.

---

10. **Use positive visualization.** This boosts goal achievement.

11. **Practice.** Practice new skills regularly. Get additional information, training, coaching, and feedback on your progress.

12. **Evaluate and revise goals as necessary.** Evaluate your progress. Experiment with new methods if you're not getting the results you want, and, if necessary, revise your goals.

13. **Persevere.** Stay the course until you succeed!

14. **Reward yourself.** Rewards are motivators. As you make progress toward your goals, do something nice for yourself.

15. **Record progress on your goals.** As simplistic as it may seem, a long series of check marks on a calendar can motivate you by providing a sense of accomplishment. Don't let missing an occasional daily goal deter you, however. Keep focusing on the ultimate goal.

> *"When we set goals, the magic begins: The switch turns on, the current starts to flow, and the power to accomplish becomes a reality."*
>
> Wynn Davis
> *The Best of Success*

Take Positive Action

When you take regular positive action (no matter how small) and make progress toward goals, you create real evidence of achievement. This increases confidence and creativity and boosts your momentum. Action fuels more action! Deliberately plan and regularly work toward your goals to maximize your success.

Say you have a long-term goal of specializing in a career field. You can take momentum-building intermediate actions, as follows:

▲ Research to learn exactly what skills you need to qualify in the specialty. Contact specialists in your area to learn what skills they require.

▲ Take courses to help you develop these skills. As you complete each course, you will be a step closer to your final goal.

▲ Get help in arranging an internship or a work-study program with a firm noted in your target specialty area.

▲ Work in an entry-level position for a firm noted in your targeted specialty area. Then get additional training or education to qualify for the specialty.

Complete Career Action 1-3

Develop Assertive Abilities

Assertive behavior is:

▲ Standing up for your rights.

▲ Expressing yourself honestly, courteously, and comfortably.

▲ Observing and respecting the rights of others.

Assertive behavior promotes equality and a healthy balance in human relationships. Assertion is based on human rights—especially the right to be treated with respect in all situations. Every person has the right to be listened to and taken seriously, to say yes or no with conviction, to express his or her opinion, and to ask for what he or she wants.

Assertive Behavior Is Critical in Your Job Search.

Why is assertiveness critical to a successful job search and career potential? Because it conveys self-esteem and capability.

Employers hire people who behave confidently and are able to convey their job qualifications comfortably and clearly. They want employees who strengthen human relations and project competence in the workplace through assertive behavior. They hire applicants who demonstrate assertiveness in interviews, resumes, and all communications. To reach your full career potential, be assertive and tactful in expressing yourself, and respect the rights of others.

Assertive Behavior Is Critical to Workplace

Success. Personality types fall into three general categories: nonassertive, aggressive, and assertive. Employers avoid hiring nonassertive and aggressive employees because they are often detrimental in the workplace.

▲ **Nonassertive People.** People who are nonassertive have difficulty expressing thoughts or feelings because they lack confidence. They may become unhappy because they permit others to abuse their rights. They project their feelings of unhappiness to others.

Success Tip

Behave assertively to enhance your interview and career success.

▲ **Aggressive People.** People who are aggressive violate the rights of others with domineering, pushy behavior. Their goal is to dominate because they fear loss of control. Overly aggressive employees drive business away; therefore, employers avoid hiring them.

▲ **Assertive People.** Assertive behavior is essential to achieving career success. Assertive people are confident, express their needs and opinions comfortably, and are sensitive to the feelings and needs of others. Employers want assertive employees because assertive behavior projects capability and promotes a healthy, productive working environment.

Building Assertiveness Skills. Being assertive requires a healthy self-esteem. Therefore, a key to improving assertiveness is strengthening self-esteem. Because all the success strategies and behaviors discussed in this chapter build self-esteem, they also enhance assertiveness.

CAREER ACTION 1-3

Practice Dynamic Goal Setting and Positive Actions

Directions: Access your Learner's CD or use a separate sheet of paper to write your responses.

1. Review and follow the guidelines for dynamic goal setting on pages 6–7. Identify a goal that is important to you.

2. Write down your goal and describe it by addressing goal-setting guidelines 1–5.

3. Identify three to five positive actions you can take in the next 10 days to achieve this goal.

4. Follow up by actually completing all 15 guidelines.

File your goal statements in your Career Management Files Binder.

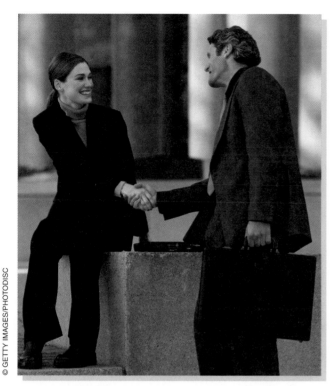

© GETTY IMAGES/PHOTODISC

Employers look for people who behave confidently and respect the rights of others.

Practicing Assertiveness. Strive to deal with others in a confident, positive way without appearing boastful or overbearing. Force yourself to be more open, to express your ideas and needs, and to perform with greater confidence. At the same time, practice show-ing respect for others more openly. The winning combination is *assertiveness + respect.*

Techniques for Developing Assertiveness. Review the following techniques for improving assertiveness. Practice expressing your feelings and needs calmly and clearly. Also demonstrate acceptance and respect for others by praising them when they perform or behave well.

1. **Initiate a friendship.** Invite a person you don't know well to have coffee or lunch. Take time to get to know him or her.

2. **Express your opinion** in a meeting or conversation, particularly when you believe strongly about the topic. Do this even if everyone else appears to disagree with you.

3. **Join a professional or service organization or club,** and volunteer to serve on a committee. What a way to network and build your assertiveness skills!

4. **Compliment someone** on a skill, a talent, an achievement, or a positive quality.

5. **Tell someone when he or she has offended you unfairly.** Evaluate first to be certain the person was actually unfair. Being overly sensitive can impair your assertiveness.

6. **Return faulty merchandise** to get an immediate replacement or a free repair.

7. **Initiate a conversation** with a stranger before or after a class, meeting, or social event. (Just try it; you'll like it!)

Complete Career Action 1-4

CAREER ACTION 1-4

Improve Assertiveness

Directions: Review the techniques for developing assertiveness just discussed. Select at least two activities for practicing assertiveness—exercises provided in the chapter or others more pertinent to your needs. Access your Learner's CD to write out a plan for improving your assertiveness skills through the exercises you have chosen, and follow through with your plan.

File your assertiveness improvement plan in your Career Management Files Binder.

Enhance Your Self-Esteem

Projecting confidence requires a healthy self-esteem (belief in your abilities and your worth). Think about how easy it is to project a confident, competent image when you feel good about yourself. By developing the success habits outlined in this chapter, you will strengthen your self-esteem.

Enhancing Your Self-Esteem. Begin by describing yourself in writing. You may want to ask a friend or family member to help. Make two lists: one of your positive traits and one of your negative traits. Which list is longer? If it's your positive list, you have a good base for self-esteem. If it's your negative list, you must work harder to develop a strong sense of self-confidence. By doing so, you will strengthen your assertive abilities because having a healthy self-esteem makes behaving assertively easy.

Next, identify negative images you want to change. Begin with the trait you think you should improve first. An example of a negative trait may be a lack of initiative, expressiveness, or organization. Improving self-image often requires developing a positive habit, such as reading more to improve vocabulary or exercising to improve fitness.

After you identify the traits you want to improve, develop an Action Plan. Write your goal in positive terms, as shown in Figure 1-2. Write your Action Plan so you can evaluate it daily. This makes progress easy to evaluate and provides reinforcement. Put a check mark on your calendar each day you make progress toward your goal. This may seem simplistic, but it is surprisingly motivational.

Action Plan

Goal: To improve my public-speaking skills by enrolling in a workshop.

Personal Action Plan for Achieving Goal: On Tuesday afternoon, I will research dates and times for public-speaking workshops offered on campus. After I have the scheduling information, I will sign up for the workshop sessions that fit my schedule. Once I have completed and participated in the sessions, I will write a summary of the skills I learned. In the summary, I will identify the three most important points to use in my public speaking. My next goal will be to practice my public speaking!

Time Frame for Action Plan: I will write the public-speaking workshop session dates and times in my planner. I will attend all sessions offered this semester.

Figure 1-2: Action Plan

PERSONAL**BEST**

Maintaining Work and Life Balance

Balancing the demands of your work and personal lives can sometimes feel like a juggling act. As you identify career goals that are important to you, consider how they affect:

▲ **Your values.** What do you consider important in your life—family, personal interests, work, education, community service, spiritual development, and so on?

▲ **Your priorities.** Based on your values, which daily tasks are the most important to you? Which are the least important?

▲ **Your physical health.** With a fit body, you are better able to deal with emotional stress and physical strain.

▲ **Your stress level.** Are your goals achievable? Be realistic about what you can accomplish in one day.

Today many employers are sensitive to the importance of personal and professional balance. They know that employees who achieve a healthy balance in life are happier and more productive. Explore with employers how you can achieve a healthy life/work balance *and* deliver top-quality results at work.

Effects of Negative Self-Esteem and Fear. A negative self-image holds you back by promoting fear of failure. It prevents you from taking risks that can lead to growth and development. The result is stagnation, even regression, but not successful development. Have you ever avoided attempting a new activity or goal because you feared failure or rejection?

Sometimes you base your behavior on imagined fears, not on facts. You allow fear to limit your full potential. Following are tips for dealing constructively with fears and enhancing your success.

1. When working on a challenging goal, such as public speaking, avoid negative images. Concentrate on developing your skills and knowledge; then plan and act positively, and visualize your success in detail.

2. Assess the situation. Get training or additional information if necessary.

3. Seek support from those who motivate you.

4. Act with courage and conviction; be persistent.

Maintaining a Healthy Self-Esteem. Because life experiences may change your level of self-esteem, you need to work deliberately at strengthening and maintaining self-esteem. A few techniques for building self-esteem are as follows:

1. **Believe it can be done, and make a commitment.** Remember how positive suggestion positively influences your subconscious!

2. **Identify your strengths** in writing, and dwell on past successes.

3. **Set written goals** for improvement, and take action.

4. **Practice positive self-talk.**

5. **Visualize your success.**

6. **Make positive action a habit.**

7. **Surround yourself with a positive environment** (positive people and positive reading, viewing, and listening materials).

8. **Look good to feel good.** Looking your best boosts your confidence, and others respond positively to a good appearance.

9. **Stay fit.** Take care of your body, mind, and spirit. Exercise, eat properly, rest, and balance work with other life activities.

Develop Proactive Skills

In his world-acclaimed book, *7 Habits of Highly Successful People,* Stephen Covey emphasizes that the way people typically approach challenging situations and tasks is a major determinant of their career success. Many choose either a proactive or reactive approach in dealing with difficulties or challenging tasks and situations. They may also fall into the habit of using one of the approaches predominantly. One of these approaches is a consistent career booster; the other, a guaranteed detriment.

Behaviors common to these approaches are outlined in Figure 1-3.

The Proactive Approach—A Synergy Booster. The proactive approach to dealing with challenges focuses on problem solution and positive action. Those who use this approach aim to resolve problems or master challenging tasks by taking full responsibility for their assignments and career growth. They actively seek resources for goal achievement. They also strive for win-win solutions that best meet the needs of all involved.

Proactive people regularly practice the nine positive success strategies emphasized in this chapter. All of these success strategies enhance your ability to take proactive steps that will boost your career success.

Typical Proactive Behaviors	Typical Reactive Behaviors
Focus on problem solution/personal growth	Focus on problems/difficulties of the situation (not on solutions) and have a generally negative attitude
Take responsibility for own behavior and for personal or team assignments and productivity	Blame others or circumstances for the difficulty or try to shift responsibility for solution to others
Seek synergistic solutions through productive relationships	Procrastinate in the face of a difficult task or problem
Employ personal motivation skills based on positive expectations	Don't seek resources for problem solution (networking, researching for useful information, and so on)
Encourage/assist others	Don't strive to motivate self or others to improve or excel
Network and strive to develop mutually beneficial relationships, share information and perspectives, and get and give support	Diminish energy of others

Figure 1-3: Typical Proactive and Reactive Behaviors

The Reactive Approach Is a Career Minimizer. The reactive approach focuses on problem avoidance and negative personal reactions. Those who fall into a reactive habit focus on problems, not on solutions. Their habitually negative behaviors greatly diminish their career opportunities and, in some cases, can lead to depression.

Both Approaches Are Contagious. Have you noticed how enjoyable it is to be around people who are typically proactive? Their positive, supportive, and action-oriented behaviors are energizing and motivating—they "rub off" on those they work and interact with. They motivate others to perform at their best, and they infuse a healthy aura that encourages creativity and increases productivity.

Rewards of Proactive Behaviors Are Great. With practice, you will increase your ability to use proactive behavior as your predominant style and enjoy greater success throughout your career. Also, by associating with other proactive people, you can mutually expand your career potential through the contagious synergy you experience. The following list summarizes the beneficial outcomes of developing good proactive skills.

▲ Enhance self-esteem/increase personal motivation

▲ Improve problem-solving skills

▲ Enhance self-esteem and professional reputation

▲ Improve ability to correct personal errors and strengthen skills

▲ Build positive working relationships that boost career success potential for all

▲ Improve performance in all endeavors

▲ Gain skills under the direction of mentors and in networking with others

▲ Increase knowledge and career resources

▲ Expand perspective

Complete Career Action 1-5

Apply the Nine Success Strategies

Use the nine success strategies emphasized in this chapter to reach your full career potential. Apply these success strategies regularly throughout your job search and career. Throughout your life, pursue your goals with an assertive belief in yourself and your rights, and practice thinking and acting positively and proactively. Success is not a one-time destination; it's a lifelong journey.

CAREER ACTION 1-5

Access the Internet and Develop a Proactive Success Action Plan

Directions: Launch your web browser and follow the steps below.

1. Access the *Your Career: How to Make It Happen* web site at http://levitt.swlearning.com. (You will be accessing this web site for numerous Career Action assignments, so bookmark its address in your web browser.)

2. Locate the **Proactive Success Action Plan** form.

3. Read the instructions and enter your answers on the **Proactive Success Action Plan** form.

4. Print your completed form, and file it in your Career Management Files Binder.

CHECKLIST

APPLYING NINE SUCCESS STRATEGIES

○ Think and act positively.

○ Visualize your positive performance.

○ Use positive self-talk.

○ Use affirmation statements.

○ Write clear short-term and long-term goals, and revise them when necessary.

○ Take regular action to achieve defined goals.

○ Practice assertive behavior.

○ Maintain self-esteem through positive thinking and actions.

○ Develop proactive skills.

CRITICAL THINKING QUESTIONS

1. How can an understanding of workplace trends give you a competitive edge in a job search?

2. Which of the nine success strategies are the most useful for attaining career planning and job search success?

3. How can projecting enthusiasm and positive expectations help you in an interview?

4. What effects do positive and negative thoughts, images, and self-talk have on performance?

5. Would you rate your own assertiveness skills as excellent, good, or needing improvement? If you need improvement, what specific actions can you take to strengthen these skills?

6. What should be compiled in your Career Management Files Binder? How will the binder be useful to you throughout your career?

 For convenient access to valuable career resources, activities, and job information links, visit the companion web site for this text: *http://levitt.swlearning.com*

TAKE A LOOK AT YOURSELF

In this chapter, you will:

- Document your education, work experience, and other activities related to a potential career to use in your job search and career development.

- Identify the career-related skills you developed through your education and work experience.

- Identify your personal, school-related, and work-related accomplishments.

 Use the Internet to complete personal assessments for planning and confirming your career choices.

"In today's job market, self-knowledge is the most important piece of a successful job search. To help you gain knowledge about different aspects of yourself, who you are, and what you want out of your life and your career, there are several types of motivational interest, workplace, and personality inventories that can be taken.

The most important result of your work is achieving personal satisfaction. The money will follow."

Henry Neils
President and Founder
Assessment.com

In Chapter 2, you take a complete inventory of your education, training, experience, accomplishments, values, work preferences, and performance traits. This personal inventory is an essential tool for developing or confirming your career target and for conveying your qualifications to potential employers.

Knowing Yourself—A Must for Your Career Success

To achieve each step throughout your career—your first job, a promotion, a job or career change—you must sell the product: you. Just as successful salespeople must know their products, you must know your qualifications and be able to communicate them clearly to employers in a resume, in a cover letter, and in interviews.

To help ensure wise job and career choices, you need to clarify what values and work environment preferences are important to you. The Chapter 2 Career Action assignments will help you thoroughly inventory your qualifications, including your training, education, skills, and work experience and identify your values and work preferences.

> *"It's not what you've got, it's what you use that makes a difference."*
> Zig Ziglar

Your Personal Career Inventory

In this chapter, all the information you compile about yourself through the Career Action assignments will form your personal career inventory. This will be an important source of information when you develop your resumes, cover letters, job applications, and more. Employers may want your inventory information when considering you for a job. Included in this career inventory are basic personal data and information about the following:

▲ Education and professional training

▲ Work experience, skills, and accomplishments

▲ People you can use as references

Record Education, Training, and Organizational Activities

The first step in compiling your personal career inventory is documenting your education and training, including dates, places, career-relevant courses and activities, skills, and accomplishments. You will also document your membership and achievements in professional and other organizations related to your

job and career targets. This information will help you identify or confirm an appropriate career choice, develop resumes and cover letters, and prepare for job interviews.

Complete this section of your personal career inventory thoroughly and accurately. Put yourself under a microscope, and look at every detail carefully. Ask people who know you well to help you document your accomplishments. Consider scholarships, honors, and awards you have received and competitions in which you have participated. In describing accomplishments, be as specific as possible. For example:

▲ Won first place in school math competition.

▲ Voted president of the senior class.

When identifying the skills and accomplishments you achieved through your education, training, and organizational activities, consider two kinds of skills (or competencies) that employers are seeking: job-specific skills and transferable competencies.

Job-Specific Skills. Job-specific skills are the technical abilities that relate *specifically* to a particular job. For example, in accounting, preparing a balance sheet by using accounting software customized for a client is a job-specific skill. Relining brakes on a vehicle is a job-specific skill for an auto mechanic. Operating medical diagnostic equipment is another job-specific skill.

Transferable Competencies. Transferable competencies are abilities that can be applied in more than one work environment. For example, both accountants and auto mechanics are required to have such transferable competencies as reading, writing, doing mathematics, and using computers. Other transferable competencies include working well with others, leading, organizing work and materials, solving problems, making decisions, and managing resources.

Complete Career Action 2-1

CAREER ACTION 2-1

Education, Training, and Organizational Activities Inventory

Directions: Access Career Action Worksheet 2-1 on your Learner's CD, or use the worksheet that begins on page 22 of this text. Complete each section of the worksheet that applies to you. Be thorough in providing details. When you have completed the assignment, file your worksheet in your Career Management Files Binder.

List Experience and Skills

In Career Action 2-2, you will document all your work and other pertinent experience and record the dates and places of these experiences. You will also list the skills and knowledge you developed and any accomplishments, achievements, or recognition you received as part of these experiences. You should include both job-specific skills and transferable competencies.

Include any paid or volunteer work (e.g., community service projects and fund-raising), internships, and cooperative education experience. Be specific about the contributions you made:

> *"All our dreams can come true, if we have the courage to pursue them."*
>
> Walt Disney

▲ Raised 20 percent more in contributions over previous year.

▲ Designed a bandwidth usage tracking tool that improved network efficiency by 45 percent.

▲ Suggested new file management procedures that reduced filing error rate by 25 percent.

Complete Career Action 2-2

Identify Job References

The final step in completing your personal career inventory is identifying job references. A job reference is someone who can and will vouch for your capabilities, skills, and suitability for a job. References are typically people who have been your instructors and coaches in school or your supervisors or coworkers in volunteer and paid work environments. Therefore, you should review your inventory of education and work experience for potential job references.

Identify people who can *and are willing* to confirm (from firsthand observation) your good performance on the job, in school, or in other activities. Employers

CAREER ACTION 2-2

Experience and Skills Inventory

Directions: Access Career Action Worksheet 2-2 on your Learner's CD, or use the worksheet that begins on page 26 of this text. Complete each section of the worksheet that applies to you. Be as specific and thorough as possible. When you have completed the assignment, file your worksheet in your Career Management Files Binder.

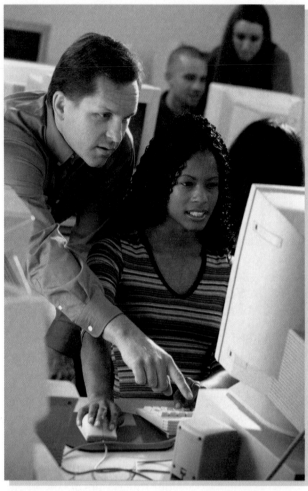

An instructor who can attest to your strong performance in school is a valuable job reference.

often want at least three job references listed on application forms. Ideally, these references are supervisors, employers, or others who know your work

well. Relatives or classmates are not appropriate references. The more references you have available, the better prepared you are for your current and future job campaign.

If you are qualified to work in two different fields, such as retail sales and accounting, you will get the best results by having one set of references targeted for each of the two fields, or a total of six references (three in the sales field and three in the accounting field). Some organizations ask for different types of references. For example, an employer may ask for personal references as well as professional references.

Use Career Action 2-3 to identify people you can use as references. Make note of how they know you and in what areas they can speak about your performance.

Complete Career Action 2-3

Self-Assessment

Also important in knowing yourself is accurate assessment of your personal values, work preferences, and job-related performance traits. Understanding the personal factors that influence your performance and job satisfaction will help you make good choices when setting job and career targets and when considering specific job offers.

CAREER ACTION 2-3

Develop a List of Potential Job References

Directions: Access Career Action Worksheet 2-3 on your Learner's CD, or use the worksheet that begins on page 28. Identify at least three (but as many as possible) potential job references from your education/training and experience/skills inventories. Also consider any contacts in professional associations. Record the names of your references, their addresses, and other pertinent contact information. Plan to contact each reference and ask him or her to write you a letter of reference. When you have completed the assignment, file your worksheet in your Career Management Files Binder.

Values

Webster's New World Dictionary defines value as "that which is desirable or worthy of esteem for its own sake; the social principles, goals, or standards held or accepted by an individual." By working in a job that matches your values, you greatly increase your chances of enjoying and succeeding in the job. Career Action 2-4 will help you identify and prioritize your values.

Work Environment

Most people spend a lot of time in their work environment. To maximize your success, identify the work environments you prefer and perform best in. For example, if you are an extrovert, you probably won't enjoy working in an isolated environment. Career Action 2-4 will help you clarify what is important to you in a work environment.

Complete Career Action 2-4

Personal Qualities and Work Performance Traits

To get the job you want, you must be able to sell your personal qualities, positive job performance traits, and enthusiasm to prospective employers. In Career Action 2-5, you will identify these qualities and traits to help you find a suitable job target match.

Identifying your personal qualities and work performance traits will also help you decide what type of work you are best suited for.

PERSONAL**BEST**

Professional Ethics

A code of ethics is a set of principles—written or unwritten—that guides your behavior. These principles are based on your personal values. For example, if you value honesty, honesty will be part of your ethical code.

How will your behavior in the workplace reflect your personal values and ethics? If everyone else plays computer games during work hours, will you? According to Kenneth Blanchard and Norman Vincent Peale, authors of *The Power of Ethical Management*, you should ask yourself three questions when faced with an ethical dilemma.

▲ **Is it legal?** Will you be breaking any laws or company policies by engaging in the activity?

▲ **Is it balanced?** Is it fair to all parties in the short term as well as the long term? Is it a win-win situation for all those involved?

▲ **Is it right?** Does the action go against your conscience? How does your decision make you feel about yourself?

Complete Career Action 2-5

CAREER ACTION 2-4

Values and Work Environment Preferences Inventory

Directions: Career Action 2-4 will help you identify and prioritize the values that are important to you. It will also help you clarify the kinds of work environments you prefer. Remember, there are no wrong answers in defining what's important to you. Access Career Action Worksheet 2-4 on your Learner's CD, or use the worksheet that begins on page 30. When you have completed the assignment, file your worksheet in your Career Management Files Binder.

CAREER ACTION 2-5

Personal Qualities and Work Performance Traits

Directions: Access Career Action Worksheet 2-5 on your Learner's CD, or use the worksheet that begins on page 33. Follow the instructions to complete Career Action 2-5. When you have completed the assignment, file your worksheet in your Career Management Files Binder.

Self-Assessment Resources

Many self-assessment resources speed up the process of making and confirming a successful career choice. (Note that some of these resources may have a fee attached to them.)

▲ **Your school's career services staff and counselors.** These specialists can provide a wide variety of aptitude and interest tests.

▲ **The Internet.** You can find useful information about careers and jobs on the Internet. Many sites offer online tools to help you assess your career interests and values and match the results with appropriate careers and jobs.

▲ **Commercial software packages.** Some commercial software packages are available on the Internet and through schools' career offices.

Complete Career Action 2-6

Success Tip

Complete self-assessments to help match your interests, values, and personality style to appropriate careers.

CAREER ACTION 2-6

Online Self-Assessment Test

Directions: Use the Internet to locate and complete two or three career-related self-assessment tests that measure your interests, values, and/or personality style. Print the results for your Career Management Files Binder. Some versions of tests to search for include The Career Key, a mini-Myers-Briggs Type Indicator quiz, and The Keirsey Temperament Sorter. Resources for this assignment include the following:

1. The *Your Career: How to Make It Happen* web site at http://levitt.swlearning.com. Access the "Links" page; then click on the "Self-assessment links" category. From there, review the self-assessment links and select assessment tests you are most interested in completing.

   Also check out the "Efficient web searching links" for more information on conducting Internet research.

2. Your favorite search engines. Conduct a search using a search string such as *self-assessment*.

When you have completed the assignment, file your worksheet in your Career Management Files Binder.

CHECKLIST

SELF-ASSESSMENT

Check each of the actions you are currently taking to increase your career success:

○ Identifying skills, abilities, work experience, values, and work preferences to achieve a good job match

○ Identifying potential references—people who can *and are willing* to confirm your good performance on the job, in school, or in other activities

○ Completing self-assessments to help match interests, values, and personality style to appropriate career and job targets

○ Using self-assessment resources—such as school career services, career counselors, the Internet, and commercial software packages—to help validate successful career choices

CRITICAL THINKING QUESTIONS

1. Why is it important in career planning and a job search to assess and document thoroughly your education, training, work experience, and accomplishments?

2. How are job-specific skills different from transferable competencies? Give two examples of each.

3. What is the important role of references in a job campaign?

4. Why is it useful to identify your work performance traits and career-related personal qualities?

 For convenient access to valuable career resources, activities, and job information links, visit the companion web site for this text: *http://levitt.swlearning.com*

CAREER ACTION WORKSHEET 2-1

Education, Training, and Organizational Activities Inventory

Directions: This inventory of your education and training contains three sections: (1) High School Inventory; (2) Post-Secondary Education Inventory; and (3) Seminars and Workshops Inventory. Complete each section that applies to you. List information related to your career target. Be thorough in documenting your accomplishments and achievements.

HIGH SCHOOL INVENTORY

Name of School: _____

Address: _____

_____

Dates of Attendance: _____ to _____ Date of Diploma: _____

Grade Point Average: _____ GED (Date): _____

1. **Career-Related Courses.** List the career-related courses you completed.

_____

_____

2. **Career-Related and Organizational Activities.** Describe your involvement in school, extracurricular, community, and other activities (examples: clubs, sports, organizations, and volunteer work).

_____

_____

3. **Career-Related Skills.** List the skills you developed in high school and through other activities. Include both job-specific skills and transferable competencies (examples: operating a computer, calculating numbers, persuading others, using specific tools/equipment, leading others, and working in a team).

_____

_____

4. **Accomplishments, Achievements, and Recognition.** List all special accomplishments, achievements, and recognition you received in high school and through other activities (examples: selected to play lead in musical production, selected to serve on state debate team, and awarded first place in math competition). List any scholarships or honors you earned. Also summarize praise you received from instructors, peers, and others.

_____

_____

Continued on next page >>>

CAREER ACTION WORKSHEET 2-1 (continued)

POST-SECONDARY EDUCATION INVENTORY

Directions: Complete one form for each post-secondary school attended. Duplicate the form if you have attended more than one post-secondary school.

Name of School:_____

Address: _____

_____

Dates of Attendance: _____ to _____ Date of Diploma: _____

Grade Point Average: _____

1. **Career-Related Courses.** List the career-related courses you completed.

_____

_____

_____

_____

_____

_____

_____

_____

2. **Career-Related and Organizational Activities.** Describe your involvement in school and extracurricular activities, in professional or other associations or organizations, in community activities, in volunteer work, and in other activities (examples: sports, clubs, offices held, volunteer work, and community projects or programs).

_____

_____

_____

_____

_____

_____

_____

_____

Continued on next page >>>

CAREER ACTION WORKSHEET 2-1 (continued)

3. **Career-Related Skills.** List the skills you developed through your classes and other activities. Include both job-specific skills and transferable competencies (examples: operating a computer, using specific software, oral and written communication, marketing, calculating numbers, persuading and leading others, working as a team member, and researching).

_____

_____

_____

_____

_____

_____

_____

_____

4. **Accomplishments, Achievements, and Recognition.** List all special accomplishments, achievements, and recognition you received for school activities. List any scholarships or honors you earned (examples: awarded second place in state business education skills competition, won scholarship, earned service award, inducted into National Technical Honor Society, prepared lesson plans that were used as model for campus, and restored two-bedroom apartment).

_____

_____

_____

_____

_____

_____

_____

_____

_____

_____

Continued on next page >>>

CAREER ACTION WORKSHEET 2-1 (continued)

SEMINARS AND WORKSHOPS INVENTORY

Directions: List the seminars and workshops you have attended. If necessary, add to the list of seminars and workshops by keying in the additional information (if you are using a computer for this activity) or by using additional paper (if you are handwriting this activity).

Name of Seminar/Workshop: _____

Offered by: _____ Date(s): _____

Career-related concepts or skills I learned: _____

Name of Seminar/Workshop: _____

Offered by: _____ Date(s): _____

Career-related concepts or skills I learned: _____

Name of Seminar/Workshop: _____

Offered by: _____ Date(s): _____

Career-related concepts or skills I learned: _____

Name of Seminar/Workshop: _____

Offered by: _____ Date(s): _____

Career-related concepts or skills I learned: _____

Name of Seminar/Workshop: _____

Offered by: _____ Date(s): _____

Career-related concepts or skills I learned: _____

CAREER ACTION WORKSHEET 2-2

Experience and Skills Inventory

Directions: Complete one form for each position or project you have had (cooperative work experience, internship, volunteer/paid work experience, military experience). Begin with the most recent experience, and continue in reverse chronological order. Two copies of the form are provided; duplicate the form for additional job experience.

POSITION TITLE: _____

Name of Organization: _____

Address: _____

Telephone Number: _____ Salary (if paid experience): _____

Circle Type of Experience: (1) Cooperative   (2) Volunteer   (3) Internship   (4) Paid Work

Dates of Employment or Involvement: _____

Supervisor Name/Title: _____

1. **Career-Related Skills.** List the job-specific skills, transferable competencies, and responsibilities you developed in this position.

   _____

   _____

2. **Accomplishments and Achievements.** List your accomplishments in this position, preferably in measurable terms (examples: increased sales by 20 percent, reduced order processing time by 15 percent by developing more efficient processing methods, named employee/volunteer of the month, and supervised evening shift of eight employees).

   _____

   _____

3. **Praise Received.** Summarize praise received from employers, coworkers, and customers.

   _____

   _____

Why did you leave? _____

Performance rating (circle one):   Excellent   Very Good   Good   Needs Improvement   Poor

Continued on next page >>>

CAREER ACTION WORKSHEET 2-2 (continued)

POSITION TITLE: _____

Name of Organization: _____

Address: _____

Telephone Number: _____ Salary (if paid experience): _____

Circle Type of Experience: (1) Cooperative   (2) Volunteer   (3) Internship   (4) Paid Work

Dates of Employment or Involvement: _____

Supervisor Name/Title: _____
_____

1. **Career-Related Skills.** List the job-specific skills, transferable competencies, and responsibilities you developed in this position.

_____

_____

_____

_____

2. **Accomplishments and Achievements.** List your accomplishments in this position, preferably in measurable terms (examples: increased sales by 20 percent, reduced order processing time by 15 percent by developing more efficient processing methods, named employee/volunteer of the month, and supervised evening shift of eight employees).

_____

_____

_____

3. **Praise Received.** Summarize praise received from employers, coworkers, and customers.

_____

_____

_____

Why did you leave? _____

Performance rating (circle one):   Excellent   Very Good   Good   Needs Improvement   Poor

CAREER ACTION WORKSHEET 2-3

Develop a List of Potential Job References

Directions: List at least three people who would recommend you to prospective employers. List more references if possible. Be sure to get their permission to use them as references during your job search.

Name: _____

Title and Organization: _____

_____

Address: _____
                    Street   City   State   ZIP Code

Telephone: _____
                            Home   Work   Fax

E-Mail Address: _____

How I know this reference: _____

Date I received permission to use reference: _____

Date of reference letter on file: _____

Date of last personal contact: _____

Name: _____

Title and Organization: _____

_____

Address: _____
                    Street   City   State   ZIP Code

Telephone: _____
                            Home   Work   Fax

E-Mail Address: _____

How I know this reference: _____

Date I received permission to use reference: _____

Date of reference letter on file: _____

Date of last personal contact: _____

Continued on next page >>>

CAREER ACTION WORKSHEET 2-3 (continued)

Name: _____

Title and Organization: _____

_____

Address: _____

            Street   City   State   ZIP Code

Telephone: _____

           Home   Work   Fax

E-Mail Address: _____

How I know this reference: _____

_____

Date I received permission to use reference: _____

Date of reference letter on file: _____

Date of last personal contact: _____

Name: _____

Title and Organization: _____

_____

Address: _____

            Street   City   State   ZIP Code

Telephone: _____

           Home   Work   Fax

E-Mail Address: _____

How I know this reference: _____

_____

Date I received permission to use reference: _____

Date of reference letter on file: _____

Date of last personal contact: _____

CAREER ACTION WORKSHEET 2-4

Values and Work Environment Preferences Inventory

PART 1: VALUES

Directions: Review the values listed below, and rank the importance of each as it relates to your career and job goals (H = high, M = medium, and L = low).

Value	Ranking (H, M, L)
1. Adventure (risk taking, new challenges)	_____
2. Education/Learning/Wisdom	_____
3. Social needs (need for relationships with people)	_____
4. Self-respect/Integrity/Self-discipline	_____
5. Helping/Serving	_____
6. Recognition/Respect from others	_____
7. Freedom/Independence (working independently with minimal supervision)	_____
8. Security (job, family, national, financial)	_____
9. Spiritual needs	_____
10. Expression (creative, artistic)	_____
11. Responsibility (reliability, dependability)	_____
12. Balance in work and personal life	_____

Others (List other values below and rank each one.)

_____   _____

_____   _____

_____   _____

_____   _____

_____   _____

_____   _____

_____   _____

_____   _____

Continued on next page >>>

CAREER ACTION WORKSHEET 2-4 (continued)

PART 2: WORK ENVIRONMENT PREFERENCES

Directions: In the boxes to the right, place a check mark next to each work environment condition you prefer.

Work Environment	Check Those Preferred
1. Indoor work	☐
2. Outdoor work	☐
3. Industrial/manufacturing setting	☐
4. Office setting	☐
5. Working alone	☐
6. Working with people	☐
7. Working with things	☐
8. Working with data	☐
9. Working with ideas	☐
10. Challenging opportunities	☐
11. Predictable, orderly, structured work	☐
12. Pressures at work	☐
13. Problem solving	☐
14. Standing while working	☐
15. Sitting while working	☐
16. Busy surroundings	☐
17. Quiet surroundings	☐
18. Exciting, adventurous conditions	☐

Continued on next page >>>

CAREER ACTION WORKSHEET 2-4 (continued)

Work Environment	**Check Those Preferred**
19. Safe working conditions/environment	☐
20. Creative environment	☐
21. Opportunities for professional development and ongoing training/education	☐
22. Flexibility in work structure	☐
23. Teamwork and work groups	☐
24. Opportunities to supervise, lead, advance	☐
25. Opportunities to make a meaningful difference or to help others	☐
26. Using cutting-edge technology or techniques	☐
27. Integrity and truth in work environment	☐
28. Stability and security	☐
29. High-level earnings potential	☐
30. Opportunities to participate in community affairs	☐

Others (List other conditions you are seeking in your job target.)

_____	☐
_____	☐
_____	☐
_____	☐
_____	☐
_____	☐
_____	☐
_____	☐
_____	☐

CAREER ACTION WORKSHEET 2-5

Personal Qualities and Work Performance Traits

Directions: Rate yourself on each of the personal qualities and work performance traits listed below by using a scale of high, average, or low (H, A, or L). For example, if you think you have a high degree of dependability, write H in the space to the right of *Dependability*. Be sure to list other qualities or traits that are important for success in your targeted career. In developing your resume and preparing to interview well, you should be able to prove that you possess these traits by giving examples of how you have used them successfully. At the end of the form, write at least five brief positive examples of how you have used these qualities or traits.

Personal Quality or Work Performance Trait	Rating (H, A, L)
1. Initiative/Resourcefulness/Motivation	_____
2. Dependability	_____
3. Punctuality	_____
4. Flexibility	_____
5. Creativity	_____
6. Patience	_____
7. Perseverance	_____
8. Humor	_____
9. Diplomacy	_____
10. Intelligence	_____
11. High energy level	_____
12. Ability to work well with a team	_____
13. Ability to set and achieve goals	_____
14. Ability to plan, organize, prioritize work	_____
15. Outgoing personality	_____
16. Ability to handle conflict	_____
17. Optimistic attitude	_____
18. Realistic attitude	_____

Continued on next page >>>

CAREER ACTION WORKSHEET 2-5 (continued)

Personal Quality or Work Performance Trait	Rating (H, A, L)
19. Enthusiastic attitude	_____
20. Willingness to work	_____
21. Orderliness of work	_____
22. Attention to detail	_____
23. Ability to manage time well	_____
24. Honesty and integrity	_____
25. Ability to multitask	_____

Others (List and rank other positive personal qualities or work performance traits.)

_____   _____

_____   _____

_____   _____

_____   _____

_____   _____

_____   _____

_____   _____

_____   _____

_____   _____

Examples: List at least five positive examples of how you have used some of these qualities and traits in the past.

_____

_____

_____

_____

_____

_____

WHAT DO EMPLOYERS WANT?

"When hiring for any position, I look for people who have a grasp of computers and good communication skills. I also look for people who can work well with others, adapt easily to change, and be creative when looking for new ways to do things."

Debbie Bornholdt
Human Resource Project Manager
QVC, Electronic Retailer
West Chester, PA

Chapter 3 identifies the skills, work attitudes, and other qualifications that employers focus on in making hiring decisions. The chapter guides you through a self-assessment from the employer's perspective. The assessment will help you identify your most important qualifications so you will be ready to present them effectively to an employer during your job search. This chapter identifies excellent career and job planning resources to help you confirm appropriate goals. Chapter 3 also explains the importance of developing a career portfolio.

What Employers Want

Employers want to hire people who will make their businesses more successful. The most desirable employees have the specific skills, transferable career competencies, work values, and personal qualities necessary to be successful in the employers' organizations. The more clearly you convey your skills as they relate to your job target, the greater your chance of landing your ideal job. Chapter 3 helps you identify these skills and qualities so you will be prepared to interview successfully.

Job-Specific Skills

Employers seek employees with job-specific skills (skills and technical abilities that relate specifically to a particular job). Two examples of job-specific skills are using specialized tools and equipment and using a custom-designed software program.

Transferable Skills and Attitudes

Change is a constant in today's business world. Strong transferable career skills are the keys to success in managing your career through change. The most influential skills and attitudes are the abilities to:

▲ Work well with people.

▲ Plan and manage multiple tasks.

▲ Maintain a positive attitude.

▲ Show enthusiasm.

Employers need workers who have transferable career competencies—basic skills and attitudes that are important for all types of work. These skills make you highly marketable because they're needed for a wide variety of jobs and can be transferred from one task, job, or workplace to another. Examples include these:

▲ Planning skills

▲ Research skills

▲ Communication skills

▲ Human relations and interpersonal skills

▲ Critical thinking skills

▲ Management skills

Take, for example, a construction supervisor and an accountant. Both must work well with others, manage time, solve problems, read, and communicate effectively. All of these are transferable competencies. Both professionals must be competent in these areas even though framing a house and balancing a set of books (a job-specific skill for each field, respectively) are not related. In every occupation, transferable competencies are as important as technical expertise and job-specific skills.

> **Complete Career Action 3-1**

CAREER ACTION 3-1

Skills and Competencies Profile

Directions: Access Career Action Worksheet 3-1 on your Learner's CD, or use the worksheet that begins on page 43 to complete the assignment. When you have completed the assignment, file your worksheet in your Career Management Files Binder.

Assessing Yourself From an Employer's Perspective

In Chapter 2, you identified specific skills you developed in school, in work, and through other activities. Chapter 3 has provided you with insights into how employers view skills and competencies. Now it's time to review your inventory and self-assessment from an employer's perspective. How would an employer categorize your skills and personal qualities?

> **Complete Career Action 3-2**

Career Planning Resources

Many convenient resources are available to speed and improve the processes of making and confirming your best career choice. Review the following resources, and place a check mark next to those you could use to improve your career planning. (Note that comprehensive sources of job information are discussed in Chapter 6. You may want to review those now because some of them can also be used as career planning resources.)

▲ **Your school's career services staff and counselors.** These counselors specialize in assisting students with career planning. They provide aptitude and interest tests, as well as current resources for and information about the job market and occupational fields.

Success Tip

Identify your job-specific skills and transferable competencies to convince employers you fit the job.

CAREER ACTION 3-2

Career Competencies Inventory

Part A: Access Career Action Worksheet 3-2 on your Learner's CD, or use the worksheet that begins on page 47 to complete the assignment. As you read the summaries of the competencies, foundation skills, and personal qualities listed, think about and check each one you've developed.

Part B: Once you have completed Part A of this Career Action, do the following:

1. Write descriptions of at least three tasks you have carried out on a regular basis in each of the following categories:

   a.   Current or past jobs

   b.   Community, school, volunteer, or other activities

2. List as many examples as possible of both task- and job-specific skills and transferable competencies you used in each of the activities you described in number 1.

When you have completed the assignment, file your worksheet in your Career Management Files Binder.

▲ **The Internet.** A wealth of career planning and job information is available through the Internet. Many sites offer online tools that assess your career interests and values and match the results with appropriate careers and jobs. The *Your Career: How to Make It Happen* web site (http://levitt.swlearning.com) links to many of these. See your school's career services office for recommendations for helpful web sites, and check out the career center web sites of your local colleges and universities.

▲ **Computerized career information systems.** With these systems, users complete a computerized questionnaire regarding their personal interests and abilities. The program then provides a list of occupations consistent with a user's answers. Other information provided may include job descriptions, hiring requirements, employment prospects, and education and training requirements. Check with your school's career counselor or state department of education to locate the nearest computerized system.

▲ **City, county, state, and federal employment or human resources departments.** For information about government occupations, contact the employment or human resources department that manages employment in your target field.

▲ **Career planning publications.** Ask your school's career services counselor or librarian for help in locating books, magazines, and articles about your field and current job target. (Many of these publications are now available online.)

▲ **People you know.** Contact people you have observed or known, people you admire, and people who have jobs just like the one you dream of. Ask them to help you explore your readiness for a similar job or career.

▲ **Volunteer work.** Volunteer experience can be a big asset when applying for the job you want. It demonstrates initiative and helps you get a feel for a job and a career. You can volunteer on a part-time or temporary basis or arrange an internship through your school.

Success Tip

Consult a variety of career planning resources to improve the processes of making and confirming your best career choice.

PERSONAL BEST

Career Competencies

Your transferable career competencies or skills are every bit as important to your success in the workplace as your job-specific skills and training. The ability to identify, communicate, and demonstrate these skills in an interview could make the difference between you and other qualified job candidates.

The SCANS Report (Secretary's Commission on Achieving Necessary Skills), published by the U.S. Department of Labor, identified the transferable competencies essential for career and business success in the twenty-first century.

Workplace Competencies

1. **RESOURCES:** Identifies, organizes, plans, and manages resources.

2. **INTERPERSONAL:** Works well with others.

3. **INFORMATION:** Acquires, organizes, interprets, and uses information.

4. **SYSTEMS:** Understands complex social, organizational, and technological systems and interrelationships.

5. **TECHNOLOGY:** Works with a variety of technologies (tools, equipment, computers).

Foundation Skills and Personal Qualities

1. **BASIC SKILLS:** Reads, writes, and performs mathematical operations; listens; and speaks.

2. **THINKING SKILLS:** Thinks creatively, makes decisions, solves problems, visualizes, knows how to learn, and reasons.

3. **PERSONAL QUALITIES:** Displays responsibility, self-esteem, sociability, self-management, integrity, and honesty.

Successful Career Planning Requires Flexibility

Changing technologies and a global economy cause some careers to become obsolete or vastly changed. Broaden your job options. Prepare to qualify for two closely related career goals (such as becoming a mathematician or a systems analyst) that require related education, training, and general capabilities. Which transferable career competencies do you have that qualify you for jobs within and between career clusters? Ask a knowledgeable career counselor to help you identify multicareer goals appropriate for your interests and abilities. Continually work at developing your career flexibility and pursuing lifelong learning.

Complete Career Action 3-3

Set Your Career Target

The work you have completed in this chapter has prepared you to set your career target. You may want to use the visualization skills from Chapter 1 to help you define your personal career objectives. Together with friends and associates, brainstorm appropriate careers. Think about work, hobbies, and volunteer experiences you have enjoyed in the past. What kind of work do you want to do? Where would you like to do this work? How much do you want to get paid for your work? What is the best career match for your unique skills, experiences, values, and interests? The form for Career Action 3-4 will help you organize your thoughts.

Complete Career Action 3-4

CAREER ACTION 3-3

Internet Career Planning Resources

Directions: Use several of the Internet resources below to search for information about your career and job targets, including descriptions of your targeted fields and jobs, salary information, employment outlook projections, and more. Prepare a written summary of your findings, or print useful information that you find. Links can be found on the *Your Career: How to Make It Happen* web site (http://levitt.swlearning.com).

▲ Bureau of Labor Statistics

▲ America's Career InfoNet

▲ JobStar

▲ Occupational Outlook Handbook

▲ collegeboard.com

▲ O*Net OnLine

When you have completed the assignment, file your findings in your Career Action Worksheet.

CAREER ACTION 3-4

My Career Target

 Directions: Access Career Action Worksheet 3-4 on your Learner's CD, or use the worksheet on page 50 to complete the assignment.

 When you have completed the assignment, file your worksheet in your Career Management Files Binder.

Success Tip

Use a variety of career planning resources to help you choose and validate appropriate career and job goals.

Your Career Portfolio

A portfolio is a collection of documents and other items that demonstrate your skills, abilities, achievements, experience, and training. The purpose of a career portfolio is to organize relevant examples of skills and achievements that you can present during interviews as proof of your qualifications. A career portfolio provides tangible proof of your qualifications. It also demonstrates important skills that employers are seeking: critical thinking, analyzing, planning, and preparation.

Examples of appropriate portfolio items include the following:

▲ An official copy of your transcript(s)

▲ Your resume

▲ Exemplary samples of your work, such as business writing, graphic artwork, and printed samples from software presentations

> *"Formulate and stamp indelibly on your mind a mental picture of yourself succeeding. Hold this picture tenaciously. Never permit it to fade. Your mind will seek to develop this picture!"*
>
> Norman Vincent Peale

▲ Evidence of specialized computer usage, such as desktop publishing and web site creation

▲ Awards

▲ Work performance evaluations

▲ Letters of reference

A more comprehensive list of appropriate items and ideas for building your portfolio are contained in the "Career Portfolio" section of Appendix B, "Career Management and Marketing Tools." Additional activities are presented later in this text to assist you in developing an effective portfolio.

Portfolio samples can be from paid or volunteer work, internships, cooperative education, clubs, community activities, and more. Begin considering what you have done or accomplished that best demonstrates your qualifications for the job you want. For example, to demonstrate your computer skills, you could include transcripts listing related coursework or a CD or portable flash drive containing examples of multimedia presentations or programming code you have developed. To demonstrate a strong background in foreign languages, you could include transcripts listing appropriate coursework and a letter of recommendation from an instructor or employer who is familiar with your language skills.

For now, you can use a folder to store appropriate portfolio items to be used later in your job search. Begin listing appropriate items in Career Action 3-5.

Complete Career Action 3-5

Success Tip

Begin listing appropriate items for your career portfolio that demonstrate your job qualifications.

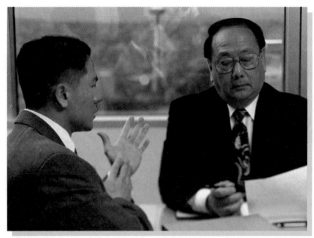

Presenting a portfolio to a potential employer helps you prove your qualifications for the job.

CAREER ACTION 3-5

List Appropriate Portfolio Items

Part A: To identify additional useful ideas for your own career portfolio, use two or more search engines to search the Internet for career portfolio information. Also check out other links available on the *Your Career: How to Make It Happen* web site (http://levitt.swlearning.com).

Part B: Access Career Action Worksheet 3-5 on your Learner's CD, or use a separate paper to complete the assignment. Take a moment now to list items that seem appropriate to include in your career portfolio. As you progress through the upcoming chapters, add other items to your list. Later you will be instructed to complete the assembly of your actual portfolio.

_____

_____

_____

_____

_____

_____

_____

When you have completed the assignment, file your worksheet in your Career Management Files Binder.

CHECKLIST

ASSESSING YOURSELF FROM AN EMPLOYER'S PERSPECTIVE

Check each of the actions you are currently taking to increase your career success:

○ Identifying job-specific skills and transferable career competencies to convince employers of appropriateness for the job

○ Using a variety of career planning resources to help in choosing and validating appropriate career and job goals

○ Preparing to qualify for two closely related career goals that require similar skills and training in order to increase your career flexibility

○ Using visualization, brainstorming, personal reflection, and other techniques to set your career target

○ Developing a portfolio of items to demonstrate job qualifications for prospective employers

○ Collecting items that will demonstrate job qualifications for prospective employers

CRITICAL THINKING QUESTIONS

1. Why is it important to develop a broad career base that is flexible enough to encompass at least two fields?

2. What career planning resources will be most helpful in your job search and career planning activities? Why?

3. Why do employers value employees who have the career competencies and foundation skills identified in the SCANS Report?

 For convenient access to valuable career resources, activities, and job information links, visit the companion web site for this text: *http://levitt.swlearning.com*

CAREER ACTION WORKSHEET 3-1

Skills and Competencies Profile

PART 1: JOB-SPECIFIC SKILLS

Directions: Review Career Actions 2-1 and 2-2 to refresh your memory regarding the job-specific skills and transferable career competencies you developed through your education, training, and experiences. Then identify and list below the 10 most important job-specific skills related to your current career target (examples: using job-specific computer software; operating specific equipment or tools; and performing specific tasks, such as mixing dental adhesives).

My Most Important Job-Specific Skills Related to My Career Target

1. _____

2. _____

3. _____

4. _____

5. _____

6. _____

7. _____

8. _____

9. _____

10. _____

In Chapter 9 (resume development) and Chapter 11 (the interview), you will be asked to prove that you have these job-specific skills by documenting examples of times you used them—providing "proof by example." Employers ask for such examples, and you need to be prepared to give them.

Continued on next page >>>

CAREER ACTION WORKSHEET 3-1 (continued)

PART 2: BASIC SKILLS AND ATTITUDES

Directions: Review the following skill categories and related transferable career competencies. Check the box to the left of each skill category that applies to you in any way. Then circle each transferable competency you have developed (from those listed after each skill category). Finally, list under *Other* any additional transferable competencies you have that relate to each category.

Skill Category

Related Transferable Career Competencies

☐ **Art:**

Drawing, designing, painting, sculpting, computer graphics design

Other: _____

_____

☐ **Athletics:**

Physical strength, physical ability, physical coordination, coaching, physical development, agility, team sports, individual sports

Other: _____

_____

☐ **Communication:**

Explaining/persuading, strong grammar/vocabulary, organizing thoughts clearly, communicating logically, listening, speaking, good telephone/reception skills, writing, knowledge of foreign languages

Other: _____

_____

☐ **Computer Technology:**

Computer operation, researching, training, testing, workflow analysis, evaluating, writing instructions, programming

Other: _____

_____

☐ **Creativity:**

Innovative, imaginative, idea person, bold

Other: _____

_____

Continued on next page >>>

CAREER ACTION WORKSHEET 3-1 (continued)

☐ **Engineering:**   Researching, testing, designing, constructing, analyzing, evaluating, controlling, electronic technology

Other: _____

_____

☐ **Human Relations:**   Counseling, diplomacy, negotiating, patience, outgoing, teamwork ability, understanding, resolving conflict, handling complaints

Other: _____

_____

☐ **Management:**   Analyzing data, directing, delegating, evaluating performance, organizing people/data/things, leading, making decisions, managing time, motivating self/others, planning, budgeting money/resources, solving problems, supervising, interviewing/hiring people, owning/operating a business

Other: _____

_____

☐ **Manual/ Mechanical:**   Good manual dexterity, building, operating, maintaining/repairing, assembling, Installing, carrying, loading, lifting, cooking, driving/operating vehicles, performing precision work, assessing spatial relationships, operating heavy equipment

Other: _____

_____

☐ **Mathematical:**   Mathematical computations, accuracy, analyzing data, mathematical reasoning, statistical problem solving, analyzing cost effectiveness, budgeting, applying formulas, collecting money, calculating

Other: _____

_____

☐ **Office:**   Keyboarding, data entry, computer operation, text processing, data processing, office equipment operation, filing/retrieving records, recording data, computing data, record keeping, telephone skills, business writing

Other: _____

Continued on next page >>>

CAREER ACTION WORKSHEET 3-1 (continued)

☐ **Outdoor Activities:**   Animal care, farming, landscaping, grounds care, boating, navigating, oceano-
graphic studies, forestry, logging, mining, fishing, horticulture

Other: _____

_____

☐ **Performing:**   Speaking, acting, dancing, singing, musical ability, comedy, conducting

Other: _____

_____

☐ **Sales/Promotion:**   Persuading, negotiating, promoting, influencing, selling, projecting enthusiasm,
organizing, handling rejection, following up

Other: _____

_____

☐ **Scientific Activities:**   Investigating, researching, analyzing, systematizing, observing, diagnosing

Other: _____

_____

☐ **Service/General:**   Serving, referring, receiving, billing, handling complaints, good customer relations, good listening skills, patience, managing difficult people, helping others, relating to others

Other: _____

_____

☐ **Service/Medical:**   Nursing, diagnosing, treating, rehabilitating, counseling, consoling, sympathizing,
managing stress/emergencies, good interpersonal skills

Other: _____

_____

☐ **Training/Teaching:**   Teaching skills/knowledge, tutoring, researching instructional content, organiz-
ing/developing content, explaining logically/clearly, demonstrating clearly, coach-
ing others, evaluating learning, addressing all learning styles, using instructional
technology

Other: _____

CAREER ACTION WORKSHEET 3-2

Career Competencies Inventory

Directions: Check the box to the left of each competency, skill, or quality you've developed, and circle the portions of the detailed descriptions that apply to you.

PART 1: WORKPLACE COMPETENCIES

RESOURCES: Identifies, organizes, plans, and manages resources

☐ **Manages Time:** Selects relevant, goal-related activities; ranks activities in order of importance; allocates time to activities; and understands, prepares, and follows schedules

☐ **Manages Money:** Uses budgets, keeps records, and makes adjustments to meet objectives

☐ **Manages Materials and Facilities:** Acquires, stores, allocates, and uses materials and/or space efficiently

☐ **Manages Human Resources:** Assesses skills and distributes work accordingly, uses coaching/mentoring skills with peers and subordinates, evaluates performance, and provides feedback

INTERPERSONAL: Works well with others

☐ **Participates as Team Member:** Contributes to group effort

☐ **Teaches Others New Skills**

☐ **Serves Clients/Customers:** Works to satisfy customers' expectations

☐ **Exercises Leadership:** Communicates ideas to justify position and persuades/convinces

☐ **Negotiates Decisions:** Works toward agreements involving exchange of resources and resolves divergent interests

☐ **Respects Cultural Diversity:** Works well with people from diverse backgrounds

INFORMATION: Acquires, organizes, interprets, and uses information

☐ **Acquires/Evaluates Information**

☐ **Organizes/Maintains Information**

☐ **Interprets/Communicates Information**

☐ **Uses Computers to Process Information**

Continued on next page >>>

CAREER ACTION WORKSHEET 3-2 (continued)

SYSTEMS: Understands complex social, organizational, and technological systems and interrelationships

☐ **Understands Systems:** Knows how social, organizational, and technological systems work and operates effectively with them

☐ **Monitors/Corrects Performance:** Distinguishes trends, predicts impacts on system operations, diagnoses deviations in systems' performance, and corrects malfunctions

☐ **Improves/Designs Systems:** Suggests modifications to existing systems and develops new or alternative systems to improve performance

TECHNOLOGY: Works with a variety of technologies

☐ **Selects Technology:** Chooses procedures, tools, or equipment, including computers and related technologies

☐ **Applies Technology to Task:** Understands overall intent and proper procedures for setup and operation of equipment

☐ **Maintains/Troubleshoots Technology:** Prevents, identifies, or solves problems with equipment, including computers and other technologies

PART 2: FOUNDATION SKILLS AND PERSONAL QUALITIES

BASIC SKILLS: Reads, writes, performs arithmetic/mathematical operations, listens, and speaks

☐ **Reading:** Locates, understands, and interprets written information, including material in documents such as manuals, graphs, and schedules

☐ **Writing:** Communicates thoughts, ideas, information, and messages in writing and creates documents such as letters, directions, manuals, reports, graphs, and flowcharts

☐ **Arithmetic/Mathematics:** Performs basic computations and approaches practical problems by choosing appropriately from a variety of mathematical techniques

☐ **Listening:** Receives, attends to, interprets, and responds to verbal messages and other cues

☐ **Speaking:** Organizes ideas and communicates orally

Continued on next page >>>

CAREER ACTION WORKSHEET 3-2 (continued)

THINKING SKILLS: Thinks creatively, makes decisions, solves problems, visualizes, knows how to learn, and reasons

☐ **Creative Thinking:** Generates new ideas

☐ **Decision Making:** Specifies goals and constraints, generates alternatives, considers risks, facilitates group decision-making processes, and evaluates and chooses best alternative

☐ **Problem Solving:** Recognizes problems, devises and implements plan of action, and facilitates problem-solving and brainstorming discussions

☐ **Knowing How to Learn:** Uses efficient learning techniques to acquire and apply new knowledge and skills

☐ **Reasoning:** Discovers a rule or principle underlying the relationship between two or more objects and applies it when solving a problem

PERSONAL QUALITIES: Displays responsibility, self-esteem, sociability, self-management, integrity, and honesty

☐ **Responsibility:** Exerts a high level of effort, perseveres toward goal attainment, and multitasks effectively

☐ **Self-Esteem:** Believes in own self-worth and maintains a positive view of self

☐ **Sociability:** Demonstrates understanding, friendliness, adaptability, and empathy; manages conflict effectively; is polite

☐ **Self-Management:** Assesses self accurately, sets personal goals, monitors progress, works well under pressure, and exhibits self-control

☐ **Integrity/Honesty:** Chooses ethical courses

Fine-Tune Your Competencies List

Directions: Review the items you identified in Career Action 3-2. Then select the 10 strongest of these transferable career competencies and basic skills related to your current job target. List them below.

1. _____   6. _____

2. _____   7. _____

3. _____   8. _____

4. _____   9. _____

5. _____   10. _____

NOTE: You will expand on this information in Chapters 9 and 11.

CAREER ACTION WORKSHEET **3-4**

My Career Target

Directions: Answer the following questions about your current career target.

1. In what career field are you planning to seek employment? (Examples: accounting, office management, health care, teaching, administration, construction, and computer technology)

_____

_____

_____

_____

2. What specific job or jobs are you targeting in your employment search? (List every job you are qualified for and interested in pursuing. Maximize your options by listing jobs within and between career fields or clusters that require transferable competencies you have.)

_____

_____

_____

_____

_____

_____

3. What specific activities are you most interested in performing in your ideal job? What energizes and excites you most?

_____

_____

_____

_____

_____

4. Are you willing to travel or relocate? Explain.

_____

_____

_____

_____

PREPARE FOR A CHANGING WORKPLACE

"When I answer career-related questions on the CareerBuilder web site, I tell people that the workplace is changing very rapidly. A positive attitude, flexibility, and a varied skill set have become the keys to success. When setting goals, be assertive for your own goals, but also for the company's goals—that is the ultimate in career development."

Nancy Porte
Director of Professional Services
The CareerBuilder Network

Chapter 4 provides an overview of topics that are critical to success in the changing twenty-first century workplace. Managing personal finances well is one key to career success. Additionally, contemporary issues in globalization, technology, teamwork, diversity and workplace equity, and ethics all play roles in career development. Use this chapter to help plan for the future and develop the competencies, skills, and resources that will best support your career success.

Manage Your Personal Finances

Many goals—a home, a car, and an education—require both personal effort and money. Managing money well is also essential for landing a job and achieving career success. In fact, many employers routinely run credit checks when screening job applicants. Credit checks have long been used to determine whether an applicant can get a loan or credit card, and they are increasingly being used as part of many employers' job application processes. Employers often will not hire applicants if their credit reports show a history of poor money management, such as late payments or defaulting on school loans or other lines of credit.

Careful and effective management of your personal finances provides many benefits: It protects your credit status, helps you avoid disqualification for employment, and helps you get accepted for future loans at favorable interest rates.

Balance Wants and Resources. Plan and control your money with a well-designed monthly budget. Required income varies with individual circumstances, and a budget will reveal the amount of money you need to survive. Knowing this figure is crucial for you to be able to negotiate salary offers.

Track Income. Tracking your sources of year-round income will help you anticipate and plan for income changes or variations. For example, you may earn quite a bit of money during the summer months but find that during the school year, income is down and expenses are up.

Track Expenses. Where does your money go? To manage your finances successfully, you need to allocate money for all your needs, including living, school, and personal expenses. Categorize and budget your expenses. If your actual expenses exceed the budgeted amounts, determine where you can cut.

Set Up a Regular Savings Plan. Making regular contributions to a savings plan will allow you to save

© GETTY IMAGES/PHOTODISC

Learn to manage your personal finances, and keep your living expenses below your income.

money to pay back college or other loans. Keep in mind you must pay a minimum amount per month on a student loan regardless of the balance. Savings will also help you accumulate the extra cash you may need if you choose a job that involves relocation. Start-up expenses (such as deposits for rent, utilities, and telephone) can be costly.

Use Credit Wisely. Establishing and maintaining good credit is a must for successful career development. Opening a credit account and using it wisely will help you build a positive credit rating.

The rewards for budgeting your income and expenses, saving money, and investing wisely include the following:

▲ Earning a good credit rating

▲ Maintaining your employment competitiveness

▲ Being able to negotiate realistic wages

▲ Keeping financial peace of mind

▲ Having money to achieve financial goals (such as a car, a home, an education, retirement security, and travel)

Complete Career Action 4-1

CAREER ACTION 4-1

Prepare Your Monthly Budget

Directions: Access Career Action Worksheet 4-1 on your Learner's CD or use the worksheet on page 64 of this text to prepare a monthly budget. When you have completed the assignment, file your budget in your Career Management Files Binder.

PERSONALBEST

Use Credit Wisely

Using credit beyond what you can afford creates a destructive cycle of more and more charging and deeper and deeper debt. Below are six tips to help you use credit wisely and protect your personal finances:

1. Avoid using credit beyond what you can afford.

2. Shop around for a credit card with good terms (such as no annual fee, grace periods, and a low interest rate). Watch out for cards that offer low initial interest rates that eventually increase, sometimes significantly.

3. Use only one credit card, and use it sparingly.

4. Pay your entire balance each month, or at least pay more than the minimum monthly payment.

5. Make sure the credit card company receives your payment before the due date.

6. Never use credit to extend your paycheck.

Use good budgeting skills, make informed choices, and exercise common sense to avoid a financial fiasco that can tarnish your credit rating for a lifetime.

Understand What Globalization Means to Your Career

Experts predict that for the first part of the twenty-first century, global trade among nations will increase three to four times faster than individual national economies. Success in this larger, more competitive market requires quality products that are innovative, timely, and efficiently produced. To meet the new challenges, many companies are restructuring as follows:

▲ Distributing design, marketing, and customer service operations across the globe

▲ Moving manufacturing plants to locations that offer the appropriate combination of education and low labor costs

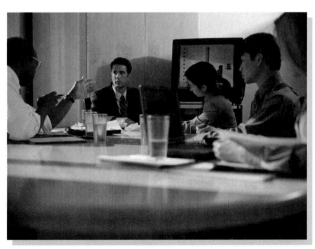

© GETTY IMAGES/PHOTODISC

To compete in today's markets, companies often assemble specialized teams to meet critical deadlines.

▲ Purchasing product components from outside suppliers

▲ Reducing the number of permanent employees

▲ Relying on specialized teams, often made up of short-term workers, to meet critical deadlines

▲ Recruiting highly skilled workers worldwide

In short, globalization is increasing competitive pressures, blurring economic boundaries, and relocating well-educated workers.

Appreciate the Major Role of Quality Assurance Programs

In the early 1980s, the European economies lagged behind those of the United States and Japan. After realizing that their many different production standards made them less competitive, Europeans began requiring suppliers of regulated products to meet the quality assurance standards adopted by the International Organization for Standardization (known as the ISO). Companies worldwide are establishing Total Quality Management (TQM) programs to achieve ISO certification. TQM programs are also referred to as Continuous Quality Improvement (CQI) programs. ISO standards have varied goals; some represent product conformance to established requirements, while others strive to achieve sustained customer satisfaction. Assure employers that you understand the importance of quality by submitting well-prepared job search documents. Study the TQM and CQI literature, and learn how the quality assurance process applies to your industry. During job interviews, ask employers about their quality assurance programs.

Provide Service for Two Kinds of Customers

TQM and CQI have taught companies that success in today's marketplace requires the satisfying of two kinds of customers—internal and external. Internal customers are employees who build on the work of coworkers and depend on receiving quality work to complete their own jobs successfully. External customers contribute to the success of companies by purchasing the final products and services. In the worldwide market, customer service means delivering satisfactory results to both types of customers.

Identify the internal and external customers for any job you consider. Research your industry so you can speak knowledgeably about current customer service issues and give examples of how you handle typical customer concerns in a positive way.

Develop a Worldwide Perspective

Meet the challenges of globalization by developing a worldwide perspective. Demonstrate an understanding of the global competitive factors of your industry, and show a willingness to learn about international cultures. Tell employers if you are willing to travel or if you speak more than one language. As trading opportunities expand, career possibilities will also broaden and require more skills and more world awareness.

Success Tip

For a successful career in a global economy, learn about the economic, political, social, and technological trends in the world, and provide quality products and service to all your customers.

Explore Contemporary Workplace Issues

The effects of globalization combined with rapid advancements in technology are swiftly changing the work environment, the pace of work, and communication methods. In a long-term trend known as "offshoring," many U.S. employers are shipping jobs overseas where cheaper labor continues to be an attractive bargain. Being adaptable, developing your skills, and staying abreast of workplace trends are essential for keeping job security and for landing a new job if yours is threatened by offshoring.

Develop Telecommuting Skills for Flexible Work Environments

One of the fastest-growing trends worldwide is the virtual corporation or office. Individuals who participate in this type of work environment are referred to as virtual employees, teleworkers, or telecommuters. The defining element of telework is the use of computers and telecommunications to change the accepted geography of work. Flexibility is the driving force behind this type of work. Some companies are reducing the number of permanently assigned desks and providing workstations equipped with network connections, telephones, and office supplies so employees who travel among company locations can plug their laptops into the company network and start working.

As a result of companies' reducing their workforces and individuals' opting to work within more flexible schedules, many organizations with surplus space available have set up work areas that they rent or make available to employees and visitors who do not have "permanent" office space.

Develop the following organizational skills and remain flexible so you can work comfortably and productively in any virtual office environment:

▲ **Planning.** Set realistic goals to ensure your productivity. Establish a schedule for your day, and stick to it.

▲ **Focus.** Be disciplined, and be able to work without supervision.

▲ **Preparation.** Set up a home office space, and use it only for work tasks. Obtain the equipment, technology, and supplies you will need. If you will be spending your own money, talk to an accountant so you will understand the tax issues involved.

▲ **Organization.** Avoid distractions. Try to set clear boundaries between work and home, but be adaptable. When a client in a different time zone calls your home office at night, you must be flexible.

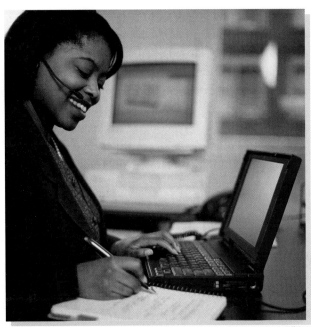

© GETTY IMAGES/PHOTODISC

Virtual offices are increasing in popularity. Employees who telecommute may not have permanent desks at their companies but instead work among various locations using laptops and other technologies.

Update Your Technology Skills and Understand Computer Networks

Technology will continue to evolve and affect all work environments at an ever-increasing pace. Incorporate technology into your career by keeping current on technological trends; by frequently updating your skills; and by maintaining a flexible, positive attitude.

> *"Once a new technology rolls over you, if you're not part of the steamroller, you're part of the road."*
> Stewart Brand

Businesses and organizations rely on networks, which use computer and communications technology to link resources and make it easy for people to find, send, and receive information. Voice and data networks can provide nearly instantaneous access to items as diverse as company records, public chat rooms, and unwanted viruses. Being able to navigate voice and data networks is essential to workplace success.

Navigate an Intranet and Extranet. Although any business may use the public Internet, many companies have private, closed computer networks called intranets. These intranets are used for internal communications to protect business information from competitive spying or sabotage. Intranets often start with electronic mail, scheduling, and collaboration applications to create an organization that extends beyond the physical constraints of buildings and walls. Companies typically restrict and/or examine incoming and outgoing data to stop the unauthorized transmission of information by company-owned, employee-operated computers. Some companies even prohibit remote access, but most issue passwords to allow employees who travel or telework to use the intranet via telephone or cable lines and modems.

When a company or an organization expands its network to include customers, suppliers, and partners outside the company or organization, it has created a structure known as an extranet. This type of network rests on three technologies: the Internet, groupware applications (such as e-mail, team areas on web sites, and newsgroups), and firewalls (security hardware and software). Why would an organization develop and implement an extranet? Because quick communication with customers and partners is an advantage in today's ever-changing marketplace.

Companies often use firewall security systems that protect their intranets and extranets and provide their employees with secure access to the Internet. Firewalls use special combinations of hardware and software to restrict the types of information that can enter and exit network systems. Firewalls can also be configured to provide network managers with usage patterns, the number of attempts to breach the system, and other information. In addition to firewalls, extranets often use some form of user identification (such as digital certificates), encryption, and virtual private networks (VPNs) that navigate through the public network.

Take Security Precautions. Anyone with a computer, a telephone or cable line, and a modem can access the Internet. Like any other society, the Internet

has its share of vandals. Companies that use the Internet to send inter- and intra-company e-mail, sponsor company web sites, or conduct monetary transactions must protect their computers with host-based security programs. These special programs are installed on each computer to protect it from unauthorized access and viruses.

Recognize Privacy Limitations on the Internet, Intranet, and Extranet. Network managers have full access to network information, including in-hosue e-mail. Even if both the sender and the receiver delete a message from their computers' memories, the message still exists in the backup files of the sending and receiving servers. Protect your privacy: Do not send private information over the Internet, and transmit only legal, ethical company business over intranets. Also, use passwords to protect the confidentiality of company information and sensitive personnel records.

Embrace New Technologies

Completely new industries have emerged to support our daily need for the use of technology. If you are not already involved with technology, you no doubt soon will work directly or indirectly with computers or some other form of the many technological advances used today. A fear of technology can reduce your productivity or restrict your ability to do a job well. If you are faced with this anxiety, take the initiative to get the training or education necessary to become comfortable with the technology you will need in your career. An attitude that embraces the smart use of technology can protect your job and keep you on the cutting edge of the workforce.

Adapt to an Increased Work Pace

Technology has increased the pace of work by reducing distance and time as barriers to communication. In the past, the pressures of decision making and the demands of work processes were buffered by the time it took for information to travel from one point to another. No one expected business information to be available quickly to all workers or to be delivered routinely to people who were traveling, on vacation, or at home.

Expectations have changed. People expect quicker results and faster decisions because information is now available swiftly from almost any location to workers at any level. The current direction is toward larger, more complex workloads. The abilities to solve problems quickly, to be resourceful, to use technology to enhance productivity, and to manage multiple priorities are now essential workplace skills, along with a willingness to work longer but more flexible hours.

Function as a Team Player

The availability of management information to all employees, the rapid rate of technological advances, and the competitive pressures of globalization have combined to result in unpredictable staffing needs and fundamental shifts in the working structures of companies. The shift is away from management-directed systems and toward "flat" team-directed systems that increase each individual's responsibilities.

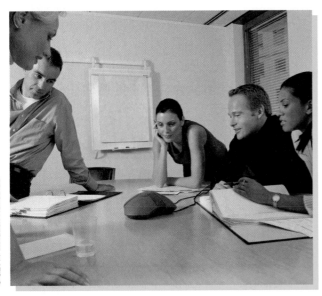

Technology increases the pace of work by eliminating communication barriers.

© GETTY IMAGES/PHOTODISC

Companies are using a skilled core group of leaders to develop strategies and goals and to manage work teams that perform the design, production, marketing, and servicing tasks. Instead of middle managers, technology now transfers information between core groups and work teams. Flatter, leaner organizations respond more efficiently to competitive pressures and create a need for flexible, problem-solving team leaders.

Working in teams results in benefits for both team members and the organization in which they work. These benefits include:

▲ **Collaboration.** People want to work well together and support one another because they identify with the team.

▲ **Communication.** Team members realize the importance of passing on the information members need to operate more effectively.

▲ **More efficient application of resources, talents, and strengths.** Team members apply themselves willingly. When one member lacks certain knowledge or competence, another is there to fill the gap.

▲ **Sound decisions and solutions made simultaneously.** A team can generate more discussion, ideas, and solutions than a single individual can.

▲ **Quality.** Team members feel pride in the team effort and ensure that each member gets what he or she needs from other team members to turn out the best possible work.

Determine Areas of Potential Employment Growth

Globalization, advancing technology, and the aging of baby boomers (the 76 million people born between 1946 and 1964) are stimulating a long-term shift from a manufacturing-based economy to a service-based economy. The U.S. Bureau of Labor Statistics (BLS) Employment projections for 2002-2012 show that professional and related occupations will grow faster and add more jobs than any other major occupational group, with 6.5 million new jobs expected by 2012. Three-fourths of the job growth in this area is expected to be among health care practitioners, computer occupations, and education and training occupations. According to the

BLS projections, the fastest-growing occupations (2002-2012) are:

▲ Medical assistants

▲ Network systems and data communications analysts

▲ Physician assistants

▲ Social and human service assistants

▲ Home health aides

▲ Medical records and health information technicians

▲ Physical therapist aides and assistants

▲ Computer software engineers, applications

▲ Computer software engineers, systems software

Pursue Education and Training. Education is more important than ever in today's job market. Most of the fastest-growing occupations require specific post-secondary education, on-the-job training, or a bachelor's degree. Your commitment to your education and training will be critical to your career success.

Consider Small Businesses. Small businesses represent a huge portion of economic growth and offer significant opportunities. According to the Small Business Administration, small businesses provide approximately 75 percent of the net new jobs added to the economy. Additionally, small businesses hire a larger proportion of employees who are younger workers, older workers, and part-time workers. These businesses are expected to continue to prosper. When planning your career, consider what small businesses have to offer. What they may lack in benefits, they may make up for in flexibility and opportunity.

Recognize the Impact of Baby Boomers' Retirements

Only 12 percent of the pre-baby-boomer generation chose to remain in the workforce after the traditional retirement age of 65. If global markets continue to expand and if boomers (who make up 52 percent of today's working population) retire at the same rate as their parents, employers could face a serious labor shortage and a rapid rise in recruitment, training, and benefit costs. Current projections, however, show

> ### Success Tip
>
> Sharpen your technological and team skills so you can work productively with flatter, leaner organizations that use the latest in computer and communications technology. Show employers that you adapt well to change by demonstrating flexibility and by focusing on problem solving.

that several factors will keep 75 to 80 percent of baby boomers working in some capacity after the traditional retirement ages:

▲ **Lack of money.** Most baby boomers older than 65 will need to work to supplement Social Security, to combat the effects of inflation, to offset reduced or nonexistent pensions, to pay rising Medicare and medical rates, and to maintain their pre-age-65 standard of living.

▲ **Healthier elderly and longer life spans.** In the 1950s, the average life expectancy was 68 years; today it is 80 years.

▲ **Personal satisfaction.** The National Institute on Aging published a survey that showed 75 percent of older workers would prefer to phase down from full-time to part-time work instead of retiring abruptly.

Understand Employee Benefit Programs

Today's employers must balance the rising cost of healthcare coverage with the need to provide attractive employee benefits packages. As a result, they take a variety of approaches that employees and job seekers must carefully consider:

▲ **Offer personalized benefits.** Employers often make fixed-amount benefit contributions that employees use to pay for choices from a variety of benefit options (such as child care; long-term care insurance; elder-care services; family-care leave of absence; work/life programs; domestic partner benefits; prepaid legal, automobile, home, and funeral insurance; and convenience or "concierge" services). These are sometimes called "defined contribution" or "cafeteria-style" plans.

▲ **Allow workers to pay for additional benefits at group rates.**

▲ **Offer flexible working schedules.**

▲ **Restructure jobs** into part-time (including shared jobs), temporary, teleworking, or contractual assignments.

▲ **Reorganize the compensation system** to reward people quickly for their performance.

▲ **Expand compensation packages** to include extra training, exposure to decision makers, and increased recognition.

Chapter 19 offers more advice on how you can make the most of company benefits.

> *"Government cannot make us equal; it can only recognize, respect, and protect us as equals before the law."*
>
> Clarence Thomas
> U.S. Supreme Court Justice

Success Tip

Research the compensation and benefits plans offered by firms of various sizes in your industry. Recognize that employers may offer attractive, unusual benefits packages to enhance wages.

Work Responsibly With Others

A complex and diverse workforce requires workers to be flexible, respect differences, and work together to increase productivity. Economic, legal, and social forces worldwide make it increasingly important to respect and value cultural, gender, and physical diversity among coworkers. Successful companies view employee differences as assets to the teamwork that ensures successful customer service in diverse markets.

Promote Workplace Equity

To meet competitive pressures today, employers are working to integrate diversity into their businesses.

Companies that meet and exceed legal requirements for workplace equity have increased productivity because employees feel valued and respected for their contributions. Most businesses with more than 15 employees have an official diversity policy to ensure compliance with the four federal laws that set the tone for workplace equity in the United States:

▲ **The (Revised) Fair Labor Standards Act (including the Equal Pay Act)** defines the 40-hour workweek, covers the federal minimum wage, sets requirements for overtime, places restrictions on child labor, and prohibits compensating men and women differently for doing the same job.

▲ **The Age Discrimination in Employment Act** prohibits companies with 20 or more employees from discriminating against employees who are age 40 or older.

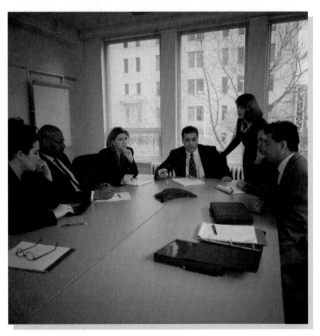

© GETTY IMAGES/PHOTODISC

Workplace diversity is an asset. Treat your coworkers with respect, and be open to their unique perspectives.

▲ **The Americans with Disabilities Act** prohibits employers with 15 or more employees from discriminating against people with physical or mental disabilities. This act also requires employers to make "a reasonable accommodation" for the needs of disabled employees as long as the accommodation does not represent an undue hardship for the employers.

▲ **Title VII of the Civil Rights Act** makes workplace discrimination with respect to race, color, sex, national origin, and religion illegal for companies that employ 15 or more people.

The most frequently reported type of discrimination covered under Title VII of the Civil Rights Act is sexual harassment. Sexual harassment occurs when one person makes continued and unwelcome sexual advances toward, requests sexual favors from, and displays other verbal or physical conduct of a sexual nature toward another person against the other person's wishes. According to the Equal Employment Opportunity Commission (EEOC), sexual harassment occurs "when submission to or rejection of this conduct explicitly or implicitly affects an individual's employment, unreasonably interferes with an individual's work performance, or creates an intimidating, hostile, or offensive work environment." This type of discrimination can occur in a variety of situations and should be thoroughly investigated once reported.

Keep the following facts in mind:

▲ Harassers and victims may be men or women, and the victim is not necessarily of the opposite sex.

▲ The harasser can be a coworker, a customer, a supervisor, or someone not connected to the employee's work. The victim is not just the target of the harassment, but is anyone who observed or learned about the harassment and was affected by it.

▲ Sexual harassment can occur even if there is no demonstrable effect of economic injury or discharge of the victim.

Promote workplace equity by demonstrating respect for others and openness to different perspectives. Further your career by relating positively to others regardless of their physical abilities, gender, race, culture, age, religion, or sexual orientation.

Respect Privacy and Confidentiality of Your Company, Coworkers, Customers, and Suppliers

Working responsibly with others includes respecting coworker, company, and customer privacy. Coworkers do not like having their privacy violated, and employers dismiss and often sue employees who "leak" proprietary information, abuse the company's computer system, or violate a nondisclosure agreement. Customers and suppliers also are assertive in protecting their confidential business information. They may take legal action against or refuse to do business with people who violate their trust.

Treat Coworkers As You Want to Be Treated. The openness of most working environments makes true privacy impossible, but the expectation of privacy remains. If you develop a reputation for being discreet and courteous, you will learn more, progress further, and become a respected member of the team.

Guard Your Company's Business Information. By accepting employment, you agree to join your employer's team and help the company succeed. Divulging proprietary information could undermine the ability of your employer to compete in the marketplace. Therefore, you have a moral and legal obligation to protect product, marketing, and management information. Before discussing work-related information with your coworkers, make sure you are in an appropriate location. Take reasonable precautions to protect important business information.

Honor Confidentiality Agreements with Customers and Suppliers. Learn about your company's policies regarding confidentiality or nondisclosure agreements. These types of agreements state that a company's representatives will not disclose or use clients' or suppliers' business information except for the legitimate purposes detailed in the agreement. Make sure you know what customers or suppliers expect you to do with sensitive information before you accept it. If you have any doubts, check with appropriate management personnel.

Develop Conflict Resolution and Problem-Solving Skills

Conflict and problems are a natural part of life. The only way to avoid them is to live in a vacuum. If you are to manage conflict and prevent it from escalating, you must develop strong interpersonal communication and problem-solving skills. Several skills are particularly critical to your success in navigating through conflict that can arise in the workplace.

To be successful at conflict resolution:

▲ Be an active listener.

▲ Define and analyze a situation and/or problem objectively.

▲ Use "I" messages to communicate how you feel without assigning blame.

▲ Understand barriers that may be preventing a solution and causing resistance, and tactfully start breaking them down.

▲ Brainstorm for solutions.

▲ Evaluate possible solutions to choose a win-win solution through which the needs of all parties are met.

▲ Maintain your integrity and professionalism.

Conflicts are most successfully resolved when communication flows well, behavior is assertive rather than aggressive, and a collaborative method is used.

To solve problems, use the following six-step process, which will focus your thinking and direct your decision making.

1. **Identify the problem.** Define it clearly and honestly, without bias. Pinpointing the problem is the first step in solving it.

2. **Gather information.** Learn as much about the problem as you can, and work with others to brainstorm as many ideas as possible for solutions.

3. **Evaluate the information.** Consider the source of all the information. Is it reliable, accurate, and unbiased?

4. **Consider alternatives.** Consider the pros and cons of each possible solution. Evaluate the costs, benefits, and potential obstacles.

5. **Select the best alternative.** Carry out the plan for your best solution, but be ready to change the plan if necessary.

6. **Evaluate results.** Monitor the results of your solution to measure its effectiveness. If the solution is not working, be ready to develop a new plan.

Practice Ethical Behavior in the Workplace

According to one dictionary, ethics means "the moral principles which determine the rightness or wrongness of particular acts or activities." Nothing will

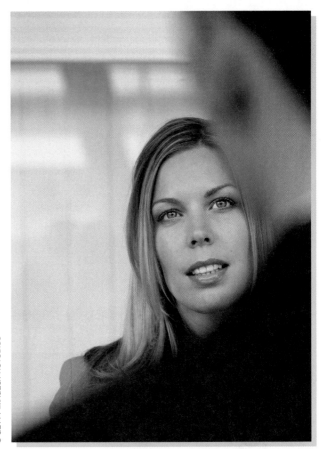

If you find yourself facing an ethical dilemma at work, maintain your integrity. Remember: Nothing will damage your career as drastically as losing your reputation for being ethical!

damage your career as drastically as losing your reputation for being ethical! In general, members of the business community expect you to be honest, open, accurate, law abiding, and trustworthy.

Make Ethical Decisions. Most people believe they know the difference between right and wrong, but applying one's own principles and maintaining one's integrity in the business world can be challenging. Aim to be fair, truthful, and responsible in your dealings, and always think through the consequences of your actions.

Refuse to Take Unethical Actions. If you know an action is wrong, refuse to do it. If you are faced with an ethical dilemma and you are not sure what to do, start by asking yourself these questions:

▲ Would I be violating any laws or policies?

▲ Do I have the proper consent?

▲ Will my decision be fair and respectful?

▲ What are the consequences of my actions? What are the risks? Will anyone benefit or suffer?

▲ How will my decision make me feel about myself? Will I be proud of my actions?

Gather as much information as you can, and ask for help from trusted experts or resources. Most companies make personnel, management, and legal resources available to employees. You also have the right to consult with your own spiritual or legal advisers.

> *"Reading about ethics is about as likely to improve one's behavior as reading about sports is to make one into an athlete."*
>
> Mason Colley
> U.S. Aphorist

If you have any reservations about an action, don't let yourself be talked into doing it. If you take an unethical action, you are the one who will have to live with the resulting loss of reputation and with the personal and legal consequences. Protect your long-term career by always demonstrating your personal integrity and professional ethics.

> **Complete Career Action 4-2**

CAREER ACTION 4-2

Use the Internet to Research Contemporary Workplace Issues

 Directions: Access Career Action Worksheet 4-2 on your Learner's CD or use the worksheet on page 66 of this text to complete the assignment.

 Use the Internet to research a workplace issue that interests you or research one of the contemporary issues listed on the worksheet.

 After you have summarized your findings, file your worksheet in your Career Management Files Binder.

CHECKLIST

PREPARING FOR A CHANGING WORKPLACE

Check each of the actions you are currently taking to increase your career success:

○ Mastering money with common sense by using a monthly budget

○ Using a two-pronged approach when preparing for a successful career in the global economy of the twenty-first century: (1) learning about the economic, political, social, and technological trends; (2) providing quality products and excellent service to customers

○ Showing employers your ability to adapt to change by demonstrating flexibility, focusing on problem solving, and working well in teams

○ Sharpening telecommuting and technology skills

○ Staying abreast of workplace trends and employment growth areas

○ Pursuing education and training opportunities

○ Researching the compensation and benefits plans offered by firms of various sizes in a target industry

○ Respecting diversity, honoring confidentiality, and maintaining high ethical standards

CRITICAL THINKING QUESTIONS

1. Why is it important to manage your personal finances well?

2. How are globalization and advancing technology changing the way people work and affecting employment growth areas?

3. What skills should you possess to deal effectively with conflict?

4. How can following the six-step, problem-solving process improve your decision making?

5. Why should you practice high ethical standards in the workplace?

For convenient access to valuable career resources, activities, and job information links, visit the companion web site for this text: *http://levitt.swlearning.com*

CAREER ACTION WORKSHEET 4-1

Prepare Your Monthly Budget

Directions: Follow the steps below using this worksheet or an electronic spreadsheet to prepare a monthly budget.

1. Add your additional item names to Column B.

2. Put appropriate amounts in Columns C and D.

3. For each numbered item, subtract Column D from Column C; place the answer in Column E. Indicate differences that are over budget with a negative (−) sign and differences that are under budget with a positive (+) sign.

4. Subtotal each category in each column.

5. In Columns C and D, put the total for line 3 on line 32 and the total for line 31 on line 33.

6. Subtract line 33 from line 32, and put the answer on line 34.

MONTHLY BUDGET PLANNER FOR MONTH OF _____

A Category	B Item	C Budgeted	D Actual	E Over (−) or Under (+)
1. Income	Wages			
2.	Other			
3.	Total Income			
4. Expenses	Rent/Mortgage			
5.	Car Payment			
6.	Child Care			
7.	Insurance			
8.				
9.	Loans			
10.				
11.	Savings			
12.	Allowance			
13.	Food/Living Items			
14.	Home Utilities			
15.				

Continued on next page >>>

Career Action Worksheet 4-1 (continued)

A Category	B Item	C Budgeted	D Actual	E Over (−) or Under (+)
16.	Telephone(s)			
17.	Cable TV			
18.	Transportation			
19.				
20.	School Expenses			
21.	Credit Cards			
22.				
23.	Medical Care			
24.	Clothes/Shoes			
25.	Hobbies/Sports			
26.	Entertainment			
27.	Charity			
28.	Gifts			
29.	Vacations			
30.	Other			
31.	Total Expenses			
32. Totals	Total Income			
33. (less)	Total Expenses			
34.	Difference*			

*If your expenses exceed your income, reassess your budget.

CAREER ACTION WORKSHEET 4-2

Use the Internet to Research Contemporary Workplace Issues

Directions: Use the Internet to research one or more of the contemporary issues listed below, or select a workplace issue that especially interests you. Use your favorite search engines or those linked from the *Your Career: How to Make It Happen* web site (http://levitt.swlearning.com). Write a brief summary of your findings below, or use a separate sheet of paper for your report.

1. **Global Perspective:** Try the search string *international and business.*

   Also search for these web sites:

   a.   Michigan State University's globalEDGE

   b.   BusinessWeek Online (Click on "Global Biz.")

   c.   United States Council for International Business (Click on "What's New.")

2. **The Workplace:** Try the following three search strings: *the workplace, computers and networking,* and *telecommuting and virtual and office.*

   Also search for these web sites:

   a.   Reengineering Resource Center (Click on "The Virtual Office.")

   b.   Webopedia (Do a search using the keyword *telecommuting.*)

3. **Tailored Benefits Packages:** Try the following two search strings: *workplace and benefits* and *work and life and benefits.* Also check the Yahoo! web site. (Click on "Business," "Employment and Work," and "Employment and Workplace Issues.")

   Also search for these web sites:

   a.   The Benefits Network

   b.   International Foundation of Employee Benefit Plans

Summary of Internet Research Findings

_____

_____

_____

_____

_____

_____

_____

ORGANIZE YOUR WINNING NETWORK

In this chapter, you will:

- Develop a list of people who can act as a personal support system to motivate you in your job search and provide moral support.

- Prepare a list of people who can act as a job search network to help you find solid job leads and provide professional suggestions for enhancing your job search preparation.

 Use the Internet to search for current job search networking tips.

"What a lot of people don't recognize, until they are faced with a job search, is that it pays to <u>stay networked</u>— particularly in good times when you don't feel the need as much to keep in touch. Staying networked on a regular basis will put you steps ahead of everyone else who has not remained connected when it comes time for a job search or getting the information or resources you need."

Rebecca Zucker
Career and Executive Coach
Career Transition and Managerial Effectiveness

Statistically, the most effective resource for finding a job is networking. Chapter 5 explains how to build a powerful job search network. This chapter guides you through the development of two important support groups to help you achieve your career goals: a personal support system to motivate you and a network of people to help identify solid job leads.

Networking Offers Big Benefits

Because it is the No. 1 source of finding a good job, smart job seekers focus heavily on networking (the process of developing relationships with people who can assist with job search strategies and in finding strong job leads). The benefits of networking are great and include the following:

▲ Focusing your job choice or career direction

▲ Tapping into jobs you would not have access to otherwise

▲ Gaining insider information about the industry, trends, and job search and hiring processes in your field

▲ Gaining access to information about specific employers

▲ Getting the chance to promote yourself

▲ Practicing your communication and interviewing skills

▲ Obtaining referrals to other people who may help you

Your Personal Support System Is Your Coaching Team

What is a personal job search support system? Your support system is the group of people who can motivate, advise, and encourage you—like a personal coaching team—during your job search and throughout your career. Good choices for your personal support system are people who are willing to provide you with motivational and instructional support (such as family; friends; school, work, or social acquaintances; former or current employers; career services staff and counselors from school; and instructors).

Success Tip

Develop a personal support system of people who can motivate and encourage you; help with resumes, job search letters, and interview practice; and act as sounding boards for job search planning.

> "There is no such thing as a self-made man. You will reach your goals only with the help of others."
>
> George Shinn

Members of Your Support System Play Many Important Roles

One support system member may help boost your commitment. Another may help soothe your ego after a job rejection. Still another support system member who is skilled in writing may help you polish your resumes and cover letters. These people sustain and motivate you when you need a push and ultimately help you reach your full potential.

Identify Your Support System Members Now!

Select your support system members for the following qualities:

▲ Ability to motivate you

▲ Ability to help develop or edit effective job search communications (good writing skills) and ability to help you practice for interviews

▲ Ability to help you find solid job leads, provide job search advice, and/or share similar experiences

Complete Career Action 5-1

CAREER ACTION 5-1

List Your Personal Support System Members

Directions: People who boost your morale and encourage you to reach your goals should be tops on your list! Review the three areas you should consider when selecting support system members. Then list the names of your personal support system members below. These people will become part of your larger job search network, which is explained in the next section of this chapter.

_____

_____

_____

_____

File this list in your Career Management Files Binder.

Develop a Large Network— The No. 1 Source of Job Leads

Did you know that 65 percent of jobs are identified through networking? Getting your ideal job is a numbers game; the more people you make aware of your search, the more solid leads you will obtain. The goals of your networking should be:

▲ To make as many people as possible aware of your job search.

▲ To make a good impression.

▲ To seek job leads and referrals to others who may help.

▲ To seek career and networking suggestions.

Networking is the top source of job leads because employers prefer to hire people who are referred to them personally (through networking). Therefore, the larger your network, the greater your odds are of finding someone who knows a viable prospective employer. So tap into this dynamic source, build your successful network, and get the word out now.

Networking Pays Off: A Case History

Consider this actual experience: After Roland completed a computer electronics training program, he sent resumes to all his prospects. Because he had overlooked a good source in his network, landing a job took him much longer than necessary. Six months into his job search, he was describing his job

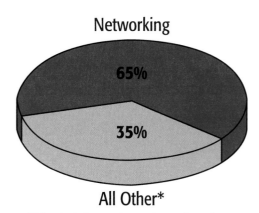

*Other includes employment agencies, ads, and miscellaneous sources.

Figure 5-1: Networking is the No. 1 source of job leads.

target to Helio, the owner of the print shop he frequented. From past experience, Helio knew that Roland's computer and technology abilities were good. A few days later, the print shop owner mentioned this to another regular customer, Patsy, who had been looking for someone with Roland's skills for five months. Patsy called Roland for an interview; as a result, Roland landed an ideal job. He could have landed the job much sooner, however, by including the print shop owner in his network from the start. Be sure to include absolutely everyone you know in your network.

Networking Sources

The network of people who can help you grows exponentially with each new contact you make. People who know you personally are the most likely to help. Your network begins with people you know who link you to others, increasing your chances of discovering good job prospects. Review the list of networking sources below to identify as many prospects as possible for your support network:

▲ Friends, relatives, and neighbors

▲ Current and former employers

▲ Colleagues or coworkers

▲ Instructors, trainers, coaches, counselors

▲ Career/job fairs

▲ Classmates and alumni from your school

▲ People you serve or meet in your work or volunteer activities (clients, customers, others)

▲ People from your place of worship

▲ Attendees and presenters at business meetings, trade shows, and conventions

▲ Members, newsletters, membership directories, and web sites of your clubs, professional and trade associations, volunteer groups

▲ Web sites, bulletin boards, news/chat groups

▲ Professionals (physicians, dentists, accountants)

▲ People with whom you do business (salespeople, clerks, others)

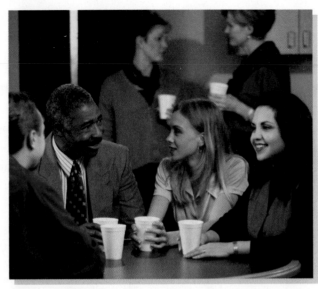

Your personal network is larger than you think. Consider contacts where you work and play.

▲ People with whom you spend leisure time

▲ Service people (letter carriers, hairdressers or barbers, librarians, mechanics, clerks, others)

▲ People with whom your children or siblings associate (parents, teachers, club leaders, others)

▲ Who else do you know? (Don't overlook anyone!) Who do they know? Also consider spouses and family members of people you know. Someone could have a connection exactly where you need it.

Networking Expands Your Potential

You could easily have 100 to 500 acquaintances. Multiply that number by two (two referrals from each person), and the potential is astounding! This is why networking is the top source of job leads. The following guidelines will help you get the most from your networking efforts:

▲ **Ask Everyone for Advice.** Go out of your way to meet people. Be friendly, smile, and introduce yourself. Ask what people do, and don't be afraid to ask for their advice. In networking, getting job leads is important. Asking directly is typically not as productive as saying, "I'm looking for a/an _____ job. Do you have any advice for finding one in _____ (industry) (company) (city)?" This approach focuses on the word *advice* and makes your contacts more inclined to help. Be courteous. Also, ask for names of referrals you can contact to seek additional information.

▲ **Put Career/Job Fairs High on Your List.** Career fairs are excellent networking opportunities because you can connect with many potential employers at one time. Check with your school's career center to find out what job fairs are offered in your area.

▲ **Participate Actively in Relevant Groups.** Join and be active in professional, trade, and other relevant associations or groups. They are valuable resources for getting job leads and keeping informed of industry developments.

▲ **Join or Start a Job Club.** A job club is a group of job seekers who meet regularly to share experiences and advice, set goals, and offer encouragement. Also known as networking or job search clubs, they can be located through newspapers, alumni and employment offices, chambers of commerce, and online. If you can't find a club that meets your needs, just start your own! Recruit members online or in community newspapers.

▲ **Make the Most of Business Cards.** Business cards are essential to networking. They look professional and allow people to stay in touch. *Always* exchange business cards when you meet new people. Later, write notes on the back of a card to help you remember how a contact might be helpful in your job search. Always keep plenty of your own cards on hand in networking situations.

▲ **E-Network.** Search for and communicate with contacts via the Internet. Check sites in your field, news groups, message boards, chat groups, e-mail, and more. Seek career and job search advice and referrals from others who may be helpful. Share information and support with other job seekers.

▲ **Network for Life.** In today's changing work world, it is essential to build and maintain strong networking relationships throughout a career, not just during a job search. Networking regularly will help you remain informed and connected in your field and ready to make a successful job change when necessary.

▲ **Remember: It's a Numbers Game.** The more people who know about your job search goals and qualifications, the greater your chance of finding the ideal job! Networking is a tremendous force multiplier. Focus your energies on network-

PERSONAL**BEST**

Networking Success Formula

To get the most from networking, take advantage of the following steps:

▲ Contact people who can help with your career preparation and job search.

▲ Treat every networking contact (whether a planned or spontaneous opportunity) with professional respect. Even if you don't believe the advice they offer is good, don't argue; just thank them for providing it. The impression you make can help or hinder the outcome.

▲ Discuss your job target with your contacts. In planned meetings, leave a copy of your resume and a brief outline of your job target and qualifications. In spontaneous situations, follow up with this same information.

▲ Respect your contacts' time.

▲ Ask for the names of at least two other people you can contact to find job leads and information.

▲ Contact these two people; repeat the process.

▲ Follow up on every lead; be persistent.

▲ Within one day, send a thank-you note on quality stationery.

▲ Stay in touch throughout your search.

▲ Let your contacts know when you get a job.

ing to expand your job search reach and to get the word out that you are looking for a job. By doing so, you will maximize your job and career development potential.

Complete Career Action 5-2

CAREER ACTION 5-2

Job Search Network List

Directions: Access Career Action Worksheet 5-2 on your Learner's CD, or create a table like the one below on a separate sheet of paper. List the names of everyone you can think of for your job search network. Be sure to include the personal support system members you listed in Career Action 5-1.

Then develop a Networking Organizer with spaces to record the following for each contact: name, mailing address, e-mail address, telephone number, dates of contact, and notes of needed follow-up.

Networking Organizer					
Name	**Mailing Address**	**E-Mail Address**	**Telephone Number**	**Dates of Contact**	**Notes/ Follow-Up**

Keep this organizer in your Career Management Files Binder.

Update Your Network List. Update your job search network list periodically. Eliminate people who, over time, are reluctant or have too many other commitments that prevent their involvement.

Establish References. During your networking, seek influential references who are willing to vouch for your qualifications. These people should be able to attest to your strong performance at work, in school, or elsewhere and to your desirable character traits and values. They also should be willing to write letters recommending you to employers. Add their names to the list of references you recorded in Career Action 2-3. Also follow the guidelines below for developing references:

▲ Only use references who have given you permission to use their names, and thank them for allowing you to use them.

▲ Only use references who would recommend you highly from firsthand knowledge.

▲ Because legal constraints may restrict your previous employers from giving a reference, ask former employees of a workplace. They may be more willing to give you a recommendation.

▲ Don't use relatives as references.

▲ Ask each reference to write a letter of reference that you can give to potential employers.

▲ Keep copies of your reference letters in your Career Management Files Binder for use during your job search.

▲ Let your references know when you will be using their names.

Prepare for Reference Checks. Potential employers will check your previous employers *and* your references. Many employers will only confirm your dates of employment, but personal references may be asked to respond to questions about your attitude, work history, job performance, ability to work with others, and work habits. Coach your references accordingly. You can't control what your references will say about you, but you should always give them information about the jobs you seek and the skills required so that they will be able to emphasize your qualifications and abilities.

Maintain Active Communication

Communicate with your network members regularly to update them on your job search progress. Ask them to recommend additional job search strategies or job leads. It is best to contact the members of your network in person. Otherwise, use the telephone or e-mail to update them regarding your job search status and to get additional assistance and encouragement from them. Every job hunter can use regular encouragement. Someday you may be able to return the favor or extend your help to another person who needs and deserves it.

> **Complete Career Action 5-3**

CAREER ACTION 5-3

Use the Internet to Search for Current Job Search Networking Tips

Directions: Search the Internet for tips on effective job search networking. You can use any of the web sites listed below (links can be found on the *Your Career: How to Make It Happen* web site), other sites you identify, or search engines. (Try using *job search networking* as keywords for your search.) Select at least two articles that interest you, and write a summary of each.

1. CareerJournal.com

2. careermag.com

3. The Riley Guide

File your research in your Career Management Files Binder.

CHECKLIST

ORGANIZING A WINNING NETWORK

Check each of the actions you are currently taking to increase your career success:

○ Developing a support system: people who motivate you and help you develop resumes and job search letters

○ Developing a large job search network to help you find job leads

○ Increasing your networking potential by identifying as many networking prospects as possible and considering many different networking sources

○ Getting the most from your networking efforts by approaching as many people as possible, joining clubs and job fairs, using the Internet, and maintaining relationships

○ Conducting organized networking appointments: reviewing your job target and qualifications, leaving a resume, asking for referrals, getting references, sending thank-you letters, and following up

CRITICAL THINKING QUESTIONS

1. What is networking?

2. What are the steps in effective networking?

3. Are neighbors and fellow club members as useful for networking as instructors or coworkers are? Explain your answer.

4. How can you make sure your references will be prepared to answer potential employer's questions about you?

 For convenient access to valuable career resources, activities, and job information links, visit the companion web site for this text: *http://levitt.swlearning.com*

chapter 6

ENGINEER AN EFFICIENT JOB SEARCH

In this chapter, you will:

 Use the Internet to research job listings and job trends.

 Identify and use printed, human, Internet, and organizational sources of job information.

- Use tools for organizing and conducting your job search efficiently.

"Now is the time to call on your network of friends and acquaintances. Take advantage of alumni, professional associations, and local career transition support groups. Visit online job sites. Search for jobs by location and by areas of interest and industry. If there's a certain company you'd love to work for, you'll probably find a job section right on the corporate site. And don't forget traditional classified ads."

Chris Miller
Founder
6FigureJobs.com™

This chapter identifies many solid resources to help you find jobs fast, including networking, direct employer contact, school career services centers, Internet sites, professional associations, and newspapers and other publications. The resources presented are based on extensive research with expert employment and placement counselors, with recent job seekers, and through the Internet. The more types of resources you use, the more job choices you will have and the more quickly you will get optimum results. Chapter 6 also provides practical, efficient tools for organizing the job search to achieve your goals quickly.

Sources of Job Leads

The following sources of job leads and related information will help you identify prospective employers. But don't limit yourself to the sources listed here. Use your imagination and some initiative. Many rewarding jobs are uncovered in personally creative ways. Your career objectives determine what sources are most useful to you.

Networking

Networking is the process of developing relationships with people who can assist with job search strategies and in finding strong job leads. Friends, relatives, and acquaintances (such as current and former employers, coworkers, and instructors) are statistically the best source of job leads for two reasons:

1. People who know you are more likely to be interested in your success. Therefore, they are more likely to help you in your job search.

2. A personal referral from a friend, a relative, or an acquaintance is highly influential with prospective employers if the employers know and respect the person referring you. Employers trust recommendations from people they know.

Since it's the most productive source of strong job leads, focus your efforts on networking (getting help from people you know) to identify prospective employers.

> *"Everyone who's ever taken a shower has an idea. It's the person who gets out of the shower, dries off, and does something about it that makes a difference."*
>
> Nolan Bushnell

Success Tip

Focus your job search energy on networking—the Number 1 source of job leads.

Direct Employer Contact: Direct Bids and Information Surveys

Applicants trained in job search techniques often find jobs through direct employer contact because they are organized and professional in making contacts by telephone, in writing, and in person. An effective technique you can use to obtain solid job leads is arranging information interviews or surveys. These are meetings you arrange to obtain general career information and advice from prospective employers or from employees holding jobs that are similar to your job target. During such meetings, many job seekers obtain job leads and the career advice they seek. Known as career information surveys, these meetings are discussed further in Chapter 7.

School Career Services Centers

School career services centers are valuable sources of job search information. Typically, these offices (a) maintain listings of local, regional, national, and global employers and job openings; (b) assist with job search skills, interviewing, and resume and letter writing; (c) arrange and schedule on-campus interviews with students and prospective employers; (d) help research employer and salary information; and (e) provide career planning and job search counseling.

Job Information Web Sites

Many web sites serve as job bank connections for employers and applicants. Several of these sites are listed in Career Action 6-1. You can access these sites and several others from the *Your Career: How to Make It Happen* web site (http://levitt.swlearning.com). Don't limit yourself to just these, however. Many web sites provide listings of job openings, opportunities to submit online resumes, and career planning and job search information.

Additionally, the vast majority of employers have web sites today. Employer web sites typically provide information about the organization, information about available jobs, and instructions for submitting applications and resumes. Chapters 9 and 10 of this text provide more information about electronic applications and resumes.

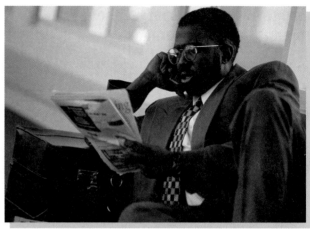

Publications of professional, technical, career, and trade associations, as well as local newspapers, are valuable sources of information about job openings and hiring trends.

> ## Success Tip
>
> Use the Internet as a job search tool. If jobs in your field are heavily advertised on the Internet, it could be a top source of job leads for you.

Leaders in Your Occupational Field

Recognized leaders in your occupational field can be excellent sources of job leads. Successful people are usually knowledgeable about the employment needs of their peers and competitors. One of them may even consider hiring you after learning of your job target and qualifications. Be sure to include this valuable source in your job search. Ask instructors in your career field for names of leaders in your area.

Professional, Technical, Career, and Trade Associations

Virtually every profession, vocation, and trade has one or more national associations to keep members informed of changing technology, methods, and trends. Such groups typically provide educational publications, workshops, and continuing education courses. They often announce job openings during meetings and in their publications.

The Internet and many libraries have information on professional, technical, and trade associations. For example, using both sources, you will find associations for information technology, accounting, writing, health care, teaching, and business management. Your career services staff and a reference librarian can help you identify organizations related to your interests and locate their web sites and publications. Check current and back issues of printed resources or Internet archives for help-wanted ads, and look for information about employment and job market trends.

Employment Directories

Directories that list employers in local areas and defined geographic regions are useful sources of job leads. Some employer specialty directories are also available in specific areas, such as manufacturing. To find such directories, check public, state, college, or university libraries; your school's career counseling center; the Internet; and area chambers of commerce.

> ## Success Tip
>
> Concentrate on direct telephone or face-to-face contact with employers. The most successful strategies involve direct contact with a hiring authority.

Want Ads (Newspapers, Other Print Media, and the Internet)

Check for job openings posted in a variety of ways:

▲ **Newspapers.** Look in the help-wanted section, the business section, and virtually all other sections of newspapers from locations that interest you. You can learn a lot about the hiring, expansion, downsizing, or start-up of organizations in an area. Many newspapers also post their classified ads on the Internet.

▲ **The Internet.** Check job listings and want ads on the Internet. The Internet allows quick, convenient access to an enormous number of sources. Search both large job listing sites and small niche sites that focus only on your career field and/or specialty. Also, check employers' web sites for job postings.

▲ **Journals and other publications.** Check the classified sections of both printed and online professional journals in your field, your school's newspaper and bulletin boards, and other publications that target job seekers.

Learn About Job Market Trends. Get the most out of printed and Internet want ads. Use them to learn about what kinds of employers are hiring and which appear to be expanding (indicated by several ads from the same organization). You can learn about the experience, additional courses, and training you need for employment or advancement in your field. Also, check employers' web sites for job postings.

Be alert for organizations that advertise actively—even for jobs that require more experience and education than you currently have. Active advertising indicates growth and job opportunities—and that other positions may be open.

Read Every Ad. Good opportunities are not always evident. Be thorough; read every listing. Advertisements don't always appear under logical job headings, and you may miss an important lead by looking only under the obvious heads.

If an advertised job differs slightly but is still related to your target, pursue the lead anyway. You could find yourself interviewing for an unadvertised job that fits your goals. Don't overlook the blind ads requesting that resumes be sent to an anonymous box number. Some companies run blind ads to limit the number of individual contacts required to review applications. A well-prepared resume and cover letter can help you land a job this way.

Review Old Ads. Search the Internet and back issues of newspapers for ads that are 12 to 18 months old. If a company was hiring three months ago, it's a job lead for you. The company may not have found the right person, may have let the last person go, or may be expanding. Contact the firm and ask to schedule a career information survey. The meeting could provide a good lead or even a job offer. (See Chapter 7 for survey details.)

Help-wanted advertisements are a limited resource for finding just the right job, but don't let a choice opportunity slip through your fingers for lack of attention. Ask family members or friends to help with the daily task of reading through them.

Success Tip

Don't limit your search to published job announcements. They represent only 15 to 20 percent of available jobs.

Don't Limit Job Search to Published Ads. As emphasized in Figure 6-1, published job openings represent only 15 to 20 percent of available jobs. While they should not be overlooked and may lead to a good job, your odds are greatly increased if you use other sources of job leads, as well.

Small Businesses

According to the U.S. Small Business Administration, small businesses represent 99.7 percent of all employers and employ 50.1 percent of the private work force. These are clear reasons to research small businesses as sources of employment. Information about

Published jobs = 15%–20% of available jobs

Look deeper: Don't limit yourself to only 20% of available jobs.

Eighty percent of available jobs are not published! Discover them through:

➡ **Networking**

➡ **Direct contact with employers**

➡ **Research**

Figure 6-1: Published job openings: just the tip of the iceberg!
Source: U.S. Department of Labor

openings with small businesses is available through chambers of commerce, your school's career services center, employer directories, and help-wanted ads (printed or online).

Complete Career Action 6-1

Private Contractors and Employment Agencies

Private contractors and employment or staffing agencies can be useful resources for finding prospective employers, particularly if the one you select specializes in your field. The operations of these organizations vary. Some focus on connecting applicants with part-time jobs, while others focus on full-time jobs.

Some employment firms connect employers and applicants to facilitate a full-time hire by the employer. Other employment firms actually serve as a permanent link between employer and employee, and the employment firm handles all human resource functions. This relieves the employer of such activities as hiring, compensation, career development, and so on. Policies vary regarding who pays fees for securing a permanent job—the applicant or the employer. Always try to negotiate in your favor. Before considering such a firm, research the following:

▲ Does the firm have a good reputation? Ask the staff at your school's career services center, employers who work with the agency to obtain employees, other job seekers, and the Better Business Bureau. Don't rely on one person's word. Also, visit the agency you are considering.

▲ How long has the employment firm been in business? What has happened to its past clients?

▲ Does the agency have expertise in placing people in your field? What employment firms are associated with the ads for the jobs you are targeting?

CAREER ACTION 6-1

Use the Internet to Find Job Listings and Information

Directions: Use the Internet to access at least four of the sites listed below. (Links are provided on the *Your Career: How to Make It Happen* web site: http://levitt.swlearning.com.) Also visit any specialty sites in your field. Browse the sites, and prepare a written report of your findings, addressing the following:

1. Describe the sites that have the most relevant information to your job target and field.

2. Summarize or print job listings you find for your field, and indicate the sources of the listings.

3. Summarize job trends and other useful information you find in this search.

Web Sites

America's Job Bank   Monster

The Black Collegian Online   NationJob Network

CareerBuilder.com   Net-Temps

EmploymentGuide.com   Saludos.com

JobCentral.com

File your report in your Career Management Files Binder.

▲ If you would accept employment outside of your local area, does the employment firm belong to a nationwide or regional system? Is it familiar with job opportunities, hiring trends, and salaries throughout the areas you would consider?

▲ What services will the employment firm provide for you, and what will it expect you to do?

▲ What are the costs to you? Get a written agreement spelling out every service you will receive, including how long counseling will take and how long you are entitled to the agency's services.

▲ Do you understand the contract? Read every word of it, and make certain you are willing to accept all the conditions. Ask the agency to clarify how it handles client dissatisfaction with job placement. Firms that guarantee a full refund are usually the most reputable.

Some employment firms focus on hiring applicants to perform contract work on a temporary or project basis. This is one of the most accessible means of reentering the job market and is a stepping stone from unemployment to employment. This arrangement offers two major benefits: (1) It gives the employer and the employee an opportunity to check for a "good fit" without the employee having to make a permanent commitment up front, and (2) the employment firm takes care of the administrative details. Many people find full-time jobs through this source by gaining experience in the temporary jobs.

To locate this type of employment firm, look in the Yellow Pages of your telephone directory or search the Internet for *employment agencies, employment contractors, employment staffing agencies,* or *temporary-help agencies.* An individual job may not fit your career target perfectly, but it can provide some outstanding benefits, including these:

▲ Entry or reentry into the job market

▲ Experience you may lack

▲ References for work done well

▲ Additions to your list of solid job leads

▲ A possible full-time job

▲ On-the-job training and hands-on practical skill development

▲ Immediate income

State Employment Services

Through the U.S. Department of Labor, each state has an employment agency that includes a job services or employment services office. You can call the main state information number and ask for the number of the employment services office.

These offices provide career counseling, job search techniques, training, referrals to upgrade training or education, and information on area job openings. Most offices maintain computerized, up-to-the-minute information on job openings in the service regions. The job hunter is not charged a fee for this assistance.

Public Agencies: City, County, State, and Federal

City, county, and state agencies employ people in a wide variety of positions. Most agencies have a civil service system that requires application and pre-employment testing through a central human resources department. Consult your local telephone directory for the numbers of these agencies, and check with your school's career services office. You can also search online for links to jobs in states that interest you. Every state has its own employment agency and web site. Check America's Job Bank (a link is provided on the *Your Career: How to Make It Happen* web site). This site is a combined effort of all state employment offices, providing online listings of both private and public job openings.

© GETTY IMAGES/PHOTODISC

Your job search is a full-time job. Focus your energy on networking—the best source of job leads.

Federal agencies have a variety of positions, and many openings are projected to occur with the retirement of a large group of federal employees. Your state's employment office can refer you to the regional federal offices in areas that interest you. Check out USAJOBS (a link is provided on the *Your Career: How to Make It Happen* web site) for information about federal jobs. Also look for federal job information under *U.S. Government* in major area telephone directories. Request federal job information from your school's career services center or your local state employment office.

Human Resources Departments in Private Industry

Contact the human resources departments of private companies to learn about current job openings. If no openings are available, ask if you can leave your application and resume for future openings. If these are accepted, ask what action you need to take to keep your file open (for example, confirming your status every six months). Also ask about other sources of job leads in your field. Some organizations offer telephone recordings about current job openings.

Career/Job Fairs

The primary reason employers go to community, industry, or school-sponsored career or job fairs is to find new talent, so go; you have to be there to be discovered! Career fairs are good sources of job leads and employer information. They are beneficial to both employers and job seekers, allowing them to explore employment matches in a more relaxed, face-to-face format. They provide the job seeker with an efficient way to contact many employers in one day. Career fairs are also offered on the Internet; look for advertisements on job listing sites and use search engines to locate online career fairs.

The following guidelines explain how to get the most out of on-site career fairs:

▲ Take copies of your resume, your business cards, and your business portfolio.

▲ Set a goal to meet at least 10 people at every career fair.

▲ Plan your remarks. Present yourself professionally and confidently. Wear business-smart clothes. Shake hands, introduce yourself, summarize your qualifications briefly, and ask pertinent questions.

▲ Before visiting your main employer targets, visit the less attractive firms to perfect your marketing pitch.

▲ To your Job Search Network List (Career Action 5-2), add the names of everyone with whom you network and add notes about any needed follow-up.

Educational Institutions

To find a teaching job, contact the human resources departments of school districts that interest you to learn about their application and hiring procedures. Also ask your school's career services staff for help in locating jobs in education. Look in telephone directories for areas you would consider.

If no openings are currently available, request permission to leave your application and resume on file for future openings. Ask how you should follow up to keep your file updated and active. Also look into the possibility of becoming certified to do substitute teaching. This can be a good way to prove your abilities and possibly work your way into a regular teaching position.

Self-Employment

The popularity of self-employment continues to grow because of organizational downsizing and task/job outsourcing to control costs.

Learn Under Another Employer First. To succeed in your own business, you must have adequate education, training, and knowledge. In addition, you can significantly improve your chances of successful self-employment by first working for someone who has succeeded in the field. Learn the plusses and minuses of a business as an employee, not as a new business owner.

Gaining experience and achieving solid accomplishments in the field first provide the credibility you need to land work contracts on your own. Self-employment is worth considering if you have related work experience and can get endorsements from people who are satisfied with your performance.

Research to Succeed. If you are seriously interested in self-employment, interview people in your field who are successfully self-employed to learn what methods they have used. Also obtain and study information about self-employment from published and Internet sources. Remember that you will need to earn enough money to cover your insurance and other items provided by many employers as benefits; in some cases, this could require 30 percent more income. Finally, before starting your own business, plan carefully, develop a formal business plan, and check with the Small Business Administration for information on starting a business.

Networking Is Essential. To succeed in your own business, you must network regularly with people in your field, potential clients, and customers. Market yourself by being active in professional or trade associations and clubs related to your career field.

Start Small and Build. A smart way to begin self-employment is to do it part-time to develop a client base and essential references. Volunteer with groups to prove your skills. Start small, keep expenses at an absolute minimum, and expand only with demand.

Success Tip

Consider self-employment if you have adequate experience; this is projected to be one of the largest sources of employment in the near future.

Nonprofit Organizations

Nonprofit organizations are good sources of jobs in public relations, solicitation, writing, management, health care, and other fields. They often offer growth opportunities, valuable work experience, and opportunities to demonstrate community service.

Examples of nonprofit organizations are the United Way, representing several organizations; the Red Cross; the March of Dimes; professional associations; federal-grant-supported projects; Head Start programs; and health clinics for migrant workers. Look under *Associations* or *Social Services Organizations* in the Yellow Pages to locate various nonprofit organizations.

Classified Telephone Directories

Collect classified sections or Yellow Pages of telephone directories from areas you would consider for employment. Most of these directories are available

on CD and the Internet (a link is provided on the *Your Career: How to Make It Happen* web site). Look for employers in your field under all related headings (check the easy-reference indexes). These sources provide comprehensive, readily available listings of current employers.

Library

Ask your local library's reference librarian for help in finding directories (business, product, company, and so on) related to your field of interest. These directories list names, addresses, telephone numbers, and general descriptions of employers in your field. Also, ask knowledgeable people in your field to suggest additional library job search resources.

Chambers of Commerce

Contact the local chamber of commerce in each of your target geographical areas. Chambers of commerce have complete, current lists of employers and often have the names and telephone numbers of company executives. Most chambers also have information on new organizations that plan to establish themselves in the area.

The Military

The military is a good source of employment and provides important training and experience. Talk with your school's career services staff and local recruiting officers to obtain information on military opportunities and to compare the offerings available.

Cooperative Education and Volunteering

You can benefit from cooperative education programs and volunteer work. By exploring these avenues, you gain important experience and references who can verify your qualifications. You also demonstrate personal initiative and commitment (both highly favorable attributes), thus enhancing your employability.

Internships

An internship—a period of supervised training in a workplace—can be one of the most important parts of a student's education. Some internships come without pay, but that doesn't mean they're not worthwhile. They can give you a chance to break into a field, work at a top company, or get valuable experience that will give you an edge in your job search. They provide excellent opportunities for networking and can even lead to full-time employment. Job seekers with internship experience have an advantage in the hiring process because they have work experience and will need less training. To get the most from an internship:

▲ **Be flexible and enthusiastic.** Offer to take on any tasks that need to be done. If you find yourself with some free time, ask your boss for another assignment.

▲ **Act like you want to be taken seriously.** Dress professionally, be punctual, never leave early, do not use office supplies or technology (including telephones and computers) for personal business, and don't date or flirt with coworkers.

Reference Reading

Excellent publications—particularly those that specialize in your field—are available to strengthen your career planning and job search efforts. Ask your school's librarian and career services staff for reference reading suggestions.

The Hidden Job Market

Numerous studies emphasize that 80 to 85 percent of job openings are never published and that personal searching is required to uncover them. Many jobs are actually created by applicants; such jobs are part of the *hidden job market*. The first step to uncovering the hidden job market is researching your target employer thoroughly. Discover where you can provide a useful service or offer moneymaking or money-saving ideas. Then present your qualifications for the job or service so convincingly that the employer is motivated to create a job for you. The hidden job market, which is discussed further in Chapter 12, is created through your own ingenuity.

Personal Awareness of Market Trends

Throughout your job search (and even before you begin your job search), look actively for job leads—from people, television, radio, newspapers, the Internet, books, and magazines and through personal awareness. Be aware of what is happening in your city and state, the nation, and the world. Notice how changing technology shapes new jobs and revises or eliminates traditional jobs. Through this awareness, you can identify emerging trends.

Major job market trends favor preventive health care, nursing, and physical therapy; network systems analysis, data communications, and computer software engineering; and social and human services, such as services for the elderly, education, government, police work, and security, to name a few. Can you market your abilities in any of these areas? What other job market trends do you see emerging?

Organizing an Effective Job Search

The energy you put into organizing your job search directly affects the speed and success of your search. The techniques that follow will help you maximize your efforts.

Compile Your List of Prospects

This chapter provides many excellent resources for identifying prospective employers. Use any of the suggestions that apply to your occupational field. Focus your job search efficiently by completing the following Career Action to identify the sources of job leads that are most appropriate for your job target.

Complete Career Action 6-2

CAREER ACTION 6-2

Job Leads Source List

Directions: To focus your list of sources of job leads, access Career Action Worksheet 6-2 on your Learner's CD or turn to page 88 and review the instructions for preparing your Job Leads Source List.

File your source list in your Career Management Files Binder.

Develop Prospective Employer Records

To identify prospective employers to contact in your job search, research each source on your Job Leads Source List (Career Action 6-2). To best organize your job search, access the Prospective Employer Record on your Learner's CD or make copies of the worksheet on page 89. File all your records in one folder, and use them to monitor your employer contacts and follow-up activities efficiently.

When it comes time to make calls or send cover letters and resumes, you can search first for the records you marked as "Hot Prospects" to maximize your potential and your time in the job search. Use colored file tags to mark hot prospects.

Narrow Your List

After completing your Prospective Employer Records, concentrate on the employers who could best use your abilities. For now, eliminate the long shots, those who offer a slim chance for employment.

If you plan to do a direct mailing in your job search, narrowing your list of prospects is especially important. (A direct-mail job search consists of mailing cover letters with requests for interviews along with your resume to prospective employers.) Don't start this type of campaign until you have completed all the reading, assignments, and activities for Chapters 1 through 10 of this book. Note that a direct mailing of unsolicited resumes is statistically not a productive job search method unless you have skills that are in high demand.

The Job Market Is Not Always Organized— You Must Be!

Employers use a variety of hiring techniques. Their processes may be simple or complex, well or poorly organized, short or long. You, the job applicant, must be well organized—even if the job market is not. As you progress through this book, your collection of job-seeking tools will grow. Use them to develop an efficient, speedy, and successful job-seeking campaign.

Planning Time for Your Job Search

If you are just finishing school, you will be competing with other recent graduates for employment. The sooner you start your job search, the greater your advantage will be. Employers sometimes view a long delay between school or your last job and application for employment as a lack of initiative or a lack of employability.

Your Job Search: A Full-Time Job

A job search campaign should include daily activities and requires a minimum of 25 to 30 hours per week. If you're currently employed and seeking another position, you must look at your job search as a second job, which means you won't have as much time to devote to it.

PERSONAL BEST

Job Search Management

The following tips will help you manage your job search time effectively:

1. Set up an organized job search headquarters so you can easily lay your hands on anything you need and follow up on leads effectively. Use labeled file folders for your job search schedules, job lead lists, prospective employer records, and so on.

2. Prepare a weekly job search schedule. Use a monthly calendar to schedule your activities one or more weeks in advance. Record the hours to be spent on your search each day.

3. Prepare a daily job search plan. Plan your daily job search activities at least one day in advance. Use the Daily Job Search Organizer on your Learner's CD or the worksheet on page 90 to plan your daily goals.

4. If possible, begin your job search while still employed part- or full-time. (Employers consider employed applicants to be more employable than the unemployed. Why? Being employed is proof that you can do a job well enough to keep it.)

5. If you aren't employed, begin your search the moment you know that you need to get a job. If you graduate in June and will need a job then, start your search preparations in January—or before!

6. Report for work on your search as you would for a job. Procrastination is the job seeker's biggest enemy.

7. Never be late. Employers expect you to be punctual for all scheduled appointments.

8. Follow up on every job lead immediately. A delay can cost you the job you are seeking.

Success Tip

Write out your job search schedule to increase your sense of commitment and to improve your organizational effectiveness.

Winning Job Search Routines

Establish a routine to help you stay focused and efficient. The following are appropriate daily activities:

▲ **Look the part every day.** Dress and groom yourself for success.

▲ **Organize your job search work area daily,** including your files, references, and related forms and materials. If possible, have a telephone and a computer in your work area.

▲ **Make telephone contacts** to arrange appointments, communicate with your network, and so on.

▲ **Work on new leads.** Research, make telephone and written contacts, and arrange appointments.

▲ **Follow up.** Write thank-you letters, review leads, and take appropriate actions.

▲ **Arrange appointments** to network and gather information for interviews.

Success Tip

Organize your job search to gain an advantage over those who don't plan an efficient search. Develop prospective employer records. Develop and follow a daily job search schedule. Be persistent. Follow up.

CHECKLIST

ORGANIZING A WINNING JOB SEARCH

Check each of the actions you are currently taking to increase your career success:

○ Focusing job search energy on networking (the No. 1 source of job leads)

○ Concentrating on direct telephone or face-to-face contacts with employers

○ Using the Internet as a job search tool

○ Not limiting the search to published job announcements, which represent only 15 to 20 percent of available jobs

○ Considering self-employment (with adequate experience)

○ Allocating time in relation to the proven success rate of the top job search strategies: networking, advertisements, and employment agencies

○ Planning and organizing the job search to gain an advantage over others and spending time on the job search every day

CRITICAL THINKING QUESTIONS

1. Why should you make a conscious effort to tell everyone about your job search?

2. How can internships help the job seeker?

3. How can you obtain employment information from organizations in private industry?

4. What sources do you think will be most useful for your job search?

For convenient access to valuable career resources, activities, and job information links, visit the companion web site for this text: ***http://levitt.swlearning.com***

CAREER ACTION WORKSHEET 6-2

Job Leads Source List

Directions: Review each of the sources of job information presented in this chapter, including the web sites you used in Career Action 6-1. Then list the sources you think would be effective in your job search. (Make additional copies of this worksheet if necessary.)

Name of Source: _____

Address of Source: _____

Internet Address: _____ E-Mail Address: _____

Telephone Number: _____

Action Plans for Using This Source: _____

Name of Source: _____

Address of Source: _____

Internet Address: _____ E-Mail Address: _____

Telephone Number: _____

Action Plans for Using This Source: _____

Name of Source: _____

Address of Source: _____

Internet Address: _____ E-Mail Address: _____

Telephone Number: _____

Action Plans for Using This Source: _____

Name of Source: _____

Address of Source: _____

Internet Address: _____ E-Mail Address: _____

Telephone Number: _____

Action Plans for Using This Source: _____

Continued on next page >>>

CAREER ACTION WORKSHEET 6-2 (continued)

Prospective Employer Record

Directions: Access this worksheet on your Learner's CD, or duplicate this page. Prepare one record for each employer you are targeting in your job search. Retain for your reference any job notice or help-wanted listing related to this job target.

Name of Organization: _____

Address of Organization: _____

Internet Address: _____ E-Mail Address: _____

Telephone Number: _____ Fax Number: _____

Job Target Title: _____

Job Target Description: _____

_____

Person to Contact (name and title): _____

_____

Source of Information: _____

Referred By (person who will refer me): _____

Hiring Status: Position Open _____   No Position Currently Open _____

Other: _____

Potential: Hot Prospect _____   Possibility _____   Long Shot _____

Dates and Methods of Contact With Employer: _____

_____

_____

Date Resume and Cover Letter Sent: _____

Date of Interview: _____

Interview Follow-up: _____

_____

Comments: _____

_____

_____

Continued on next page >>>

CAREER ACTION WORKSHEET 6-2 (continued)

Daily Job Search Organizer

Directions: Access this worksheet on your Learner's CD, or duplicate this page. Record the name of the employer, the person you plan to contact, and the job target. Record the form of contact (personal visit, phone call, letter, or Internet contact) and the purpose of the contact. Summarize other job search goals you plan for the day. Complete the last three sections of the worksheet at the end of the day, including a summary of your progress, a list of new job leads, and any necessary follow-up (sending a thank-you note or resume, for example). Also note whether you achieved the purpose of each contact made.

Date: _____ **Number of hours to be spent on job search:** _____ **From:** _____ **To:** _____

Employer, Name of Contact, and Job Target	Form of Contact (personal visit, phone call, letter, Internet contact)	Purpose of Contact	Purpose Achieved (Yes/No)
1.			
2.			
3.			

Other Goals for Today (research, contact support system or network, schedule appointments, and so on):

_____

Summary of Progress Made: _____

New Job Leads: _____

Follow-up/Next Steps: _____

INVESTIGATE JOB, APPLICATION, AND HIRING PROCEDURES

"We select the applicants for our branch of Microsoft from a corporate resume database. This database is made up of all of the resumes that are submitted online through our Microsoft web site. I can run a query on the type of experience and job skills I am looking for, and the computer will do a search for me."

Carrie Fellhoelter
Senior Human Resource Administrator
Microsoft Corporation
Dallas, Texas

In this chapter, you learn more about existing jobs that are similar to the one you are targeting and about the application and hiring procedures that are typical in your field. You complete two surveys to obtain this information directly from people who work in your career field. These are your first outside Career Action assignments. You also use the Internet to locate additional tips regarding current hiring and job application procedures. The information you obtain will help you land your ideal job. Finally, Chapter 7 guides you through the preparation of your Job Qualifications Profile, which will help you develop content for successful self-marketing in networking, resumes, cover letters, and interviews.

The Career Information Survey

Through the Career Information Surveys in this chapter, you'll gain a decided advantage over your competition by meeting with people who hold jobs that are similar to your job target. Professionals in your field can provide valuable inside information and advice to help you realize your career goals. Through your meetings, you'll gain:

▲ **Practice.** You will go directly to the business community as you research and network. You will schedule appointments and practice communicating about your career and job targets—terrific preparation for actual interviews!

▲ **Information.** You will obtain important current information about the scope of jobs and the hiring procedures in your field. You may even get valuable job leads.

▲ **Competitive Edge.** You will have the edge over applicants who don't complete these activities.

To complete your Career Information Surveys, you will contact two people who hold jobs that are similar to your job target. You'll meet them at their work sites to learn about their jobs and the hiring procedures used by their employers. This will help prepare you for a successful job search in your field.

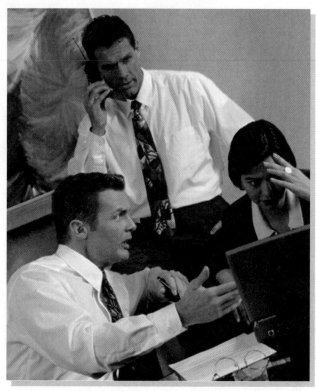

© GETTY IMAGES/PHOTODISC

You can learn a lot about a workplace by watching how people interact. Be observant. Does the place you're visiting seem like a place you'd like to work?

Success Tip

Gain an advantage over the competition by meeting with employees in your field who hold jobs that are similar to your job target. They can provide valuable advice and give you information about the scope of their jobs and the organization's hiring procedures.

Prepare Sample Questions for Career Information Surveys

To prepare for your survey meetings, write a list of questions to ask your contacts. Following are some sample questions:

A. Questions Regarding Job Scope and Career Development

1. Is the firm privately owned, a government agency, or a nonprofit organization? (Ask only if you don't already know.)

2. What are the main goals of the organization? Is it a product- or service-oriented firm? (Ask only if you don't already know.)

3. What skills, education, experience, and knowledge are required to qualify for a position such as yours?

4. What personal qualities or traits are important in your work?

5. What are your specific duties?

6. What do you like the most/least about your job?

7. What is the average starting salary range for a position such as yours?

8. What employee benefits are offered in this position (health insurance, retirement savings programs, others)?

9. What future changes do you anticipate in this field?

10. What additional or ongoing education or training do you need to achieve your career goals?

11. Does the employer offer on-the-job training for employees in your position? If so, what does it involve?

12. Does the employer encourage continuing education for your position? If so, what kinds of programs are available, and does the employer pay the associated fees?

13. Would it be possible to get a written description of your job if one is available?

14. What professional or other associations would you recommend joining to stay informed about this career field?

15. What publications would you recommend (books, journals, and so on)?

16. Could you suggest other people to help me with my research?

17. Do you have any advice for me about planning my career and job search?

B. Questions Regarding Application, Interview, and Hiring Procedures

1. What are the general application procedures for positions such as the one I will be seeking?

2. Do you have an employment application form I could see, or may I keep a copy of one to review as a reference?

3. What are the organization's typical interview procedures (one person interviewing the applicant, team interviewing, multiple interviews, typical length of interviews, testing)?

4. What types of questions are typically asked during interviews? Are applicants asked to give specific examples of how they have used the required job skills or how they have handled specific work situations?

5. What do you think is important to show in a resume for a position such as the one I will be seeking?

6. What advice do you have for me about preparing and interviewing successfully?

Study the Work Environment of Your Contacts

Through careful observation at a job site, you can learn about the working conditions for the type of job you want. Therefore, prior to a survey, you should also write a list of questions about the work environment that you will answer yourself. Following are some examples:

1. What type of work area does my contact have? Does my contact work at a desk, share office space, or use some other type of work space?

2. What equipment and software does my contact use?

3. Is the work environment appropriate for the type of work?

4. Is the environment quiet, noisy, slow paced, or fast paced?

5. Does my contact interact with others? If so, with whom and how often?

6. What type of dress is appropriate?

7. Is the atmosphere formal or informal?

8. Are work areas neat and clean or cluttered?

Spot a Top Place to Work

Be alert to the work atmosphere, and listen for revealing comments from your contacts. Employees of desirable workplaces may mention freedom, trust, pride, teamwork, fair pay and benefits, opportunities for growth, recognition, and fairness in management. Ask about and watch for these characteristics during your meetings. Keep these qualities in mind as you select your actual job prospects.

Now prepare your own questions about the job and work environment.

Complete Career Action 7-1

CAREER ACTION 7-1

Career Information Survey Worksheet

 Directions: Develop a Career Information Survey Worksheet by preparing two sets of questions:

1. Prepare the career information questions you will ask your contact during a survey meeting (questions regarding the job, career development, and hiring procedures).

2. Prepare the work environment questions you will answer for yourself through observation.

Some of the sample questions listed earlier may apply to your field, but you should prepare additional questions that are relevant to your field. The goal is to clarify your understanding of the particular job, the occupational field, the typical work environment, and the hiring procedures. Leave adequate space after each question to record the information you obtain. Place the questions in a professional binder to use during your surveys; projecting a professional image is important in all outside assignments!

File your survey questions in your Career Management Files Binder.

Make an Appointment for a Survey Meeting

To make a survey appointment, contact at least two organizations that employ people in your field. Making the initial contact in person is preferable. If you can't do that, use the telephone, but first review the telephone techniques outlined in Chapter 12.

Success Tip

Dress and act professionally in all outside assignments to project competence and encourage job leads.

Ask to speak with someone whose job is similar to your job target. Emphasize that you are carrying out an assignment from your instructor or doing research in your field. Explain that you want to learn about your occupational field as part of your career plan-

ning research. *Do not say you're looking for a job.* Strangers are more likely to help you with career planning research than with getting a job. Follow the guidelines below:

1. **Be clean, neat, and properly dressed if you make your appointment in person.**

2. **Introduce yourself.**

3. **State your purpose**—completing an assignment from your instructor at (name your school). If you are using this book independently, state that you are conducting career research.

4. **Request an appointment** to ask a few questions (those you prepared in Career Action 7-10) about the person's job and the occupational field.

5. **Confirm the date and time.** If you're making your initial contact in person, the individual may offer to meet with you immediately. Be prepared by having your binder and questions with you!

6. **Thank the person for his or her time and assistance.**

Connect With Hard-to-Reach Employers

Some organizations are not as accessible for career survey meetings. If your target employer is such an organization, follow the guidelines below to identify people with whom you can meet for a survey.

▲ **Turn to your network.** Ask everyone in your job search network (friends, family, school counselors, and so on) to help you identify someone who works in your targeted employment field—a person you can meet with to gather career information. Your network may provide opportunities that would not otherwise be available to you.

▲ **Search the Internet.** Many firms have computerized hiring processes and provide application and hiring information through their company web sites or through third-party job bank/job-posting web sites. If your target employer falls in this category, obtain the company and/or third-party Internet addresses, search for the application and hiring information, and print your findings or prepare a written summary to submit as your report for Career Action 7-2.

▲ **Choose a closely related employer target.** If you are unable to schedule an appointment to meet with your preferred employer, schedule a meeting with a closely related organization. Face-to-face meetings give you the valuable business communication practice necessary to outdistance your competition.

Success Tip

Use the Interent to research job descriptions and hiring practices of hard-to-reach employers.

Complete Career Action 7-2

CAREER ACTION 7-2

Internet Research of Hiring Procedures

Directions: Identify at least two major company or organizational web sites that offer information regarding application and/or hiring processes. When you reach your target sites, search for information about jobs, application processes, resume submission, and so on. Prepare a summary report of your findings.

Web resources for finding major employers:

▲ Using a search engine (accessible through the *Your Career: How to Make It Happen* web site at http://levitt .swlearning.com), enter the names of the employer companies or organizations (private; nonprofit; or state, county, or city government) you are researching to find links to their web sites.

▲ Visit job listing and industry information sites, and search for organization names or job titles. The following sites and others are accessible through the *Your Career: How to Make It Happen* web site.

   ▲ USAJOBS (for information about federal jobs)

   ▲ WetFeet.com

File your research in your Career Management Files Binder.

PERSONAL**BEST**

Career Information Survey Meeting

Take your career information survey meetings seriously. If you make a strong first impression, you could gain job leads from the meetings. Some people actually obtain job offers. Maximize your information-gathering sessions by following these tips:

▲ Dress and act professionally. (See Chapter 11 for appropriate grooming guidelines.)

▲ Be courteous, friendly, and professional.

▲ Arrive on time.

▲ Learn your contact's name. Use it when you first meet, when you leave, and in follow-up.

▲ Begin by restating your reason for being there.

▲ Ask well-prepared open-ended questions. Let your questions show that you did your homework.

▲ Move quickly through your prepared questions, and avoid wasting time.

▲ Take brief notes of your contact's answers. Don't write out every answer completely, however. (Do this as soon as possible after the meeting.)

▲ Practice active listening skills.

▲ Pay attention to body language—both yours and your contact's.

▲ Obtain the names of other individuals you can contact.

▲ Be alert for job leads, and accept help enthusiastically. Do not make a direct bid for a job. (If you do, you risk offending your contact.) You asked to schedule a career information meeting, not an interview!

▲ Apply the nine success strategies that were presented in Chapter 1. Conduct your career information survey meetings with energy, enthusiasm, and attention to detail.

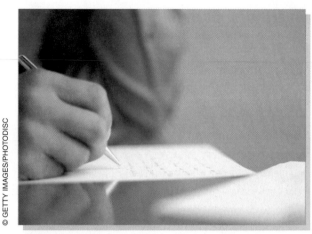

Promptly write thank-you letters to the people who helped you with your career information survey meetings.

Complete Career Action 7-3

Follow Up the Meeting

Within one day of your survey meeting, write follow-up thank-you letters to the people who helped you. Use good-quality stationery, and handwrite or key the letters neatly. If a contact offers to help you with a job lead, hand deliver or mail a copy of your resume to him or her within a week. (This person could become a key part of your job search network!) If you don't have a resume, prepare one using the guidelines in Chapter 9.

Job Qualifications Profile: A Snapshot to Persuade Employers

The Job Qualifications Profile organizes the qualifications information you summarized about yourself in Chapters 2 and 3. It gives you a solid description of your abilities and how they relate to your job target. This is exactly what employers need to see evidence of a good match between the job and the applicant—you! Follow the steps below to start developing this summary and preparing yourself for a successful job search:

1. **Clearly identify your job target.** If you have not yet done this, a career counselor can help you. Also, refer to Chapter 3 to identify other sources of career planning information and assistance.

CAREER ACTION 7-3

Participate in a Career Information Survey Meeting

Directions: Schedule and conduct your career information survey meeting(s). Use a separate sheet of paper to write the answers to the questions you prepared in Career Action 7-1.

▲ Schedule as many of these meetings as possible; the benefits of obtaining current information and possible job leads are great.

▲ Also consider contacting people in your field who screen, interview, and hire job applicants to discuss the job hiring processes in particular. This could put you closer to a future job interview if you perform impressively during your information-gathering meeting.

▲ Small companies often have only a few employees; the owner of a company may also be the company's hiring authority.

2. **Write a clear description of your targeted job.** Obtain job descriptions from prospective employers. If this isn't feasible, ask your school's career counselor or librarian to help you locate a general description of your job target in the *Dictionary of Occupational Titles,* published by the U.S. Department of Labor. For more complete descriptions of major occupations, refer to the printed version of the *Occupational Outlook Handbook* or link to the online version through the *Your Career: How to Make It Happen* web site.

3. **Refer to the information you compiled in Chapters 2 and 3.** This information will help you complete the rest of the Job Qualifications Profile, outlining your abilities as they relate to your job target.

4. **Copy or print Career Action Worksheet 7-4 for multiple job targets.** If you're looking for employment in more than one field or area, prepare one Job Qualifications Profile for each target. Develop the broadest possible career planning base by including as many options as possible.

Your Job Qualifications Profile will be a valuable resource throughout your lifetime for writing your resume and letters and for preparing for interviews for each job you target. As you develop new skills and gain more experience, training, and education, your goals will change or expand. You can repeat the self-analysis exercises in this book at any time during your career. Your Job Qualifications Profile will result in a well-organized summary of the qualifications that relate directly to your current job target. This profile provides the snapshot of your qualifications necessary to persuade an employer to hire you for the job you want.

Complete Career Action 7-4

CAREER ACTION 7-4

Job Qualifications Profile

Directions: Access Career Action Worksheet 7-4 on your Learner's CD, or turn to page 99 to review the instructions for preparing your Job Qualifications Profile.

File your completed Job Qualifications Profile in your Career Management Files Binder.

CHECKLIST

INVESTIGATING THE JOB, APPLICATION, AND HIRING PROCEDURES

Check each of the actions you are currently taking to increase your career success:

○ Contacting employees in the field to get current information about the scope of their jobs and their employers' hiring procedures

○ Dressing and acting professionally in all outside assignments to project competence and encourage job leads

○ Using the Internet to research job descriptions and hiring information of hard-to-reach employers

○ Following up with contacts and people who participate in survey meetings by sending them thank-you letters (within one day) and copies of your resume

○ Developing a Job Qualifications Profile to help in successfully marketing yourself to employers

CRITICAL THINKING QUESTIONS

1. What benefits can you gain by conducting career information survey meetings?

2. What is the most significant information you obtained from your Career Information Surveys?

3. What methods can you use to connect with hard-to-reach employers?

4. How can you use your Job Qualifications Profile information in your job search and interviews?

 For convenient access to valuable career resources, activities, and job information links, visit the companion web site for this text: *http://levitt.swlearning.com*

CAREER ACTION WORKSHEET 7-4

Job Qualifications Profile

Directions: Supply the information requested on this Job Qualifications Profile. Refer to your completed Career Actions from Chapters 2 and 3. Print Career Action Worksheet 7-4 from the Learner's CD or copy this page to develop a summary for each of your job targets.

1. Title of job target:

   _____

   _____

   _____

2. Description of job:

   _____

   _____

   _____

3. My education and training related to the job target:

   _____

   _____

   _____

4. My work experience related to the job target:

   _____

   _____

   _____

   _____

5. My accomplishments related to the job target:

   _____

   _____

   _____

   _____

Continued on next page >>>

CAREER ACTION WORKSHEET 7-4 (continued)

6. Praise or recognition I have received related to the job target:

_____

_____

_____

7. How my skills and transferable competencies relate to the job target:

_____

_____

_____

_____

8. How my values relate to the job target:

_____

_____

_____

9. How my work environment preferences relate to the job target:

_____

_____

_____

10. How my personality traits relate to the job target:

_____

_____

_____

_____

11. What appeals to me about this job:

_____

_____

_____

chapter *8*

RESEARCH PROSPECTIVE EMPLOYERS

In this chapter, you will:

Use Internet, printed, and people resources for researching prospective employers, your job target, and your career field.

• Expand your job search and career planning vocabulary by reviewing descriptions, employment applications, job advertisements, and selected newspaper and journal articles.

"Understanding company culture is key to job success. By doing research before you accept a job, you will be a more educated employee with a reduced learning curve. You may also save yourself from the aggravation and disappointment commonly associated with job dissatisfaction. It is a worthwhile investment of your time."

Samer Hamadeh
President and CEO
Vault, Inc.

Chapter 8 explains how to gather current information about your field and about prospective employers so you can customize your job search communications and emphasize your related strengths and suitability for a job. Many resources for researching employers are presented, including recognized leaders in a field, career or job fairs, Internet sites, libraries, and professional or trade associations. Doing this research gives you a major advantage over those candidates who don't.

Complete Industry, Employer, and Job Research for Big Payoffs!

Research gives applicants a competitive edge. Employers nationwide say that applicants who research employers well increase their employability as much as 25 percent! Figure 8-1 shows the competitive advantage you can gain over other applicants by doing employer research.

The advantages of researching your career field and potential employers affect the success of your job search in many ways:

▲ **Competitive Edge.** Employers view candidates who don't have solid knowledge of the employers' businesses or industry as weak choices. If you are prepared to discuss products and industry facts with employers, you will show that you have made a sincere effort to learn about the organization and the marketplace. Many applicants don't invest their time and energy in researching employers. If you do, you will have the competitive edge.

▲ **Better Career Decisions.** Having current knowledge about employers, industries, and job targets allows you to make informed career decisions and assess your interest in and qualifications for specific jobs.

▲ **Improved Ability to Market Your Skills and Get Hired.** Researching employers improves your ability to discuss specifically how your qualifications match the employers' purposes, goals, and needs. Employers are most willing to invest training resources in applicants who demonstrate initiative and commitment through their research of the employer and the industry.

▲ **Compensation for Lack of Experience.** Industry knowledge helps you compensate for lack of actual or extensive job experience.

▲ **Increased Confidence.** Being well informed helps you feel more confident, communicate more clearly, and project greater competence.

Figure 8-1: This applicant-rating graph illustrates the power of research.

© GETTY IMAGES/PHOTODISC

Visiting a potential employer is a good way to gather information and get a personal perspective on the company.

Learn What You Should Know

Strengthen your employability by improving your knowledge in the following three areas:

1. **Information About the Occupational Field.** Learn about the current and predicted trends, general educational requirements, job descriptions, growth outlook, and salary ranges in the industry.

2. **Information About Prospective Employers.** Learn whether the organizations are publicly or privately owned. Verify companies' names, addresses, and products or services (current and predicted, as well as trends); histories; cultures; reputations; performance; divisions and subsidiaries; locations (U.S. and global); predicted growth indicators; number of employees; philosophies and procedures; predicted job openings; salary ranges; and listings of managers in your targeted department. Also learn about their competitors and customers.

3. **Information About Specific Jobs.** Obtain job descriptions; identify the required education and experience; and determine the working conditions, salaries, and fringe benefits.

Success Tip

Gain the competitive advantage by researching employers; they expect you to be knowledgeable about the job, the company, and the industry.

Use Many Sources of Information

This section identifies resources for industry, company, and job information.

People Resources

People are strong resources for learning about the character and function of an organization and for gathering general information about an industry. If your target employer is a small organization, its people are typically the best research resources.

Employees of Your Target Employer. Current and former employees know about hiring procedures; employee satisfaction levels; job descriptions and responsibilities; skills, education, and experience required for jobs; company objectives; salaries; and advancement opportunities. Don't rely only on opinion, however, particularly if it's extremely negative or overly positive.

Your Target Employer. When possible, visit your target employer to get a personal perspective. Be sure to dress appropriately. Ask for literature about the organization, such as a brochure, mission statement, strategic plan, or stockholder's report. If appropriate and affordable, try the company's product or service to increase your knowledge about it.

Customers, Clients, or Patients. Ask customers, clients, or patients for their opinions of the employer's service, reliability, products, and general reputation.

Competitors. Research the competitors of your target employer to learn about the industry. Compare positions available, pay rates, and benefits, as well as the education, skills, and experience required.

Instructors, Professors, and Counselors. These people are often knowledgeable about local employers and industries. Since they may serve as job references for you, be professional, punctual, and reliable when dealing with them.

Schools' Career Services Centers. Schools' career services centers generally have comprehensive resources for learning about industries, specific companies, specific jobs, local employers, and more.

> *"The next best thing to knowing something is knowing where to find it."*
> Samuel Johnson

Recognized People in the Field. Successful people in your field are excellent resources for learning about the industry and prospective employers. Complete Career Action 8-1 to learn more about your career field through discussions with experienced leaders. It could lead you directly to the job you are hoping for!

Complete Career Action 8-1

Career/Job Fairs

As noted previously, career/job fairs offered by communities and schools and on the Internet are valuable sources of employer information. It could take hundreds of hours to visit the number of individual companies that you can access in one day at a career fair.

Use fairs to gather company literature, to find out directly what job skills and knowledge are required, to learn keywords you can emphasize in your resume, and to schedule interviews.

Libraries

Check out the reference sections of college, university, or public libraries to find extensive employer and industry information available in printed, microfilm, and electronic format. Reference librarians can help you locate appropriate resources.

The following resources will help you complete your research and preparation:

▲ Company pamphlets, brochures, and annual reports

▲ *Dun & Bradstreet's Million Dollar Database*

    ▲ *Thomas Register of American Manufacturers*

    ▲ *Standard and Poor's Stock Reports*

    ▲ *Value Line Investment Survey*

    ▲ *Moody's Manuals*

    ▲ *Business Periodicals Index*

▲ *Readers' Guide to Periodical Literature*

▲ *Job Choices*—excellent magazine of the National Association of Colleges and Employers; check schools' career services centers to locate a copy

▲ *Occupational Outlook Handbook*—published by the U.S. Department of Labor, Bureau of Labor Statistics; usually available in schools' career services centers

▲ Area telephone directories

▲ Newspaper and journal articles

▲ *Fortune* and *Forbes* magazines and *The Wall Street Journal*

▲ *Standard and Poor's Register of Corporations, Directors and Executives*

Also ask reference librarians for assistance in locating international business information if your target employer has international holdings or is based outside the United States.

CAREER ACTION 8-1

Contact Recognized People in Your Field

Directions: Follow the five steps below to research trends and information sources in your industry. In this activity, you will conduct meetings with industry leaders to gather industry information so you can communicate well during your job search, making you a more persuasive candidate. The purposes of these meetings are to learn all you can about your career field and to identify methods of updating your industry information and skills.

Remember: Do not ask for a job or an interview during these meetings.

Steps for Researching Trends and Information Sources in Your Industry

1. Contact at least two people in your target industry who are recognized for their ability and accomplishments. Ask your schools' career services staff, instructors, family, and friends to suggest people to contact.

2. Call and ask whether your contacts can meet with you to discuss career development questions. Schedule a time, date, and place to meet.

3. Be well dressed and on time. Such meetings can lead to referrals or job offers.

4. Project professionalism. Keep your neatly prepared survey questions in a professional binder. (Sample questions are listed below; add others of your own. Refer also to Career Action Worksheet 8-1 on your Learner's CD.)

5. Be prepared to discuss your findings in class, or write a summary report.

Sample Questions for Career Action 8-1

1. What current trends do you think are the most important in the industry? Where can I learn more about these trends?

2. To remain well informed about the industry:

    a.   What publications (books, periodicals, and so on) do you recommend?

    b.   What web sites do you recommend?

    c.   What professional or trade associations do you recommend?

3. What skills, education, and experience are necessary for my job target?

4. What new terminology or industry buzzwords do you suggest I know to be well prepared? (This information will be useful in Career Action 8-3.)

5. How did you succeed in the field? Would you recommend the same or a similar approach for me?

6. What other suggestions can you give me to improve my employability in the field (further education, training, research, reading, and so on)?

File your findings in your Career Management Files Binder.

PERSONAL**BEST**

Using the Internet for Research

The Internet is exploding with public and private web sites that offer information about industries and employers. Use the Web to gather information about products and services, corporate history, recent trends, and more. Links to the sites listed below can be found on the *Your Career: How to Make It Happen* web site (http://levitt.swlearning.com).

"Researching Companies Online" by Debbie Flanagan: This is an excellent site with multiple links and tips for online employer research.

Search engines: Use search engines to conduct general searches for specific employers or specific career topics. Use the sites to find recent news about your industry and target companies.

Financial sites: Use financial sites to find sales and earnings information and recent news about public companies. Examples are the American Stock Exchange, the New York Stock Exchange, and the NASDAQ Stock Market.

Employer sites: Visit the sites of employers that interest you. Always check out the "Jobs" or "Careers" and "What's New" or "News" pages to get the most current information. Mine the entire sites, searching for nuggets of information you can use during your job search to demonstrate your knowledge and Internet skills.

As you cruise the information superhighway, remember that while the Internet is valuable and sometimes the most up-to-date information source, many facts that are vital to evaluating an employer can be found only in print sources. The Internet often provides summaries of topical information, while the full text is available through library research. In addition, employer web sites only emphasize the employers' positive aspects, so don't rely on them alone.

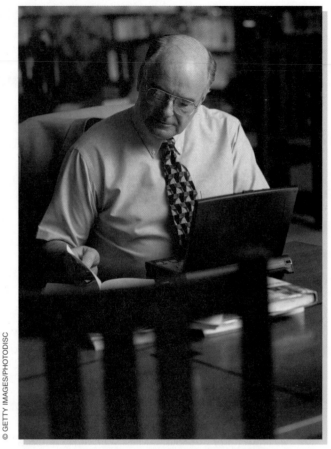

© GETTY IMAGES/PHOTODISC

Use your library's printed and electronic resources to find articles and information on employers that interest you.

Research Local and Small Firms

If you want a job with a local or small firm, the following are good resources for your research:

▲ People in the field

▲ The area chamber of commerce

▲ The area Better Business Bureau

▲ Local newspapers

▲ Telephone directories

▲ Local libraries

Also learn about the occupational field in general (local, national, and global trends; professional or trade associations; and so on).

Professional or Trade Associations

Nearly every industry has professional or trade associations that provide journals, newsletters, and reports on current industry information and related trends. Many have membership lists, which are good resources for finding prospective employers. Employers are impressed with applicants who know about their industry associations and publications.

Enhance your employability by joining a well-known professional or trade association in your field and reading its publications. Many have student chapters or memberships. Such extra effort can give you the power to outdistance your competition. Check the *Encyclopedia of Associations* to locate major associations in your field. Also use the Yahoo! site to find professional or trade associations. A link to Yahoo! can be found on the *Your Career: How to Make It Happen* web site (http://levitt.swlearning.com).

Develop and Expand Your Career-Related Vocabulary

A strong career-related vocabulary projects competence. Employers view such a vocabulary as a good indicator of job and industry knowledge. Therefore, it is important that you continually expand your job- and career-related vocabulary. Career Action 8-3 is designed to help you do this. Your vocabulary can help or hurt your career; start now to build a vocabulary that enhances your career success.

Success Tip

Develop and regularly expand your job/career-related vocabulary to demonstrate competence and knowledge.

Complete Career Action 8-2

Complete Career Action 8-3

CAREER ACTION 8-2

Printed, People, and Internet Resources for Employer Research

Directions: Use printed, people, and Internet resources to research at least two companies that interest you. Learn about the companies' products or services, objectives, locations, salaries, and trends, and research any other details that interest you. Prepare a written summary of your findings.

Resources:

1. *Your Career: How to Make It Happen* web site (http://levitt.swlearning.com). From the main menu, select "Links." Then click on "Researching Companies Links."

2. For additional research and resource ideas, refer to Career Action Worksheet 8-2 on your Learner's CD or on pages 111–114 of this text.

File your research in your Career Managment Files Binder.

CAREER ACTION 8-3

Job Search and Career Development Vocabulary

Directions: Follow the steps below to create a vocabulary list, and use the terms to shine in your resumes, cover letters, interviews, and follow-up communications:

1. Obtain two general job descriptions for the type of job you are seeking. Get them directly from employers, from people currently working in similar jobs, from job postings, or from the Internet. If you can't find at least two written descriptions, obtain verbal descriptions from people who work in your field, and write them out. Also get one or more general job descriptions for your job target from the *Occupational Outlook Handbook*.

2. Obtain at least two blank applications for the type of job you are seeking. Note that some employers only provide applications online. Visit the web sites of such employers to obtain copies of their applications.

3. Obtain at least two advertisements for positions that are similar to your job target. Check newspapers, professional journals, the Internet, your career services center, and so on.

4. Carefully read through the job target material you obtain. Underline all action verbs (for example: *compile, analyze, operate, supervise*) and all keywords or nouns used to describe required or related skills, education, and experience, including the specific names of software programs or computer-related knowledge (for example: *operator, operation, accounts receivable, instructor/ instruction, writing, analyzing, designing, evaluation, management, computing, computations, Word, Excel, UNIX*). Underline vocabulary, abbreviations, special terminology, and buzzwords that are unique to your field.

5. Make a list of these terms, spelling each word correctly, and include their definitions. If you don't know the definition of a term, find it. Categorize the terms as follows: (a) action verbs, (b) keyword nouns, (c) specialized terminology, (d) abbreviations, and (e) industry buzzwords.

6. File this vocabulary list in your Career Management Files Binder, and add to it whenever possible.

Success Tip

Competing applicants with equal education, training, and experience are judged on their verbal and written command of industry vocabulary. Develop a strong vocabulary to improve your chances of landing your ideal job.

Apply Your Industry, Employer, and Job Research

Apply the information you obtain from your research as you write your resumes and cover letters and as you interview. Complete all the Career Action assignments in Chapter 8 to gather this essential information.

Review the information from Career Action 8-2 and the corresponding worksheet on your Learner's CD to identify resources for answering specific research

© GETTY IMAGES/PHOTODISC

A vast amount of career information is available from a number of sources. Schools' career services staff and reference librarians can help you identify those sources.

Learn About the Interviewer *Before* You Are Interviewed

Get the interviewer's name from the company when you schedule an interview. If you know anyone who works or worked with the interviewer or who knows him or her personally, contact that person to learn as much as you can about the interviewer.

Know What to Research

In researching the interviewer, learn as much as you can about the following:

▲ The interviewer's special interests or activities

▲ The interviewer's work philosophy, goals and objectives, and achievements

▲ The general development of the interviewer's career

If possible, find out how the interviewer prefers to be contacted for a job (by letter, in person, by telephone, by e-mail). This information can help you approach the interviewer in his or her preferred style and can help you phrase your remarks to meet his or her interests and needs.

In small organizations, people who know the interviewer are the best resources for providing information about him or her. Don't press an assistant, a receptionist, or another employee too hard for information about the interviewer, however. Word may get back to the interviewer! If you are courteous, you may learn some useful information, but tread lightly; avoid coming across as pushy.

questions. Don't limit yourself to the resources listed in this textbook. Ask your school's career services staff and reference librarians to help you identify the most valuable resources for your career objectives. Ask members of your network for help in obtaining the most current and useful employer information.

Refer to Chapter 9 to see how you can use the information you find in your research to prepare powerful targeted resumes.

Research Interviewers

Round out your research by learning about the interviewer. This can strengthen your competitive position by providing you with information that helps you communicate comfortably and connect positively during an interview.

Success Tip

Research to learn all you can about the interviewer so you can communicate comfortably and connect positively during your interview.

CHECKLIST

RESEARCHING PROSPECTIVE EMPLOYERS

Check each of the actions you are currently taking to increase your career success:

○ Gaining a competitive advantage by researching to learn about prospective employers who expect you to be knowledgeable about the job, the company, and the industry

○ Using many sources of current job information, including people in your field, job fairs, libraries, online sources, and associations

○ Developing and regularly expanding your job/career-related vocabulary to demonstrate competence and knowledge

○ Obtaining the most current and useful employer information and using it to develop targeted resumes and cover letters and to prepare for successful interviews

○ Researching to learn about the interviewer so that you can make a positive connection with him or her during the interview

CRITICAL THINKING QUESTIONS

1. What are the advantages of researching your occupational field and your targeted job?

2. How can your vocabulary help or hurt your career?

3. What should you try to learn about an interviewer?

4. What are at least two web sites you have visited that provide useful information about employers? Give at least two examples of the types of information you have found at each site.

 For convenient access to valuable career resources, activities, and job information links, visit the companion web site for this text: *http://levitt.swlearning.com*

CAREER ACTION WORKSHEET 8-2

Printed, People, and Internet Resources for Employer Research

Note: Links for the web sites listed below can be found on the *Your Career: How to Make It Happen* web site (http://levitt.swlearning.com).

Questions About the Industry

1. What is the general job description for your occupational career choice?

    References: (a) schools' career services staff, (b) *Occupational Outlook Handbook,* (c) reference section of library

    Internet: (a) schools' career services web sites, (b) *Occupational Outlook Handbook* online, (c) employers' web sites

    _____

    _____

    _____

2. What is the occupational outlook projection for your field? (Will occupational opportunities grow, diminish, stay the same? By what percentage? Over what period of time?)

    References: (same as #1)

    Internet: (same as #1) and America's Career InfoNet

    _____

    _____

    _____

3. What is the current general salary range for your occupational field and job target?

    References: (a) people in the field, (b) *Occupational Outlook Handbook,* (c) school's career services staff

    Internet: (a) same as #1—at the *Occupational Outlook Handbook* site, select the title of your occupational cluster, choose the title of your field (and a subtitle if necessary), and click on "Earnings"; (b) JobStar—click on "Salary Info"; (c) Salary.com

    _____

    _____

4. What occupations are closely related to your first occupational choice?

    References: (a) *Occupational Outlook Handbook,* (b) school's career services staff

    Internet: (same as #1)

    _____

    _____

Continued on next page >>>

CAREER ACTION WORKSHEET 8-2 (continued)

Questions About Prospective Employers

1. What are the products or services of the prospective employers you have identified?

   References: (a) people in the field, (b) *Dun & Bradstreet's Million Dollar Database,* (c) annual reports of the employers, (d) *Moody's Manuals*

   Internet: (a) employers' web sites–look for products, services, and annual reports; (b) "Researching Companies Online" by Debbie Flanagan; (c) *Your Career: How to Make It Happen* web site (http://levitt.swlearning.com)–click on the "Links" button, and then select "Researching Companies Links"; (d) Monster; (e) Hoover's Online; (f) search engines

   _____

   _____

   _____

2. What are the size, location, sales assets, and stock market standing of the employer organizations, and how many employees do they have?

   References: (a) people in the field, (b) *Dun & Bradstreet's Million Dollar Database,* (c) *Standard and Poor's Buyers' Compendium of American Industry,* (d) companies' annual reports

   Internet: (a) all sources listed in #1, (b) financial information web sites

   _____

   _____

   _____

3. Have the companies shown consistent and substantial growth? What are the financial and competitive positions of the companies in the industry?

   References: (a) people in the field, (b) companies' annual reports, (c) *Fortune* magazine, (d) *Forbes* magazine, (e) *The Wall Street Journal,* (f) *Value Line Investment Survey,* (g) *Dun & Bradstreet's Million Dollar Database*

   Internet: (a) all sources listed in #1, (b) annual reports of the employers, (c) *Your Career: How to Make It Happen* web site (http://levitt.swlearning.com)–click on "Links" and then on "Financial Information Links"

   _____

   _____

   _____

Continued on next page >>>

CAREER ACTION WORKSHEET 8-2 (continued)

4. Who are the competitors?

   References: (a) people in the field, (b) *Dun & Bradstreet's Million Dollar Database,* (c) telephone directory Yellow Pages, (d) chambers of commerce, (e) *Fortune* magazine, (f) *Forbes* magazine, (g) *The Wall Street Journal*

   Internet: (a) "Researching Companies Online" by Debbie Flanagan, (b) WetFeet.com, (c) Vault.com, (d) SuperPages.com—a national online Yellow Pages directory

   _____

   _____

   _____

   _____

5. What are the current trends in the industry, and are technological changes occurring or anticipated in the field?

   References: (a) people in the field, (b) professional and trade associations, (c) publications in the field, (d) *The Wall Street Journal*

   Internet: (a) employers' web sites; (b) America's Career InfoNet; (c) InternetNews.com—click on "Business"; (d) web sites of professional, trade, and other associations in the field; (e) Internet search engines

   _____

   _____

   _____

   _____

   _____

   _____

   _____

   _____

   _____

   _____

   _____

   _____

   _____

   _____

Continued on next page >>>

CAREER ACTION WORKSHEET 8-2 (continued)

Questions About the Job Itself

1. What is the title of the position you are seeking?

   References: (a) the company or organization–check with the human resources department or the department or employer you are targeting, (b) people who are currently in the field and knowledgeable about your job target

   Internet: (a) employers' web sites–check under *human resources, employment opportunities,* and so on; (b) other sites you found useful in the previous questions

   _____

   _____

   _____

   _____

2. What are the description, duties, and responsibilities of the job, and what are the required skills, education, and training?

   References: (a) the employer organization (many provide written job descriptions on request), (b) employees of the company or people who work in similar jobs

   Internet: (a) employers' web sites–check under *human resources, employment opportunities,* and so on; (b) other sites you found useful in the previous questions

   This question will help you identify the requirements of the position so you can relate your qualifications for the job in your search communications. Do your research carefully, and be complete in your answer. You are the one who benefits!

   _____

   _____

   _____

   _____

   _____

   _____

   _____

   _____

   _____

   _____

   _____

PREPARE A WINNING RESUME

In this chapter, you will:

- Identify the elements of a winning resume.

- Identify critical differences among print, electronic, and web resumes.

- List appropriate keywords to use in your resumes.

- Write a clear, appropriate job objective.

- Outline the content for your print resume.

- Prepare and evaluate a print resume draft, make corrections, and produce a final resume.

- Create an electronic resume.

 Use the Internet to access and research job/resume-posting web sites.

"A resume is written to impress, not to inform. Think of it as a marketing tool, not a historical record. It is valuable real estate—use it for your most impressive information. If you don't list any accomplishments in your resume, chances are no one will call you.

Visual presentation is as important as, if not more important than, resume content. No one is going to take the time to read a traditional resume that is poorly presented."

Peter Newfield
President
Career-Resumes.com

Chapter 9 shows you how to write and deliver resumes that get you interviews. A good resume is your key to getting an interview. Most employers choose candidates to interview based largely on their resumes. Employers' selections are based on a quick visual screening or computerized search of the resumes they receive. Employers look for a match between their needs and the applicants' qualifications. Your resume must be written so that it passes an initial screening and a more detailed analysis. This chapter explains how to create resumes that will pass these tests.

What Is a Resume?

A resume is a short document that details your qualifications for a particular job or job target. As a job applicant, you need at least two resume versions: a print resume and an electronic resume. In some fields, having a web resume is also an asset. These three types of resumes are described in Figure 9-1, "Resume Types, Purposes, and Preferred File Formats." Specific instructions for preparing each type of resume are presented later in this chapter.

Today, many employers use web-based applicant-tracking systems or in-house programs to electronically scan resumes into applicant- or resume-tracking and search software. These programs search resumes for keywords—terms that represent the qualifications the company has instructed the software to search for. The purpose is to identify applicants with the required qualifications for specific jobs.

Resume Type	Purpose	Preferred File Format
Print resume	To be delivered as a printed resume with an attractive visual presentation *(Note: Some employers use software capable of scanning print resumes into a searchable database to identify job matches.)*	Microsoft® Word (.doc), WordPerfect® (.wpd), Rich Text Format (.rtf), or Portable Document Format (.pdf) Word processed with visually attractive layout for human readers *(Note: All print resumes should be scannable—specifically formatted to scan cleanly into a database.)*
Electronic resume	To be transmitted electronically and clearly (by e-mail or through online resume builders or e-forms) For employer use in compiling, searching, and maintaining a resume database for hiring purposes	ASCII or Plain Text
Web resume	To be posted as a web document designed to showcase the applicant's HTML skills May include a portfolio of artistic, specialized computer, and other abilities (for example, graphic art, CAD drawings, video or musical performance clips)	HTML

Figure 9-1: Resume Types, Purposes, and Preferred File Formats

Print Resume

A print resume is a word-processed resume designed:

▲ To be visually appealing.

▲ To be delivered as an e-mail attachment, by regular mail, in person, or by fax.

▲ To be scanned clearly into a database by computer software.

A print resume is created using a word processing program. Currently, the following formats are the most acceptable: Microsoft Word (.doc) or WordPerfect (.wpd), a word-processed resume containing full formatting; and Rich Text Format (.rtf), a resume version less vulnerable to viruses that is word processed and saved as an .rtf file, but which may not retain full formatting. A print resume may also be converted to a Portable Document Format, or PDF, file (.pdf), which retains all formatting, is invulnerable to viruses, and is compatible across all platforms, but which may be difficult to search for keywords. Always ask employers exactly which format they prefer, and comply with their preferences.

Because some word processing formatting elements don't scan well, print resumes should be carefully formatted to omit features and characters that may not scan correctly. Instructions for accomplishing this are provided later in this chapter.

© GETTY IMAGES/PHOTODISC

Your resume may be circulated to managers within a company via e-mail or fax.

> "People often say that motivation doesn't last. Well, neither does bathing—that's why we recommend it daily."
>
> Zig Ziglar
> American Sales Trainer, Author, Motivational Speaker

Electronic Resume

An electronic resume is an ASCII or plain text document designed to be delivered via e-mail or an online e-form. This type of resume must be completely stripped of word processing codes and is, therefore, a plain-looking document. Electronic resumes must be specially formatted (explained later in this chapter) so that they can be transmitted electronically to employers, be easily read on screen through e-mail programs, and be transmitted directly to resume-tracking programs for processing. Because electronic resumes save employers the scanning step, many employers prefer them over the other resume formats.

Web Resume

A web resume is formatted in HTML so it can be posted on the Internet as a web document. The web resume looks like an attractive print resume but can contain more sophisticated graphics. It is designed to showcase the applicant's HTML skills and may also link to a web portfolio of artistic, specialized computer, and other abilities (for example, graphic art, charts, CAD drawings, and video or musical performance clips).

What Makes a Winning Resume?

A winning resume is one that gets you a job interview. The following scenario illustrates how employers process resumes and what features help candidates land interviews:

▲ ABC Company receives your resume (along with resumes from many other candidates) in response to a job advertisement. The company electronically searches all resumes and stores the contents in an electronic database for easy analysis, distribution, and retrieval.

▲ Resumes are typically reviewed to select candidates who appear the most qualified. This review and selection process may be done by a human resources staff person or by software that searches resumes for keywords.

▲ The selected resumes are reviewed again and may be circulated (in hard copy format or online) to the hiring authorities. These people choose the candidates who appear the most qualified and are likely to work well with the existing employees.

From this scenario, you can infer that a winning resume achieves four objectives:

1. It quickly shows that the candidate has the qualifications necessary for the job.

2. It demonstrates that the candidate can meet the employer's needs.

3. It suggests that the candidate is someone who is likable and works well with others.

4. It appeals to both human and electronic reviewers.

Figure 9-2, "Four Keys to Writing a Winning Resume," provides guidelines for achieving these four key objectives in your resume. Review these guidelines to get a sense of how to best focus the content of your resume to obtain positive results. The remainder of this chapter walks you through all the stages of preparing, writing, formatting, and submitting a winning resume.

Prepare to Write Your Resume

Before you begin writing your resume, you should do the following:

▲ Complete a thorough inventory of your education and skills (see Chapters 2 and 3).

▲ Determine the kind of work environment in which you thrive.

▲ Set a career target (see Chapter 3).

▲ Perform research to identify specific companies or job titles that interest you.

If you haven't already completed Chapters 2 and 3 of this book, do so before beginning to write your resume.

Success Tip

Begin the resume-writing process by taking an inventory of your qualifications.

Four Steps to Preparing Your Resume

Writing a resume well enough to get an interview typically does not happen on the first try. It requires completing these four carefully planned steps:

1. Decide on your job objective.

2. Choose the most appropriate resume layout.

3. Organize carefully and write forcefully.

4. Fine-tune each section of your resume.

Don't rush the process. If you skip or skimp on any of these steps, you will greatly diminish your chance of achieving the purpose of your resume: getting the interview and, ultimately, the job.

FOUR KEYS TO WRITING A WINNING RESUME

KEY	WHY	HOW
1. Quickly show that you have the qualifications for the job.	The first cut in resume reviews takes only seconds. Your qualifications for a job must be readily apparent.	Include a clear job objective. Include a qualifications or capabilities section at the top of your resume. List the most pertinent data first.
2. Demonstrate that you can meet the employer's needs.	Once your resume is past the initial qualifications review, employers want to know if you can apply your skills to solving their problems.	Show your knowledge of the job and employer in your resume. Include examples of work-related accomplishments (for example, reduced errors, saved money, and increased sales/productivity).
3. Suggest that you are likable and work well with others.	Employers want to work with people who have positive personal and performance traits.	Emphasize your enthusiasm, cooperation, and dependability. Stress activities, teamwork, and leadership in organizations. Include words such as *accurate, cooperative, creative, flexible, organized,* and *self-directed*.
4. Pass both human and electronic reviews.	Many employers scan and process resumes electronically. Resumes are read and assessed only by humans in some organizations.	Include keywords throughout your resume to pass electronic reviews. Use action words to describe your accomplishments and to appeal to human readers. Format your resume for clear scannability.

Figure 9-2: Four Keys to Writing a Winning Resume

Step 1: Decide on Your Job Objective

The first step in writing a successful resume is specifying a concise job objective that describes the job you are seeking. Your entire resume will be organized around this objective. Deciding on a clear job objective, such as *medical technician*, will help you determine the best way to organize your resume, select appropriate keywords, and present your experience. Detailed instructions for writing an effective job objective are provided later in this chapter under "Step 4: Fine-Tune Each Section of Your Resume."

Step 2: Choose the Most Appropriate Resume Layout

The most common resume layouts are:

▲ Reverse chronological

▲ Functional

▲ Combination

Deciding on a clear job objective, such as *medical laboratory technician,* will help you determine the best way to organize your resume, select appropriate keywords, and present your experience.

Review the following descriptions of these resume layouts, and determine which one best meets your needs.

Reverse Chronological. Use this layout to show skills, work experience, and logical career progression that are directly related to the job target. Choose this layout to emphasize steady, related work experience without major employment gaps or numerous job changes. At the top of the resume, place the information category that best supports your job objective. List your employment history in reverse chronological order with the most recent experience first, and stress the major accomplishments and responsibilities of each position. Avoid repeating details that are common to several positions. (See Figure 9-6 on page 141.)

Functional. Use the functional layout if you lack work experience that is directly related to your job target. This layout is also appropriate if you have gaps in employment. Instead of showcasing your work history, it highlights your capabilities that are related to the job target. Clearly emphasize your skills that relate to the job objective, and substantiate them with measurable accomplishments. Use separate paragraphs to emphasize each skill category. Arrange the paragraphs in order of importance to the objective, listing the most important skill first. (See Figure 9-7 on page 142.)

Combination. Capture an employer's attention by immediately emphasizing the match between your skills and the position requirements. Consider the combination layout if you want to emphasize your skills or if you have limited experience. List your skills just below the job objective. Then incorporate your accomplishments in a reverse chronological list of job experiences. Add credibility

> *"What we do for ourselves can get us by. What we do for others is what gets us ahead, whether in our profession, spiritual pursuits, or relationships."*
>
> Dr. Vincent Muli Wa Kituku

by linking your achievements with specific employers and time periods. Place your education summary where it best supports your objective. If your education is more closely related to the skills required for your target job, place your educational information before your work experience information. (See Figure 9-8 on page 143.)

Success Tip

Choose the resume layout that best supports your job objective.

Step 3: Organize Carefully and Write Forcefully

Use the following general guidelines as you write and edit your resume.

Write Concisely and Clearly. Convey your qualifications as clearly and concisely as possible, but don't omit pertinent information and cost yourself the interview. Use phrases, not complete sentences.

You can write more concisely if you avoid clichés, dated expressions, and overly complex terms. Some common examples and alternatives are shown below.

Cliché/Dated	Concise
at this point in time	now
ballpark figure	estimation
explore every avenue	explore the options
last but not least	finally
left no stone unturned	used every possible method

Complex/Wordy	Concise
utilized	used
endeavor	try
equitable	fair
initiated	started

Use Numbers and Specific Examples of Accomplishments. Your resume will be clearer and more powerful if you use specific terms and examples to describe your accomplishments. Notice the more forceful impact the following specific examples have.

General/Vague	Specific
reduced costs significantly	reduced costs by 20 percent
the leading producer	top producer of 60 employees

The most persuasive resumes describe the applicants' accomplishments with numbers, percentages, and dollar amounts to emphasize how the accomplishments could meet the prospective employers' needs. Use numbers whenever possible to enhance the credibility of your achievements.

Notice how the numbers in the second example below strengthen the accomplishment:

▲ Processed more orders than any other member of the work team.

▲ Processed **40 percent** more orders than any other member of the work team.

Try adding the word *that* to an accomplishment statement, as shown in the following examples. If necessary, use an estimated measurement (*approximately, averaged, up to,* or *more than*).

▲ Developed a new filing system that reduced filing time by 25 percent.

▲ Developed stock procedures that reduced backorders by 50 percent.

Success Tip

Use numbers, percentages, and action verbs to describe your accomplishments forcefully.

PERSONAL**BEST**

Identify Marketable Assets

When hiring, employers look for applicants who have demonstrated accomplishments in skill and knowledge areas that are relevant to the job requirements. To identify your marketable assets, apply the following questions to your paid jobs, volunteer work or involvement in organizations, and classroom and other experiences.

1. How have I increased my skills and/or knowledge?

2. How have I solved problems or made decisions or recommendations? Were the results effective? Explain in measurable terms (numbers, percentages, and so on).

3. Have I organized or planned tasks, activities, and projects? Explain.

4. Did I work well under pressure and meet critical deadlines? Explain.

5. Have I used technology? How? Have I been innovative? How?

6. Have I cut costs or increased revenues? Explain clearly using measurable terms.

7. What equipment and software can I operate proficiently?

8. How can I measure the results of my work (number of customers served, percentage increase in production, percentage decrease in costs or errors, and so on)?

9. Did I work with a team? How did I contribute? Did I lead others? Explain.

10. What reports and documents have I written?

11. Have I helped train, develop, or motivate others? Explain.

12. Did I manage money for a group? Explain your activities clearly using measurable terms that demonstrate your accuracy and reliability.

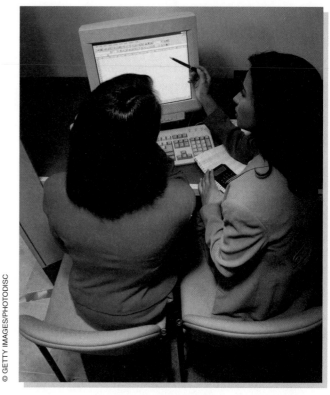

© GETTY IMAGES/PHOTODISC

In your resume, emphasize your marketable assets that will add value to the employer's organization.

Use Action Verbs, and Omit *I* and *My*. To satisfy resume-search software, you need to include keywords, which are usually nouns that reflect the employer's needs. Ultimately, however, you want a person to view your resume, so you also need to include action statements that use verbs and are persuasive to human readers.

Action statements need not be complete sentences. Employers want to find the important information quickly. Omit *I*, *me*, and *my* to increase your conciseness and avoid sounding like a braggart. (The employer already knows the resume is about you.) Use action verbs and phrases to show that you take initiative and actively participate in problem-solving and decision-making processes (*wrote proposal, improved process, increased sales*). Notice how the specific action verbs in the second example below convey a stronger image.

▲ My duties included reviewing marketing trends, analyzing statistical data, and preparing annual sales reports.

▲ **Conducted** extensive market research; **analyzed, diagrammed,** and **reported** results of sales data; and **wrote** annual sales reports.

Use a thesaurus to find just the right words to convey your qualifications accurately and clearly. Notice the use of more specific action verbs (*designed* and *implemented*) in the second example below. Specific verbs clearly describe the applicant's scope of responsibility and convey a greater sense of accomplishment.

▲ **Started up** the inventory-tracking system.

▲ **Designed** and **implemented** the inventory-tracking system.

▲ **Organized** and **trained** volunteers who solicited contributions and **raised $55,000** for citywide "elder-help" campaign.

▲ **Coordinated** school's student-body elections and **reduced** final ballot processing time by **25 percent.**

Use Keywords Strategically. Keywords (which represent the required skills, knowledge, and capabilities for a position) are words and phrases that employers search for when reviewing resumes manually or electronically. Think of keywords as the magnets that draw attention to your resume, and include as many appropriate keywords in the qualifications section as possible.

Keywords name attributes that qualified candidates must have. Appropriate keywords for your job target include industry terminology and specific words or short phrases that are gleaned from the employers' job descriptions and ads. Review the web sites and publications of specific companies and professional associations in your industry to identify relevant keywords. These words describe employer-valued qualifications. A list of sources follows to help you identify appropriate keywords to include in your resume.

▲ Job titles

▲ Skills/specialties

▲ Education, certifications, licenses, and coursework

▲ Work and volunteer experience

▲ Community and other clubs/activities

▲ Computer/software/hardware skills and specialized tools

▲ Relevant personal qualities

▲ Industry buzzwords, jargon, and acronyms

▲ Accomplishments

▲ Industry/professional organizations

▲ Awards

Include keywords throughout your resume, and repeat critical keywords. The more keywords the resume–search software identifies, the more likely it is that your resume will be selected and you will be called for an interview.

Also use synonyms for keywords; employers may use different terms in their search criteria. For example, *budget* may be a synonym for *forecast*, *BA* for *Bachelor of Arts*, and *supervisor* for *manager*.

Computerized resume-search programs typically seek nouns. In searching for AutoCAD drafters, for example, the software may look for nouns (and noun synonyms) such as *CAD, engineer, AA degree, certified drafter, Computer-Aided Drafting, AutoCAD, wiring diagrams,* and *physics.*

Figure 9-3, "Keyword Search Samples," provides examples of keywords that resume-tracking software would search for to fill two different positions.

Complete Career Action 9-1

Success Tip

Keyword choices are critical. An employer may not read your resume unless it first gets several hits in a computer search. Getting a hit means that the software matches a keyword in your resume to one that it is seeking.

Position Title	Sample Keywords
Accountant	CPA, audit, accounting, accounts receivable/payable, statistics, spreadsheet, finance, systems training, computer, database, team player, B.B.A. Accounting, accurate, project leader, customer relations, accounting database, tax code, ethics, Sarbanes-Oxley compliance, data integrity
Web Specialist	HTML, web development, web hosting, web design, PHP, VB.NET, Java, SQL, Dreamweaver, Flash, database management, server administration, security, firewalls, FTP, Internet imaging, web design internship, American Association of Webmasters (AAWM), Western Regional Graphics Award

Figure 9-3: Keyword Search Samples

CAREER ACTION 9-1

Identify Appropriate Keywords

Directions: Access Career Action Worksheet 9-1 on your Learner's CD or use a separate sheet of paper to complete this assignment.

1. Prepare a comprehensive list of appropriate keywords to use in your resumes (industry terms; acronyms; and terms describing your job positions, experience, education, skills, and so on).

2. Use the Internet as a primary resource in your research. Also use any of the resources listed below to identify appropriate keywords.

3. Print a report that includes your list of keywords and a list of the resources you used to identify them.

4. File your summary report in your Career Management Files Binder for future reference.

Resources for Identifying Keywords for Your Resume:

▲ The *Your Career: How to Make It Happen* web site at http://levitt.swlearning.com (click on "Links" and "Career planning and job search information links" to find information about resumes and keywords)

▲ Job advertisements and descriptions for positions you are considering (online or in written publications)

▲ Web sites of employers you are considering

▲ Government publications such as the *Occupational Outlook Handbook* (check the online version, too)

▲ Professional associations in your field (check their web sites, publications, and meetings)

▲ Internet search engines to search for job descriptions

▲ Online encyclopedias and dictionaries

Tailor Your Resume to the Specific Opening.
Employers expect resumes to be tailored to specific positions. Use word processing software to tailor your resumes to specific job titles, job advertisements, and employers. The targeted resume is 100 percent more effective than the one-size-fits-all resume. Here are ways you can tailor your resume:

▲ Use keywords in your job objective and throughout your resume that match those in the job ad.

▲ Identify the name of the company, organization, or industry.

▲ Use appropriate industry terminology.

Success Tip

Tailor your resume to meet the needs of the employer. Match your resume to the job description. Use specific industry and job-related terms.

Limit Your Resume to One or Two Pages. Keep your scannable print resume to one page unless you have extensive work experience; in that case, two pages are acceptable. Employers prefer brief print resumes. Make every word count, and emphasize how you can meet the employer's needs. Electronic resumes are often longer for reasons discussed later in this chapter. The content, however, should always be as concise as possible.

Step 4: Fine-Tune Each Section of Your Resume

As you write your resume, apply the writing guidelines provided earlier in this chapter. Include the sections that are most appropriate for your resume, and present them in the order that best fits your target employer's needs.

Contact Information. Provide your name, mailing address, telephone number (including message phone), e-mail and web addresses (if appropriate), and fax number. Place all your contact information at the top of the resume.

Note that many employers are turned off by applicants who use unprofessional e-mail or web address names. To avoid losing a job opportunity, be sure your address names are professional, not cutesy or crude.

Job Objective. The job objective is a statement of your employment goal. Place your job objective directly below your contact information. The job objective:

▲ Should be stated as a job title or type of work desired.

▲ Should reflect the needs of the employer based on your research.

▲ Can also include one or more of your most important job-specific skills and areas of specialization.

The job objective helps employers match you to appropriate job openings. If you have more than one job objective, write a separate resume for each.

▲ **Job Objective:** Waiter in an exclusive restaurant where knowledge of international cuisine is an added value.

Tailor your objective as much as possible. The general objective above could be tailored to an advertisement for a waiter in a French restaurant:

▲ **Job Objective:** Waiter in a four-star French restaurant where knowledge of the French language and cuisine is an added value.

Complete Career Action 9-2

CAREER ACTION 9-2

Write Your Job Objective

Directions: Write a job objective for your target job. You may want to use one of the job descriptions you collected earlier as a reference for this assignment. Address the needs stated in the job description you are referencing.

Qualifications Section and Keyword Emphasis.
The qualifications section should highlight why you are the candidate for the job. The qualifications section is a focal point for employers, so use it to emphasize specific, relevent skills and capabilities and related accomplishments, such as:

▲ Skills with and knowledge of software/hardware

▲ Years of experience in a specialized field or knowledge of specialized skills

▲ Relevant credentials and degrees

▲ Relevant accomplishments in work or volunteer experiences, community involvement, and other activities

Review the Career Action assignments you completed in Chapters 2 and 3 to extract qualifications, skills, desirable personal traits, and other attributes you can list as keywords that best match your job target. Present them in the qualifications section in order of importance as they relate to your job objective. Format the qualifications section as a bulleted list to draw attention to each item; for example:

▲ Graphic and multimedia design, including streaming audio/video, analysis graphs, and custom web graphics

▲ General ledger, inventory control, and accounts receivable and accounts payable experience

▲ Proven team-player skills demonstrated in three successful internship projects

In the body of your resume (under the appropriate section, such as work experience, education, or related activities), provide proof of the qualifications you have listed in the qualifications section.

If you don't have strong work experience related to your job objective, use the functional resume layout and the qualifications summary to emphasize your accomplishments and skills in areas other than paid work experience.

> *Success Tip*
>
> Choose the right words. Use a thesaurus to find the best words to describe your capabilities and accomplishments.

Work Experience. For a reverse chronological layout, list your most recent job first, and end with the earliest job you held. (For the functional and combination resumes, review Figures 9-7 and 9-8 on pages 142 and 143 to see how work experience is presented.) For each job, list the dates of employment; the employer's name, city, and state; the job title; and a brief results-oriented description of the job. Organize your descriptions so they begin with the results and benefits of your work. Give specific examples of your accomplishments, such as increased sales, decreased costs, and reduced errors. Quantify where possible (with a percentage, with a specific dollar figure, with a number of items produced or sold, and so on), for example, "Increased sales by 45 percent through skillful negotiation with automative clients."

> *"Use the right word, not its second cousin."*
> Mark Twain

If you have held increasingly more responsible jobs with one employer, show this to demonstrate your reliability and ability to learn and achieve on the job. List only new responsibilities and accomplishments for each promotion. Continuing job duties will be assumed by the reader. (See Figures 9-17a and 9-17b on pages 160-161 for an example.)

If you have little work experience, list your part-time and summer work, internships, school projects, volunteer work, and community involvement. Emphasize all your accomplishments and the skills you developed through these experiences—even if they don't relate directly to your job target. For example, if you just graduated and you worked throughout your schooling, one accomplishment might read as follows:

▲ Earned 65 percent of school expenses working part-time during school year and full-time during summers.

This demonstrates positive working ability, initiative, and potential for learning. Employers consider these qualities real pluses, particularly in entry-level applicants.

Success Tip

Tailor your resume to best support your objective.

Other Experience. Use this section to highlight other experience that is pertinent to your job objective. Include activities such as membership, leadership (offices held), and awards earned in professional or trade associations; honorary groups; and social, service, and school organizations. All these activities show that you are well rounded and able to work with others.

Instead of the heading "Other Experience," consider options that may be more appropriate for you, such as "Awards and Honors," "Volunteer Work," "Community Service," "Certificates Earned," "Activities," and "Professional Associations."

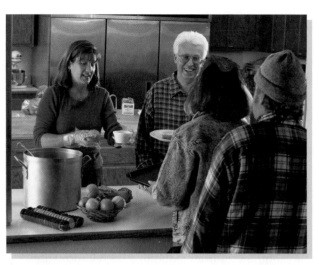

© GETTY IMAGES/PHOTODISC

If you have limited relevant work experience, list internships and school, community, and educational activities and achievements on your resume.

Education. List your education in reverse chronological order. List the names of technical schools, colleges, and universities you have attended; the years of attendance; and the degree(s) or certificate(s) earned. Include relevant certifications, specialized training, and seminars.

If you are (or will be) a recent graduate with limited work experience, highlight school activities, internships, and achievements in the education section. Support your job objective by listing related major(s), minor(s), and courses. For example, a liberal arts student with courses in business will benefit from listing the business courses when applying for a business job.

If you have several years of work experience related to your job objective, emphasize and list your work experience first. Then condense the education section of your resume.

Research your target employer to find out whether you should list your GPA on your resume. If your cumulative GPA is low but your GPA in your major is high, list your major GPA only. If your overall GPA is high and you graduated with honors, put this information on your resume. It won't hurt.

Military Service. Include on your resume any military experience that is relevant to your job objective, emphasizing pertinent training, responsibilities, and accomplishments. Highlight any rapid progressions, significant promotion(s), and special commendations. Usually, military service is listed in the experience section. If you have an exemplary record, however, you can place it under a separate heading. Don't use military jargon; use civilian terms.

Personal Data. Omit information about height, weight, age, gender, marital status, race, religion, and so on, from your resume. Fair employment laws prohibit employers from requesting such information. Do not include a photograph of yourself. In an effort to avoid discrimination, many employers will not consider a resume with an enclosed photo.

References. Generally, you should not include references on your resume. Research to learn whether your target employer wants you to submit references (names of people who can attest to your work abilities and personal qualities). Employers expect applicants to have references but differ in their preferences regarding when and how they want to see a reference list. Have a separate reference sheet prepared that includes the names, titles, addresses, and contact information for all your references. Then you are ready to provide it to employees when they request it. A model reference sheet is provided in the Model Documents folder on your Learner's CD.

Complete Career Action 9-3

CAREER ACTION 9-3

Outline Your Resume

Directions: Now that you have reviewed the resume-writing guidelines, you are ready to develop your own resume. Access Career Action Worksheet 9-3 on your Learner's CD or use the worksheet on page 165 to create a resume outline. Gather the following completed worksheets to help you with this activity:

▲ The documentation of your education and training, skills, and so on (Career Action Worksheets 2-1, 2-2, 2-3, 2-4, and 2-5)

▲ Your Job Qualifications Profile (Career Action Worksheet 7-4)

Prepare an outline of your resume. Use Career Action Worksheet 9-3 to outline your resume, or create a draft in a word processing program, using the worksheet as a reference.

Once you've completed the worksheet, number the sections of the outline, ranking them in order of importance and relevance to your job objective. Present the material in your final resume in this order. For example, if your education is more relevant to your job objective than your work experience, place the education information before the work experience information. File your completed worksheet in your Career Management Files Binder.

Format Your Resume Correctly

The next step in creating a resume is using your outline as a reference in drafting and formatting the actual resume. As noted earlier in this chapter, you should prepare at least two versions of your resume—a scannable print resume and an electronic resume.

Format Your Print Resume

The scannable print resume is designed to be delivered by e-mail, by regular mail, by fax, or in person. Produce your scannable print resume using a word processing program such as Microsoft Word or Corel WordPerfect.

Customize Your Resume. Tailor your print resume to individual employers by using terminology and descriptions that address the needs stated in their notices and advertisements of job openings. Also customize your resume for employers who specifically request your resume.

Make Your Print Resume Easy to Scan. Since some companies scan hard copy resumes and convert them to ASCII documents for storage and processing, you need to make your print resume scannable by using

formatting that is both attractive to the eye and easy for computers to scan.

A scannable print resume must be stripped of certain word processing codes that scanners may not be able to read clearly. If characters touch one another, for example, they don't scan well. The following "do's and don'ts" explain how to format your resume so it will scan clearly and keep you in the running for an interview.

DO:

1. Do use a clean overall format. Visual legibility is extremely important.

2. Do use a simple, standard font such as Times Roman. Keep the font size between 11 and 14 points. The ideal font sizes are 12 point for body text and 14 point for headings.

3. Do add a space before and after slashes (for example, HTML / XML).

4. Do use only one space after periods and at the ends of sentences.

5. Do use acceptable character enhancements and codes, such as bolding, centering commands, solid bullets, and regular and indent tabs.

6. Do print your resume on a laser or inkjet printer in black ink on one side of white or light-colored 8 1/2-inch by 11-inch paper. Standard copy machines don't produce copies of high enough quality to ensure scannability.

DON'T:

1. Don't use a highly formatted style such as a newsletter layout or columns. Scanner software assumes that the text reads conventionally from left to right across the page in one column.

2. Don't use special justification (adjustable spacing between characters). Use the standard left-margin alignment so that each letter is clearly visible.

3. Don't use underlining, italics, shadows, white letters on a black background, or colored text. These can blur or corrupt the scanned message.

4. Don't use parentheses; use a hyphen following a telephone number area code.

DEANNA ETTINGER

Make sure your print resume is scannable. Avoid formatting that does not scan clearly.

5. Don't include graphic images, and avoid vertical and horizontal lines and boxes. (You can use one horizontal line if you leave adequate white space above and below it so the line doesn't touch and blur any letters.)

6. Don't fold or staple the resume. (Creases and staple marks can cause scanning errors.)

Examples of scannable print resumes are shown in Figures 9-6, 9-7, 9-8, 9-9, 9-10, 9-13, 9-15, 9-16, 9-17a, and 9-17b.

Use an Attractive, Appropriate Design. The general design of your print resume provides employers with their first impression of you. Give your resume a professional look.

▲ Do not use the heading RESUME at the top of your document.

▲ Single-space the body of your resume, and double-space or triple-space between sections or items in the resume. (Remember: Your final resume should be only one page in length unless you have extensive work experience.)

▲ Use white or light-colored 8 1/2-inch by 11-inch paper.

▲ Frame your resume attractively. Ideally, use 1-inch margins on all sides.

▲ Use white space effectively. Areas of white space draw attention to important parts of your resume, giving it an organized, uncrowded look.

▲ Format headings in all capital letters and bold, and indent text to emphasize resume parts. (Don't overdo this, however.)

The sample resumes (Figures 9-6 through 9-17b) on pages 141-162 provide models to help you prepare your own winning resume. Examine the content and format of each resume and the summaries provided. Mark the examples that are most useful for your needs.

Complete Career Action 9-4

CAREER ACTION 9-4

Draft Your Print Resume

Directions: Review the sample resumes on pages 141-162. Mark the sections of these models that are useful to you. Resumes typically should contain all the standard sections listed below. The optional sections should be included when they support your main job objective or when an employer requests them.

Standard Resume Sections:

▲ Name and Contact Information   ▲ Job Objective   ▲ Work Experience

▲ Qualifications or Capabilities   ▲ Education   ▲ Other Experience or Activities

Optional Resume Sections:

▲ Military Service   ▲ Personal Information   ▲ References (rarely needed)

Prepare a written draft of your scannable print resume using your resume outline from Career Action 9-3 as a reference. Be selective about the quality and quantity of information you include. Make every word count. Emphasize your qualifications and measurable accomplishments, and include appropriate keywords. File your draft in your Career Management Files Binder.

Revise the Content. After you have drafted your resume, review it, paying careful attention to every detail and marking areas that could be improved.

Once you have reviewed your draft, rewrite your resume, strengthening each area you marked. Eliminate unnecessary words; substitute stronger, clearer terms for weak ones. Your goal is to answer *yes* to all the resume questions in Figure 9-4.

After reviewing your draft, check the writing guidelines presented earlier in this chapter. Then complete Career Action 9-5, "Critique Two Resumes," and Career Action 9-6, "Complete Your Print Resume."

Complete Career Action 9-5

Complete Career Action 9-6

Resume Checklist

Objective

✔ Does the objective include the job title or required abilities specified by the employer?

Qualifications

✔ Do your qualifications contain keywords that name requirements for the job?

✔ Are the qualifications relevant to your stated job objective? Are all your major strengths included?

Education

✔ If your education supports your job objective better than your work experience, have you placed the education section first (or vice versa)?

✔ Have you emphasized courses, internships, degrees, certificates, and so on, that best support your objective?

✔ If your GPA is impressive, have you included it (overall or major/minor related to your job objective)?

Work Experience

✔ Does each job listing contain the employer's name and address (city and state) and your job title?

✔ Does each job listing describe your responsibilities and specific accomplishments?

✔ Are your job descriptions written using specific action verbs and keyword nouns that support your job objective?

✔ If your work experience is limited, have you included relevant paid and nonpaid internships and volunteer or other pertinent activities?

Related Activities

✔ Have you included your involvement in professional and other organizations that support your job objective?

✔ Have you included relevant awards, achievements, and offices held?

The Big Picture

✔ Is the overall design appealing?

✔ Is the content correct (grammar, spelling, and punctuation)?

✔ Is the content logically organized and presented in order of importance to your objective?

Figure 9-4: Resume Checklist

CAREER ACTION 9-5

Critique Two Resumes

Directions: Assume you're evaluating candidates for an entry-level job as an accountant for a major accounting firm. You are to write a summary comparing and evaluating the resumes of two top applicants—Alex Valenzuela and Ralph Greenwood. Their qualifications are almost identical. However, one has documented his qualifications more convincingly than the other.

Read their resumes (Figures 9-18 and 9-19 on pages 163 and 164). Determine which resume is more effective, and explain why in your summary. Be thorough, keeping in mind that your resume will be scrutinized in the same way during your job search. Use a separate sheet of paper or Career Action Worksheet 9-5 on your Learner's CD to complete this assignment. File your summary in your Career Management Files Binder.

CAREER ACTION 9-6

Complete Your Print Resume

Directions: Use a word processor to prepare your final print resume. (If you hire an expert to prepare your resume, be sure to request an electronic copy so you have the file for future revisions or updates.)

Proofread and edit the content until the resume is perfect. Make sure your print resume is scannable. Avoid formatting that does not scan clearly. File your resume in your Career Management Files Binder.

If you want more ideas for your resume, check out the "Links" page on the *Your Career: How to Make It Happen* web site (http://levitt.swlearning.com). Check out the "Career planning and job search information links." (Look for sites that have the "Resumes" indication.) Also check with your school's career services center, which is typically an excellent resource for developing a resume.

Evaluate Your Resume. Once you have revised your resume, proceed to the critical evaluation step. Careful proofreading and evaluation are essential.

Recruit help from one or two objective members of your support system who have good writing and proofreading skills. Ask these people to review and critique your resume carefully. This assistance is vital to developing a successful resume.

Success Tip

Prepare and evaluate your resume draft, make corrections, and develop a perfect final resume.

Prepare and Format Your Electronic Resume

Some employers request that candidates submit electronic resumes. The features of electronic resumes are described below.

Larger organizations and high-tech companies are more likely than smaller organizations to require electronic resumes. As a job applicant, you need to clarify with employers exactly which resume format they prefer: a print resume that is delivered by hand, by mail, by fax, or as an e-mail attachment, or an electronic resume that is submitted at a web site or in the body of an e-mail message. Always provide your resume in the preferred format.

ASCII Text Format. The primary difference between a print resume and an electronic resume concerns the formatting. Electronic resumes are relatively plain and unattractive because they must be ASCII (also called .text, Plain Text, or Text Only) documents. These documents are stripped of all word processing codes so they can be transmitted correctly in the body of an e-mail message or processed by an employer through an applicant- or resume-tracking program.

Keyword Emphasis. Using appropriate keywords throughout your electronic resume is important because electronic resumes are often electronically searched for keywords. Design your electronic resume to generate the highest possible number of keyword hits from resume-search software.

Keyword choices are critical. Review the information about keywords presented earlier in this chapter under the heading "Step 3: Organize Carefully and Write Forcefully."

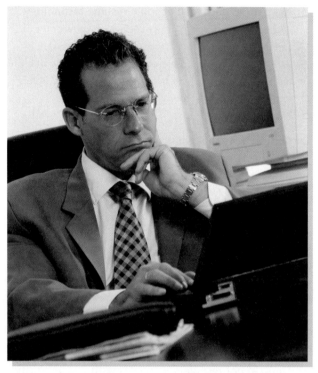

© GETTY IMAGES/PHOTODISC

Format your electronic resume carefully to ensure that the receiver views a clean-looking document. Include relevant keywords to generate as many hits as possible by resume-search software.

Important Tips for Electronic Resumes. As you prepare your electronic resume, keep the following tips in mind:

1. **Use standard section headings.** Use standard headings like those in a print resume—for example, OBJECTIVE, QUALIFICATIONS, EXPERIENCE, EDUCATION, and RELATED ACTIVITIES.

2. **Use keywords throughout.** Using appropriate keywords throughout your electronic resume is essential. Spell all keywords correctly. (Search software will not generate positive hits on your resume if the keywords aren't spelled correctly.)

3. **Emphasize nouns.** Include noun forms of industry-specific terms, such as *accountant* rather than *accounting*. Also use nouns that describe strong interpersonal skills, such as *team player*. Search software frequently looks for noun forms.

4. **Back up your file.** Using a new filename, save your resume in ASCII format (on your hard drive and on a disk or CD) so you can customize it for specific employers.

Success Tip

Use appropriate keywords in all your resumes to highlight your critical skills for potential employers.

5. **Keep up to date on electronic resume technology.** Technology changes quickly; keep your knowledge of scanning and electronic resume technology current by verifying employers' preferences and doing research on the topic. Check out the Internet resources listed in this chapter and on the *Your Career: How to Make It Happen* web site.

6. **Contact potential employers.** Ask whether you should fax or mail a scannable print resume or attach one to an e-mail message as a backup to your electronic resume. Find out who should receive your resume, and address your cover letter (see Chapter 10) to that individual. Sending a backup scannable print resume gives you an opportunity to sell your qualifications in a visually appealing format.

Electronic Resume Formatting Guidelines. Get the edge on the competition by formatting your electronic resume correctly. Demonstrate superior knowledge and preparation. Use correct formatting so employers do not receive documents with wildly erratic line lengths and unreadable text.

Since all word processing codes are stripped out of electronic resumes, be sure to format your resume to compensate for the loss of bold text, bullets, and other formatting capabilities. Follow the instructions below to be sure your resume meets an employer's expectations. The instructions assume that your scannable print resume was created with word processing software.

1. **Follow the employer's directions.** Obtain and read all employer instructions for creating and sending an electronic resume. If you have questions, send an e-mail message or call to request clarification.

2. **In your word processor, open the file containing your scannable print resume.**

   a. Highlight the text, and change the font to Courier 12 point. This monospaced font is the most reliable font for accurate e-mail transmission because each character is the same width, making it possible to determine stable line lengths.

   b. Eliminate multiple columns.

   c. Limit line lengths to 65 characters, including spaces. Longer line lengths often transmit unevenly.

   d. Clean up the formatting:

      ▲ Replace bullets with asterisks or hyphens.

      ▲ Use all caps for headings.

      ▲ Use blank lines between sections to make the content more readable.

      ▲ Eliminate special characters, such as the copyright symbol (©), the ampersand (&), and mathematical symbols.

   e. Use the Save As command to give the document a new name and to save it as "Text Only with Line Breaks" or "MS-DOS Text with Layout."

   f. Close the file, and exit the word processing program.

3. **IMPORTANT: Open the document in your standard text-editing program, such as Microsoft Notepad. (Do not open it in your word processing program.)** A standard text-editing program creates the cleanest electronic resume.

   a. Place your name on the first line with no other text. (Resume-search programs look only for a name on this line.)

   b. Start all lines at the left margin.

   c. Use uppercase letters for headings, but use a standard mix of uppercase and lowercase letters throughout the body of the document.

d. Place each telephone number on a separate line. Label each one, such as "home phone," "work phone," or "message phone."

e. Consider the length. The specialized formatting may cause your electronic resume to become two or three pages long in your standard text-editing program. Don't worry about keeping the resume to one page in this program; however, try to limit the document to two pages.

f. Save your resume again as a .txt document. Leave the file open.

4. Open your e-mail program, and create a new message.

5. To ensure clean transmission, make sure your format is set to Plain Text format (not Rich Text or HTML).

6. Return to your standard text editor (Notepad), and select (highlight) all the resume text. Then copy and paste it into your e-mail message window. Or paste the text into the resume field at an employer or recruitment web site.

7. In the e-mail subject line, include the job title and/or the reference number of the position for which you are applying.

8. Insert your electronic cover letter (see Chapter 10). In the e-mail message window that contains your electronic resume, place the cursor above your resume and paste in a copy of your electronic cover letter. Do not send a resume without a cover letter or a short message indicating that your resume is included.

9. Key a line of asterisks under your electronic cover letter to mark the end of your cover letter message and the beginning of your resume.

10. Clean up any odd spacing or other formatting problems. (See the "Transmitting Your Electronic Resume" section on page 136 for distribution instructions.)

Review the sample electronic resumes (Figure 9-11 on page 148 and Figure 9-12 on page 150) to see how these resume formatting guidelines are applied.

Develop a Winning Web Resume

A web resume is created in HTML and published to the Internet. This resume format is more flexible than the others because it supports more sophisticated elements, such as animated graphics, soundclips, and video clips. It is a good tool for displaying your expertise in computer technology (HTML, web site and graphic design, and more). Web resumes can also be creative sales tools for people who want or need to display their artistic abilities, such as photographers, artists, singers, models, architects, and graphics and computer specialists.

Web resumes are most commonly used in the high-tech industry, but they are also used in other fields. Research to determine whether a web resume is appropriate in your career field. Also note that a web resume should be used in addition to—not as a substitute for—your print and electronic resumes.

Comprehensive information describing the purposes and benefits of web resumes; tips for writing their content; and guidelines for publishing, verifying, and distributing them are provided on the *Your Career: How to Make It Happen* web site (http://levitt.swlearning.com). Also, refer to the sample web resume (Figure 9-14) shown on page 154.

Distributing Your Resume

After developing your resume, you'll want to distribute it effectively to meet the preferences of employers and achieve your ultimate goal: getting interviews.

Providing Your Resume to Your Network and to Employers

Give your resume to the members of your job search network in the format they prefer (electronic, word-processed e-mail attachment, or hand-delivered print resume, for example). Providing your resume to your network members gives them the information they need to help you find prospective employers.

Follow an employer's instructions for the preferred resume format and method of delivery: standard or overnight mail, fax or electronic transmission, or hand delivery.

Transmitting Your Electronic Resume

After you have created an electronic resume and placed it in an e-mail message with an electronic cover letter, you should practice transmitting the message. Send your electronic resume and cover letter or e-mail introduction to a friend and to yourself to see how well the documents survive the cyberspace transfer before you actually send them to an employer. You may need to adjust the spacing and format a bit. If necessary, find someone with more experience in creating and sending electronic resumes to help you tweak your resume until it transmits cleanly.

If Asked to Send Your Resume as an E-Mail Attachment

Some employers ask applicants to send a word-processed resume as an e-mail attachment so they can print it and provide a hard copy to hiring specialists. If you are requested to do this, ask what word processing software and operating system (Windows or Mac, for example) are preferred.

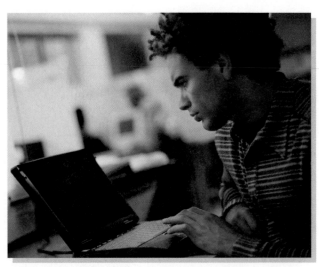

© GETTY IMAGES/PHOTODISC

Follow an employer's instructions regarding its preferred resume format and method of delivery (standard or overnight mail, fax or electronic transmission, or hand delivery).

Follow the employer's requirements exactly to be sure the receiver can download your resume in a readable form. In your e-mail message, explain which word processing software and operating system you used.

Posting Electronic Resumes Correctly

Follow the guidelines below for posting electronic resumes to the Internet (through the web sites of employers or recruitment companies that list jobs and accept online resumes from applicants):

▲ Follow the web site's instructions exactly.

▲ If the web site provides an open block for your resume, copy your electronic resume and paste it into the block.

▲ If the web site provides a fill-in-the-blanks resume form, copy and paste appropriate sections of your electronic resume into the form. If you need to key in new text, proofread it carefully before sending it.

Refer to Figure 10-10 on page 190 of Chapter 10 for more information.

Complete Career Action 9-7

CAREER ACTION 9-7

Create and Post Your Electronic Resume

Part A: Following the formatting guidelines presented, convert the print resume you created in Career Action 9-6 to an electronic resume. Be sure to give your electronic resume a different name so you still have the original file to use for your print resume.

Format your electronic resume carefully to ensure that the receiver views a clean-looking document. Include relevant keywords to generate as many hits as possible by resume-search programs.

Follow the employer's instructions and preferences regarding resume format and method of delivery (standard or overnight mail, fax or electronic transmission, or hand delivery).

Part B: Research and practice online resume posting. Access the *Your Career: How to Make It Happen* web site at http://levitt.swlearning.com, and click on the "Links" button. Locate the "Job recruitment links" category, and choose one or more resume-posting web sites (such as Monster, America's Job Bank, The Black Collegian Online, African-American Career World, and Saludos.com) to review the instructions for creating and posting an online resume. Also review each of your prospective employers' web sites, and follow the instructions for resume preparation and submission. If you prefer, use other resume-posting sites for this exercise. Practice completing an online fill-in-the-blanks resume form or pasting your electronic resume into an open resume block. Print your resume and other pertinent pages before you submit your resume, and place them in your Career Management Files Binder.

Reinforce Your Resume with a Call

Don't rely on resumes alone to get interviews. It's a mistake to send out several copies of your resume and then wait for the telephone to ring. Two to three days after sending a resume, follow up with a phone call to make sure it was received. If you mail your resume, wait about a week to call. Your call reminds the receiver about you, demonstrates initiative, and increases your name recognition.

Special Resume Reminders

To ensure that your resume gets the best possible results, heed these reminders.

Be honest. An untrue statement could eliminate you from further consideration for a job. Employers reject resumes with false information. Do not volunteer negative information about yourself, however. If you were fired from a job, don't list this on your resume. Discuss this during an interview, if necessary.

Omit references to salary. Reserve any discussion of salary until after you've had adequate opportunity to discuss your qualifications in an interview. Presenting your salary expectation in your resume weakens your negotiating position. If employers require your salary expectation, use broad numbers, such as "the mid-thirty thousands."

Career Change Resume Tips

You will probably make more than one career change in your lifetime. This will require you to revise your resume to fit the new career objective. A realistic new career target is one for which you have already developed relevant, related skills. (You'll learn more about making a career change in Chapter 20.) To revise a resume for a new career, refer to the following tips:

1. Make a list of all your work-related skills, knowledge, and experience.

2. Use a colored pen to place a check mark in front of each item on your list that matches or closely matches the needs of your new career target.

3. If necessary, change the wording of the items you checked to better fit your new career target. Use a thesaurus and your new career research to identify appropriate keywords. For example, when changing from a classroom teacher to an industry trainer, the terms *trainer*, *facilitator*, and *presenter* are more appropriate than *teacher*.

4. Create new skill and experience headings for your resume by grouping related items from your updated skills list into categories. Create a heading that describes each category.

5. Now that you have appropriate content, begin drafting and refining your new career resume. In other words, once you have completed this exercise of identifying appropriate content for a new job objective, you can begin revising your existing resume to match your new job objective. See the excerpts from the "before" and "after" resumes shown in Figure 9-5.

Success Tip

When making a career change, revise your resume to fit your new career objective. Change terminology and headings to reflect the new industry, update your skills list, and remove any irrelevant information.

Excerpts From "Before" Resume	Excerpts From "After" Resume
Job Objective: Service manager in multiline dealership	**Job Objective:** Insurance adjuster in automotive collision repair industry
Auto Repair Customer Service Scheduled appointments, performed preinspections, achieved upgrade sales on 95 percent of accounts, quoted estimates, wrote work orders, performed postrepair inspections, explained statements to customers, and increased referrals from customers by 43 percent.	**Claims Management** Scheduled client appointments, determined mechanical and auto-body damages within 45 minutes, negotiated repairs with clients and insurance companies, prepared job documentation (pictures, work orders, billing), performed postrepair inspections, and explained statements.
Parts Management Managed ordering and stocking of mechanical and auto-body parts inventories, selected suppliers and negotiated vendor discounts that averaged 25 to 30 percent below wholesale, reconciled shipping invoices to billing statements, and approved payments.	**Cost Containment** Obtained clients' permission to use appropriate aftermarket and/or rebuilt parts on 98.7 percent of jobs; located replacement parts; negotiated price, delivery, and discounts, averaging 25 to 30 percent below wholesale; returned unused parts for credit; reconciled billing discrepancies; approved payments.

Figure 9-5: Compare Excerpts From "Before" and "After" Career Change Resumes

Internet Resources for Resume Information

The Internet is a rich resource for finding useful resume writing and formatting suggestions. You can use your favorite search engine to research specific questions you may have. You can also check out online resumes in your field for content ideas that may be appropriate for your own resume. Quality sites offering useful resume development advice include the following (links can be found on the *Your Career: How to Make It Happen* web site):

▲ eResumes.com

▲ eResumeIQ.com (web resumes)

▲ Quintessential Careers

▲ Susan Ireland Resumes

▲ The Riley Guide

▲ Monster

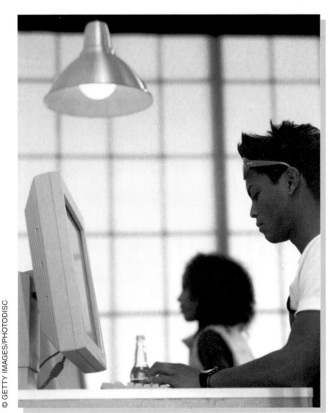

Harness the power of the Internet to locate useful information on resume trends and techniques.

© GETTY IMAGES/PHOTODISC

Success Tip

Use the Internet to locate resume preparation tips and as a means for delivering your electronic resume.

Sample Resumes

The following sample resumes are provided on pages 141-164:

▲ Figure 9-6: Reverse Chronological Resume Sample (Administrative Assistant)

▲ Figure 9-7: Functional Resume Sample (Administrative Assistant)

▲ Figure 9-8: Combination Resume Sample (Administrative Assistant)

▲ Figure 9-9: Scannable Print Resume (Health Information Technician)

▲ Figure 9-10: Scannable Print Resume (Computerized Accounting Systems Auditor I)

▲ Figure 9-11: Electronic Resume (Information Systems Analyst I)

▲ Figure 9-12: Electronic Resume (Network Support Technician)

▲ Figure 9-13: Scannable Print Resume (Receptionist)

▲ Figure 9-14: Web Resume (Web Specialist)

▲ Figure 9-15: Scannable Print Resume (Private Security Guard)

▲ Figure 9-16: Scannable Print Resume (Medical Assistant)

▲ Figure 9-17a: Scannable Print Resume (Marketing Product Line Manager)

▲ Figure 9-17b: Scannable Print Resume, page 2 (Marketing Product Line Manager)

▲ Figure 9-18: Resume for Career Action 9-5 (Applicant #1)

▲ Figure 9-19: Resume for Career Action 9-5 (Applicant #2)

CHECKLIST

PREPARING A WINNING RESUME

Check each of the actions you are currently taking to increase your career success:

○ Writing a clear, appropriate job objective to focus the entire resume

○ Tailoring the resume to support the job objective effectively

○ Choosing the resume layout that best supports the job objective

○ Using numbers and action verbs to describe your accomplishments

○ Tailoring the resume to meet the needs of the employer and matching the resume to the job description by using specific terms and industry terminology

○ Preparing and evaluating the resume draft, making corrections by applying effective writing techniques, developing a perfect final resume

○ Using appropriate keywords

○ Formatting an electronic resume carefully to ensure clear transmission to and receipt by the employer

○ Using the Internet to locate resume preparation tips and to deliver an electronic resume

CRITICAL THINKING QUESTIONS

1. When should an applicant use separate job objectives or resumes?

2. In what order should you present your resume data to best support your job objective?

3. Why is listing related capabilities immediately below the job objective effective?

4. How are electronic resumes transmitted to employers?

 For convenient access to valuable career resources, activities, and job information links, visit the companion web site for this text: *http://levitt.swlearning.com*

KIMI R. OKASAKI
148 Barrister Avenue, Tucson, AZ 85726
• 520-555-0136   • kokasaki@provider.net

OBJECTIVE

Administrative Assistant for MegaMall Property Management Company

EDUCATION

Associate of Applied Science, 2006, Westfield Community College, Tucson, AZ
• Major: Administrative Office Technology, GPA 3.6

Related Courses and Skills
• Advanced Word Processing (Word, WordPerfect)
• Keyboarding at 75 words per minute
• Spreadsheet (Excel, Quattro Pro) and Database Management (Access)
• Records Management
• Bookkeeping I and Computerized Bookkeeping (QuickBooks Pro)
• Ten-key at 250 strokes per minute
• Presentation Software (PowerPoint, Presentations)
• Office Management
• Internet Software (Explorer, Netscape)
• Experienced in use of PDF files and FTP.

EXPERIENCE

Community Volunteer, Tucson, AZ   **December 2001-2005**
• **National Diabetes Foundation:** Developed and customized spreadsheet report to track results of three fund-raising activities, reducing reporting time by 50 percent. Used Excel.
• **Secretary-Treasurer, Valley Elementary School Parent-Teacher Organization:** Published electronic newsletters, answered e-mail, maintained correspondence, maintained books for two years, and satisfied yearly CPA audits. Used Word, PDF files, FTP, and QuickBooks Pro.
• **Meals on Wheels:** Using Access, designed and maintained information database to enable Meals on Wheels to study the participation of 1,200 people.

Katz Department Store, Tucson, AZ   **March 2000-December 2001**
• Sales Supervisor, Part-time: Supervised four sales clerks; trained new sales employees. Computed daily cash receipts, balanced two registers, attained highest part-time sales volume, and had fewest sales returned.

Value Variety, Tucson, AZ   **Summers 1998, 1999**
• Sales Clerk, Floater: Provided complete customer service in sales and returns; coordinated weekly inventory deliveries.

Figure 9-6: Reverse Chronological Resume Sample (Job Objective–Administrative Assistant)

KIMI R. OKASAKI

148 Barrister Avenue, Tucson, AZ 85726   520-555-0136   kokasaki@provider.net

---

OBJECTIVE

Administrative Assistant for MegaMall Property Management Company

EDUCATION

Associate of Applied Science, 2006, Westfield Community College, Tucson, AZ
• Major: Administrative Office Technology, GPA 3.6

PROFESSIONAL SKILLS

Document Preparation: Expert using Word, WordPerfect, PowerPoint, and Presentations. Enter text at 75 words per minute. Integrate tabular data and graphics into documents using Access, Excel and Quattro Pro. Write, format, and proofread printed and electronic business correspondence, reports, and newsletters. Research topics on the Internet (Netscape, Explorer). Experienced in use of PDF files and FTP.
> • Published electronic newsletters and maintained correspondence for Valley Elementary School Parent-Teacher Organization (VES-PTO) for two years.

Spreadsheet Management: Develop and maintain Excel and Quattro Pro spreadsheets.
> • Developed spreadsheet to track results of three fund-raising activities for the National Diabetes Foundation that reduced reporting time by 50 percent.

Database Management: Configure, maintain, and generate reports with Access.
> • Designed and maintained an information database to enable Meals on Wheels to study the participation of 1,200 people.

Bookkeeping: Perform manual (ten-key at 250 strokes per minute) or computerized (QuickBooks Pro) bookkeeping functions from journal entry to end-of-period reports.
> • Maintained books for VES-PTO for two years and satisfied yearly CPA audits.
> • Computed daily cash receipts and balanced two registers as part-time sales supervisor of a department store.

Human Relations: Successfully cooperate with store managers, representatives of delivery companies and community organizations, and the general public.
> • Held positions of responsibility in three community organizations over the last three years.
> • Worked in two department stores: promoted to supervisor, trained new sales clerks, coordinated weekly inventory deliveries, provided customer service in sales and returns, attained highest part-time sales volume, and had fewest sales returned.

EXPERIENCE

Community Volunteer, Tucson, AZ	December 2001-2005
Katz Department Store, Tucson, AZ	March 2000-December 2001
Value Variety, Tucson, AZ	Summers 1998, 1999

Figure 9-7: Functional Resume Sample (Job Objective–Administrative Assistant)

KIMI R. OKASAKI

148 Barrister Avenue, Tucson, AZ 85726

520-555-0136   kokasaki@provider.net

OBJECTIVE

Administrative Assistant for MegaMall Property Management Company

RELATED QUALIFICATIONS

- Word processing in Word and WordPerfect
- Spreadsheet generation with Excel and Quattro Pro
- Database design and maintenance using Access
- Experienced in use of PDF files and FTP.
- Keyboarding at 75 words per minute
- Write and proofread printed and electronic business correspondence, reports, newsletters
- Presentation preparation using PowerPoint and Presentations software
- Internet research and e-mail correspondence using Netscape or Explorer
- Bookkeeping using QuickBooks Pro and ten-key at 250 strokes per minute
- Proven ability to work successfully with store managers, delivery companies, community organizations, and the general public

EDUCATION

Associate of Applied Science, 2006, Westfield Community College, Tucson, AZ
- Major: Administrative Office Technology, GPA 3.6

EXPERIENCE

Community Volunteer, Tucson, AZ   **December 2001-2005**
- **National Diabetes Foundation:** Developed and customized spreadsheet report to track results of three fund-raising activities, reducing reporting time by 50 percent. Used Excel.
- **Secretary-Treasurer, Valley Elementary School Parent-Teacher Organization:** Published electronic newsletters, answered e-mail, maintained correspondence, maintained books for two years, and satisfied yearly CPA audits. Used Word, PDF files, FTP, and QuickBooks Pro.
- **Meals on Wheels:** Using Access, designed and maintained information database to enable Meals on Wheels to study the participation of 1,200 people.

Katz Department Store, Tucson, AZ   **March 2000-December 2001**
- Sales Supervisor, Part-time: Supervised four sales clerks; trained new sales employees. Computed daily cash receipts, balanced two registers, attained highest part-time sales volume, and had fewest sales returned.

Value Variety, Tucson, AZ   **Summers 1998, 1999**
- Sales Clerk, Floater: Provided complete customer service in sales and returns; coordinated weekly inventory deliveries.

Figure 9-8: Combination Resume Sample (Job Objective–Administrative Assistant)

SONYA REED
2332 Clovis Boulevard • Savannah, GA 31401
912-555-0109 • sreed@provider.net

OBJECTIVE

Health Information Technician position requiring the ability to perform detailed tasks, to change priorities quickly, and to communicate well

QUALIFICATIONS

- Registered Health Information Technician, 2006
- Family practice receptionist, 1.5 years; awarded Superior Service Certificate twice
- Five-month internship as assistant to Health Information Technician, Community Hospital
- Associate of Science, 2006

EDUCATION

Associate of Science, 2006, Savannah College of Georgia, Savannah, GA
    Major: Health Information Technology   GPA 3.6
    Related Courses and Skills
        • Medical Terminology • Clinical Classification Systems • Health Information Management
        • Health Delivery Systems • Health Data • Introduction to Health Law and Ethics
        • Human Disease Mechanisms • Word • Excel • Access • PowerPoint • Explorer • Outlook
        • Health Care Reimbursement • Alternative Health Care Settings • Business Communications

CERTIFICATION

Registered Health Information Technician, 2006

EXPERIENCE

- **Community Hospital, Savannah, GA**   **January 2006-May 2006**
  Clinical Internship. Under the direction of the Health Information Director, assisted Health Information Technician in reviewing and assigning diagnosis codes and DRGs. Abstracted appropriate information and retrieved medical records. Assisted chiefly with Medicare/Medicaid coding for three months. Checked charts into and out of records department.

- **Family Practice Partnership, Savannah, GA**   **July 2004-December 2005**
  Evening Receptionist. Answered telephone, scheduled appointments, and kept waiting room neat. Checked in patients, obtained insurance and billing information, and pulled charts for nurses. Copied requested records for transport to other medical offices. Provided cheerful, efficient service to patients; awarded Superior Service Certificate in 2004 and 2005.

ASSOCIATIONS

Community Hospital Volunteer, 2004 to Present
American Health Information Management Association, 2004 to Present

Figure 9-9: Scannable Print Resume (Job Objective–Health Information Technician)

Summary of Information Emphasized in Figure 9-9: Reed

1. Objective

Sonya uses an industry-standard job title to state her job objective concisely. To capture the attention of employers and to advertise her work-related characteristics, she includes job-related competencies that her targeted employers list in job postings.

2. Qualifications

Sonya includes several terms that both humans and resume-search software programs typically search for when filling a health information technician position. She emphasizes her Registered Health Information Technician certification first because it is a primary requirement for the job she is seeking. She also highlights her relevant work experience and her hospital internship assisting a health information technician. She includes her associate of science degree because it is a keyword that is also likely to be included in an electronic search of her resume.

3. Education

Sonya puts her degree near the top of the resume to reinforce her job qualifications. She worked evenings during the two years she was in school and still earned a respectable GPA, so she includes this information in her resume. In addition, she lists classes from her major that are especially pertinent to employers and includes the computer programs she knows.

4. Certification

Because Sonya just graduated and has limited work experience, she places her national certification in its own section of the resume to emphasize her qualifications and to show that she takes her profession seriously.

5. Experience

Sonya's internship through Savannah College of Georgia allowed her to work and learn at a local hospital. Because her internship lasted five months, provided hands-on experience, and is pertinent to her job objective, Sonya places it in the Experience section of her resume. Notice how Sonya describes her activities using industry-specific terminology.

Although Sonya's job at the family practice clinic was at a medical facility, she did not have any responsibilities that are directly applicable to her current job objective. She puts her award for superior service at the end of her job description to demonstrate that her job performance is above average.

6. Associations

The association on Sonya's resume reinforces her interest in the medical field. She adds her volunteer work because she knows her target employers value and promote community service.

DONITA SILVA

1247 Madison Road, Columbus, OH 43216   614-555-0100   dsilva@provider.net

---

OBJECTIVE

Computerized Accounting Systems Auditor I

QUALIFICATIONS SUMMARY

- Education in accounting practices and computer systems
- Programming competence in C, C++, C#.NET, and Visual Basic.NET
- Practical experience in EDP accounting applications
- Proficient in Word, Excel, Access, and Windows
- Proven interpersonal skills in an auditing environment
- Experience in AS/400, MS Server 2000, MS Server 2003, and Novell LAN operations

EDUCATION

Bachelor of Business Administration, 2006   • Renton College, Columbus, OH
• Major: Computer Information Systems   • Minor: Internal Auditing

Relevant Courses of Study:
• Analysis, Design, and Auditing of Accounting Information Systems
• Internal Auditing   • Information Systems Auditing   • Accounting Applications
• Database Management   • Advanced Corporate Finance   • Cost Accounting

Senior Internship: American Interstate Bank
Under the supervision of the managing field auditor of American Interstate Bank, performed internal audits on the safety-deposit box operations of five local branches. Reviewed the audit findings with the branch managers. Compiled final report and presented it to the managers.

EXPERIENCE

Alexander & Swartz, Columbus, OH   **9/05 to Present**
Part-time Assistant Staff Auditor: Assist in audits of cash, accounts receivable, and accounts payable for midsized firms that use AS/400s. Interface with clients and write audit reports as member of the Business Services Assurance and Advisory team.

Micronomics Company, Columbus, OH   **6/02 to 9/05**
Part-time Programmer's Assistant: Designed, documented, coded, and tested C program subroutines for order-entry system on Novell PC network. Achieved a 95 percent average program-accuracy rate on test runs. Cataloged and filed new programs and program patches for the company's software library. Also used MS Server 2003.

Renton College, Columbus, OH   **9/00 to 6/02**
Computer Operator Aide. Using MS Server 2000, copied files for backup. Verified accuracy of reports and scheduled print sequences. Recommended schedule changes that improved efficiency of backup procedures by 28.5 percent.

ASSOCIATIONS

Information Technology Management Association, 2001 to Present
Columbus Computer Club, 2000 to Present

Figure 9-10: Scannable Print Resume (Job Objective–Computerized Accounting Systems Auditor I)

Summary of Information
Emphasized in Figure 9-10: Silva

Note: Figures 9-10 and 9-11 illustrate how to tailor a resume for two different job objectives. Because this employer prefers it, Donita uses a one-page scannable resume.

1. **Objective**	The title Computerized Accounting Systems Auditor I is clearly understood in the field.
2. **Qualifications**	Donita incorporates keywords in this section to highlight the education, specialized knowledge, and practical experience she possesses that relate directly to the Computerized Accounting Systems Auditor I job objective. She shows that she can be productive immediately.
3. **Education**	Because the job Donita wants requires expertise in two fields—computer systems and accounting practices—she emphasizes the courses she took that combine the skills from both areas. She addresses the requirements of her job objective by stressing the auditing experience she obtained through the class project. She also emphasizes her proven interpersonal skills, which are critical to acquiring and retaining clients.
4. **Experience**	*Alexander & Swartz.* Donita provides proof of her interpersonal skills and on-the-job auditing skills in computerized accounting. She supports the most important qualifications needed for her job objective.
	Micronomics Company. By stating a measurable accomplishment, Donita shows that she gets results.
	Renton College. The addition of another concrete accomplishment strengthens her credibility as an achiever.
5. **Associations**	Membership in professional organizations related to the job objective demonstrates a commitment to remaining current with trends in the field. This is something employers value highly.

```
DONITA SILVA
1247 Madison Road
Columbus, OH 43216
614-555-0100
dsilva@provider.net

OBJECTIVE

Information Systems Analyst I position in a financial environment requiring
system design, programming, investigation, reporting skills

QUALIFICATIONS SUMMARY

*       Education in computer systems and accounting practices
*       Proven interpersonal skills and team skills in a financial setting
*       Programming competence in C, C++, C#.NET, and Visual Basic.NET
*       Practical experience in EDP accounting applications
*       Proficient in Excel, Word, Access, and Windows
*       Experienced in AS/400, MS Server 2000, MS Server 2003, and Novell
        LAN operations

EDUCATION

Bachelor of Business Administration, Renton College, Columbus, OH, 2006
* Major: Computer Information Systems, *Minor:  Internal Auditing

*Relevant Courses of Study: System Analysis and Design, Systems Development,
Quantitative Analysis, Advanced Programming, Data Communications, Database
Systems, Advanced Corporate Finance, Information Systems Auditing,
Statistical Techniques

*Senior Internship: J. Kemp Marketing Associates
Installed a five-PC Novell LAN, three printers, and associated software
(MS Office) for 2 small marketing services businesses. Assisted the consulting
systems analyst in customizing proprietary statistical program for marketing
research applications.

EXPERIENCE

Alexander & Swartz, Columbus, OH                              9/05 to Present
Part-time Assistant Staff Auditor: Assist in audits of cash, accounts
receivable, and accounts payable for midsized firms that use AS/400s.
Interface with clients and write audit reports as member of the Business
Services Assurance and Advisory team.

Micronomics Company, Columbus, OH                              6/02 to 9/05
Part-time Programmer's Assistant: Designed, documented, coded, and tested
C program subroutines for order-entry system on Novell PC network. Achieved
a 95 percent average program-accuracy rate on test runs. Cataloged and filed
new programs and program patches for the company's software library. Also
used MS Server 2003.

Renton College, Columbus, OH                                  9/00 to 6/02
Computer Operator Aide. Using MS Server 2000, copied files for backup. Verified
accuracy of reports and scheduled print sequences. Recommended schedule changes
that improved efficiency of backup procedures by 28.5 percent.

ASSOCIATIONS

Information Technology Management Association, 2001 to Present
Columbus Computer Club, 2000 to Present
```

Figure 9-11: Electronic Resume (Job Objective–Information Systems Analyst I)

Summary of Information
Emphasized in Figure 9-11: Silva

1. **Objective**

The title Information Systems Analyst I is clearly understood in Donita's field, specifies the level of authority she is qualified to handle, and clarifies her area of interest and expertise. She highlights pertinent skills, implying flexibility, thoroughness, and responsibility.

2. **Qualifications**

Because computer systems and accounting practices are primary skills required in financial work, Donita highlights these skills to meet the Information Systems Analyst I job objective. Accenting mainframe languages and hardware, microcomputer software, and experience in order entry and accounting applications stresses her flexibility. She emphasizes the hardware, operating systems, and program languages with which she is experienced to demonstrate her ability to use these skills immediately.

3. **Education**

Donita highlights the courses she took that best support this job objective. The practical experience she gained in a directly related internship demonstrates her scope of knowledge and dependability. She omits her moderate GPA.

4. **Experience**

Alexander & Swartz. Donita uses action verbs and highlights her responsibilities and knowledge. She backs up her claim to have "proven interpersonal skills and team skills in a financial setting."

Micronomics Company. Donita's claim to be skilled in program design and coding is supported with a measurable achievement.

Renton College. Donita reinforces her image for getting results by stressing another accomplishment (28.5 percent increase in efficiency).

5. **Associations**

Donita's memberships demonstrate her interest in and commitment to continued professional growth.

```
DANIELLE RYAN
1205 Koch Lane
Seattle, WA 98115
206-555-0124
dryan@provider.net

OBJECTIVE

Network Support Technician for multilocation network

QUALIFICATIONS SUMMARY

* Education in network support technology
* Competent with peer-to-peer networks, UNIX and Linux operating systems and
command line utilities, TCP/IP, LAN, WAN, and Network utilities
* Familiar with menu utilities, system backups, ANSI C fundamentals,
VPN (Virtual Private Network), V Standards, VNC (Virtual Network Computing),
and wireless networking and security
* Practical experience with Word, Access, Excel, Windows 2000/XP/XP
Professional, MS Server 2003, and Novell
* Experienced in building token-ring networks and intranet and extranet
technology
* Proven ability to work successfully in teams
* Excellent communication and interpersonal skills
* Highly skilled in multitasking, flexible, and adaptable

EDUCATION

Associate of Applied Science, Computer Network Support Technology, Seattle
Technology College, Seattle, WA, May 2006
 Related Courses and Skills
 * Peer-to-Peer Networking Structures * WAN
 * TCP/IP LAN Transport System * UNIX * ANSI C * Linux * Telephony
 * Remote Computing * Network System Administration
 * Wired and Wireless Networking Technologies * Client/Server Architecture
 * Interpersonal Communications * Technical Report Writing

Internship, TechNet, Inc., Seattle, WA                   January-May 2006
Technician Internship: Assisted technicians in installing and reconfiguring
multilocation wireless extranets. Assisted in implementation.

EXPERIENCE

**ComputerStop SuperStore, Seattle, WA                  May 2004-Present
Installation and Repair Technician, Part-time: Assemble computers, install
hardware and software upgrades, provide in-store and on-site repairs to
computers and peripherals. Named "Employee of the Month" three times in 18
months.

**Seattle Technology College                 September 2004-January 2006
Computer Lab Technician, Part-time: Assisted faculty and students with
hardware- and software-related problems. Assembled, installed, and added PCs
to the network throughout campus. Answered 95 percent of trouble calls
within 90 minutes.

ASSOCIATIONS

Tech CORPS, Volunteer, 2004-Present
PC Users Club, 2001-Present
```

Figure 9-12: Electronic Resume (Job Objective—Network Support Technician)

Summary of Information
Emphasized in Figure 9-12: Ryan

Danielle wants a job in a medium- or large-sized firm that has an extensive network. Many of the firms she would like to work for recruit IT (Information Technology) employees through Internet job listing sites, so Danielle prepares a cyberfriendly electronic resume. She pays particular attention to formatting:

a.   Using no word processing codes.

b.   Using only standard characters that are available on the keyboard.

c.   Using a 12-point Courier font.

d.   Using a 6.5-inch line length.

e.   Saving the resume as an ASCII or Plain Text file for easy transmission.

1. **Objective**	Danielle has researched the job market and knows the types of positions that are open to people with her skills. She writes a concise, targeted job objective. Employers reviewing resumes can immediately identify which jobs match her qualifications.
2. **Qualifications**	Because Danielle knows that electronic resumes are often sorted and selected by resume-search software programs, she loads her Qualifications section with keywords that emphasize her hardware/software knowledge and experience as well as her strong interpersonal skills. She wants any resume-search program to mark her resume for further evaluation, so she includes industry-specific terms that will increase the number of hits her resume receives.
3. **Education**	In addition to her degree, Danielle lists relevant courses she has taken. Because the course names are long, she separates them with asterisks and spaces. The course listings also use industry terminology to support knowledge claims in the Qualifications section and to create other opportunities for search programs to choose Danielle's resume.
	Danielle puts her internship experience in the Education section. Her exposure to a networking configuration different from the traditional wired configuration is important because it expands her capabilities in employers' eyes.
4. **Experience**	Danielle's experience is complementary to her job objective. Notice how she uses measurable accomplishments that are meaningful to employers. She knows employers want to hire people who meet deadlines and produce quality results.
5. **Associations**	Tech CORPS is made up of individuals and businesses that donate and/or install computers, software, and networks in schools and other educational institutions. Danielle's community service relates directly to her job target, shows her commitment to her community, and helps her stay current in her field.

Mike Banta
415 S. 23rd #43
Fresno, CA 93701
209-555-0152   mbanta@provider.net

OBJECTIVE	Seeking a receptionist position for a reliable person who has a strong work ethic
QUALIFICATIONS	• Windows, Word (Advanced), Outlook • Keying at 45 words per minute • Ten-key at 245 strokes per minute • Excel and Access data entry • Formating business correspondence • Filing: alphabetic, numeric, geographic • Operating high-speed collating copy machine • Multiline telephones

EDUCATION	State University, Fresno, CA
	    Office Occupations, Certificate, August 2006
	
	McCaine Adult Education Center, Clovis, CA
	    MS Word: Levels I & II, June 2005

WORK EXPERIENCE	Fruitland West, Fresno, CA Summer 2005 Cherry Sorter Received a raise the second day for being one of the three fastest workers. Always arrived on time; promoted to Head Sorter. Trail Mushroom, Clovis, CA 2001 to 2004 Crew Leader Promoted to Crew Leader in 2002. Calculated weekly time cards and posted daily attendance records for 16 to 20 people. Left when company closed. Picker Picked and sorted mushrooms 35 percent faster than the company average.

Figure 9-13: Scannable Print Resume (Job Objective–Receptionist)

Summary of Information Emphasized in Figure 9-13: Banta

Note: Figure 9-13 illustrates Mike's excellent job of translating personal attributes—strong work ethic and reliability—into measurable benefits for an employer.

1. **Objective**

Mike states a clear job objective and stresses his strong personal attributes that enhance his job performance.

2. **Qualifications**

Mike positions his skills at the top of his resume to assure the prospective employer that he is qualified for the entry-level job stated in his objective. Notice how the keying and ten-key skills are described in measurable terms that are meaningful to an employer.

3. **Education**

Mike lists his most current schooling first. The Education section explains where Mike learned the skills that are related to the job objective on his resume.

4. **Work Experience**

Because his work experience is limited and not directly transferable to the receptionist position he is seeking, Mike emphasizes on-the-job accomplishments that demonstrate his value to the employer:

"Received a raise the second day for being one of the three fastest workers. Always arrived on time; promoted to Head Sorter."

"Promoted to Crew Leader in 2002. Calculated weekly time cards and posted daily attendance records for 16 to 20 people."

"Picked and sorted mushrooms 35 percent faster than the company average."

John Chang

jchang@provider.net

**6487 West Street
Davis, CA 56915
649-555-0177**

Objective

Web Specialist

Qualifications Summary

- Comprehensive web site development
- Web site hosting and registration; server administration
- SQL and Access database management
- Graphic and multimedia design, including streaming audio/video, analysis graphs, maps, and custom web graphics
- Network administration in Windows 2000/XP/XP Professional, MS Server, 2003, UNIX, Linux, and Solaris

Computer Qualifications

Internet/Web Applications	Programming	Multimedia
Microsoft IIS	HTML, XML	Adobe Photoshop
SQL Server, My SQL	SQL	MPEG Video Encoding
Security and Firewalls	ColdFusion	Real Media Encoding
Adobe Acrobat	ASP, ASP.NET, VB.NET	ArcView Mapping
Dreamweaver, Flash	PHP	MP3 Compression
HTTP and FTP servers	Java	Adobe Illustrator
Multi Router Traffic Graphing	Perl	

Education/Certification

Associate of Applied Science in Internet Information Systems Technology, 2006
Twin Peaks Technical College, Twin Peaks, CA
Relevant Courses Completed: Extensive programming courses, server design, database management, network security, Internet imaging

- **Microsoft Certified Database Administrator (MCDBA)**

Work Experience

Please see web portfolio for examples of my work.

National Geographic Information Center, Boise, ID
Assistant Webmaster, Summer 2004 and Summer 2005
Updated the main databases and maintained a public Internet interface using Macromedia Dreamweaver and Active Server Pages.NET (ASP.NET). Created and more efficiently redesigned several branched sites, including photo galleries, statistics tables, and PDF document posting areas and archives. Produced geologic prediction analysis graphs using information gathered from remote automated geology stations. Designed a web interface for LAN bandwidth usage tracking, improving network efficiency by 45 percent.

- *On-the-Spot Award received for extra effort, Geographic Festival, 2005*

Perez Construction and Development, Boise, ID
Web Design Project, Summer 2005
Created entire web site for a small business in construction and land development training, which included setup, design, site registration, and site hosting.

Associations

American Webmasters' Association, 2003-Present
ASP Programmers Club, 2004-Present

Other formats of this resume: Printable: (pdf) (doc) Electronic text: (ASCII)

Figure 9-14: Web Resume (Job Objective–Web Specialist)

Summary of Information Emphasized in Figure 9-14: Chang

1. **Objective**

   The title Web Specialist is commonly understood in John's career field.

2. **Qualifications**

   John summarizes his industry-specific qualifications in a bulleted list immediately following the job objective. To capture the attention of employers, he also uses an eye-catching table of key applications, programming languages, and multimedia programs to emphasize the large number of programs relevant to his job objective that he is qualified to operate.

   Keywords emphasized. The names of these programs also serve as relevant keywords that are included in the downloadable electronic version of John's resume, likely generating hits by resume-search software programs.

3. **Education**

   John's recent degree in Internet Information Systems Technology implies currency in the requisite knowledge base and satisfies the basic educational requirements for the position.

4. **Experience**

   To provide evidence supporting his qualifications claims, John repeats important keywords and uses synonyms for keywords he listed in the Qualifications section. Examples include the following: database, Dreamweaver, ASP.NET, web site development/site registration, site hosting, web graphics/analysis graphs.

   Measurable accomplishments. John includes a strong measurable accomplishment in the National Geographic Information Center description: "Designed a web interface for LAN bandwidth usage tracking, improving network efficiency by 45 percent." He also mentions the On-the-Spot Award for extra effort awarded to him by the Geographic Festival.

5. **Associations**

   Membership in two nationally-recognized professional organizations that are relevant to the job objective demonstrates John's active involvement in remaining up-to-date in the fast-changing, high-tech career field. Employers are interested in this quality when hiring for a web specialist position.

Thomas Stanley
123 Forest Drive
Springfield, NY 14201
716-555-2457
tstanley@provider.net

OBJECTIVE

Private Security Guard position requiring the ability to perform safety, security, and surveillance procedures; current licensing; and excellent communication skills

QUALIFICATIONS AND CERTIFICATION

- New York State Security Guard License, 2006
- Carrying Concealed Weapons (CCW) License, 2006
- First Aid and CPR Certification, 2006
- Physical Fitness Specialist, 2006
- Fire Prevention and Safety Training, 2005
- Burglary Prevention Training, 2005
- Practical experience in closed-circuit video surveillance and switchboard operations
- Proficiency in Windows, Word, Excel, PowerPoint, and Outlook

EDUCATION

Crown Community College, Buffalo, NY
Associate of Applied Science, 2006
Major: Criminal Justice GPA: 3.75

EXPERIENCE

Buffalo Juvenile Justice Center, Buffalo, NY   **Summer 2005**
Juvenile Corrections Internship
Under the direction of the Juvenile Corrections Officer, monitored and ensured the safety and security of juvenile detainees. Enforced facility safety and security rules. Escorted juvenile offenders to classes, counseling sessions, and work-release programs. Conducted security checks, searches, and pat downs. Maintained an error-free performance record with no security breaches.

County Fairgrounds, Hamburg, NY   **Summer 2004**
Grounds and Maintenance Supervisor
Supervised groundskeeping and maintenance crew of eight work-released detainees for the County Sheriff's Department. Quickly resolved worker disagreements and scheduling issues using training in conflict resolution techniques. Completed evaluations and submitted thorough and timely paperwork to the Sheriff's Department.

Baker Sporting Goods, Buffalo, NY   **April 2003 to May 2004**
Security Guard, Part-time
Monitored customers and employees to maintain internal and external loss-theft control. Conducted closed-circuit video surveillance of store and building exterior. Responded swiftly to all employee and customer security and safety requests. Performed switchboard operator duties. Wrote and submitted daily loss prevention reports.

Figure 9-15: Scannable Print Resume (Job Objective–Private Security Guard)

Summary of Information
Emphasized in Figure 9-15: Stanley

1. **Objective**	Thomas states a clear, targeted job objective using a job title that is clearly understood in the field. To capture the attention of employers and emphasize his qualifications, he includes job-related competencies that match those listed in employers' job postings.
2. **Qualifications and Certification**	Thomas lists his qualifications and certifications in a clear, bulleted list. Because security guard positions can have several certification requirements, he is careful to include all the relevant certificates and licenses he has, along with dates to show that they are current. He uses many industry keywords and stresses experience and training that show his emphasis on safety, fitness, and security. He also lists his practical experience in video surveillance, switchboard operations, and computers because security guards are often asked to perform a variety of surveillance and communication tasks.
3. **Education**	Thomas reinforces his qualifications by placing his degree near the top of his resume. He highlights his Criminal Justice major and includes his respectable grade point average.
4. **Experience**	Thomas's work experience shows that he can be productive immediately in a job in the security field. His internship at the local Juvenile Justice Center gave him experience in juvenile corrections, and in his description, he focuses on safety and security procedures. Thomas describes his work activities using industry-specific terminology. He includes an accomplishment statement that emphasizes his error-free performance record.
	In his description of his summer job at the County Fairgrounds, Thomas includes an accomplishment statement emphasizing his use of conflict resolution and interpersonal skills, both of which are important security guard qualifications. He also describes his ability to complete and submit essential paperwork.
	Although Thomas's job at Baker Sporting Goods was a part-time position, it gave him practical experience in a variety of common security guard tasks. He explains his activities using keywords and industry-specific language and emphasizes his ability to manage multiple surveillance and communication tasks.

Sheree Washington
5077 Pine Run
Orlando, FL 32773
407-555-8125
sheree_washington@provider.net

OBJECTIVE

Medical Assistant position requiring experience in front office and back office procedures; current certification; and fluency in Spanish

QUALIFICATIONS

- Certified Medical Assistant, 2006
- Associate of Science, 2006
- Four-month Medical Assisting internship with front office administrative and back office clinical experience
- Medical records management experience in ICD-10 coding, alpha- and color-coded filing systems
- Medical terminology courses
- Medical insurance experience
- Spanish language fluency

EDUCATION

Associate of Science, 2006, College of Applied Careers, Orlando, FL   Major: Medical Assisting

Related Courses and Skills

- Human Anatomy and Physiology
- Clinical and Diagnostic Procedures
- Medical Office Practices
- Patient Relations
- Phlebotomy
- Medical Law and Ethics

- Pharmacology and Medication Administration
- Laboratory Techniques
- EKG and Basic X-Ray
- Business Communications
- Medical Terminology
- Microsoft Office 2003

CERTIFICATION

- Certified Medical Assistant, 2006
- CPR/BLS Certificate, 2006

- IV Therapy and Blood Withdrawal Certificate, 2006
- Basic X-Ray Machine Operator License, 2006

EXPERIENCE

Dr. Jean Esteban, 106 Seminole Way, Sanford, FL   **January 2006 to Present**
Assistant Office Manager, Part-time. Greet and register patients. Answer telephone and schedule appointments. Maintain records for all patients, including active and inactive files. Reduced report generation time by 30 percent by implementing a new system for producing reports for insurance records. Handle insurance billing and collecting. Use spreadsheet, database, word processing, and Internet software programs.

Seminole Medical Center, Orlando, FL   **September 2005 to December 2005**
Medical Assisting Internship. Greeted and registered patients. Prepared patient charts. Conducted patient interviews and recorded patient history summaries. Maintained supplies and instruments, and readied examination rooms. Answered telephones and scheduled appointments. Assisted physicians with vital signs and diagnostic testing, minor laboratory testing, and EKGs. Received Standards and Procedures Award for maintaining a safe and healthy work environment.

ASSOCIATION

American Association of Medical Assistants

Figure 9-16: Scannable Print Resume (Job Objective–Medical Assistant)

Summary of Information
Emphasized in Figure 9-16: Washington

1. **Objective**

Sheree uses an industry-standard job title to state her job objective concisely and clearly. To capture the attention of employers and emphasize her qualifications, she includes job-related competencies that match those listed in employers' job postings.

2. **Qualifications**

Sheree includes several terms that readers and software programs will search for when seeking a Medical Assistant candidate. She lists her qualifications in a clear, bulleted list and emphasizes her Certified Medical Assistant certification by listing it first. She includes her practical experience in medical terminology and medical records management and highlights her ability to speak a second language, which is an increasingly important patient communication skill. She includes her degree in the Qualifications category because it is a keyword that is likely to be used in an electronic search of her resume.

3. **Education**

Sheree reinforces her qualifications by placing her degree near the top of her resume. She highlights her Medical Assisting major. She also lists classes from her major that are especially pertinent to employers and includes comptuer programs.

4. **Certification**

Because Medical Assistant positions can have several certification requirements, Sheree is careful to include all the relevant certificates and licenses she has along with dates to show that they are current. She places her national certification near the top of the resume to emphasize her qualifications and to show that she takes her profession seriously.

5. **Experience**

Although Sheree's current part-time job in a doctor's office is in a medical facility, her duties are mostly adminsitrative (front office). She uses industry-specific terminology and emphasizes her contact with patients and medical records experience. She also includes a strong accomplishment statement providing evidence of her ability to save time and implement valuable new procedures.

Sheree's internship allowed her to work and learn at a local hospital. The internship lasted four months, provided hands-on experience, and is directly applicable to Sheree's job objective, so she places the description in the experience section of her resume. Note how she describes her duties in industry-specific terminology. Sheree mentions her Standards and Procedures Award at the end of the description to show that her job performance is above average and to highlight her attention to a safe and healthy environment, which is a primary job requirement.

6. **Association**

The association noted on Sheree's resume reinforces her strong interest in the medical field and shows that she takes her profession seriously.

LAURENT CHACON

1015 Cambridge Way, Houston, TX 77001

409-555-0191   Fax 409-555-0192   lchacon@provider.net

OBJECTIVE

Marketing Product Line Manager for wireless data communications company

QUALIFICATIONS

- Managerial and technical education: BSEE, MBA
- Strong skills in marketing strategies development and implementation
- Remote conferencing technology, Windows NetMeeting, videoconferencing
- Knowledgeable and professional interaction with customers, sales force, engineers, and manufacturing personnel
- Team leader for product line introduction
- Proven project management skills, PERT and Gantt charts, Microsoft Project
- Proficient with LANs (wired and wireless), WAN hardware and protocols, T-1, T-3 Carrier networks, analog and digital telecommunications transmissions, UNIX, C++, Visual Basic, Linux, real-time embedded software
- Skilled presenter and proficient in PowerPoint development and delivery
- Experienced in RFP and RFQ processes
- Skilled in use of Word, Excel, Access, wireless technology, VPN, Novell certification

PROFESSIONAL EXPERIENCE

NETLINK INC, Dallas, TX   **1998-Present**

- **Marketing Manager, Southwest Division**   **2004-Present**

  Manage marketing operations in Texas, Nevada, Arizona, and New Mexico. Supervise a sales and service force that has an average annual growth rate of 50 percent and participate in executive-level strategic planning meetings. Direct the development and implementation of marketing plan for a banking application of LAN/WAN products; results so far include sales to 50 percent of the Southwest Division customer base. Led team whose 2005 sales strategies have doubled NETLINK's market share in the finance industry and expanded the customer base in hospitals by 80 percent.

- **Sales and Service Manager, Southwest Division**   **2001-2004**

  Supervised account executives and increased district sales by 150 percent in two years. Directed on-time, underbudget openings of offices in Houston and Dallas. Improved customer satisfaction 100 percent through systems-support teams that provide four-hour turnaround on service calls. Analyzed competitive forces in the Southwest and reported findings at quarterly planning meetings with upper management.

Figure 9-17a: Scannable Print Resume (Job Objective–Marketing Product Line Manager)

- **Engineering Product Development Coordinator**   **1998-2001**

  Member of company start-up team developing ultra-fast, self-contained, secure, low-power wireless transmission technologies. Coordinated hardware and firmware integration. Supervised component testing, provided engineering support for component production, and assisted in real-time embedded software development. Acted as marketing interface during technical presentations to customers.

University of South Texas, Houston, TX
Small Business Development Center   **1996-1998**

- **Intern: Technical Industries**
  Guided by the Center Director, assisted small businesses specializing in technical products to establish vendor sources, design and implement testing procedures, solve production problems, and train workers in manufacturing techniques.

EDUCATION

- University of South Texas, Houston, TX   MBA, 1998
- Mid-State College, Austin, TX, cum laude   BSEE, 1995

ASSOCIATIONS

- National Association of Consulting Engineers, 2001-Present
- Information Technology Management Association, 2005-Present; President, 2006
- American Society for Quality Control, 2003-Present
- Member, Board of Directors, Texas Red Cross, 1999-Present

Figure 9-17b: Scannable Print Resume, page 2 (Job Objective–Marketing Product Line Manager)

Summary of Information
Emphasized in Figures 9-17a and 9-17b: Chacon

Note: Laurent's extensive experience justifies a two-page resume.

1. **Objective**

The focused job objective reflects Laurent's ability to state goals clearly.

2. **Qualifications**

The managerial, leadership, and technical capabilities that make Laurent an effective and productive leader in this field are summarized here. These include his managerial and technical degrees, strong marketing skills, presentation skills, telecommunications and computer skills, and project-management skills.

3. **Professional Experience**

NETLINK INC: *Marketing Manager.* Laurent emphasizes measurable achievements because this field is very results-oriented. Laurent proves the competencies he claimed in the Qualifications section.

Sales and Service Manager. Laurent documents leadership, marketing strategies, and customer service achievements. Referring to the management level of the business-planning team emphasizes the scope of responsibility he has on the job, as well as the respect he has earned.

Engineering Product Development Coordinator. This position is vital to Laurent's success because it gives him credibility with technically knowledgeable customers and with the engineering and manufacturing elements of an organization.

University of South Texas, Small Business Development Center: *Intern.* This internship is valuable because it reassures employers that Laurent understands the structure and scope of the entire business process.

4. **Education**

Laurent has credible, impressive professional experience and does not need to emphasize the specific courses he has taken. He places the Education section near the end of the resume because, at this point in his career, employers are more interested in his accomplishments than his education.

5. **Associations**

Membership in related professional organizations demonstrates a commitment to remaining current with field trends—a quality respected by employers. Employees who contribute to the business community enhance an organization's image.

ALEX VALENZUELA

2440 Windom Way, Apt. 34   Los Angeles, CA 90063   213-555-0165   avalenzuela@provider.net

OBJECTIVE	Staff Accountant, Audit Division

QUALIFICATIONS

- Experienced in invoicing, accounts receivable, accounts payable, general ledger, inventory control, Sarbanes-Oxley compliance
- Self-starter, team player, goal-oriented, willing to travel
- Attention to detail, accuracy, and deadlines
- Strong communication, problem-solving, and customer service skills
- Proficient in Word, Excel, Access, Outlook, Windows, QuickBooks Pro
- Work with PC network in client-server environment

EDUCATION

Bachelor of Business Administration, Accounting, 2006
University of Los Angeles, Los Angeles, CA   GPA 3.5
Relevant courses of study:

- Analysis and Design of Accounting Information Systems
- Information Systems Auditing • Managerial Accounting
- Cost Accounting • Tax Accounting • Fianancial Accounting
- Intermediate Accounting I, II, III • Commercial Law

Senior Internship, 12/05 to 4/06
Project Leader: Coordinated student team analyzing inventory system of a small trailer manufacturing company. The recommented just-in-time ordering and improved parts control systems reduced yearly carrying costs by 55 percent.

EXPERIENCE

O'Keefe and Associates, Los Angeles, CA   **9/04 to Present**
Part-time Bookkeeper: Use Quickbooks Pro to invoice clients, post income and expenses, process accounts payable, reconcile general ledger accounts, and prepare monthly balance sheets and P&L statements. Update expense-tracking spreadsheets for each client. Using Excel, reconcile monthly bank statement. Initiated shorter invoicing cycle and introduced discounts for prompt invoice payment; reduced A/R cycle to 35 days.

Rand and Company, Los Angeles, CA   **6/02 to 8/04**
Part-time Retail Sales Clerk: Sold 175 percent of quota.
Awarded "2003 Outstanding Employee/Customer Relations" certificate.

ACTIVITIES

Vice President, Beta Alpha Psi Accounting, 2006
Member, Information Science Association, 2003 to Present
Member, Debate Team, 2002 to 2004

Figure 9-18: Resume for Career Action 9-5–Applicant #1 (Staff Accountant, Audit Division)

Ralph Greenwood

6780 Greenbriar Street,   Los Angeles, CA 90067

Education:
University of Los Angeles, Los Angeles, CA
B.B.A., Accounting, June 2006
Grade Point Average: 3.5

Major Courses of Study:
Commercial Law, Cost Accounting, Economics, Principles/Management,
Auditing, Statistical Techniques, Programming Systems, Principles/Finance,
Managerial Accounting, Systems Analysis & Design, and Intermediate Account-
ing I, II, III

Experience:
January to May 2006
Department of Accounting, University of Los Angeles, Senior Internship:
Coordinator of student team. Analyzed inventory system of a small retail
store. Recommendations to adopt just-in-time ordering and improved stock
control saved company a significant amount of time and money.

2004-Present
Westworth and Company, Los Angeles. Part-time Bookkeeper.
Responsibilities include: invoicing customers, posting income and
expenses, handling accounts receivable and payable; preparing income
statements and balance sheets, operating PC computer in client-server
network with Microsoft software and Quickbooks Pro; reconciling bank
statements; and updating client expense-tracking spreadsheets. Shortened
time needed to invoice clients and to receive payments.

2002-2004
Tueller's Men's Shop, Los Angeles. Part-time sales. Duties included:
making retail sales; maintaining merchandise displays; assisting with
inventory; assisting with cashing out; maintaining orderly stockroom.

June 2000-February 2002
Woodland General Nursery, Los Angeles. Stock maintenance staff. Duties
included: unloading new merchandise; arranging merchandise in assigned
locations; maintaining orderly and clean grounds; carrying and loading
purchases for customers; dispensing with disposable containers and other
waste. Assisting with watering, feeding, spraying, and general care of
nursery items.

Other Activities:
Beta Alpha Psi—Accounting, officer; Member, *University of Los Angeles*
Student Center—2004-2005; *University of Los Angeles Swim Team*, member,
2002-2004.
Hobbies: Swimming, reading, piano, travel.

References:
University of Los Angeles Career/Placement Center, 1300 J Street, Los
Angeles, CA 90063

Figure 9-19: Resume for Career Action 9-5—Applicant #2 (Staff Accountant, Audit Division)

CAREER ACTION WORKSHEET 9-3

Resume Outline

Name: _____

Address: _____

_____

E-Mail Address: _____

Telephone Number: _____

Pager/Message Number: _____

Fax Number: _____

Web Site Address: _____

JOB OBJECTIVE: *(Refer to the sample job descriptions you were instructed to collect earlier.)*

_____

_____

_____

_____

RELATED QUALIFICATIONS: *(Use terms and keywords that are related to your target job to describe your capabilities and accomplishments.)*

_____

_____

_____

_____

_____

_____

_____

_____

Continued on next page >>>

CAREER ACTION WORKSHEET 9-3 (continued)

WORK EXPERIENCE: *(State your accomplishments in measurable terms, if possible. Start with the most recent job, and list each job in reverse chronological order, ending with the earliest work experience you had.)*

Dates Employed: From _____ To _____

Company Name: _____

City: _____ State: _____ ZIP Code: _____

Job Title and Description: _____

_____

_____

_____

Dates Employed: From _____ To _____

Company Name: _____

City: _____ State: _____ ZIP Code: _____

Job Title and Description: _____

_____

_____

_____

Dates Employed: From _____ To _____

Company Name: _____

City: _____ State: _____ ZIP Code: _____

Job Title and Description: _____

_____

_____

_____

Continued on next page >>>

CAREER ACTION WORKSHEET 9-3 (continued)

Dates Employed: From _____ To _____

Company Name: _____

City: _____ State: _____ ZIP Code: _____

Job Title and Description: _____

_____

_____

_____

EDUCATION: *(If you have attended more than one school, list the schools in reverse chronological order—the most recent one first. Do not list high school if you have higher-level schooling unless the high school is considered very prestigious.)*

Name of School	**City, State**	**Degree(s)/Certificate(s)**	**Years Attended**

(Job seekers with little or no work experience should expand the education section.)

Major(s): _____

Minor(s): _____

GPA: _____

Relevant Courses of Study: _____

_____

_____

_____

SCHOOL-RELATED ACTIVITIES: *(Organizations, clubs, tutorial experience, class projects, honor groups, internships, leadership, and so on)*

_____

_____

_____

Continued on next page >>>

CAREER ACTION WORKSHEET 9-3 (continued)

OTHER RELATED ACTIVITIES/EXPERIENCE: *(Internships; volunteer work; membership or leadership in professional or trade associations, community organizations, social organizations, and service clubs; and so on. List the name of the program or organization. Include a brief summary of your experience, accomplishments, and activities, as well as the dates you were involved.)*

_____

_____

_____

_____

_____

_____

MILITARY SERVICE: *(If applicable, list the branch of service, your highest rank, training received, areas of specialization, major duties, skills and knowledge developed, and location of service.)*

_____

_____

_____

_____

_____

INTERESTS: *(List interests that are related to your job target and demonstrate well-rounded qualities, including interaction with people, manual dexterity, intellectual pursuits, artistic ability, physical fitness, strength, continuing education, and personal/professional development.)*

_____

_____

_____

_____

_____

_____

PERFECT THE APPLICATION AND COVER LETTER

In this chapter, you will:

- Discuss and practice effectively completing an application for employment.

 Use the Internet to search for additional cover letter strategies that may be useful to you.

- Write an effective cover letter that includes a request for an interview.

"Through their resumes and cover letters, applicants should project the qualities of focus on total customer satisfaction, quality, and neatness, which are essential in the luxury hospitality industry. Employees are hired based on a selection process to ensure each person's philosophies are in line with those of The Ritz-Carlton."

Anand Rao
Corporate Director of Organizational Development
The Ritz-Carlton Hotel Company, L.L.C.

You will be screened into or out of an interview (and a job) on the basis of your job search package: resume, cover letter, and employment application. If you carefully completed the activities in Chapter 9, your resume should be top-notch. This chapter presents tips and activities for preparing winning employment applications and cover letters. Remember: The qualified job applicant who does only an average job of preparing these documents is screened out; applicants with equal qualifications who prepare these documents well remain in the running for the job. Chapter 10 explains how you can stay in the running by completing an application correctly, writing a results-oriented cover letter, and using the Internet to search for additional useful tips in these areas.

Preparing the Employment Application

In this section, you will learn how to complete an employment application correctly and professionally. This will help ensure that your application passes the screening process so you can stay in the running for the job.

How Important Is It?

Employers use employment applications to obtain standard information from all applicants. Many job seekers think of the application as something to get through quickly so they can get on with the interview. Wrong! This idea can be fatal to your job search. Employers consider application forms, cover letters, and resumes carefully. They use these documents to select interviewees and to weed out people who don't look qualified on paper. Do not underestimate the importance of the application!

Visit a company you are interested in, and ask for a job application form. Take it home to study and complete.

Success Tip

Follow the instructions on an application exactly, and make your application perfect. It's a primary screening tool.

Recognize Differences in Application Forms

Employers design their application forms to obtain the information they consider most important to making hiring decisions. This includes some information that applicants might omit from their cover letters or resumes. By obtaining the same information from all applicants, employers can more fairly compare the applicants' backgrounds and qualifications. The cover letters and resumes expand on the applicants' qualifications and either improve or lessen their chances of getting interviews. The application, therefore, is an essential tool for screening candidates.

Many employers computerize applicant information by scanning applications and filing the information electronically. Some have applicants fill out and submit computerized applications. Applications are searched electronically for specific categories of information (job objective, educational background, work experience, and so on). Employers use these categories of information to compare applicants. If you omit important information, your application may be passed over. One of the most important things to remember when preparing an employment application is to *follow the instructions exactly!*

Both the length and complexity of application forms vary greatly. Some are relatively simple; others are more complicated. Often technical jobs require comprehensive application information.

Some organizations use long, complex applications with questions requiring detailed answers. These are designed to test applicants' endurance (a desirable employee trait). Additionally, some organizations include questions that require applicants to summarize their philosophies of the job or occupational field, thus testing the applicants' knowledge and personal values.

As you prepare applications for employment, treat every question seriously and answer it completely. Even if an application is long, maintain high quality in all your answers. Those who don't are the first to be eliminated in the screening process. If the application is extremely long, complete it at home. Take two or three days to work out the best possible answers.

Get an Application Ahead of Time

Whenever possible, don't fill out the application in the employer's office. Why? Because you need to practice fitting your answers in the spaces provided on the form. (Often space is limited and you have to abbreviate information.) You also need time to word your answers well. Employers judge applications on neatness, completeness, and accuracy, as well as on the quality of the answers. It usually takes more than one try to achieve the wording and effect you want.

Keep the following tips in mind when completing an application:

▲ Read and follow directions. Prepare each section carefully.

▲ Make your answers neat and legible.

▲ Use the correct lines or spaces for your answers.

▲ Practice on a copy of the application, squeeze in as much positive information about yourself as possible, and abbreviate to fit the information in the spaces provided.

▲ Answer every question. Use N/A (not applicable) if a question does not pertain to you. This shows that you did not overlook the question or skip it purposely.

▲ Use correct spelling, grammar, and punctuation. Use specialized terminology correctly. (You never get a second chance to make a good first impression!)

▲ Include a second telephone number of a person who is readily available and willing to take messages for you. You can't afford to miss calls from prospective employers!

▲ Make certain all information is accurate (dates, addresses, telephone and fax numbers, names, and so on).

▲ Be honest. Employers check the facts and immediately eliminate a candidate who has supplied false information.

▲ Date and sign the application. Some organizations invalidate an application if it is not signed and dated.

> *"The closest to perfection a person ever comes is when he fills out a job application form."*
> Stanley J. Randall

Copy the Application and Use It as a Draft. Get the application ahead of time, make a copy of the original, and use the copy as a working draft. Ask the employer to mail an application to you, or access the company's web site to see if you can download and print an application. If you can't get an application ahead of time, get one from a competitor or a closely related organization and practice filling it out. You can use it as a guide if you are required to fill one out in your target employer's office.

Read the Directions First! By reading through the entire application, from the beginning to the end, you can see how requests for information may be interrelated, which will help you determine which items require more or less detailed answers. You will also avoid duplicating information, ensure that you write information in the right places, and learn what other information you may need before completing the application.

As you read your practice copy, use a colored pen to mark all special directions so you don't overlook or misunderstand any of them while completing the application. If you don't fully understand a portion of the application or if you do not know exactly what type of information the employer is seeking, call and ask. Following directions is important to employers.

Be sure to demonstrate this ability when you apply for a job!

Complete Each Section of the Application Carefully

Suggestions for effectively completing the major parts of a typical application are presented in this section.

Personal Information. Look at the first part of the sample application shown in Figure 10-1, and notice the following:

▲ The last name is to be listed first, followed by the first name, and then the middle name or initial. Most applications are designed this way. Don't make a bad first impression (immediately demonstrating that you can't follow directions) by listing your names in the wrong order.

▲ This application asks only for a permanent address. Some applications call for a current address and then a permanent address. If your application calls for both, as a courtesy, you should repeat your current address under the permanent address section rather than leave it blank.

▲ The applicant listed a second telephone number where messages can be received. (Good! If you are out pounding the pavement for a job, you can still get the call for an interview by listing an alternative phone number.)

▲ Because the applicant had never applied to or been employed by the company, neither box was checked in the associated portion of the personal section of the application. The applicant wrote N/A in the box labeled "Where and when?"

▲ The applicant indicated with a check in the "No" box that no relatives were employed by the organization. If check boxes were not an option, the applicant could have written N/A (not applicable) next to the request to list the names of any relatives employed by the organization.

▲ The e-mail address provided by the applicant allows the prospective employer to contact the applicant immediately.

E-mail addresses are requested because they provide a timely way to reach an applicant without playing "telephone tag."

As an alternative to using N/A for questions that do not apply to you, type or use a black ink ballpoint pen and a ruler to draw a line through the response area.

Success Tip

Do a top-notch job of preparing your application. The application is a primary applicant-screening tool.

Position Objective. Figure 10-2 shows the position information section of a job application form. Note the following tips for filling out this section:

▲ Be sure to list a definite position objective, position title, or position number. (A number may be assigned to an open position if the job opening is posted on the organization's web site or elsewhere.) Employers are not impressed with applicants who list "anything" as the position desired. This hints of desperation, a lack of confidence, or a lack of focus or direction.

▲ Because salary is such an influential factor in employment, use "negotiable" as the reply to the question of salary desired. Don't risk eliminating yourself before you have a chance to present your qualifications in an interview. Save any discussion of salary until the employer has expressed a definite interest in you. (Besides, the employer could have more money in mind than you say you will require. Why lose such an advantage up front?) If the position is advertised at a set and nonnegotiable salary, list that figure in the "Salary Desired" response area.

If you can start work right away, write "Immediately" under Date Available. If you are currently employed, note that you will need two weeks' notice. Your circumstances and preferences will determine your answers to the remaining position questions.

ABC Company

APPLICATION FOR EMPLOYMENT

This application is used in the selection process and both pages must be completed. Attach extra sheets if necessary (references to resumes are NOT acceptable).

A P P L I C A N T   I N F O R M A T I O N

Last Name	First Name	M. I.	Social Security Number	Home Phone	Alternative Phone
Martinelli	Elizabeth	S.	606-00-0088	208-555-0106	208-555-0170

Permanent Address – No. & Street	City		State	Zip	Date
6518 Willow Way	Boise		ID	83706	01/15/--

Have you previously	☐ applied to OR ☐ been employed by ABC Company?	Where and when? N/A	E-mail Address emartinelli@provider.net

Do you have relatives working for the ABC Company? ☐Yes ☒No If yes, give names and departments where they work.

Figure 10-1: Personal Information Section

P O S I T I O N

Position Desired	Salary Desired (per month)
Sales Supervisor	Negotiable

Willing to relocate? ☒ Yes ☐ No	Do you want ☒ Full-time ☐ Part-time	Date Available for Work Immediately

Figure 10-2: Position Information Section

Education. Your education will be covered in a section that is similar to Figure 10-3. Remember the following points when filling out this section:

▲ The sample lists one high school and one community college. If you attended more than one high school, list the most recent one you attended, and indicate the year you received your diploma. List your GPA only if it is requested or if it is high. If you have attended more than one post-secondary educational institution, list the most recent one first and work back to the

first one you attended. If necessary, attach a separate keyed list of additional schools you attended.

▲ If space is provided to list subjects of study, research, special skills (such as a foreign language), or other activities, list examples of your capabilities and activities that relate to your job objective.

Employment History. The employment history (or work experience) section of the sample application is shown in Figure 10-4. An explanation of the entries follows.

EDUCATION						
Highest Educational Level Completed:						
Name of School	Location	From	To	Degree or Diploma	Major	Minor
High School *Idaho Falls High School*	*Idaho Falls, ID*			*Diploma*		
Community College *Central Community College*	*Boise, ID*	*9/04*	*1/06*	*A.A.*	*Marketing*	
College or University						
Graduate School						
Special Training						
Languages Other Than English (if required in employment announcement):	Speak *Spanish*			Read *Spanish*		Write *Spanish*

Figure 10-3: Education Information Section

▲ If your application provides enough space, include key words and use action verbs to describe your accomplishments in results-oriented terms—just as you would in your resume.

▲ Use brief, positive phrases to explain why you left a job—for example, "returned to school," "changed careers," "reorganization," "employment ended," "business closed," or "took a position with more responsibility." Avoid negative language, such as "quit," "personal conflict," "late for work," "fired for no reason," or "lawsuit." These types of responses will cause an employer to question your abilities and judgment.

If you were fired from a job, be as brief and as positive as possible, and leave longer explanations for the interview. Be prepared to describe what happened in unemotional and professional language. Take responsibility for your actions (don't blame others), explain what you learned from the situation, and explain how you could have handled the situation differently. It may help you to write out an explanation, but your best chance at getting a job will come from explaining the situation to an employer in person. It also will be essential for you to have a reference who will give you a solid recommendation.

References. Whenever possible, tie your references directly to your work experience. Most prospective employers value good references from former reputable employers because former employers know firsthand how you performed at work. Notice in Figure 10-5 how the first two references are tied to the employment history shown in Figure 10-4.

Some applications specify that your references be people other than former employers or supervisors. In this case, you should not list former employers! This is an example of why it is so important to read every word of an application carefully. Remember: You must talk to your references in advance and get their permission to use their names and contact information on an application.

EMPLOYMENT HISTORY & RELATED EXPERIENCE

List present or most recent experience first. Include armed services experience and volunteer work.

Employer Name *Kevington's Emporium (Part-time)*	Employer Address *3315 Front Street* *Boise, ID 83705*		Dates (Mo./Yr.) From *12/03* To *Present*
Position Title *Assistant Sales Supervisor*	Supervisor *Charlie Wu*		Phone *208-555-0131* Ext. *125*
Reason for Leaving *Still employed*	Salary: Start *9.00/hr* End *11.58/hr*		No. Hours Per Week: *20*

Duties:

Training, supervising, and scheduling staff of six

Promoted to Assistant Sales Supervisor after only six months

Employer Name *Crown Sportswear (Part-time)*	Employer Address *1800 Orchard Street* *Boise, ID 83704*		Dates (Mo./Yr.) From *5/03* To *11/03*
Position Title *Sales Clerk*	Supervisor *Connie Pratt*		Phone *208-555-0114* Ext. *418*
Reason for Leaving *Took new job*	Salary: Start *8.50/hr* End *8.50/hr*		No. Hours Per Week: *10-15*

Duties:

Sales, customer service, and design and setup of all merchandise displays

Performed managerial and closing duties for store three nights a week

Employer Name *Value Market Variety (Part-time)*	Employer Address *460 Park Way* *Idaho Falls, ID 83402*		Dates (Mo./Yr.) From *12/00* To *3/03*
Position Title *Sales Clerk*	Supervisor *Tevia Levitt*		Phone *208-555-0199* Ext. *420*
Reason for Leaving *Moved to college location*	Salary: Start *7.00/hr* End *8.25/hr*		No. Hours Per Week: *15*

Duties:

Sales, customer service, and inventory stocking tasks

Selected "Customer Service Employee of the Month" twice in one year

Figure 10-4: Employment History Section

REFERENCES				
Name	Address	Telephone	Occupation	Years Known
Charlie Wu (Kevington's Emporium)	3315 Front Street Boise, ID 83705	208-555-0131 Ext. 125	Sales Manager	2 years
Name	Address	Telephone	Occupation	Years Known
Tevia Levitt (Value Market Variety)	460 Park Way Idaho Falls, ID 83402	208-555-0199 Ext. 420	Supervisor	3 years
Name	Address	Telephone	Occupation	Years Known
Dr. Robert Cornwell	Business Department Central Community College 8500 College Way Boise, ID 83704	208-555-0143	Professor, Marketing and Sales	2 years

Figure 10-5: References Section

Request to Contact Your Current Employer. As shown in Figure 10-6, if an application asks for permission to contact your current employer, answer *yes* only if your current employer is aware of your job search and approves. Otherwise, protect your current job with a reply of *no*.

Background Information Check. Because employers are constantly monitored by regulatory agencies to ensure they are obeying the law, you may be asked on an application if you are legally available for work in the United States. You may also be asked if you have a criminal history that includes a felony or misdemeanor charge. Answer these questions truthfully, and indicate "will discuss at interview." Your best option is to explain any negative history in person, where you must be prepared to take responsibility for your actions and explain what you learned and how you have improved yourself.

Applicant Statement. Be sure to date and sign an application. (Be careful to list the correct year.

Incorrectly dating an application is a common error and can affect the time the application is retained in an active file.) And remember: Some employers do not consider an application valid unless it is signed.

Prepare for Completing an Application On-Site

If you must complete an application on the employer's premises, have the following items with you for easy reference:

▲ Your completed sample application to be used as a guide

▲ Two or three black ink pens

▲ Your Social Security card, driver's license, proof of citizenship, certificates, union card, grade transcripts, and related items that are pertinent to your occupational field (to verify the accuracy of the data you must record)

▲ Your resume (as a reference for details)

▲ A pocket dictionary and a calculator

ADDITIONAL INFORMATION
◆Are you currently employed? ☒ Yes ☐ No ◆May we contact your employer? ☒ Yes ☐ No ◆May we contact your former employers? ☒ Yes ☐ No
Can you (if accepted for employment) provide proof of your legal right to remain and work in the U.S.? ☒ Yes ☐ No
A separate affidavit on felony and misdemeanor convictions is REQUIRED to be completed on the attached form.
I hereby certify that all statements on this application are true and complete to the best of my knowledge and belief. If employed, I understand that any untrue statements on the above record may be considered grounds for termination.
Date *01/15/--*   Signature *Elizabeth S. Martinelli*

Figure 10-6: Applicant Statement

Check Your Work. Once you have completed an application, check it thoroughly for accuracy, neatness, completeness, and quality of answers. You will have completed a winning application if you can answer *yes* to the following questions:

▲ Did you follow all the directions?

▲ Did you print in black ink or key information correctly? (Black ink copies best.) Or, did you use a computerized application form and then print and check the final results carefully before submitting the application?

▲ Did you answer all the questions?

▲ Is the application completely free from errors?

▲ Did you use complete and accurate addresses in the references section?

▲ Is the content of every answer correct and well phrased?

▲ Does the application look attractive and neat?

▲ Did you sign and date the application?

Submit Your Application at the Appropriate Time

Turn in or mail an application to the appropriate person at the correct location. (Be sure to note if the application form has a deadline, and be careful to submit your application on time—or better yet, early!)

The best time to submit employment applications depends on the status of job openings with your prospective employers, whether the employers will give you applications ahead of time, and the employers' preferences. Once again, your research on the industry and prospective employers is essential.

"The only place where success comes before work is in a dictionary."
Vidal Sassoon

Resources for obtaining this information include current employees of the firms, the human resources departments of the firms, knowledgeable experts in the field, the area chambers of commerce, and your school's career services staff.

Unless your research indicates that an employer does not want candidates to submit unsolicited applications, obtain an application and submit it with your resume and cover letter. This shows that you have more initiative than applicants who don't bother to do this. Some employers consider the unsolicited submission of applications to be too pushy, however, so be sure to do your research first.

Complete Career Action 10-1

CAREER ACTION 10-1

Complete an Actual Application or a Sample Application

Directions: Using the guidelines presented in this chapter, print and complete the application for employment form on your Learner's CD. If at all possible, obtain and complete an actual application from an employer in your target industry—even one from your actual target employer. Using an application from your target industry provides the best preparation and practice. Complete the application for practice, and use it as a model when you fill out actual applications for employment.

File the application in your Career Management Files Binder.

Jump-Starting Your Cover Letter

Your cover letter introduces you to a prospective employer. It must be well written, be designed to get the reader's attention and interest, and provide information that convinces the reader to interview you and consider you for employment. Review the section on good writing style and organization in Chapter 9. These techniques also apply to writing a good cover letter.

Most employers expect a cover letter because it demonstrates the type of professionalism and initiative they want in an employee. Sending or taking your resume to an employer without a cover letter could cost you further consideration for employment.

Tailor the content of your cover letters to fit each employer. In addition, vary the content somewhat, depending on whether you are:

1. **Responding to an advertised opening for a specific job.** Figure 10-7 is an example of a cover letter responding to an advertised job opening.

2. **Contacting someone whom a member of your job search network has suggested (sending a networking cover letter).** See the example in Figure 10-8.

3. **Writing to a potential employer who has not advertised a job opening.** See the example in Figure 10-9. Note: A two-column comparison of the employer's

requirements and the applicant's matching experience is a highly effective technique!

Tailoring Your Letter

A cover letter should highlight your most important qualifications and stress how those qualifications can meet the employer's needs. Cover letters that are not tailored to meet an employer's needs are often eliminated. Customize every cover letter.

Demonstrate Your Knowledge of the Organization/Industry. Make your cover letter personal yet professional. Use your company research to personalize your letter. Mention your interest in a new or popular product of the organization; the expansion of the firm; recent organizational accomplishments; the company's reputation for reliability, quality, its product, or customer service; the firm's humanitarian efforts; or a special achievement of the person you're writing to or the organization in general.

Don't Overdo It. Don't use words that are too emotional for a business setting—for example, "I love to design computer graphics to enhance specialized publications." Say instead, "I recently read in *Advertising Age* about the award your organization won for Outstanding Use of Computer Graphics in a Specialty Catalog."

KIMI R. OKASAKI
148 Barrister Avenue, Tucson, AZ 85726
520-555-0136   kokasaki@provider.net

April 20, 20—

Mr. George O'Donnell
Office Manager
MegaMall Property Management Company
P.O. Box 555
Tucson, AZ 85726

Dear Mr. O'Donnell:

EXPERIENCED ADMINISTRATIVE ASSISTANT, JOB #4864

Please accept my application for the administrative assistant position advertised in last Sunday's edition of the *Arizona Bugle*. As a Scout Leader involved in a promotional project last fall, I appreciated MegaMall's offer to let us hold our event in the center of the mall at no charge. I would welcome the chance to work in such a civic-minded organization.

I am an energetic, detail-oriented person who has strong administrative and computer skills, retail and community service experience, and the ability to work well with people from all walks of life. In addition, I have held positions of responsibility in four community organizations over the last eight years and was chosen as the 2005 National Diabetes Foundation Volunteer of the Year.

As you can see from my resume, I thrive in a busy atmosphere that involves many different tasks, the opportunity to work with people, the satisfaction of meeting deadlines, and the chance to excel. I would enjoy the opportunity to talk with you about how I can help MegaMall Property Management with its administrative needs. I will call you next week to request an appointment, or you may call me at your convenience at the number above. Thank you for your consideration.

Sincerely,

Kimi Okasaki

Kimi Okasaki

Enclosure

Figure 10-7: Cover Letter Responding to an Advertised Job Opening

Juan Tejada
2440 Windom Way, Apt. 34
Los Angeles, CA 90063
213-555-0156   jtejada@provider.net

June 29, 20—

Ms. Stephanie Nolan
Manager, Auditing Staff
Nolan Henry O'Leary Public Accountants
1410 Granada Avenue, 7th Floor
San Francisco, CA 94115

Dear Ms. Nolan:

Meagan Gerena at Smythe and Associates indicated that you are interested in hiring an accounting graduate with experience in the field. My degree and special interest are in Accounting/Information Systems. Please consider me for a place on your well-respected auditing team, which the *San Francisco Business Reporter* recently named one of the Top 10 auditing firms in the area.

During the last two years, I have worked for a CPA firm where I was able to develop a wide range of accounting and accounting-related skills. My responsibilities included:

- Performing full-charge bookkeeper duties, such as opening, posting, and closing the books; completing federal and state corporate tax returns; and creating templates using Excel.
- Assisting a consultant in upgrading software for a customized accounting system.
- Creating a procedures manual that identified common operating, maintenance, and troubleshooting situations that could occur between the two operating systems and provided directions and steps for reconciling those problems in a timely and cost-effective way.

During my senior year at the University of Los Angeles, I had the chance to lead an internship research team. We studied the operations of a local accounting firm and assisted its auditors in the audit of several clients. These experiences cemented my interest in auditing as a career.

I am confident in my ability to make a positive contribution to Nolan Henry O'Leary Public Accountants and am enclosing my resume for your review. I will call next week about your interview schedule, or you may reach me at the contact information above. Thank you for your time and consideration.

Respectfully,

Juan Tejada

Juan Tejada

Enclosure

cc: Meagan Gerena, Smythe and Associates

Figure 10-8: Networking Cover Letter (Bullet Style)

CHRISTOPHER LIPSMEYER
846 Cameron Way
Phoenix, AZ 85012
(602) 555-0160   chris–lipsmeyer@provider.net

December 10, 20—

Mr. Gary Whaley
District Sales Manager
Computeriferals Company
1 Computer Way
Rallings City, NY 10099

Dear Mr. Whaley:

Computeriferals has earned my respect. I have used and repaired peripherals from most of the leading manufacturers in my studies as a Business Systems/Computer Repair major and in my job as a sales representative at ComputerChoice. I know you build quality products, and I want to sell quality products—Computeriferals.

Careful review of my qualifications and the requirements of a sales representative at Computeriferals suggests that I am well qualified for a sales position with your organization.

Your Requirements	**My Experience**
■ Ability to handle multiple prospects	■ Expanded customer base from 137 to 183 accounts in the past year—a 34 percent increase
■ Proven ability to meet sales goals	■ Increased yearly sales from $743,000 to $1,236,000—exceeded goal by 66 percent
■ Ability to expand sales in existing accounts	■ Negotiated a new $250,000 service contract for an existing client with five locations
■ Strong communication and follow-up skills	■ Attained 100 percent customer retention through a service-first approach and frequent communication

The expanding market for Computeriferals presents an appealing challenge. Even if you have no current sales openings, I would appreciate meeting with you to discuss your requirements. My resume is enclosed for your convenience. I will call next week to request an appointment, or you may reach me at the contact information above. Thank you for your time.

Respectfully,

Christopher Lipsmeyer

Christopher Lipsmeyer

Enclosure

Figure 10-9: Cover Letter Inquiring about an Unadvertised Position (Two-Column, Comparison-List Style)

Emphasize How You Can Meet the Employer's Needs. Identify in your cover letter the employer's needs that are outlined in the job opening announcements or advertisements. If your current job target deals only with accounting, a vague listing of accounting qualifications and computer specialization will not be as effective as a reference to strong accounting abilities (with the computer specialization referenced as a backup).

Also, if you are considering more than one position, such as an accounting technician and a computer specialist, highlight the appropriate skills, experience, and education for each job you are targeting.

Success Tip

Tailor your cover letter to the employer's needs, and make sure that it is error free. Applicants who write good letters stay in the running!

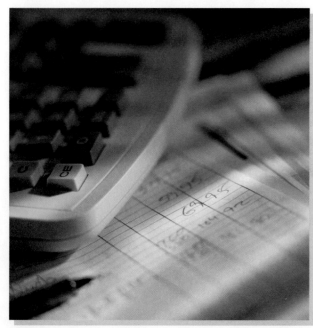

© GETTY IMAGES/PHOTODISC

In your cover letter, emphasize your specific skills and abilities that meet the employer's needs for the particular job.

Addressing Your Letter

Some organizations don't accept unsolicited applications, resumes, or cover letters. Often applicants who address communications to the human resources department get a form letter stating that no applications are currently being accepted.

Find Out Who Hires. To boost your chances of getting an interview, address your letter to the person who has hiring authority for the position (particularly the one who would be your supervisor—the department head, manager, or person who would supervise your work). Never address your cover letter "To Whom It May Concern." This type of salutation may target your letter for the wastebasket.

How do you get the right person's name? If you don't yet know who to address your cover letter to, consider one of these methods:

▲ Call your target employer and say that you are doing career research and want to address a letter of inquiry to the person who specializes in your career area. Get the person's full name and title, and verify the spelling and mailing address. When you call, introduce yourself, get the name of the person you talk with, and thank that person by name for his or her help. Always say that you are a student or are doing research. The person you speak to could possibly help you later, and using names establishes a courteous, friendly tone.

▲ Go to the human resources office (if your target employer has one). Ask whether there is an organizational chart you could use for your career planning class or personal research. The chart should provide you with the name of the department head to whom you should address your cover letter.

If this method seems inappropriate for your job search, ask members of your job search network to help you devise a workable approach. Use your creative ability and dare to be different, but always be courteous and professional.

Success Tip

Contacting the department head of your target job personally can get you in the door sooner.

The Human Resources Department or the Specific Department Head? If you send your cover letter and resume only to the human resources department, the person who heads the department you are interested in might never see them. On the other hand, if you send your letter and resume directly to the person you would work for, your chances of getting an interview will be greatly increased, but the human resources department may resent being circumvented.

How do you handle this situation? If the employer is accepting applications, send one letter and resume to the human resources department and one letter and resume to the department head. Indicate in your letters that you have sent similar communications to each party. At worst, both letters wind up in the human resources department. If the employer is not officially accepting applications, send your cover letter and resume to the department head only. If it is persuasive enough, you could still get an interview!

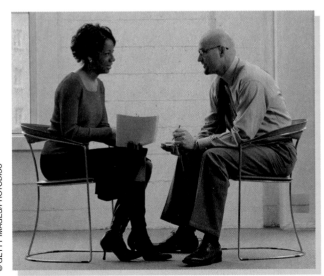

If you write a convincing cover letter, the employer will be eager to talk with you.

PERSONAL**BEST**

Writing Effective Cover Letters

▲ Create a positive first impression. The cover letter is the first thing that meets the reader's eye. Give it the same consideration and careful preparation as you do your resume.

▲ Use effective writing techniques, and project a friendly, energetic, and professional image.

▲ Address your letter to the appropriate person, and use his or her correct full name and title (no abbreviations except *Mr., Dr.,* and so on).

▲ Relate your qualifications to the needs and interests of the prospective employer. Emphasize what you can do for the organization.

▲ Don't use overblown or empty words to describe your abilities. Use specific, measurable terms; for example, "My program increased reported customer satisfaction by 35 percent."

▲ Project confidence in your qualifications, and show interest and enthusiasm for the job.

▲ If the job will likely require you to relocate, state your willingness to move.

▲ Emphasize your skills as a team player. Don't try to convince the employer that you are a one-person miracle worker.

▲ Incorporate specialized terminology from your industry and job target where appropriate.

▲ Use a word processor, and print your letter on high-quality paper. Format your letter in an acceptable business style.

▲ Hand-sign every cover letter.

▲ Be certain the final letter is perfect—no errors! Proofread and proofread again!

© GETTY IMAGES/PHOTODISC

Developing Winning Cover Letter Content

Be courteous to the employer by keeping your cover letter brief (four or five paragraphs—no longer than one page). Be sure your cover letter does not duplicate exactly the data in your resume. (What busy employer wants to read the same thing twice?) Also make sure that the contents of your resume and cover letter do not contain contradictions.

Content of a Cover Letter

Follow these guidelines to ensure that your cover letter has winning content:

▲ If you had any previous communication with the person you're writing to, refer to that communication to help him or her remember you.

▲ If you have a contact who knows the person you are writing to, mention your contact's name in the letter.

▲ Explain how you learned of and why you are interested in the employer, and state the type of position you are seeking.

▲ Include at least one sentence that shows your knowledge of the company. This demonstrates initiative and interest.

▲ Emphasize your qualifications for the job. Include two to four results-oriented descriptions of accomplishments and capabilities that show how you can benefit the employer and handle the job.

▲ State that your resume is enclosed.

▲ Include a request for a meeting or an interview (not a bid for a job), even if no openings are available now.

▲ Include a courteous closing sentence.

The Opening

Begin by introducing yourself and stating your purpose. Explain how you know of the employer and why you are interested in the particular organization. State the type of job you are seeking.

If you are responding to an announced job opening, mention the position you are applying for and explain how or where you heard about it. If you learned about the opening through an advertisement or announcement, include the date of the notice and where you found it (newspaper, Internet job posting, professional journal, employment agency, or the company's human resources department).

If you know someone who would be influential and recognized by the reader, get that person's permission and reference his or her name in your letter.

The following excerpt is from a networking cover letter sent by Kimi Okasaki, who is seeking an administrative support position. Kimi mentions the name of a person who is well known to the addressee.

> "Carmine Garduno from the Health Services Bureau recommended that I talk with you about the possibility that you may need an administrative support person with experience in educational and community activities. Your new five-year educational and community plan is soundly developed. I believe my five years of experience as a volunteer in the Valley Elementary School Parent-Teacher Organization (VES-PTO) and the Diabetes Foundation would be useful in helping you achieve success in the plan."

Your Sales Pitch

This section of the cover letter focuses on your qualifications for the job. Make this paragraph a results-oriented summary of your assets, specifically highlighting two to four accomplishments that demonstrate your suitability for the job. You must be able to verify these accomplishments with evidence. Do not duplicate information exactly from your resume. Whenever possible, use bullets to highlight the qualifications you most want to emphasize to capture the reader's attention, as shown in the letter in Figure 10-8. A short paragraph explaining your accomplishments, as shown below, is also suitable.

> "Through my volunteer work, I learned about the disease-prevention techniques your department teaches to day-care workers. The potential to combine helping families, defeating disease, and doing work I enjoy is irresistible. I recently completed an Associate in Science

degree, majoring in Information Management Technology, with an overall GPA of 3.5. As Secretary-Treasurer of the VES-PTO, I used Excel and Word to generate and merge letters and address labels for 500 student families."

Another effective way to highlight your qualifications is in a two-column, side-by-side comparison of the employer's requirements and your experience. This style is sometimes referred to as comparison-list style or a T-letter. The cover letter in Figure 10-9 illustrates the comparison-list style. This format is attractive and reader-friendly and makes your qualifications stand out.

The Closing

In the closing, ask for a meeting or an interview—not a job. Research shows that an active close (in which you say that you will call to request a meeting or an interview) leads to more interviews. A passive close (in which you request that the reader call you), however, can lead to higher-quality interviews and may prevent the reader from putting your letter aside to wait for your call. A third approach, which is used below, combines the strengths of both styles.

"Enclosed for your review is my resume. I would appreciate meeting with you and discussing the possibility of our working together. I will call you on Thursday to check on your availability, or you may reach me at 555-0136. I would welcome the

Success Tip

In your cover letter, state the position you are applying for, highlight your related capabilities, and request a meeting or an interview.

opportunity to contribute to the community outreach efforts of the Department of Disease Prevention.

Sincerely,
Kimi Okasaki"

Complete Career Action 10-2 and 10-3

Personal Review and Edit of Your Letter

Review and edit your cover letter draft by using the colored pen system recommended for the development of your resume. Be choosy—or downright hypercritical—about the words you use. Every word counts!

Outside Critical Review

Ask a member of your network who has strong communication skills and knows your background to critique your letter. Most people find it difficult to critique their own resumes and cover letters because they overlook important aspects (such as punctuation, omission of details, and so on) while concentrating on the wording. Your critic may think of additional items you should include that you have overlooked. Sources for outside reviewers and critics include:

▲ **A hiring expert you know** who can tell you how your cover letter stacks up against the ones he or she reviews and how you can improve yours.

▲ **A professional friend or acquaintance** who knows you and your work well enough to help you clarify confusing statements or to spot where you have omitted or neglected to emphasize important information or qualifications.

▲ **A professional who does not know you well** to serve as a final test for your cover letter; he or she must read the letter to learn about you. Choose a good writer who will give you honest criticism, not someone who will automatically say the letter is "fine." You want solid suggestions for improvement.

Complete Career Action 10-4

CAREER ACTION 10-2

Use the Internet to Research Cover Letter Strategies

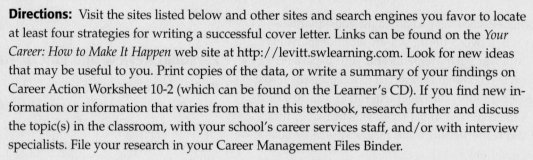

Directions: Visit the sites listed below and other sites and search engines you favor to locate at least four strategies for writing a successful cover letter. Links can be found on the *Your Career: How to Make It Happen* web site at http://levitt.swlearning.com. Look for new ideas that may be useful to you. Print copies of the data, or write a summary of your findings on Career Action Worksheet 10-2 (which can be found on the Learner's CD). If you find new information or information that varies from that in this textbook, research further and discuss the topic(s) in the classroom, with your school's career services staff, and/or with interview specialists. File your research in your Career Management Files Binder.

Monster
(Click on "Get Career Advice.")

CareerLab
(Click on "Cover Letter Library.")

CareerJournal.com
(Enter "cover letter" in search window.)

JobStar

Gary Will's WorkSearch

Quintessential Careers
(Click on the "Featured Career Article" link, "Career Articles," and "entire catalog of articles.")

The Riley Guide

CAREER ACTION 10-3

Create a Cover Letter Outline and Draft

Part A: Access Career Action Worksheet 10-3 on your Learner's CD or use the worksheet that begins on page 193 to organize and outline your basic cover letter (keeping in mind it should be tailored to fit each employer's needs). Don't try to write a perfect letter at this point; just work on getting the essence of your message on paper. You will refine it later. Review the sample cover letters provided in Figures 10-7, 10-8, and 10-9 for guidance.

Part B: Using your cover letter outline and related job target research information, compose a cover letter draft. Make it concise, tailored to the employer's needs, and courteous. Most importantly, make sure it demonstrates how you can benefit the employer. File your draft in your Career Management Files Binder.

CAREER ACTION 10-4

Prepare Your Final Cover Letter

Directions: Polish your cover letter draft, emphasizing your qualifications and making the content clear and concise. Use a thesaurus to find words with just the right shades of meaning. As you prepare your final cover letter, remember that, just as with a resume:

IT MUST BE PERFECT!

After your cover letter is complete, review it with thorough attention to detail; even one error can eliminate you in the employer's paper screening.

When you think your letter is perfect, ask an outside critic to review it one more time slowly and carefully, looking for even the smallest error. This is critical to the success of your cover letter. Print the final letter on top-quality paper.

File a copy of your final cover letter in your Career Management Files Binder.

Distributing Your Complete Job Search Paper Package

Once you have completed your resume and cover letter and know how to complete an employment application, you will be ready to submit a solid job search paper package (application, resume, and cover letter).

How you distribute your job search documents is also important. Consider the following tips regarding distribution:

▲ **Regular Mail.** If you mail your documents, put them in a large envelope so you don't have to fold them. If the employer faxes or scans your letter after receiving it, any folds in the paper can cause errors in the process.

▲ **E-Mail or Fax.** Some employers may specify that they want you to e-mail or fax the documents; do what they say! Follow the e-mail guidelines provided in Chapter 9.

Preparing an Electronic Cover Letter

The emergence of the electronic job market has created the need for the electronic resume discussed in Chapter 9. In addition, many employers require electronic cover letters to be transmitted through e-mail or posted on their web sites.

Listed below are some of the key strategies for preparing and writing an electronic cover letter:

1. **Stick with a plain style of text.** Even if your e-mail allows you to enhance the appearance of the text, keep it simple and plain. Use an easily readable font, such as Verdana or Georgia, in black and 12-point size, and make sure the background is plain and white.

2. **Make sure the lines have no more than 65 characters.** If your line length is longer than this, you risk the text fragmenting unevenly on multiple lines on the receiver's screen.

3. **Keep your cover letter concise, but clear.** Your e-mail cover letter should be only two to three paragraphs and under 150 words. It should reveal your interest and sell the target employer on one or two of your outstanding capabilities.

4. **Follow standard business letter guidelines.** Even though e-mail is less formal than a paper letter, you should not omit parts of the letter such as the salutation or closing.

5. **Entice readers with your subject line.** Always include a brief, but informative, subject line. The subject line of your e-mail should stimulate the reader to continue reading your letter. Consider a subject line such as, "Experienced CPA for Auditing Director" rather than "Re: Job No. 3872."

6. **Make the most of keywords.** Focus on keywords and skill sets that will increase the chances of your letter being retrieved in a database search. Because of the possibility of a database search, it is more important to use noun phrases than action verbs in an electronic cover letter.

7. **Provide sufficient contact information to the prospective employer.** This includes your name, address, and phone number.

8. **Do not attach files to an e-mail cover letter.** Some organizations actually block e-mails that contain attachments.

9. **Follow company guidelines, and submit only what they ask for.** Check the company's web site for guidelines rather than risk sending something they don't want.

10. **Proofread.** Spell check and proofread again before you hit the send button.

Transmit your electronic cover letter in one of two ways: (1) copy and paste it into your e-mail program, and send it to the employer as an e-mail message or (2) paste it into the cover letter block in the job application section of the employer's web site. Regardless of which way the letter is sent, if it is not well written, it will not arrive at its intended destination: the hiring desk.

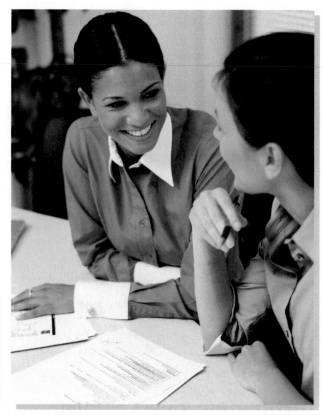

© GETTY IMAGES/PHOTODISC

Ask a member of your network who has strong communication skills to critique your cover letter carefully.

Success Tip

Format electronic cover letters to transmit correctly: Follow the employer's instructions, and save as plain text.

Maximizing Your Online Job Search

The following six steps explain how to conduct a savvy online job search.

Step 1: Define Your Specific Job Target

To access the job listings and/or post a resume on most job recruitment sites, applicants must first complete a registration or resume posting form. The applicant/job matching software used by most job listing sites requires applicant information to match to the job openings:

▲ **Keywords.** These are search terms describing the type of job you are seeking. Use terms that describe the skills, experience, and abilities you have that are required in jobs you want to pursue.

▲ **Desired employment industry.** You will typically be asked to specify the industry in which you are seeking employment.

▲ **Geographical preference.** You will need to specify one or more geographical areas in which you would like to work.

▲ **Desired salary.** Some sites require that you include the salary range you are seeking.

Step 2: Get the Edge With Employer/Industry Research

Performing employer and industry research is well worth your time for several reasons: Research demonstrates initiative on your part; employers prefer to hire people who know about their organizations; research provides common-ground information that helps you communicate easily and knowledgeably with interviewers; and research helps you avoid choosing a job that is not right for you.

Step 3: Prepare Electronic Resume/Cover Letter and Web Resume/Portfolio

You will definitely need a well-prepared electronic resume and cover letter. If appropriate for your career field, you may also want to develop a web resume and web portfolio. See Chapter 9 for details on the development and transmission of these.

Step 4: Find Online Job Listings

Many good job listing sites are available on the Internet. Resources for finding these include employers' web sites (the best resource, if available—try entering the name of an employer followed by *.com* in your Internet browser); the *Your Career: How to Make It Happen* web site (see "Job recruitment links" on the "Links" page); and the "Job Listings" section of The Riley Guide site (see the *Your Career* web site).

Step 5: Apply Online

Job listing and employer sites vary. Some require applicants to paste their resumes into an open resume block. Others require applicants to build their resumes online. Still others require the completion of an online application only—no resume is required in this case. Follow each web site's instructions exactly. See Chapter 9 for more details about submitting resumes online. Before you hit the transmit, send, or submit button, print copies of all forms you have completed, proofread them carefully, and make any needed corrections. Reprint if corrections were made; then file your final forms as a reference.

Step 6: Follow Up

Get the edge on your competition by following up as outlined below.

▲ **Call the employer directly.** Ask for the human resources department, and state that you are responding to the company's online job advertisement. (Give the source of the ad, the date, the job number, and so on.) If you have applied online, ask for the name, phone number, and mailing and e-mail addresses of the hiring decision maker.

▲ Call and/or send an e-mail to the decision maker. Let him or her know of your application and interest in the job.

Review the key steps for online job application illustrated in Figure 10-10.

Tapping Into Your Network for Job Leads

Employers base their hiring decisions largely on trust. They are most likely to hire people they know or who are referred by people they know. For this reason, your job search network is the No. 1 source of solid job leads.

Step	Action	Process
1	**Define your job target** so you can complete job search forms on recruitment sites.	Identify keywords you can provide in keyword fields for job matches on recruitment sites. Identify your preferred geographical locations, employment industry, and salary range (if required).
2	**Research employers.**	Review Chapter 8, "Research Prospective Employers." Research employers' web sites. See the "Links" pages on the *Your Career: How to Make It Happen* web site for employer, salary, and relocation information.
3	**Prepare an electronic resume and cover letter.** Also prepare a web resume and e-portfolio, if appropriate for your job target.	Prepare and transmit properly formatted electronic resumes and cover letters tailored to each employer's needs, including targeted keywords (see Chapter 9). If appropriate, prepare a web resume and an online portfolio.
4	**Find online job listings.**	Check employers' web sites. Check job listing sites. See the "Links" pages on the *Your Career: How to Make It Happen* web site.
5	**Apply online.**	Follow the sites' job application instructions carefully. Register or fill out the access screens on job listing sites with your job target information (Step 1 above). Post your electronic resume and cover letter as required by the sites. Before submitting the final online application, print a copy for your files.
6	**Follow up, if possible.**	Call the employer; indicate that you have applied online to a specific job ad. Contact the decision maker, if possible.

Figure 10-10: Key Steps for Online Job Application

Networking Process

Once you complete your job search package, contact your network to expand your employment options. Because network members are statistically the strongest source of job leads, they can form the bridge to your perfect job. Follow the networking guidelines below for best results. They are listed in order of preference for maximum results.

1. **Make an appointment to meet in person.** Make appointments with the most viable of your networking members. Appointments get the best results. In each meeting, briefly review your job objective and ask for recommendations. Give each person a copy of your cover letter and resume, asking for feedback on the content and quality. Be organized; respect the person's time.

2. **Make a telephone call.** If you can't arrange an appointment, make a telephone call. Briefly review your job objective and ask for recommendations. Ask whether you can send a copy of your cover letter and resume to get your contact's feedback.

3. **Send a networking letter.** If you can't arrange a meeting or reach the person by telephone, send a networking letter (see instructions below).

Networking Letter

A networking letter tells your network about your job search goals and requests specific help with the process. It contains a basic informational core and personalized comments tailored to the recipient. The employment success rate from networking letters is high.

Your networking letters should include the following features:

▲ A friendly, enthusiastic, and confident tone

▲ A professional format with no errors

▲ A complete but concise message that clearly identifies your job target and job search goals

▲ A request for specific help

▲ A reference to your resume

Tailor your networking letters by considering the individual strengths of your network members. Ask a good writer for advice on improving your resume. Ask for help in identifying specific employers or finding direct job leads. You can also request meetings with some network members to brainstorm strategies.

Following Up With a Telephone Call

Applicants who follow up by calling employers after sending cover letters and resumes are dramatically more successful in obtaining jobs. Two important reasons for this are (1) employers see follow-up as an indication of initiative and confidence, and (2) a busy employer may actually intend to call an applicant but get sidetracked. Applicants who call save the employer time and often speed the hiring decision.

Call about three or four days after the employer receives your letter, and say something like this: "This is Jennifer Ortiz calling from Raleigh. I sent you a letter and resume regarding the system support programming job and wanted to make sure you received it." This simple telephone call is often a deciding factor in getting an interview. Improve your odds by making this call.

Success Tip

After sending your job search package, follow up with a telephone call to increase your chances of securing an interview.

CHECKLIST

PERFECTING APPLICATIONS AND COVER LETTERS

Check each of the actions you are currently taking to increase your career success:

○ Making your applications perfect

○ Tailoring your cover letters to specific employers; making sure the cover letters are error free

○ Stating the position you are applying for, listing your related abilities, and requesting a meeting or an interview

○ Formatting your electronic cover letters correctly

○ Distributing a complete job search paper package or maximizing your online job search process

○ Using the networking process to find solid job leads— via appointments, telephone calls, and networking letters

○ Following up your cover letters with telephone calls

CRITICAL THINKING QUESTIONS

1. What are the possible consequences of not filling out an employment application completely and according to the instructions?

2. Should you mention a salary figure in an application? Explain.

3. Think of a probable employer with whom you would like to interview. How can you find out to whom you should address your cover letter? Write the name, title, and address of the person in your answer.

4. What are at least three features of an electronic cover letter?

For convenient access to valuable career resources, activities, and job information links, visit the companion web site for this text: *http://levitt.swlearning.com*

CAREER ACTION WORKSHEET 10-3

Create a Cover Letter Outline and Draft

Part A: Cover Letter Outline

Your Personal Letterhead: _____

(Include name, address, _____

phone number, and e-mail.) _____

_____

_____

Date: _____

Name, Title, Organization, _____

and Address of Recipient: _____

_____

_____

_____

Salutation: Dear _____

_____:

Paragraph 1, _____

Opening: _____

(Include the name _____

of a referral if _____

you have one; _____

state your _____

position _____

objective.) _____

_____

_____

_____

Continued on next page >>>

CAREER ACTION WORKSHEET 10-3 (continued)

Paragraph 2,

Your Sales

Pitch:

(Tailor it to

the opening.

Where appropriate,

use bullets or side-by-side

columns to

highlight strong

job-relevant

qualifications.)

Paragraph 3,

Closing:

(State that

your resume is

enclosed and

request a meeting or an

interview. Include

your telephone

number or refer to the

contact information in your

letterhead. Thank the reader.)

Complimentary   Sincerely,

Close:

_____

(Key your name here.)

INTERVIEW LIKE A PRO

In this chapter, you will:

- Prepare appropriate interview responses to demonstrate enthusiasm and interest in a position and an organization.

- Identify nonverbal behaviors that will enhance your interview performance.

- Prepare a 60-Second Commercial for an Interview.

- Identify the core elements of successful interviewing and ways to succeed in an interview.

- Summarize the fine points for interview success that are applicable to your job search and career planning.

 Use the Internet to locate interview strategies and summarize your findings.

> *"I am constantly interviewing potential candidates for all kinds of positions. My advice is to really listen in an interview. If you don't understand a question, ask the interviewer to clarify exactly what he or she is looking for instead of just trying to talk, hoping you've answered the question."*
>
> Beth C. Hare
> Fidelity Search Group, Inc.

You have learned how to present yourself well on paper through the application, cover letter, and resume. Now for the main event: the job interview. The practical interview techniques presented in this chapter work. They are based on widespread, ongoing research with professional interviewers who represent diverse employment fields and organizations. Research also includes the thorough review and testing of successful job-seeking program techniques.

Know the Core Elements of Successful Interviewing

You are screened into an interview because you appear qualified on paper. The employer uses the interview to learn whether you have the personal qualities needed to fit into the organization and to further confirm your work performance qualifications.

The First 30 Seconds Count

People often form opinions about others within 30 seconds of first meeting them! For this reason, the first 30 seconds can make or break an interview. Interviewers say they form strong opinions about an applicant in the time it takes the applicant to walk across the room, say "Hello," and sit down. Read on to learn how to make those 30 seconds work for you!

Interview and interpersonal communications experts have studied what applicants can do to make a favorable first impression and to best project professionalism and competence during interviews. They report that the attitudes, image, and appearance applicants project during interviews are as influential as their skills in getting ahead. Projecting strength in these areas gives job applicants a decided edge over their competition, as you can see in Figure 11-1.

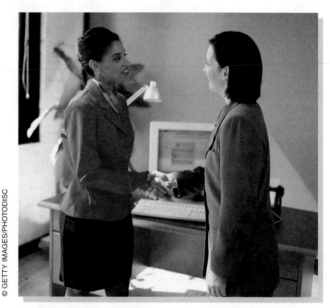

© GETTY IMAGES/PHOTODISC

Be at your best from the moment you arrive at an inteview. The first 30 seconds count!

Applicants Are Screened on Paper First

You are selected to interview on the basis of your resume, cover letter, and application. Employers request these beforehand so they can review your education, work experience, and qualifications and compare them with those of other applicants. Employers don't have time during interviews to evaluate this information in detail.

The Interview Focuses on You as a Person

One main purpose of the interview is for the employer to get to know the applicant as a person. Your image and appearance are the first things the interviewer will evaluate, and a first impression can influence the entire interview. Your attitude (the essence of your personality), however, is the biggest factor determining your success in the interview. Job qualifications also count during the interview, and your responsibility is to summarize them well.

Your Attitude—The No. 1 Factor

Attitude is the No. 1 factor that influences an employer to hire. Following are ways you can exhibit a good attitude:

Impact on Interviews	
Areas:	Approximate Impact on Interview:
1. Attitude	40 percent
2. Image and Appearance	25 percent
3. Communication (verbal/nonverbal)	25 percent
4. Job Qualifications	10 percent

Figure 11-1: Impact on Interviews

1. **Concentrate on being likable.** As simple as this may seem, research proves that one of the most essential goals in successful interviewing is to be liked by the interviewer. Interviewers want to hire pleasant people whom others will enjoy working with on a daily basis. Do the following to project that you are highly likable (these actions are detailed later in this chapter):

   ▲ Be friendly, courteous, and enthusiastic.

   ▲ Speak positively.

   ▲ Use positive body language and smile.

   ▲ Make certain your appearance is appropriate.

2. **Project an air of confidence and pride.** Act as though you want and deserve the job—not as though you are desperate.

3. **Demonstrate enthusiasm.** An applicant's level of enthusiasm often influences the employer as much as any other interviewing factor. The applicant who demonstrates little enthusiasm for a job will never be selected for the position.

4. **Demonstrate knowledge of and interest in the employer.** Saying "I really want this job" is not convincing enough. Explain why you want the position and how the position fits into your career plans. You can cite opportunities that may be unique to the firm or emphasize your skills and education that are highly relevant to the position.

5. **Perform at your best every moment.** There is no such thing as "time out" during an interview. While in the waiting area, treat the assistant or receptionist courteously; learn and use his or her name. (An interviewer often requests this person's opinion of the applicants.)

6. **Remember: An interview is a two-way street.** Project genuine interest in determining whether you and the employer can mutually benefit from your employment.

Success Tip

Project enthusiasm and a positive attitude in interviews. Often a less experienced applicant with more enthusiasm for a job is hired over competitors who are more qualified but less enthusiastic.

Complete Career Action 11-1

Image and Appearance

Have you ever looked at a display of CDs or books and been drawn to one with an appealing cover? The same concept applies in interviews. Remember: By the time you have walked into the room and sat down, the interviewer has decided whether you will be considered for the position. Your image and appearance help determine the first impression you make and may count for as much as 25 percent of the employer's positive or negative hiring decision.

CAREER ACTION 11-1

Project Enthusiasm, Positive Attitude, and Interest

Directions: Access Career Action Worksheet 11-1 on your Learner's CD or use a separate sheet of paper to complete this assignment. Prepare a list of statements you can use in an interview that demonstrate sincere enthusiasm and interest in the job, company, and other relevant aspects of your target employer. Back up your statements by referring to your research.

File your worksheet in your Career Management Files Binder.

Know How the Outer Package Helps the Sale.

Cosmetic firms are well aware of the impact of the package; some people spend six times as much for the package as they do for the product inside! Products that are packaged attractively far outsell those that are not.

Dress Conservatively.

Most interviewers expect applicants to wear businesslike clothes when they apply for office or professional positions. For men and women, a conservative suit of quality fabric is generally appropriate. For women, a conservative, tailored dress or coordinated skirt and blouse with a matching jacket are also appropriate. In some cases, women who wear slacks to an interview lower their chances of being hired.

Whenever possible, visit your target employer before the interview to observe the working atmosphere, conditions, and dress code. Use this information to determine how to dress for your interview. A word of caution: Even if the employer permits casual dress on the job, you should demonstrate initiative and enhance your professional image by dressing more formally for the important business meeting—your interview. This projects respect for the employer, which increases your likability.

Appear Clean, Pressed, and Perfectly Groomed.

Make sure your clothes are clean, pressed, in good repair, comfortable, and well fitted. (Clothing or shoes that are too tight restrict comfortable, poised movement.) Visit top-notch clothing stores, and get help from experienced salespeople in selecting a coordinated interview outfit. You don't have to buy your outfit in an expensive store; you can usually duplicate it closely in a less expensive shop. Be immaculately groomed from head to toe. Be a model of cleanliness, and always use a deodorant: "Never let 'em see you sweat!"

Use Color to Your Advantage.

Color is the most dynamic tool for dressing to enhance your appearance. Learn which colors best complement your skin, eyes, and hair. A good way to do this is to note when you receive compliments on a color you wear.

Traditionally, blue and gray are reliable color choices for interview suits, jackets, slacks, and skirts. Strengthen your image by using your best colors in your accessories—scarves, ties, shirts, blouses, and so on.

Research Dress Expectations.

A business suit is not appropriate for every interview. Base your clothing choice on your employer and career field research. Would a sport coat and dress slacks be more appropriate for your target employer, or would less formal slacks and a neat shirt and tie be better? Would a skirt and blouse be more in line with the target employer? Never dress too casually. T-shirts, jeans, tennis shoes, and other casual or faddish items cost applicants the job.

Success Tip

Smile and project professionalism. Dress and groom yourself neatly and appropriately.

Cover Tattoos, and Lose the Nose Ring and Baseball Cap.

If you try to make a bold statement against business-world conformity, you can probably kiss the job good-bye. People who sport visible tattoos or body piercings; unnatural hair or makeup styles; ball caps; or too many earrings, bracelets, or rings to an interview might as well stay home. Many organizations have grooming policies that prohibit radical hairstyles and visible body piercings and tattoos. In a recent Vault.com survey, 58 percent of managers reported that they would be less likely to hire an applicant with visible tattoos and body piercings. Show employers that you conduct yourself professionally and dress accordingly.

Review the pictures of job applicants on page 199. Based on their outfits, which applicant do you think is more likely to get a job in a professional business or office setting? Why?

Look Alert!

Being well-rested projects a healthy, alert image; get plenty of sleep the night before an interview. Taking good care of yourself with a healthy diet, exercise, and adequate rest is an important lifetime investment in a successful career.

Even though casual attire may be appropriate for some business offices, it is inappropriate when interviewing for a business or office position.

A conservative suit is appropriate when interviewing for a business or office position.

Smile! Nothing leaves a better impression of likability than a pleasant smile at the point of meeting the interviewer and throughout the interview.

Verbal Communication

Start your verbal communication off right by using the interviewer's name in your greeting. This conveys respect, which enhances your likability. (In some cases, more than one person will interview you at a time. See Chapter 13, "Be Prepared for Any Interview Style.") Learn and use the names of everyone who will be interviewing you.

State Your Name and the Position You're Seeking. When you enter the interviewer's office, begin with a friendly greeting and state the position you're interviewing for: "Hello, Ms. Levine, I'm Bella Reyna. I'm here to interview for the accounting position." If someone has already introduced you to the interviewer, simply say, "Good morning, Ms. Levine." Identifying the position is important because interviewers often interview for many different positions.

Use a Pleasant Tone of Voice. It isn't always what you say that creates a positive or negative reflection of your attitude, but how you say it. Using a pleasant tone of voice (friendly, courteous, and energetic) also enhances your likability.

Record Yourself for Practice. Ask a friend to conduct a practice interview with you to evaluate your tone of voice. Have your friend ask you some of the sample questions from Chapter 14. Tape your questions and answers, and listen to them; then decide where you can improve. If your voice is high-pitched, work on lowering it; if you speak too softly, increase your volume; and so on. Above all, speak in a warm tone with energy.

Focus on How You Fit the Job. Near the beginning of an interview, as soon as it seems appropriate, ask a question similar to this: "Could you describe the scope of the job and tell me what capabilities are most important in filling the position?" The interviewer's response will help you focus on emphasizing your qualifications that best match the needs of the employer.

Use Positive Words and Phrases. One of the most important interview goals is to keep the content completely positive so the interviewer's final impression is "Yes, this is the person for the job!" Use a positive vocabulary, and eliminate all negative terms.

Emphasize Your Strengths—Even When Discussing an Error You Have Made. Emphasize your strengths and abilities that are relevant to the job. Although you want to avoid bringing up past short-comings, do not try to dodge one that comes out during an interview. Face it head-on, and explain what you learned from the experience. Turn a potential negative into a positive by demonstrating that you learn from your mistakes.

> *"Remember that a person's name is, to that person, the sweetest sound in any language."*
>
> Dale Carnegie

If the interviewer asks you about the circumstances of an error you made, explain briefly; don't make excuses or blame others. Remember: The interviewer is human too and has probably made his or her share of mistakes. You will create a better impression by being honest, candid, and sincere.

Do not lie during an interview, and be prepared to state why you left previous employment if you're asked. Do not speak unfavorably about your former supervisor or firm. Interviewers may believe that you would do the same after leaving their companies. Maintain your business and professional integrity throughout the interview.

Speak Correctly. Grammatical errors can cost applicants the job. Use correct grammar; word choice; and a businesslike vocabulary, not an informal, chatty one. Avoid slang, and *never* use profanity or derogatory terms. When under stress, people often use pet phrases (such as "like" and "you know") too often. This is highly annoying and projects immaturity and insecurity. Ask a friend or family member to help you identify any speech weaknesses you have. Begin eliminating these poor speech habits now.

Avoid Credibility Robbers. Avoid using words and phrases that rob you of credibility and make you sound indecisive or unbelievable. Eliminate the following credibility robbers from your vocabulary:

▲ ***Just* or *only*.** Used as follows, "I *just* worked as a waiter" or "I *only* worked there on a part-time basis" implies that you are not proud of your work or that you don't consider the work meaningful. All work is meaningful; it demonstrates initiative. Leave out these credibility robbers.

    ▲ ***I guess.*** This makes you sound uncertain—definitely not the image you want to project!

    ▲ ***Little.*** Don't belittle your accomplishments, as in "This is a little report/project I wrote/developed."

▲ ***Probably.*** This suggests unnecessary doubt: "The technique I developed would *probably* be useful in your department." This statement sounds more convincing: "I believe the technique I developed would be useful in your department."

This is a small sample of words and phrases that can diminish your image, but it is designed to illustrate the concept of credibility robbers. Ask members of your support system to help you identify other verbal credibility robbers and to remind you when you use them.

Meet Business Etiquette Expectations. Business etiquette refers to expected professional behavior in business, and it is based on courtesy and cultural norms. Etiquette blunders include leaving your cell phone ringer on during a business meeting and licking gravy off your fingers during a business lunch. Appropriate business etiquette is important in conducting global business successfully; an unintentional etiquette breach can quickly squash a delicate international transaction. For example, in Asia, presenting a business card using only one hand is considered rude.

Business etiquette is a key factor in hiring. Your behavior in an interview gives your potential employer clues to how you'll treat clients and customers. For example, during an interview lunch, one applicant lost the job when he wiped his nose with his napkin. Any error in etiquette can cost you the job during an interview situation.

Etiquette expectations are getting more attention in the interview process. To learn more about this topic, conduct an Internet search for current tips on business etiquette.

Heed These Additional Tips. The following are additional tips for effective communication in an interview:

▲ **Keep the interview businesslike.** Do not discuss personal, domestic, or financial problems. The purpose of the interview is to explore how well your qualifications and interests match the needs of the employer. This is where you need to focus your remarks.

▲ **Try to demonstrate a sense of humor.** Most employers look for job applicants with a sense of humor. Humor is an important factor in working well with other people and is a sign of intelligence. Use humor only when appropriate, however, and don't tell jokes; they're not suitable for an interview. Never use profanity or off-color humor. Making yourself the subject of the humor is usually safe, but be careful not to make yourself look bad.

▲ **Don't ramble.** Be concise—but not curt—with your replies. Rambling is frequently a nervous response. Answer questions with required information, adding anything you think is relevant or especially important; then stop talking or ask your own question.

▲ **Focus on your goal.** Keep coming back to the main purpose of the interview: determining how you and the employer can mutually benefit from your employment. If the conversation strays too far from this subject, bring it back in the right direction. Get feedback from the interviewer to determine how you're coming across. Stop and ask: "Do you think my skills in that area would be helpful to you?" If the answer is yes, you know you're on the right track. If the answer is no or unclear, clarify how you are qualified for the job.

> ## Success Tip
>
> Keep your verbal communication positive, focused on how you fit the job, and courteous.

Body Language

Through life experiences, people become experts at sending and interpreting nonverbal messages. Nonverbal communication, or body language, is powerful. A severe frown can melt the warmest smile; a yawn during a speech speaks for itself. What emotions or qualities do you associate with these behaviors: (a) hands on hips and glaring face, (b) extreme fidgeting, (c) lack of eye contact, (d) slouched posture, (e) uplifted posture, (f) pleasant smile, (g) limp handshake?

See How Body Language Packs a Punch! Body language has the greatest impact of the three sources of communication (verbal communication, voice qualities, and nonverbal communication); it carries more influence than the words you say. To succeed in interviews, keep your body language positive.

During an interview, your body language is a major factor. If you speak persuasively but your body language conveys arrogance, lack of enthusiasm, excessive nervousness, or other negative messages, the interviewer typically will be more influenced by your negative body language than by what you say.

In face-to-face communication, the three elements that affect the listener or receiver are verbal communication, voice qualities, and nonverbal communication. The impact of each is illustrated in Figure 11-2. Because body language affects communication so greatly, you should focus on sending positive nonverbal messages to maximize your interview effectiveness.

Even though words have the smallest impact in communication, the content of your speech must be appropriate for the situation. (This is where your research pays off.) You must also speak correctly (to project professionalism and competence). A glaring grammatical error could vaporize your chances for a job.

Use Positive Body Language to Your Advantage.

Follow the easy body language pointers below. They will speak well for you during your job search and will help you achieve important goals throughout your career. Also pay attention to the body language of others.

1. **Relax.** If you're tense, your body language will project that tension.

   a. Most importantly, be well rested for the interview so you will be alert.

   b. Complete your research on the industry, organization, and interviewer ahead of time. Stop preparing the night before the interview; at that point, relax and let your preparation pay off the next day.

   c. On the day of the interview, exercise; do some stretching, running, or yoga, for example. Exercise is one of nature's best techniques for relaxing your body and your mind. Be sure to allot adequate time in your day to do some form of exercise prior to an interview. You will have more energy and feel more relaxed. Also, fuel yourself with a light, healthy meal before an interview so you won't feel hungry or tired.

   d. During the interview, occasionally change your position in your seat; this relaxes muscular body tension and breaks the rigid feeling that nervousness can cause.

   e. Don't hurry your movements, and breathe deeply to aid relaxation. This will help you project confidence and will also reduce your anxiety.

   f. Smile—it's an effective tension breaker (for you and the interviewer)!

   g. Visualize your success in detail. Project enthusiasm and likability; concentrate on your capabilities.

2. **Give a firm handshake.** Because touch is the keenest physical sense, your handshake will greatly bolster or detract from your credibility. The best handshake is firm and is accompanied by confident eye contact and a pleasant smile.

3. **Make eye contact.** Making good eye contact is essential to achieving effective communication. It conveys that you really care about what the person has to say. It also conveys confidence, intelligence, competence, and honesty. This doesn't mean that you should glue your eyes to the interviewer; it means that you should look at the interviewer, especially when he or she is talking. Break the eye contact at natural points in the discussion. Avoid letting your eyes dart back and forth around the room. If you are extremely uncomfortable looking directly into the eyes of the interviewer, look at his or her forehead. This gives the impression of looking into his or her eyes. In a group interview, periodically make eye contact with each person.

4. **Maintain good posture.** Good posture conveys that you're composed, respectable, alert, and strong. Sit, stand, and walk with your head up and your back straight. Slouching conveys that you're bored, disinterested, lazy, or unintelligent. Crossing your arms and legs may be interpreted as being closed or stubborn.

5. **Maintain a pleasant facial expression.** Aim for a pleasant, uplifted facial expression. Avoid frowning, licking your lips, clenching your jaw, or any other nervous or downturned expression.

Figure 11-2: Three Sources of Communication and the Impact of Each

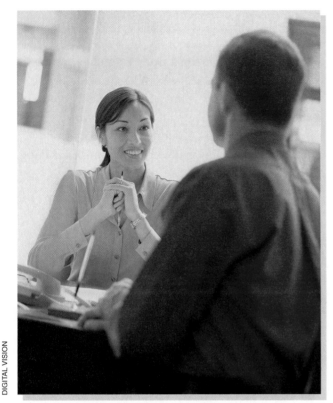

DIGITAL VISION

Use assertive eye contact and a pleasant facial expression.

6. **Don't fidget.** Fidgeting is distracting and makes you look nervous, self-conscious, and unsure of your ability to get the job. Avoid behaviors such as drumming your fingers, jiggling your leg, playing with your hair, or rubbing your chin.

7. **Mirror the communication behaviors of the interviewer.** Some people have intense, highly energetic body language and voice qualities, while others are more relaxed in both. People are most comfortable communicating with others who have styles similar to their own. Subtly mirror, or match, your interviewer's style, speed, and tone of voice, but don't overdo it. Never mirror negative behavior. Much has been written about this technique of mirroring communication behaviors (called neurolinguistic programming)—more than can be included here. Consider reading more about this skill and developing the technique.

Communicate Trustworthiness. During an interview, conveying trustworthiness, which also conveys believability, is essential. Interviewers will not hire people they think are untrustworthy.

Conveying trust is almost entirely a nonverbal function. Trust is conveyed through positive nonverbal messages that convince the listener's emotional brain center. Trust is a dynamic emotional response that is learned in infancy and childhood and remains permanently embedded in the brain. As children, we learned to trust people who projected caring, competence, warmth, and self-confidence through their body language. As adults, we still evaluate the trustworthiness of others in the same way.

How can you convey the trustworthy and believable qualities of warmth, caring, competence, and self-assurance? By adopting the following hallmarks of positive nonverbal communication:

▲ A firm, warm handshake

▲ A pleasant facial expression and direct eye contact

▲ Erect posture (while sitting, standing, and walking)

▲ Head and shoulders help upright at all times

▲ Occasional head nodding and gesturing to convey agreement and emphasis

▲ An energetic, pleasant tone of voice

▲ A brisk, purposeful walk

Develop Assertive Body Language. Concentrate on sending assertive messages and eliminating passive or aggressive nonverbal habits. Three styles of body language are defined below.

1. **Assertive Body Language.** This body language is relaxed, open, and confident. It agrees with and supports your words and conveys competence, self-assurance, caring, and credibility.

2. **Passive Body Language.** This body language looks nonenergetic and diminishes your credibility by conveying insecurity, weakness, anxiety, and a lack of self-assurance and competence.

3. **Aggressive Body Language.** This body language appears brash and overbearing and sends offensive messages that convey hostility, pushiness, intimidation, and a domineering attitude.

Observe Additional Body Language Tips. Pay attention to the following nonverbal communication do's and don'ts:

DO

▲ Do sit with your body slightly to the side, rather than directly facing the interviewer. This tends to promote an attitude of openness and a relaxed atmosphere.

▲ Do keep your hands apart to avoid fidgeting. Rest them on the arms of the chair, and keep them still. Keep your hands relaxed, not in tight fists.

DON'T

▲ Don't bring your hand to your face; this may be interpreted as insecurity.

▲ Don't nod your head too much or tilt it to one side. Both actions detract from your message.

▲ Don't grimace or frown, and don't blink too frequently.

To practice developing positive body language, arrange a videotaped practice interview. Review the tape, watching carefully for body language that needs correction.

Complete Career Action 11-2

Watch Your Interviewer's Body Language. Watch to see what the interviewer's body language is saying. The interviewer may lean forward, signaling you to expand on what you are saying. If the interviewer shuffles papers, looks around the room, or gives other nonverbal cues that you should finish speaking, heed the signal.

Keep listening and watching to determine whether what you are saying is clearly understood. Retreat from a subject if you observe that it's not being well received.

Success Tip

To project trust and credibility quickly, use positive body language in the first 30 seconds of and throughout the interview. Use a pleasant facial expression, good posture and eye contact, and a strong handshake.

CAREER ACTION 11-2

Body Language Self-Inventory

Directions: Access Career Action Worksheet 11-2 on your Learner's CD or turn to page 216 to complete the Body Language Self-Inventory. This assignment will help you identify passive and aggressive body language habits that you can begin eliminating to increase the effectiveness of your communications.

File your worksheet in your Career Management Files Binder.

PERSONAL**BEST**

Listening Skills

While you may think of the interviewing process primarily in terms of talking, listening is just as important. You need to listen to the interviewer carefully to learn important details about the job requirements, the organization, and the department so you can respond appropriately. Follow these tips to become a more effective and active listener:

▲ Address the interviewer using his or her proper name.

▲ Communicate with undivided attention; resist distractions.

▲ Nod as appropriate.

▲ Repeat or summarize the main ideas.

▲ Ask questions as appropriate to clarify meaning.

▲ Listen "between the lines" for the underlying messages.

▲ Don't argue or interrupt.

▲ Maintain eye contact (but not too intensely).

▲ Maintain an "open" position (don't cross your arms or legs; keep your hands unclenched).

▲ Maintain the same eye level as the interviewer (sit or stand as appropriate).

Listening: The Silent Power Play

Concentrate on listening to every word the interviewer says. Never interrupt him or her; that is considered rude. If the interviewer asks a question you don't understand, politely ask him or her to repeat it. If you don't understand the question fully, you won't be able to respond adequately.

Silence Is Sometimes Used as a Power Play. The interviewer asks you a question, you provide the proper answer, and the interviewer does not respond. This is a technique interviewers sometimes use to test applicants' confidence and ability to handle stress or uncertainty.

If you experience this silence power play, do not retract your statement; just wait calmly. You have no obligation to continue talking if you answered adequately. By doing this, you will pass the "test" and project a mature, confident image. Break a long silence by asking whether the interviewer needs more information or by asking a related question. Be prepared to handle silence.

You Can Also Use Silence. If you are asked a difficult question, answering too quickly and without enough thought can be detrimental. You're entitled to think carefully about a question and prepare a response. The employer wouldn't want you to solve problems on the job without adequate thought and planning. Avoid long pauses in a telephone- or video-based interview, however; such pauses can be perceived as slow thinking abilities.

Emphasizing Your Qualifications

In an interview, you need to convince the interviewer that you are the best-qualified person for the job. If you don't, you won't be hired. To convince the interviewer, focus on how your skills and experience can benefit the employer. The way you handle the discussion of your qualifications will be a determining factor in whether you get the job.

Getting hired can be compared to making a sale. In this case, the products are you and your capabilities. You complete the "sale" by effectively emphasizing how your capabilities can benefit the employer.

Develop and Use a 60-Second Commercial.

To help make the sale, develop a 60-Second Commercial, a power-packed summary of the benefits you offer. As a starting point, think of times you provided benefits to an employer or a volunteer organization. Employers are persuaded to "buy" (hire) the person who can offer benefits in one or more of these areas:

▲ Increasing sales/profits/productivity

▲ Decreasing costs

▲ Saving time

▲ Solving problems

▲ Increasing convenience

▲ Enhancing image

▲ Improving relationships

▲ Increasing accuracy or efficiency

Give Examples of Measurable Accomplishments and Transferable Competencies. The key is to provide evidence of your capabilities, or proof by example. For instance, if you are skilled at improving work efficiency, give specific examples of how you applied this ability. Use numbers to boost your credibility. For example,

NO: "I work efficiently."

YES: "I developed an order processing system that reduced processing time by 20 percent."

Since employers are looking for flexible employees, you should also emphasize your transferable competencies, such as your ability to handle diverse responsibilities, manage yourself (attendance, punctuality, and problem solving), and work well with others.

Highlight Group Skills, Problem Solving, and Multi-Tasking. Emphasize your ability to work successfully with others on a team by providing examples of projects you worked on with coworkers in the past. Be prepared to explain the contributions you made to the group and how you were able to solve a problem or resolve group conflicts. Similarly, identify any particularly complex projects you handled in past jobs. Be ready to explain the variety of tasks they involved and how you were able to manage multiple priorities at the same time.

Be sure your 60-Second Commercial represents you authentically. If it doesn't, it can lead to a mismatch

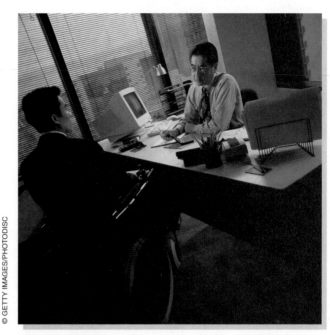

© GETTY IMAGES/PHOTODISC

During an interview, use your 60-Second Commercial to focus on your qualifications for the job.

between you and the employer. A lack of honesty can eliminate you from the competition; don't sell what you can't deliver.

Keep Your Commercial Concise. Assume that your target employer requires you to summarize your job qualifications in a 60-second videotape. Just as in a television commercial, your interview commercial must be short, relevant, and convincing.

Tailor Your Commercial to Each Employer. Career Action 11-3 guides you through the development of a persuasive summary of your qualifications tailored to each employer.

Review the 60-Second Commercials in Figure 11-3. See how they focus on employer benefits, emphasizing results-oriented accomplishments and transferable competencies. Notice how they are phrased in the proof-by-example format and are concise phrases rather than complete sentences. (In an actual interview, you should use complete sentences.)

Complete Career Action 11-3

60-SECOND COMMERCIAL SAMPLE #1

Job Target: Sales representative with Axion Inc., a consumer product company

Experience Credentials: Two years in retail sales at Computer Logistics, Inc.

Education Credentials: B.A. in sales and marketing

Proof of Benefits Provided

▲ Increased school newspaper revenues by 22 percent as advertising assistant

▲ Voted "Most Helpful Clerk" by customers in Service Excellence contest at Ralston Pharmacy

▲ Received performance ratings of "excellent" in accurate, quick sales for two years at Computer Logistics

Related Job Skills/Preferences

▲ Highly skilled in record keeping, use of personal computers, business math

▲ Enjoy travel; open to relocation

Transferable Competencies

▲ Maintain a professional appearance and have good communication skills

▲ Strong interpersonal relations skills

60-SECOND COMMERCIAL SAMPLE #2

Job Target: Graphics/text specialist position with Action Publishers

Experience Credentials: Worked 18 months as graphics/text processing assistant at Westville State College Print Center

Education Credentials: Associate of Applied Business Degree, Westville State College

Proof of Benefits Provided

▲ Worked with team to develop priority scheduling method, resulting in 99 percent on-time delivery

▲ Developed three graphic-intensive brochures that were selected by school for national student recruitment campaign

Related Job Skills/Preferences

▲ Key 70 wpm

▲ Skilled in English usage

▲ Proficient in Word, Excel, graphics design, and desktop publishing software

▲ Operate personal computers, printers, networks, and other office equipment

▲ Enjoy all aspects of document/graphic development

Transferable Competencies

▲ Punctual, self-starter, resourceful in information management, skilled in computer technology, excellent team skills

Figure 11-3: 60-Second Commercial Samples

CAREER ACTION 11-3

60-Second Commercial

Directions: Access Career Action Worksheet 11-3 on your Learner's CD or follow the steps outlined below to prepare your own 60-Second Commercial. File your completed 60-Second Commercial in your Career Management Files Binder.

1. **Prepare a rough draft.** On a separate sheet of paper, prepare a rough draft of your basic commercial.

2. **Use short phrases, not full sentences.** The goal is to say the most about your qualifications in the fewest possible words.

3. **Name your target job position and employer.**

4. **Briefly summarize your education and training.** Use your resume and Career Action 2-1 (Education, Training, and Organizational Activities Inventory) as references.

5. **Focus on "Proof of Benefits Provided."** Provide relevant examples of your work performance and accomplishments and successful use of your job-specific skills. Whenever possible, use numbers or percentages to describe your successes. Also emphasize the benefits you can provide for the employer.

6. **List your job skills and transferable competencies that are most relevant to the job target.** Refer to Career Actions 3-1 and 3-2 to review your job-specific skills and transferable competencies.

7. **Tailor each commercial.** Use your commercial draft as a base, and tailor it to each target employer. Practice delivering your commercial aloud, but don't memorize it word for word. (You don't want to sound as though you are reading a script or lacking energy.) Take a copy of your commercial with you to an interview. If you have a momentary memory lapse, quickly scan the commercial, but don't read from it directly.

Focus and Polish the Content. Your aim is to prepare a brief, polished summary of your qualifications. The heart of your 60-second sales message should emphasize how you can benefit the employer. It is your interview billboard saying "Here's what I can do for you!" This helps the interviewer focus on the strengths you have to offer.

Deliver Your 60-Second Commercial. To create an opening for your commercial, ask the interviewer to review the scope of the job responsibilities and the reason for the opening. Pay attention to the answers. If necessary, probe further to clarify what the employer really needs. Then discuss the benefits you can offer to meet those needs. Pick from your master 60-Second Commercial the items that best fit the needs expressed by the interviewer—that's good selling!

Be ready for any situation; practice delivering the full-length (60-second) version of your commercial as well as a shorter one (a 30-second version). Remember: The more often buyers see or hear a sales message, the more likely they are to buy. Whenever possible, weave your commercial into the interview—perhaps the longer version first, followed later by the shorter one. Don't overdo it, however; twice is probably enough.

If the person interviewing you isn't an experienced interviewer, you may have to take the initiative to deliver your commercial. An untrained interviewer may never ask you directly about your qualifications. Be sure you present them in the interview.

Complete Career Action 11-4

CAREER ACTION 11-4

Summary of Core Areas of Successful Interviewing

Directions: Write a summary discussing how you can apply the interview strategies presented thus far in Chapter 11 in your own job search. Explain specifically how you can apply the techniques related to each of the following:

1. Attitude
2. Image and Appearance
3. Verbal Communication
4. Nonverbal Communication
5. Listening
6. Job Qualifications

File your summary in your Career Management Files Binder.

Success Tip

Help interviewers remember your strengths: Always deliver your interview commercial—even if you only get 30 seconds to do so!

Use Your Portfolio Items and Interview Marketing Kit

Interviewers agree that applicants who prepare well for interviews gain a decided advantage over those who don't; those who prepare always perform better. By preparing well, you will project professionalism and organizational skills and increase your own sense of readiness.

> *"When your work speaks for itself, don't interrupt."*
> Mark Twain

Select Portfolio Items

Before each interview, select the items that are most appropriate for your current job target from your career portfolio (see Chapter 3's "Your Career Portfolio" section; also see "Career Portfolio" and "Interview Marketing Kit" in Appendix B: Career Management and Marketing Tools). Place the portfolio items you select in the Interview Marketing Kit described below.

Prepare and Use an Interview Marketing Kit

To round out your interview preparation, assemble an Interview Marketing Kit. Use a professional-looking binder or small attaché case to carry selected portfolio and other items with you to an interview. A regular briefcase is not recommended because interviewers may view it as overkill. The items to include in your kit are listed in Figure 11-4.

Well in advance of an interview, prepare your 60-Second Commercial and the list of questions you want to ask. For guidance in developing your questions, refer to the "Plan Now: Your Questions Count!" section in Chapter 14. Arrange the portfolio items in your Interview Marketing Kit to best show how your abilities relate to the employer's needs.

INTERVIEW MARKETING KIT CONTENTS

1. **Items from your career portfolio that pertain to the interview**

   ▲ Job-related samples of your work, if applicable (from your work and/or educational or training experience)

   ▲ Required certificates, licenses, transcripts, or other related documents

   ▲ Spare copies of your resume

   ▲ Letters of recommendation

   ▲ List of references appropriate for the job

2. **A copy of your 60-Second Commercial** summarizing your qualifications for the job (skills, education, and experience)

3. **A notebook with a list of pertinent questions** you can ask during the interview (see Chapter 14)

4. **Professional preparation items**

   ▲ Pens and pencils

   ▲ An appointment calendar

Figure 11-4: Interview Marketing Kit Contents

Practice Using Your Marketing Materials

To capture an interviewer's attention, refer first to an item that represents one of your most outstanding accomplishments. Save another exceptional item to use toward the end of the interview to leave a favorable last impression.

Practice using your Interview Marketing Kit items so the actual delivery will be smooth. Have a friend give you a mock interview, and practice referring to your portfolio items at key points during the interview.

Suppose an interviewer asks, "How important do you think it is to keep up with changing technology?" To this you can reply "I think it is very important, and I have taken several classes to update my software skills." You can then provide an appropriate example of how you have kept up to date with technology in your field. By rehearsing, you will be able to work the portfolio items into an interview naturally.

Success Tip

Be prepared and organized; take with you an Interview Marketing Kit that contains items from your career portfolio and other items you may need in the interview.

Use Portfolio Items Wisely

Relying only on your portfolio items to convince an interviewer of your qualifications is a big mistake. It's like a speaker relying on only one set of slides. The focus of the interview is still on you. Your personal appearance and your nonverbal and verbal communication skills are essential. The portfolio items are visual aids to add further dimension to your qualifications.

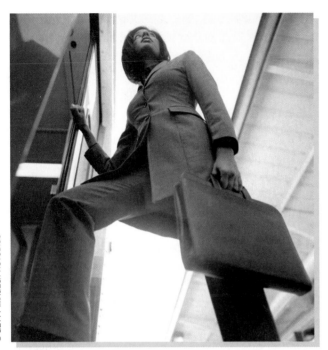

Be prepared: Head to an interview with your Interview Marketing Kit in tow.

Do not misrepresent yourself in your portfolio items; the work must be your own. Be prepared to reproduce the work if requested to do so during pre-employment testing. Select your portfolio items to match specific employers and jobs. Do not use every item in your primary portfolio for every interview.

An important part of your research is learning whether your target employers would likely be interested in reviewing your career portfolio during interviews. Some employers prefer not to review portfolios during interviews.

Refer to Your Portfolio Items and Take Notes

Before you refer to any portfolio items in your Interview Marketing Kit and before you take notes, ask whether the interviewer has any objections to your doing so. Pay attention to the answer, and follow the interviewer's wishes.

An exception to this rule is referring to your appointment calendar. If you need to schedule a follow-up meeting or an activity, having your appointment

book handy is essential. You should confirm any future appointments immediately. Doing so at a later time could result in a lost opportunity; an interviewer may want to make a future commitment while you're still in the interview.

Prepare an Interview Survival Pack

With a little planning, you can avoid an interview-sabotaging experience. Prepare a separate survival pack that contains personal hygiene items (toothbrush and toothpaste, comb, even deodorant); a spare tie or nylons; and anything else you may need to look, smell, and be your best under any circumstances. Put your gear in a zippered pouch that fits neatly into your Interview Marketing Kit. Or, if you travel by car, store it there.

Limit Interviews to Two a Day

After two interviews in a day, an applicant's performance levels typically drop. Don't jeopardize your chances of getting a job; take a breather and gear up for the next day.

Avoid Interview Disqualifiers

The following is a list of important reminders. Avoid committing any of these blunders. Any one of them could cost you the job:

1. Don't sit down until the interviewer invites you to; waiting is courteous.

2. Don't bring anyone else to the interview; it makes you look immature and insecure.

3. Don't smoke.

4. Don't put anything on or read anything on the interviewer's desk; it's considered an invasion of personal space.

5. Don't chew gum or have anything else in your mouth; this projects immaturity.

6. If you are invited to a business meal, don't order alcohol. When ordering, choose food that's easy to eat while carrying on a conversation.

7. Don't offer a limp handshake; it projects weakness. Use a firm handshake.

Wrap Up the Interview in Your Favor

To wrap up the interview in your favor, clarify what to expect next in the interview process and restate your qualifications.

Clarify What to Expect Next

You must know what to expect next in the interview process. Before you leave the interview, clarify:

▲ What, if anything, you should do in the way of follow-up.

▲ How long you should expect to wait before the hiring decision is made. (If you're considering another job, this is especially important.)

▲ How the interviewer prefers you to follow up (by telephone, by letter, or in person).

The following sample dialogue shows how to get this information:

> **You:** When should I expect to hear whether I am selected for the position?
>
> **Interviewer:** We'll notify all applicants of our decision within two weeks.
>
> **You:** Do you mind if I check back with you?
>
> **Interviewer:** I prefer that you don't until we notify you.
>
> *or*
>
> **Interviewer:** No, I don't mind.
>
> **You:** How would you prefer I do that—by telephone, by mail or e-mail, in person?
>
> **Interviewer:** I prefer that you telephone my assistant.

You are clarifying *how* you will be notified of the hiring decision, *when* you will be notified, *whether* the in-

> *"We judge ourselves by what we feel capable of doing, while others judge us by what we have already done."*
>
> Henry Wadsworth Longfellow

terviewer objects to your checking back, and *how* the interviewer prefers that you check back. In every instance, you are helping yourself in the job campaign.

Use the Clincher

As you near the close of an interview, make a point of leaving your interviewer with a clear picture of how you fit the job. Bring the interview full circle by asking a question similar to this example in a courteous tone:

> "Would you please summarize the most important qualifications you're looking for in filling this position?"

Once the interviewer has answered, you can restate your skills, experience, and other assets that meet the employer's needs. (Run your 60- or 30-Second Commercial one more time.) This important clincher gives you one last chance to make the sale—to market the products (you and your qualifications for the job). People remember best what they hear first and last in any communication.

Close the Interview Skillfully

Some applicants lose the race for a job by not clearing the final hurdle: closing the interview skillfully. Don't let your posture, attitude, or verbal and nonverbal communication slip for even a moment. Use the following techniques to close an interview skillfully:

▲ Watch for signs from the interviewer that it's time to wrap up. Signs include asking whether you have any further questions, tidying up papers on the desk, pushing the chair back, or simply sitting back in the chair. Heed the cue. Don't make the interviewer impatient by droning on at this point.

▲ If the interviewer is not skilled at interviewing, help wrap up the interview smoothly by asking, "Is there anything else you need to discuss with me? I know you are busy, and I appreciate the time you have given me for this interview."

▲ Request a commitment from the interviewer to notify you when an applicant has been selected. Imply that this is not the only job you are considering: "By what date will you make your decision on this position? I'd appreciate knowing within the next two weeks so I can finalize my plans."

▲ Before you leave, determine any follow-up activities the interviewer expects from you. If a second interview is arranged, write down the date, time, place, and names of all of the people who will be interviewing you. If you are expected to provide additional information, credentials, references, or work samples, make a note and verify what you are supposed to do before you leave.

▲ If you're seriously interested in the job, say so! Just as in effective sales, the person who asks is the most likely to receive. Interviewers are impressed by applicants' expressions of interest; candidates who directly express their interest strengthen their position. Offer a simple statement—for example, "I'd be pleased to be a part of this organization" or "After talking with you, I'm convinced this is the job I want, and I believe my qualifications would be an asset to the XYZ Corporation. Please consider me seriously for this position."

▲ As you leave, remember to use the interviewer's name: "Thank you for providing me with this interview, Mr. Carpenter."

Success Tip

Close the interview skillfully. Pay attention to the interviewer's signals for closure. If possible, run your commercial one more time to focus on your capabilities. Find out how you should follow up and when a hiring decision will be made.

▲ Be conscious of your posture as you stand up, keeping your shoulders back and your head up. A warm smile and a firm handshake confirm your friendly and positive attitude. Once you leave the interviewer's office, you are still interviewing! Thank the receptionist or assistant by name, and add a brief parting greeting.

Review Figure 11-5 to reinforce your understanding of the areas that employers consider the most important during an interview.

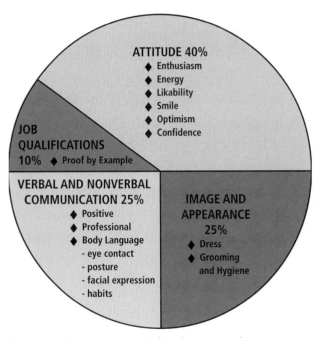

Figure 11-5: How You Are Rated During an Interview

Complete Career Action 11-5

Complete Career Action 11-6

CAREER ACTION 11-5

Summary of Fine Points for Interview Success

Directions: Access Career Action Worksheet 11-5 on your Learner's CD or use a separate sheet of paper to write a summary of how you plan to apply the information presented in this chapter to your own job search. Address the following items in your summary:

1. **Your Interview Marketing Kit.** What will yours consist of?

2. **Your Interview Survival Pack.** What should yours contain?

3. **Interview Disqualifiers.** Which apply to you?

4. **How to Wrap Up the Interview in Your Favor.** Summarize how you plan to wrap up an interview favorably. Explain how you will determine what method of follow-up contact the interviewer prefers.

5. **Close the Interview Skillfully.** Summarize how you plan to end an interview.

File your summary in your Career Management Files Binder.

CAREER ACTION 11-6

Use the Internet to Research Interview Strategies

Directions: Visit the web sites listed below (links can be found on the *Your Career: How to Make It Happen* web site at http://levitt.swlearning.com), visit other sites you favor, and/or use search engines to locate and summarize at least four strategies for effective interviewing. Look for new ideas that will be useful to you. Write a summary of your findings. If you find new information, research further and discuss the topic(s) in the classroom, with your school's career services staff, and/or with interview specialists. File your research in your Career Management Files Binder.

Search strings and topics to look for: *interview tips, techniques, or strategies and interview portfolios*

The Black Collegian Online (Click on "Monthly Issues.")

CareerJournal.com (*The Wall Street Journal*)

Quintessential Careers

CareerBuilder.com (Click on "Advice & Resources.")

Job-Interview.net

JobWeb
(National Association of Colleges and Employers)

Monster

CHECKLIST

INTERVIEWING LIKE A PRO

Check each of the actions you are currently taking to increase your career success:

○ Projecting enthusiasm and a positive attitude in interviews

○ Projecting professionalism; smiling, dressing neatly and appropriately, and being clean and neat

○ Using positive verbal communication; using positive terms; and avoiding grammatical errors, slang, and credibility robbers

○ Using positive body language in the first 30 seconds of and throughout the interview to project trust and credibility quickly

○ Making the sale by delivering a polished interview commercial that emphasizes your qualifications and includes measurable accomplishments whenever possible

○ Being prepared and organized; taking to the interview an Interview Marketing Kit that contains appropriate portfolio items

○ Closing the interview skillfully; paying close attention to the interviewer's signals for closure; running the commercial one more time to focus on your capabilities; and finding out how to follow up and when a hiring decision will be made

CRITICAL THINKING QUESTIONS

1. What aspects of the applicant do interviewers focus on the most?

2. How can a job applicant demonstrate a positive attitude during an interview?

3. What negative nonverbal habits are the most important for you to eliminate to improve your interview abilities?

4. What is the most important information an applicant must convey to an interviewer?

5. What are the two most important pieces of information you should include in your 60-Second Commercial?

 For convenient access to valuable career resources, activities, and job information links, visit the companion web site for this text: *http://levitt.swlearning.com*

CAREER ACTION WORKSHEET 11-2

Body Language Self-Inventory

Part 1

Directions: Review the following descriptions of nonverbal communication behaviors, and place a check mark next to each item that describes your body language habits. Review your answers, and circle any habits that are aggressive or passive. Make a list of these behaviors. Then, in Part 2, prepare a list of the habits you think are the most important to change. Finally, take action to correct these habits, and get others to remind you when you exhibit them.

POSTURE

Behavior	Style	Behavior	Style
☐ comfortably upright	Assertive	☐ overbearing, intimidating	Aggressive
☐ relaxed, balanced	Assertive	☐ wooden, tight	Passive
☐ open, not constricted	Assertive	☐ slumped shoulders	Passive
☐ overly stiff	Aggressive	☐ slumped back/spine	Passive
☐ arms/legs crossed	Aggressive		

HANDSHAKE

Behavior	Style	Behavior	Style
☐ appropriately firm	Assertive	☐ held too long	Aggressive
☐ connect between thumb/first finger	Assertive	☐ limp	Passive
☐ shake from elbow through hand	Assertive	☐ shake from wrist through hand	Passive
☐ held for appropriate length of time	Assertive	☐ held too briefly	Passive
☐ a "bone-crushing" grip	Aggressive	☐ grasping fingers only	Passive

FACIAL EXPRESSION

Behavior	Style	Behavior	Style
☐ open, relaxed, pleasant	Assertive	☐ clenched jaw	Aggressive
☐ frowning	Aggressive	☐ wrinkling forehead	Passive
☐ moody, sulking	Aggressive	☐ biting or licking lips	Passive
☐ tight upper lip, pursed mouth	Aggressive	☐ continual smiling	Passive

Continued on next page >>>

CAREER ACTION WORKSHEET 11-2 (continued)

EYE CONTACT

Behavior	Style	Behavior	Style
☐ comfortably direct	Assertive	☐ constantly looking down	Passive
☐ staring off, bored expression	Aggressive	☐ blinking rapidly	Passive
☐ sneering, looking down nose	Aggressive	☐ frequently shifting focus	Passive
☐ direct stare	Aggressive	☐ no eye contact, avoidance	Passive

VOICE QUALITIES

Behavior	Style	Behavior	Style
☐ distinct and clear	Assertive	☐ too loud	Aggressive
☐ controlled, but relaxed	Assertive	☐ arrogant or sarcastic	Aggressive
☐ warm, pleasant tone	Assertive	☐ dull or monotone	Passive
☐ energized/suitable emphasis	Assertive	☐ whiny tone	Passive
☐ too rapid	Aggressive	☐ too soft or too slow	Passive
☐ too demanding or urgent	Aggressive	☐ too nasal	Passive

GESTURES

Behavior	Style	Behavior	Style
☐ natural, not erratic	Assertive	☐ hands on hips	Aggressive
☐ occasional gestures to emphasize	Assertive	☐ wooden gestures	Passive
☐ occasional positive head nodding	Assertive	☐ tilting head to one side	Passive
☐ open hand (conveys trust)	Assertive	☐ bringing hand to face	Passive
☐ leaning toward speaker	Assertive	☐ too much head nodding	Passive
☐ pointing finger	Aggressive	☐ fidgeting	Passive
☐ clenched fists	Aggressive		

Continued on next page >>>

Career Action Worksheet 11-2 (continued)

DISTRACTING NONVERBAL HABITS

Behavior	Style	Behavior	Style
☐ drumming fingers	Passive	☐ fiddling with any object	Passive
☐ use of fillers (um, uh, you know)	Passive	☐ rubbing beard or mustache	Passive
☐ jiggling leg/arm	Passive	☐ biting nails	Passive
☐ fiddling with hair/glasses	Passive	☐ scratching	Passive

OTHER HABITS (List other similar habits you have.)

Behavior	Style	Behavior	Style
_____	_____	_____	_____
_____	_____	_____	_____
_____	_____	_____	_____

Part 2

Directions: Review your self-assessment; then list the negative nonverbal habits you plan to change. List them in order of importance (with the most important change first).

MY GOALS FOR IMPROVING NONVERBAL COMMUNICATION

1. _____
2. _____
3. _____
4. _____
5. _____

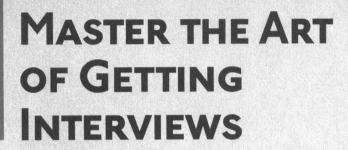
MASTER THE ART OF GETTING INTERVIEWS

In this chapter, you will:

- Develop written scripts for interview requests to be made through personal visits or by telephone.

- Practice delivering your request for an interview.

Use the Internet to research job search telephone strategies.

> *"Present yourself with confidence when communicating with a potential employer. Your own confidence will help convince them that you are the best person for the job. A genuine sense of enthusiasm conveys the high energy and interest level that employers want. Enthusiasm also helps sustain you during the job search process, encouraging you to follow up, maintain contact, and keep a positive outlook—all things that, ultimately, will distinguish you from the crowd."*
>
> Charlene Crusoe-Ingram
> Vice President of Organization and People Development
> Coca-Cola USA

To land your target job, you first need to get an interview. Sound strategies for succeeding in this essential job search step are outlined in Chapter 12. Techniques for arranging interviews directly and indirectly are presented.

Direct Requests for Interviews

You can use four direct methods of contacting employers for an interview:

▲ Personal visit

▲ Telephone call

▲ Standard letter

▲ Internet communication

Once you identify a promising employer prospect, your goal is to get an interview. Statistically, the most productive methods of getting an interview are face-to-face contact and telephone contact. Don't write a letter when you can call, and don't call when you can make a personal visit. If you can't visit or call, a standard letter or Internet communication is appropriate. Review the 60-Second Commercial, resume, and cover letter that you prepared earlier. Tailor your request for an interview to each prospective employer by emphasizing your strengths and experience that are most relevant to the employer's needs.

Developing Verbal Effectiveness in Interview Requests

To increase your success rate in landing interviews, focus on being courteous, likable, professional, persuasive, and resourceful. Follow the guidelines below to project likability and professionalism in face-to-face and telephone interview bids:

▲ Use a friendly tone and moderate pitch and speed.

▲ Use correct grammar.

▲ Speak distinctly and confidently.

▲ Eliminate slang and annoying filler expressions (*um, uh,* or *you know*).

▲ Be courteous.

▲ Communicate your message clearly and concisely.

▲ Emphasize your qualifications before requesting an interview.

© GETTY IMAGES/PHOTODISC

Personal contact—in person or by phone—is the best way to make a bid for an interview.

Respect the person's time. Most businesspeople will have only a few minutes for your visit or call. If you sense that this is not a good time, say something like, "I'd be glad to call/visit you at a more convenient time, if necessary." Remain composed and professional. Do not act inconvenienced or become irritable.

Success Tip

When requesting an interview, emphasize your qualifications before you make the request to give the receiver a reason to answer *yes.*

Focusing Your Interview Request

The focus of an effective interview request should be on how your abilities can benefit—or even be essential to—the employer. Identify for yourself what advantages your specific qualifications provide, and then translate those advantages into benefits for the prospective employer. Performing employer research is vital and should include finding out who is in charge of the department that could benefit the most from your abilities. This is the target person for your interview request.

Review the 60-Second Commercial you developed in Chapter 11 (Career Action 11-3.) Use a brief modification of it as the foundation for your request for an interview.

Making a Request Through a Personal Visit

Making a direct request for an interview through a personal visit is statistically the most successful method of getting an interview. It is difficult for people to ignore you when you're standing in front of them. Here are some guidelines for making a successful request for an interview in person:

1. **Research the firm thoroughly beforehand.**

2. **Dress for the part.** Dress and groom yourself as though you are going to an actual interview.

3. **Be prepared.** Take your Interview Marketing Kit (Chapter 11) with you, including your 60-Second Commercial and your resume.

4. **Pay special attention to the gatekeeper** (the person standing between you and the employer): This may be an administrative support person, a supervisor, or a human resources staff member. Actively and courteously seek that person's help (see "Breaking Gatekeeper Barriers" later in this chapter).

5. **Present the most concise, action-packed version of your 60-Second Commercial,** and then request an interview.

6. **Thank your contact by name** for his or her time and consideration.

If you don't get an interview, ask for a referral to another department or company that may need your abilities.

Study the example on page 221 of a request for an interview made during a personal visit to an employer. The applicant highlights her qualifications, demonstrates her knowledge of the employer and the industry, and expresses her interest in the job—just the right approach!

Success Tip

When you make a request for an interview in person, prepare as though you are going to an actual interview. The first impression you make will influence the outcome.

Complete Career Action 12-1

The following paragraphs represent a sample script that someone applying for an administrative support

CAREER ACTION 12-1

Develop Your Personal Request for an Interview

Directions: Read the sample request for an interview on the next page. Then write or key a script that would be appropriate to use when requesting an interview with your prospective job target(s). File your script in your Career Management Files Binder.

position in a medical center might use to make an in-person request for an interview. Please note that there are four parts to this request.

SAMPLE IN-PERSON REQUEST FOR AN INTERVIEW

▲ **The Opening.** "Hello, Mr. Selland. My name is Jaleesa Williams. My instructor, Gerald Johnston, recommends your Information Services Department at Saint Mary's Hospital for its well-organized systems design. I recently completed my education at Mesa College, earning two A.S. degrees—one in Information Management Technology and the second in Medical Administrative Assisting."

▲ **The 60-Second Commercial Excerpt.** "I worked for 18 months as a clerical assistant in the Business Office at Lewis State College while attending school. I'm proficient in Word, Excel, Access, PowerPoint, and Outlook software and have received MOUS certification in each of these software packages. I operate personal computers, networks, and general office equipment. I also type at 70 words per minute and am skilled in English usage."

▲ **The Request.** "I've developed some time-saving methods for creating templates and macros that are appropriate for your department. Would you have time for me to review them with you today, or would one day next week be more convenient?"

▲ **The Close.** "Next Tuesday at 10 a.m.? I appreciate your willingness to meet with me so soon, Mr. Selland. I look forward to meeting with you then. Thank you and good-bye."

Success Tip

Prepare a script and practice asking for an interview before you make a real request.

Requesting an Interview by Telephone

The telephone can be a powerful ally. It demands immediate attention from the person who answers it and reduces the time you need for initial inquiries because delivery is instantaneous. It also can be as informal as you wish and allows for two-way communication. Use the telephone to survey employers and to determine whether they're viable targets for employment. Follow up with personal visits to the most likely prospects.

Using the Telephone Persuasively

Your telephone communication skills will affect your success throughout your career. You can develop these skills just as you develop any other skill. To make persuasive job search telephone calls, follow the methods outlined in the "Personal Best" feature, the "Organizing and Placing Telephone Calls" section, and the sample script on the next two pages.

Your telephone communication skills are important to your career success. Develop good telephone skills so you can use your voice to project confidence and enthusiasm and make a positive impression.

PERSONAL**BEST**

Telephone Skills

Your voice is your personality over the telephone. It makes an immediate impression that can portray you as friendly or distant, confident or timid, relaxed or nervous. These tips from the Dallas, Texas, Online Women's Business Center can help you improve your telephone presence.

▲ Smile when you speak on the telephone. The muscles used to smile actually relax the vocal cords and create a pleasant tone of voice. Try it!

▲ Don't talk on the phone with food or gum in your mouth. Don't drink while talking on the phone, either. The sounds of drinking and eating are amplified over phone lines.

▲ When you place a call that you know might be lengthy, ask if it's a good time to talk before you dive into your spiel.

▲ Know what you want to say before making an important call. Practice the words aloud until they feel comfortable.

▲ Don't read from a script during a call. Either memorize your script as an actor would, or use notes to guide you from one idea to another.

▲ Don't check your e-mail or catch up on other activities while on the phone. The person you're talking with will know you're distracted.

▲ Listen and respond to the person on the other end of the line. When you focus on him or her rather than on what you're going to say next, the phone call becomes more conversational.

▲ Evaluate your voice. Make a tape recording of yourself speaking on the telephone. Is your voice too shrill or strained? Do you speak in a monotone? Are you too quiet or too loud? Do you speak too quickly? Too slowly? Do you speak clearly?

Organizing and Placing Telephone Calls

To prepare for and place effective telephone calls for your job search, follow the steps outlined below.

1. **Determine the purpose of your call.** Is your purpose to get the name of the hiring individual? Is it to request information about the position? Is it to request an interview?

2. **Learn all you can about the organization before calling.** Get the name of the person you need to contact before you call to request an interview. You may need to make a preliminary call to get this information.

3. **Write out your script completely.** Summarize the key points you need to cover prior to placing the call. Pattern your script after the samples in this chapter, and refer to your 60-Second Commercial. List all the information you need to obtain from your contact. The script or outline is essential. It helps you organize your message, making you sound intelligent and well prepared. It also provides a good reference in case you forget something.

4. **What do you say when someone answers the telephone?**

   a. Identify yourself. "Hello, this is Brenda Bernstein." Support personnel who screen calls are immediately suspicious of callers who don't give their names or state why they are calling. Therefore, be straightforward to eliminate any suspicions instantly.

   b. Identify your purpose for calling. Deliver your request for an interview, or use a practiced indirect strategy for getting through to the employer.

   c. Get the name of the person who answers. Ask, "Could I please have your name in case I need to talk with you again?" Write the name down. Using this person's name may make him or her more receptive to helping you.

   d. Clarify the details. Clarify any follow-up activities you are instructed to complete (pick up an application, supply additional information or references, keep an appointment, and so on). Verify the time and place of any meetings, and get the correct spelling and pronunciation of the names of people you will meet.

e. Thank the person you speak to by name.

If you need practice before actually calling for an interview, refer to the samples of indirect strategies for getting an interview on pages 225 and 226. You can ask all the sample questions by telephone or request a meeting to discuss them in person. Study the telephone script for an interview request that follows. The job seeker's qualifications, knowledge of the employer and the industry, and interest in the employer are incorporated.

Like the sample script for an in-person request for an interview, the telephone request for an interview consists of four parts. This sample script shows what might be said in a telephone conversation about trying to secure an interview for a sales representative position.

SAMPLE TELEPHONE REQUEST FOR AN INTERVIEW

▲ **The Opening.** "Hello, Ms. Hope. This is Stephen Rogowski. I've recently completed research comparing the product quality and service records of computer network manufacturers. I'm impressed with the results XYZ Company has achieved, and I'm interested in learning about your sales representative position."

▲ **The 60-Second Commercial Excerpt.** "I'm completing my degree in sales and marketing at Lewis State College and have two years of successful retail sales experience. I also was the advertising assistant for our school paper and increased sales by 18 percent this year."

▲ **The Request.** "Would it be possible to arrange a meeting with you to discuss your sales goals and how I might contribute to them?"

▲ **The Close.** "Thank you, Ms. Hope. I look forward to meeting with you next Tuesday, the 18th, at 2:30. Good-bye."

Complete Career Action 12-2

CAREER ACTION 12-2

Develop and Practice Your Telephone Request for an Interview

Part A: Write or key a script that would be appropriate to use when making a telephone request for an interview with your prospective job target(s). File a copy of your script in your Career Management Files Binder.

Part B: Turn to your support system for assistance. Do some role-playing, and follow the guidelines below. Deliver your telephone request for an interview to your support system helper.

1. Tape record your delivery, play it back, critique it, and improve on it where necessary.

2. Request your helper to ask you questions that require more information about your qualifications.

3. Practice responding when your helper makes excuses for not scheduling an interview.

4. Practice presenting your qualifications persuasively.

5. Practice turning objections into acceptance.

6. Persevere.

Requesting an Interview by Letter

If you are relying on your cover letter and resume to attract interviews and you have prepared these documents well, you are ready to make an interview request.

First, find out which method is appropriate for your target employer: sending your request by regular mail, by fax, or by e-mail. As a general rule, e-mail is appropriate for a first communication only under these circumstances:

▲ In communications with peers

▲ When it has been requested

▲ With high-tech or Internet-oriented companies

Second, review the instructions for preparing and distributing a cover letter provided in Chapter 10. You may want to use e-mail and a letter to cover both bases. By using both media, you give extra emphasis to your message and increase the likelihood that your request will be read.

If you don't receive responses from your cover letter and resume within a week to 10 days, reinforce the request through a telephone call or personal visit.

Responding to a Job Posted on the Internet

If you find a job posted on the Internet through a general job listing site or a specific employer's web site, follow the instructions provided exactly. Often employers want you to e-mail or fax your resume and a cover letter to them. They may use a special code to identify a specific job opening; be sure to include any such code in your cover letter. They may also have an online resume form you can fill out or a block into which you can paste your resume or letter. All of these options become your technical "request for an interview."

Indirect Strategies for Landing Interviews

To reach an employer, to bypass a gatekeeper, or to find the hidden job market, you may need to use an indirect strategy that will lead to a request for an interview. Indirect requests for interviews are especially important during times of high job competition.

Getting Through to the Employer

When job competition is high, many employers are flooded with applicants. In response, they may issue a temporary no-hire policy, which makes personal contact difficult because employees are instructed to notify applicants that no interviews are being scheduled at that time.

> *"The people who get on in the world are the people who get up and look for circumstances they want, and if they can't find them, make them."*
>
> George Bernard Shaw

In a situation like this, you need to use initiative and persistence. Develop a persuasive reason to contact the person with hiring authority in your target organization.

Using an indirect strategy can create opportunities to meet people in your target organization who can arrange an interview for you. While you should not make a direct request for a job during a meeting that is arranged indirectly, you can discuss your experience and abilities. By doing so, you may actually convince your contact that you would be an asset to the organization, which is exactly your intention! Also ask whether the employer may need your skills in the future or if your contact could suggest another organization or department that may need someone with your qualifications.

Meet to Discuss Resources Related to Your Field

The indirect strategy samples that follow provide natural leads into discussing your qualifications. One effective indirect strategy is to arrange a brief meeting with a prospective employer to discuss professional associations and publications in your field. Once you meet, ask the following questions:

▲ What professional association(s) would keep me informed of industry developments, technological advances in the field, and emerging trends?

▲ Which professional publications or Internet resources deal specifically with our field?

▲ Who else could I speak with for further advice on this topic?

Ask for Assistance with Your Career Preparation

If you have limited work experience related to your job target, call a prospective employer to ask for assistance with your career planning and educational preparation. The conversation you have with the employer may be similar to one of the two samples below:

"Hello, Mr. Cuevo. This is Celia Lee. I'm completing an assignment for a career planning course and would appreciate your assistance with some of my research. I'm seeking opinions from people who are recognized and experienced in the field of (your field), which is why I'm calling you. My skills lie in the area(s) of _____. Could you help me identify positions within (your career field) for which these skills would be most useful? I'd also appreciate your recommendations regarding any additional course work and preparation I may need."

"My major is _____, and my career objective is _____. I would appreciate your helping me identify elective course work or a minor (another minor) that would strengthen my educational preparation and support my career goal."

If you are seeking help in developing your resume into one that prospective employers will not pass over, you can place a telephone call to an employer and ask for his or her help in the following manner:

"Hello, Ms. Pappas. This is Nhon Tran. You've been highly recommended to me by Dr. Ivarsen of the

Computer Information Systems Department of Nevada College. I'm developing a professional resume and would very much appreciate your critiquing it."

Follow Up

Four to six months later, you should follow up on your telephone call requesting information about additional preparation to make you more employable and/or your telephone call requesting help in developing your resume. The conversation may be similar to the following:

"Hello, Mr. Cuevo. This is Celia Lee. You gave me some excellent advice six months ago. Would you consider evaluating my job preparation now?"

Ask to arrange a meeting, and then approach the meeting as you would an interview—totally prepared! Remember: This person advised you earlier. If

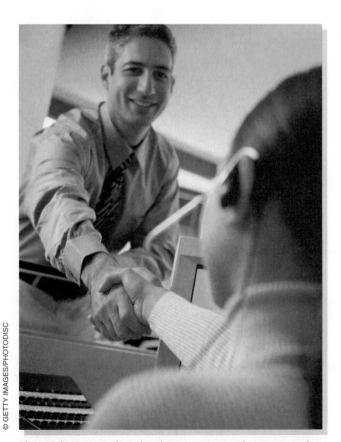

© GETTY IMAGES/PHOTODISC

The gatekeeper can be a barrier or a resource in your pursuit of an interview.

you followed the advice, he or she may consider hiring you for demonstrating initiative and intelligence. (After all, it was his or her advice, so it must be good!)

Breaking Gatekeeper Barriers

The gatekeeper (the administrative support person, receptionist, or human resources staff member) who must screen all job applicants can help, hinder, or destroy your chances of obtaining a job with the organization. This person's influence on your job campaign can be considerable, so you need to use good diplomacy skills when communicating with him or her. The following recommendations will help you establish a good relationship with the gatekeeper:

▲ Express respect for the organization, perhaps referring to its reputation for professionalism, reliability, or leadership. A gatekeeper who is happily employed with the organization will likely agree with your comments and may help you.

▲ Make as much of an effort to get the gatekeeper on your side as you do to get the employer to hire you. Be personable, courteous, and enthusiastic.

▲ As you would in an interview, notice the gatekeeper's surroundings. An interested comment from you about a family portrait, a wall decoration, or a desk item can relax the conversation. If the gatekeeper seems receptive, you can discuss your job search; you may receive useful assistance!

▲ Ask for the gatekeeper's help in arranging an interview with the employer, indicating your awareness of busy schedules. Ask the gatekeeper to suggest the best time to contact the employer. Ask if you could speak with someone else who could tell you more about your areas of interest.

▲ At the end of your conversation, address the gatekeeper by name and thank him or her for the assistance. Remember the importance of developing a good rapport with all gatekeepers. Your efforts to do so may help you considerably in your job search campaign.

Success Tip

Treat gatekeepers (administrative support personnel and receptionists) courteously and professionally. They are often the keys to connecting with the hiring authority.

Uncovering the Hidden Job Market

Seek to uncover the hidden job market mentioned in Chapter 6. The hidden job market is comprised of jobs that are not advertised. In fact, some employers may be unaware that they have positions you could fill. It's up to you to make an employer aware of your potential and possibly create a job in the process.

> *"If you only knock long enough and loud enough at the gate, you are sure to wake up somebody!"*
>
> Henry Wadsworth Longfellow

Research and Prepare. To uncover the hidden job market, you need to research carefully and learn as much as possible about the employer's products or services, structure, and so on. Then you need to:

▲ Analyze how your qualifications can be useful—or even essential—to the employer.

▲ Prepare a dynamic 60-Second Commercial that emphasizes how you can benefit the employer and get someone who is skilled in writing to help you polish it.

The key is to identify how you can provide a useful service or save or make money for the organization.

Find out who is in charge of the department that can use your assets—your hidden job market target. Practice and polish your hidden job market sales pitch. A member of your support system can help you by playing the role of your contact and critiquing your presentation.

Emphasize the Need for Your Capabilities. Armed with thorough employer research and a 60-Second Commercial that illustrates how you can benefit the firm, you may uncover a job that the employer hasn't even considered.

Think big! The hidden job market is limited only by your imagination. You have nothing to lose and everything to gain by tapping into this market in your bid for an interview.

Going Through the Human Resources Department

If your target employer has a strict policy requiring all applicants to be processed through the human resources department, you may have to follow the required procedure. Usually, the first step in such a procedure is submitting an application, a resume, and a cover letter.

If the organization is interviewing, the first interview will likely be a screening interview given in person by a member of the human resources staff. One purpose of the screening interview is to verify the information in your cover letter, application, and resume. You will also be judged on your self-confidence, composure, intelligence, and personality. Projecting energy, enthusiasm, and confidence is essential during a screening interview.

Note, however, that many screening interviews are conducted by telephone to save time and money. Also, some screening interviews are even conducted by telephone screeners who may not actually work for that employer. (The screening interview is discussed in further detail in Chapter 13.)

If you perform well during a screening interview and your qualifications appear to be adequate, you may be scheduled for a departmental interview. If the employer doesn't have an opening in your area, find out how to keep your file active and how you can remain informed of the hiring status for the position.

Using Employment Agencies/Contractors

If you are planning to use employment or staffing agencies or employment contractors in your job search, your job interviews will be arranged by them. Read each agency's agreement thoroughly to be certain you are satisfied with the method of interviewing. Clarify the procedure carefully before agreeing to it. Review the information on employment and staffing agencies and employment contractors presented in Chapter 6.

Developing a Plan When Your Target Job Is Not Open

If your preferred employer is not scheduling interviews because the company has no openings, reevaluate your goal.

If your ultimate goal still is to work for this organization and you think a position is worth waiting for, develop an effective waiting plan. The following guidelines may help:

1. **Take another job during the waiting period.** This work experience can increase your value. During your interim job, you can polish your current skills, develop new ones, and establish a reputation as a valuable employee.

2. **Follow up.** Call your target employer after you have been in your interim job for some time and when you think the employment opportunities have improved. Ask whether the employer would consider reevaluating your qualifications in light of your new experience, or ask for additional suggestions to improve your employability.

3. **Check back periodically.** Call the human resources department of your target employer to remain informed of the hiring status and to reaffirm your interest. This helps keep you first in line for openings.

If you consider more than one organization to be a prime employer, don't let one discouragement slow you down. Review the techniques presented in this chapter, and rally your efforts toward your next target. Preparation, practice, action, and perseverance pay off!

If you have a screening interview with a human resources staff member, be sure to project poise and enthusiasm.

Success Tip

Make calls, send letters, and search the Internet. Successful achievement never starts with *if*, *but*, or *later*.

Complete Career Action 12-3

CAREER ACTION **12-3**

Use the Internet to Find Strategies for Getting Job Interviews

Directions: Conduct an Internet search to find additional tips for getting job interviews. You may want to look for special tips on using the telephone effectively in a job search. Look for new ideas that are specifically useful to you. Write a summary of your findings, and file your research in your Career Management Files Binder.

Use the following Internet resources or others of your choice to conduct this search. Links can be found on the *Your Career: How to Make It Happen* web site at http://levitt.swlearning.com.

Quintessential Career

Monster

CareerLab

Job-Interview.net

CareerJournal.com

CHECKLIST

MASTERING THE ART OF GETTING INTERVIEWS

Check each of the actions you are currently taking to increase your career success:

○ When requesting an interview, emphasizing your qualifications before you make the request to give the receiver a reason to answer *yes*

○ When making a request for an interview in person, preparing as though it were an actual interview because the first impression you make can influence the outcome

○ Preparing a script and practicing asking for an interview before making a real request

○ Treating gatekeepers courteously and professionally because they are often the key to connecting with the hiring authority

○ Tapping into the hidden job market because resourceful applicants create jobs by researching employers' needs and by showing exactly how their abilities meet those needs

CRITICAL THINKING QUESTIONS

1. What method of making a request for an interview do you think will be the most effective in your job search? Why?

2. What are some advantages to making requests for interviews by telephone rather than by letter?

3. Why is it important to establish a good relationship with a gatekeeper? What are three strategies for doing so?

4. Get creative. Think of an employer you could realistically target for a hidden job market position. What are the needs of this employer, based on your research? What special skills and knowledge do you have that represent a hidden job you could perform to meet the employer's needs?

 For convenient access to valuable career resources, activities, and job information links, visit the companion web site for this text: *http://levitt.swlearning.com*

chapter *13*

BE PREPARED FOR ANY INTERVIEW STYLE

In this chapter, you will:

- Conduct direct employer research to learn about the styles of interviews used in your field.

Use the Internet to search for additional information on interview styles.

- Prepare a summary of the information from this chapter and from your research that is most pertinent to your job search.

"We give a one-on-one interview the first time we interview an applicant. If we bring them back for a second interview, we have two people interview them. Usually, we can get more in-depth in the second interview because the applicant is less nervous. If we are seriously considering hiring the person, we will send them to a staff member that is equal to their level to ask any questions and ensure a good match."

Ron Taylor, CPA
Partner
Robinson, Maynard & Associates

While employers use several styles of interviews, there are two basic approaches to interviewing: structured and unstructured. Sometimes these approaches are combined within one interview. At other times, the interview falls into one of the two categories. Once you have a job interview scheduled, you will greatly improve your chance of success if you find out what style of interview will be used. Usually, the human resources department or receptionist will explain the general interview style and process to you.

The Interview Connection

In every interview, try to give the interviewer a picture of your personal attributes as well as your experience, skills, and other job qualifications. Make your verbal and nonverbal messages positive, incorporating posture, facial expressions, and voice qualities that convey competence, friendliness, energy, and enthusiasm. This helps the interviewer feel comfortable and creates an open tone, which improves the chance for a successful interview. An open tone helps both you and the interviewer relax and improves the natural flow of conversation. When under less tension, you can better communicate the information necessary for a good interview.

The Structured Interview

The structured interview is often used by professional interviewers who work in the human resources department or are part of a corporate team, panel, or other trained interviewing group. The interviewer typically uses a planned pattern of questioning, sometimes recording the applicant's responses and making notes on a checklist or an interview rating form. Many interviewers use the same list of questions for each job applicant to ensure fairness. The approach is formal and focuses on obtaining factual information. Because it is highly structured, this approach doesn't always give the interviewer adequate information about the applicant's personality and attitudes.

> *"The spirit, the will to win, and the will to excel are the things that endure."*
> Vince Lombardi

Success Tip

Be friendly, courteous, and positive to establish a good rapport with interviewers and to help relax the tone of overly structured interviews.

The Human Resources Department (Screening) Interview

Large organizations often require applicants to be interviewed first through the human resources department. The screening interview is used to identify qualified applicants for the next level of interviews and to screen out those who don't have the basic qualifications required for the job. Your objectives in this type of interview should be to make your qualifications clear and to try to find out who will make the final hiring decision.

To save time and money, some employers conduct screening interviews by telephone. A recent study by the Society for Human Resource Management shows that some screening interviews are also being outsourced—especially by small companies with limited human resources staff. In these cases, the interviewers may not actually work for the employer, so do not assume that they will be knowledgeable about the company or able to answer all of your questions.

If the interviewer doesn't give you the information you need during the interview, politely ask who will make the final hiring decision. If you are qualified for the job, this will accomplish two things: The interviewer will feel more obligated to arrange an interview for you with the hiring authority, and you can attempt to arrange the interview if the human resources department does not.

While it's best to work through regular organizational channels, try to arrange the interview yourself if going through the regular channels isn't successful. Some employers are impressed with an applicant who doesn't give up, while other employers may be annoyed by an applicant who doesn't follow protocol. If the human resources department will not help you, setting up your own interview is worth a try—and you just might get the job! Take this approach with care, however; be assertive, not aggressive.

An interviewer may use a rating sheet to evaluate each applicant. Review Figure 13-1 on the next page, a typical inter-view rating form, and notice the categories of evaluation.

Your goal in a screening interview is to be scheduled for the next required interview. If the screening interviewer does not tell you, ask what to expect next, who is responsible for making the final hiring decision, and when this decision will be made.

As a rule, you should expect to have no fewer than two interviews with an employer before a hiring decision is made. Some organizations have three or four rounds of interviews before selecting an applicant. A hiring decision is rarely made during the first interview. If you are scheduled for a follow-up interview, you're definitely in the running, so review and

polish your interviewing skills. Keep your chin up and your smile broad, and go for the win!

The Behavioral Interview

In a behavioral interview, the interviewer asks questions aimed at getting the applicant to provide specific examples of how he or she has successfully used the skills required for the target job. This helps the interviewer evaluate the candidate's experience and behavior as indicators of his or her potential for success. In fact, behavioral interviewing is said to be 55 percent predictive of future on-the-job behavior. If you have completed the activities in Chapter 11, you are ready to handle this style of interview. Your 60-Second Commercial contains the proof-by-example descriptions of your capabilities that are most relevant to the target job. This is exactly what an interviewer is looking for in a behavioral interview.

In a behavioral interview, the interviewer is looking for evidence of skills in the following three areas:

▲ **Content skills**—work-specific skills, such as computer programming, CAD, and medical transcription.

▲ **Functional or transferable skills**—skills used with people, things, or information, such as good communication skills or math skills. These are applicable from one job to another.

▲ **Adaptive or self-management skills**—personal characteristics, such as being dependable, a team player, a self-directed worker, a problem solver, or a decision maker.

The following are examples of typical behavioral interview questions:

▲ Give me an example of how you managed conflict well.

▲ Give me an example of a time when you had to go above and beyond the call of duty to get a job done.

▲ Describe your leadership experience. Give examples that show your leadership style.

▲ Describe exactly how you used this software, equipment, or tool in the past.

In a behavioral interview, the interviewer may ask you to provide an example of how you have managed conflict in the past. Be prepared to answer this question.

INTERVIEW EVALUATION

Applicant: _____ Date: _____

Position: _____

	POOR	FAIR	GOOD	VERY GOOD	EXCELLENT
Resume, Application, Cover Letter					
Attitude, Interest, Enthusiasm					
Communication Skills					
Knowledge of Job/Company					
Education/Training					
Related Experience					
Team/Interactive Skills					
Leadership Ability					
Coping Ability (stress, conflict, time demands, and so on)					
Motivation/Goals					
Judgment, Decision Making, Maturity					
Organizational/Planning Skills					
Demonstrated Performance/ Achievements					
Appearance (appropriate dress, grooming)					

Comments: _____

Conclusion: Considering the observations made above and the applicant's qualifications, do you think this person should be considered for the position?

Yes__ No__ Reservations: _____

Interviewer's Signature: _____

Figure 13-1: Typical Interview Rating Form

Success Tip

In behavioral interviews, provide the proof-by-example descriptions of your capabilities and include relevant parts of your 60-Second Commercial.

The Campus Interview

Some organizations give campus interviews to graduating students in such fields as engineering, electronics, business management, law, accounting, computer information systems, and marketing. These are prearranged screening interviews, and the techniques used vary depending on the organization. They are usually structured interviews, but several styles may be used, including the stress interview, the "tell me about yourself" interview, and the panel interview. Each of these styles is explained in detail later in this chapter.

Campus interviews are generally scheduled through a school's career services office. The schedule is closely observed, and the interviewer is forced to evaluate each candidate quickly. (The average interview time is 20 to 30 minutes.) In this type of interview, you should keep your remarks as concise and to the point as possible. Most interviewers are professionally trained and know how to guide applicants through the fact-finding process. Let the interviewer take the lead, and respond as concisely as possible without omitting pertinent information about your qualifications.

"Things turn out best for people who make the best of the way things turn out."

John Wooden

The Board or Panel Interview

In a board or panel interview, you talk with more than one person at one time. Focus on the person questioning you at the time, but don't ignore the others. Being relaxed and projecting a self-assured

attitude are important. Review the information about attitude and relaxation presented in Chapter 11.

Before a board or panel interview, obtain and memorize the names of every member of the panel. Then during the interview, draw a diagram of the interviewers as they are seated, and label the seats with their names (see Figure 13-2). At the close of the interview, thank by name and shake hands with each interviewer as you leave.

The Team Interview

A team interview may be given by a group of three to five employees. Usually, these employees are trained in interviewing techniques. They meet prior to the interview to determine the subject areas that each team member will cover with the applicant. A few common questions may be asked by all the team members to give the applicant more than one opportunity for adequate expression.

In this type of interview, the applicant meets individually with each member of the team; the team and the applicant do not meet together at one time. After the interviewing is completed, the team members meet to discuss the applicant's performance. Using common criteria, they assess the information from the individual sessions and their reactions before identifying the best candidate.

Team interviews give applicants a chance to meet with several people who may be their peers or supervisors on the job. This type of interview ensures a personality fit and increases the applicant's chances of establishing rapport with one or more members of the team.

Another team interview tactic is for several team members to use a panel interview format. This method is used when a future hire will be working directly with several managers. Having a candidate meet with several people at once saves time. For an out-of-town candidate, meeting several interviewers in a single sitting eliminates the need to travel to the prospective employer multiple times, thus saving money and time.

Before a team interview, learn the names of the members and, if possible, learn something about their areas of expertise. Use this information to enhance your performance. Also, be sure to give consistent answers to the individual members' questions.

Figure 13-2: Seating Diagram for a Panel Interview

The Stress Interview

A stress interview is usually structured and is designed to test the applicant's behavior, logic, and emotional control under pressure. This type of interview is not used routinely. It makes it more difficult to assess applicants' job qualifications and personal attributes because the applicants often become guarded in response to the stress. Stress interviews are generally reserved for jobs that involve regular pressure. Some stress questions, however, are routinely asked in other types of interviews—even informal ones. Every job has a crisis situation occasionally.

A skillful interviewer may use some stress techniques in combination with an unstructured interview approach to get a well-rounded picture of your personality. Some techniques used in stress interviewing

include (a) remaining silent following one of your remarks, (b) questioning you rapidly, (c) placing you on the defensive with irritating questions or remarks, and (d) criticizing your responses or remarks.

An interviewer may use a stress technique unintentionally. If you encounter one, do not react negatively. Take a deep breath, demonstrate control, and be courteous. This type of behavior earns perfect marks in a stress test! (Refer to Chapter 14 for specific examples of stress questions and suggested responses.)

The "Tell Me about Yourself" Interview

In a "tell me about yourself" interview, the interviewer takes a few minutes to build rapport with the applicant and then says, "Tell me about yourself." Be prepared to handle this type of interview effectively. Once the interviewer makes this request, he or she comments just enough to encourage the applicant to keep talking. The purpose is to see whether the applicant focuses on his or her qualifications for the job and how the employer would benefit by hiring the applicant. Do not ramble on about your life history; this is a sure way to disqualify yourself on the spot. Ask questions such as "What exactly do you want to know about— my work experience, educational experience, skills, or extracurricular and community activities?"

Your objective in this case is to highlight your positive qualities (personal attributes, accomplishments, skills, pertinent training, work experience, and so on). After you think you have covered these topics, ask, "Would you like me to clarify or expand on any area for you?" This helps you focus on the information the interviewer wants.

> ### Success Tip
>
> If an interviewer says "Tell me about yourself," focus completely on your qualifications for the job. Don't talk about your life history.

© DIGITAL VISION

Be prepared to take an interview call at any time. Stand up, smile, and speak directly into the mouthpiece while you're talking to project an energetic and positive tone.

The Corporate Ladder Interview

Large organizations sometimes schedule corporate ladder (or multilevel) interviews. The first rung of the ladder is the human resources department interview, which screens for applicants who are qualified to progress to the next step. The next interview is usually with a divisional manager or department head and is more detailed and specific regarding your relevant qualifications, skills, and experience.

From this step, you may have one or two more interviews, perhaps with a department manager, followed by the immediate section supervisor for the position. Each step will be progressively more specific in evaluating your suitability for the job. If you are asked the same question by more than one person, try to elaborate creatively while maintaining consistency. The key is to keep your enthusiasm high. This is an endurance test, so keep fueling yourself with positive thinking and expectations. And lean on your support system!

The Telephone Interview

A telephone interview is a cost-effective screening technique. If you expect to be interviewed by telephone, prepare by getting a member of your network to role-play the interviewer. Practice delivering your 60-Second Commercial and answering typical interview questions.

If you have submitted resumes or applications, you must expect a call from an interviewer at *any* time. Make sure you have a businesslike outgoing voice mail message with your name and/or phone number, and make sure all housemates know to answer the phone professionally and take messages if necessary. Return calls promptly, and be prepared either to interview immediately or to leave a message with your full contact information and your availability. The following tips will help you succeed in a telephone interview:

1. Be prepared to take an interview call at any time. Post your resume and 60-Second Commercial where you can refer to them easily. Also, have paper and a pen handy, so you can write down names and information and keep a log of your calls. If you need a moment to collect yourself, politely ask the interviewer to hold for a moment while you move to a quiet location. Eliminate all distractions and background noise.

2. Focus on why you are interested in working for the prospective employer (on the basis of your research and understanding of the employer's products or services, current developments, philosophies, and so on).

3. Be professional, courteous, and friendly; let the caller lead the conversation, but ask questions of your own.

4. Stand up, smile, and speak directly into the mouthpiece while you're talking; this gives your voice more energy and a pleasant tone. Never smoke, eat, or chew gum while on the telephone.

5. Beware of yes/no answers. They give no real information about your abilities.

6. Be factual in your answers; be brief yet thorough.

7. If you need time to think about a question, avoid using repetitive phrases to buy time. Instead, simply say, "Let me think about that."

8. Use the "clincher" technique described in Chapter 11: Ask what skills, knowledge, and qualities the employer is looking for in filling the position. While the interviewer answers, jot down the qualities you have that match; then describe them to emphasize how you meet the employer's needs.

9. As you wrap up the interview, ask what the next steps are. Tell the interviewer that you are available for a face-to-face interview at his or her earliest convenience.

10. Follow up. Call back one or two days later, thank the interviewer for his or her time, and restate your interest in the position. If necessary, leave this message by voice mail, or send an e-mail or a fax.

The Computer-Assisted Interview

Some companies use computer-assisted interviews to screen applicants. The applicant is taken to a computer workstation and given instructions on how to complete the interview. The interview typically consists of 50 to 100 computerized multiple-choice and true/false questions that are scored automatically. Some computer-assisted interviews include essay questions that are reviewed by recruitment specialists or managers. Answer questions just as you would in a face-to-face interview. Be sure to:

▲ Emphasize your related skills, but don't exaggerate. Be concise, avoiding overly long responses or a negative focus on a topic.

▲ Be consistent in your answers; some programs search for contradictions.

▲ Avoid pausing too long before responding; some systems flag abnormally long pauses.

The benefits of computer-assisted interviews include ease and cost effectiveness of data collection, consistent gathering of information from all applicants to keep the playing field level, and avoidance of personal bias from the interviewer. The primary drawback is that computers are not capable of assessing personal qualities such as attitude and enthusiasm. These qualities can be observed in follow-up interviews, however.

The Internet Computer-Assisted Interview

The Internet computer-assisted interview is a version of the regular computer-assisted interview. The Internet interview is useful for long-distance applicant screenings because it saves travel time and other expenses.

In an Internet interview, the employer contacts you and gives you a password. Through the Internet, you log on to the company's in-house network (using the password) and complete an interview that is essentially the same as a computer-assisted interview.

Success Tip

In computer-assisted interviews, be consistent in your answers and avoid long pauses before responding.

The Task-Oriented Interview

In a task-oriented interview, the applicant is asked to demonstrate his or her skills by performing specific tasks. This type of interview gives employers a chance to assess applicants' skills and knowledge in a realistic—rather than theoretical—way. It also gives applicants a chance to showcase their abilities and to assess their interest in the type of work they would be doing. If your target employer uses this style of interviewing, try to find out what types of skills you are expected to demonstrate, and practice them beforehand.

The Internet Video Interview

An Internet video interview involves the use of two-way video to conduct a "face-to-face" interview over the Web. Cameras are attached to computers at two separate locations. This method is being used frequently to save money and time for organizations. Many major corporations, colleges, and universities are set up to offer real-time video interviewing.

To save time and money, an employer may ask you to participate in an Internet video interview.

To succeed in this type of interview, follow the guidelines for standard face-to-face interviews outlined in Chapter 11. Be sure to dress appropriately, project energy, maintain eye contact with the camera, use positive body language, use good posture, and avoid fidgeting.

You may want to practice this type of interview with a member of your support group to increase your comfort level with it.

Complete Career Action 13-1

CAREER ACTION 13-1

Research Interview Styles

Part A: Personal Contact Research

Directions: Contact at least two organizations in your field that are similar to your target employer, and arrange a brief meeting with each to research their interview styles. Make sure they understand that this is not a request for an interview. Follow the guidelines for conducting a successful outside assignment provided in Chapter 7, as well as the steps below.

1. During your meetings, ask your contacts to describe the style of interviewing they use to evaluate applicants for positions similar to the one you are targeting.

2. Ask what criteria (skills, experience, education, personal qualities) they use to evaluate applicants.

3. Ask for specific examples of applicants' positive and negative actions and comments.

4. Take notes of any information you find useful.

5. As always, act professionally and thank the people who help you. Follow up by sending thank-you notes.

Part B: Internet Research

Directions: Use the following Internet resources or others of your choice to search for information on the interview styles you expect to be the most prevalent in your field (links can be found on the *Your Career: How to Make It Happen* web site at http://levitt.swlearning.com). Summarize the key points you find useful or print relevant articles.

File your research in your Career Management Files Binder.

CareerJournal.com   Quintessential Careers

The Riley Guide   Yahoo! HotJobs

The Unstructured Interview

The unstructured interview approach is generally taken by people who are not professionally trained in interviewing. It tends to be more informal and conversational in tone than a structured interview approach. The unstructured approach is often used by the owners or managers of small businesses. In a small organization, interviewing job applicants is just one of many responsibilities of the interviewer; it is not the primary job assignment, as it is in the case of a human resources specialist in a large organization.

Success Tip

The most important thing to do in an unstructured interview is to be sure you present your qualifications thoroughly. If an untrained or unstructured interviewer doesn't focus on extracting this essential information, make sure you bring it out!

Unstructured interviewing is often more successful than structured interviewing at bringing out the personal qualities of an applicant (attitudes, feelings, goals, and human relations skills). The questions in unstructured interviews are usually open-ended to encourage the interviewees to express their personalities, background, and goals. Success or failure in this type of interview is more often based on the ability of the job seeker to communicate than on the content of his or her answers.

An untrained interviewer may not be skilled in discussing job qualifications, so the conversation may get bogged down by unimportant details. In this situation, you need to be the "professional interviewee." You can aid the interviewer by asking questions to learn about the full scope of the job and by communicating all your skills, experience, and attributes that apply to it.

PERSONAL BEST

Managing Stress

The ability to manage stress well is key to your success in today's ever-changing workplace. It's also key to your success in stressful interviewing situations. If you can anticipate stressful situations ahead of time, you can manage the stress they cause more effectively. These tips will help:

▲ **Rehearse.** Practice for a stressful event in advance so you can polish your performance and build confidence. Be sure to work on communication and thinking on your feet by practicing tough questions.

▲ **Plan.** Learn specific techniques for dealing with stress, such as positive visualization. Also, being organized, prepared, and punctual will help you minimize anxiety and make a good impression.

▲ **Keep it in perspective.** If an event seems big, put it in its place. How important is the event, really, in light of your ultimate goals? To put it in perspective, compare it with bigger events in your mind.

▲ **Get the information you need.** A lack of information can negatively affect your ability to perform. If you are uncertain about what's expected in a job or in an interview setting, ask for the information you need.

▲ **Think positively.** Practice the nine success strategies you learned in Chapter 1. Positive thinking, visualization, positive self-talk, goal setting, and self-esteem builders can all work together to combat stress.

▲ **Take action.** Exercise, yoga, breathing exercises, good health, and good nutrition can help you relax and release stress. Also, get a good night's sleep before an important interview to be sure you're energetic and alert.

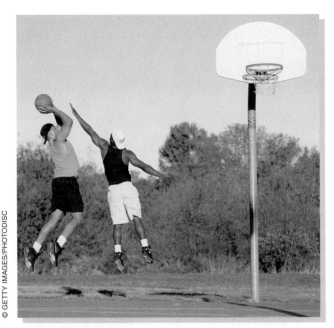

Engaging in physical activity is a good way to help you relax and keep up your energy for a successful interview.

the professional interviewee. You can always learn something beneficial or use the opportunity to polish your interviewing skills. Don't give up during an interview; it could cost you a future reference or a good job lead from the interviewer. If you have a bad interview, chalk it up to experience.

The Unsuccessful Interview

As a general rule, a job applicant must have several interviews before a good job is offered. Getting a top-notch job is a full-time job that often requires several interviews and some rejections. Harness the energy of negative feelings from rejections, turning them into a positive force. Fueling your determination will help you land the job you want the most.

Again, remember that you can learn from interviews. If you aren't offered a job, ask the interviewer to suggest ways you could improve your interviewing skills or to explain whether you appear to be lacking in any area of skill, training, or experience. Attaining this information is the starting point for succeeding in your next interview.

The Bad Interview

Some interviews are not good; in fact, some are grim. After learning the details of a job, you may be convinced that you don't want it. The interviewer may be inept at interviewing, making it difficult for you to perform well. Do not stop trying. Do your best to be

Complete Career Action 13-2

CAREER ACTION 13-2

Summarize Interview Styles That Are Pertinent to Your Field

Directions: Review all the information in this chapter and your findings from Career Action 13-1. On a separate sheet of paper or using the form on your Learner's CD, prepare a written report that includes the following information:

1. Describe the interview styles you expect to be the most prevalent in your field.

2. Describe techniques you have learned that will help you succeed in these types of interviews.

File your report in your Career Management Files Binder.

CHECKLIST

PREPARING FOR ANY INTERVIEW STYLE

Check each of the actions you are currently taking to increase your career success:

○ **Overly structured interview:** Being friendly and positive to establish rapport and a relaxed tone

○ **Behavioral interview:** Providing proof-by-example descriptions of your capabilities

○ **Screening interview:** Finding out what the next step is and who will make the hiring decision

○ **Board, panel, or team interview:** Learning and using the names of all the interviewers

○ **Stress interview:** Remaining calm and not reacting negatively

○ **"Tell me about yourself" interview:** Focusing completely on your job qualifications

○ **Multilevel or corporate ladder interview:** Keeping your answers consistent and maintaining energy

○ **Telephone interview:** Posting your resume and your 60-Second Commercial close by, standing up, smiling, and eliminating distractions

○ **Computer-assisted interview:** Giving consistent answers and avoiding long pauses

○ **Unstructured interview:** Presenting your qualifications thoroughly

CRITICAL THINKING QUESTIONS

1. How can job seekers benefit by learning what style of interview is typically used by their target employers?

2. What benefits can you gain by trying to relax the atmosphere of a highly structured interview?

3. What style(s) of interviewing do you expect to be the most prevalent in your job search? What techniques can you use to maximize your performance in these types of interviews?

For convenient access to valuable career resources, activities, and job information links, visit the companion web site for this text: *http://levitt.swlearning.com*

chapter 14

NAVIGATE INTERVIEW QUESTIONS AND ANSWERS

In this chapter, you will:

- Use the Internet to search for additional information on interview questions and answers.

- Write out appropriate answers to frequently asked and challenging interview questions.

- Write effective questions to ask during an interview.

- Employ strategies for your best question-and-answer performance.

"A long-term focus and commitment to succeeding are items I use to evaluate a prospective candidate. Specific questions regarding advancement opportunity and business development are key indicators that the individual is looking for a career, not merely a job."

Michael R. Slyby
Managing Director
MetLife Financial Services

The core of an interview is the question-and-answer period. It should include questions and answers from the interviewer and from you. To ace an interview, you should generally let the interviewer take the lead. Interviewers usually consider applicants' efforts to control the interview to be rude. You should, however, ask questions—for two reasons: (1) to verify that this is the employer you want to work for and (2) to demonstrate initiative and preparation. Chapter 14 presents a comprehensive overview of common interview questions, tips for answering these questions effectively, and samples of meaningful questions to ask.

Focus on Your Job Qualifications

Persuasively discussing your strengths and how they can benefit the employer requires some preparation. Consider the positive capabilities and personal qualities your coworkers, supervisors, instructors, and others have recognized in you. Review your 60-Second Commercial (Chapter 11) and your resume. Write out examples of your positive performance that are related to the target job's requirements.

What examples demonstrate your organizational skills and orderly mind? Have you developed improved methods of performing tasks or working with people? How have you motivated people successfully? Can you cite examples of effective problem solving? Are you creative? Can you give examples of handling detail work well? Are you dependable and cooperative? What activities have you been involved in that demonstrate each of these qualities? Are you flexible, able to work independently without regular supervision, and able to work effectively in a team? Choose these types of examples to showcase what you can do for the employer. Focus on proving your qualifications by example in the question-and-answer period of your interview.

Prepare for Interviewer Questions

Questions asked by interviewers generally fall into four categories:

▲ General information questions

▲ Behavioral questions

▲ Character questions

▲ Stress questions

Study the following lists of the most common interview questions and suggested answers. In Career Action 14-2, you will write your own responses. Writing and rehearsing this script will help you answer questions successfully during an interview.

Success Tip

Focus on proving by example. Respond persuasively to questions about your abilities; give measurable examples of successfully applying them in work, school, and other activities.

General Information Questions

General information questions are asked to obtain factual information about you. They usually cover your skills, education, work experience, and so on.

1. **Why do you want this job?** (Be prepared; every employer wants to know the answer to this question.)

   Suggested Answer: "My skills and experience are directly related to this position, and my interest lies especially in this field." Relate examples of your experience, education, and/or training that are pertinent to the job you are seeking; select appropriate examples based on your employer and job research. Emphasize your interest in developing your career in this area. Don't say you want the job because of the pay and benefits. If you are impressed with and knowledgeable about the reputation of the firm, say so, and add that you would be pleased to be a part of the organization. Don't overdo it, however. Keep your answer to the point, remembering that the objective is to show what you can do for the company.

2. **What type of work do you most enjoy?**

   Suggested Answer: Play your research card; name the types of tasks that are involved in the job you are interviewing for. Demonstrate how you are qualified for the position.

3. **What are your strongest skills?**

   Suggested Answer: Review your abilities and accomplishments and your 60-Second Commercial. Use them to develop your answer. Again, try to relate your skills to those required in the position for which you are applying.

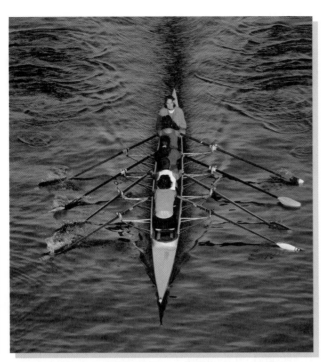

© GETTY IMAGES/PHOTODISC

Describe school or sports activities and accomplishments in other jobs when responding to questions about teamwork, character, and personal strengths.

4. **What are your long-term career goals, and how do you plan to achieve them?**

Suggested Answer: While this is usually a general information question, it can become a stress question if you trap yourself by appearing overly aggressive, too ambitious, or lacking in ambition. Employers want a commitment in return for their training investment. They may not consider you if they think you won't be happy in the job for a reasonable amount of time or see the job only as a fast springboard to something better. Emphasize your strengths, state that your goal is to make a strong contribution in your job, and explain that you look forward to developing the experience necessary for career growth.

Employers are impressed with employees who show initiative because they often perform better than those who have no plans for self-improvement. Mention your plans to continue your education and expand your knowledge to become a more valuable employee.

5. **Are you a team player?**

Suggested Answer: Teamwork is highly valued in today's workplaces, so a positive answer is usually a plus. Give examples of your successful team roles (as a leader, as a member, and as a partner) at school, on the job, and in clubs or other activities.

6. **Do you have a geographical preference? Are you willing to relocate?**

Suggested Answer: If the job requires relocation, this question is important. If you have no objection to relocating, make this perfectly clear. If you do have objections, this could be a stress question. Be honest in your answer. If you don't like being mobile, say so; otherwise, you will undoubtedly be unhappy in the job.

7. **Under what management style do you work most efficiently?**

Suggested Answer: "I am flexible and can be productive under any style. The management style I enjoy working with the most is _____." (This answer shows that you are flexible and casts no negative connotations. It also answers the primary question.)

Success Tip

Prepare and rehearse responses to typical interview questions. The result can enhance your interview and career success.

Behavioral Questions

The behavioral job interview is used widely today and is based on the premise that past performance is the best predictor of future behavior. Behavioral interviews probe applicants' specific past performance and behaviors through behavioral questions such as "Describe one of the most challenging assignments you've had. How did you handle it?" This may be followed by several more in-depth probes aimed at getting further details, such as

"Explain what problems you encountered. How did you overcome them?" Some behavioral questions probe for negative experiences. In responding to these, focus on what you learned from the experience or what actions you took to improve the situation.

Experience Scenarios. To prepare for behavioral interviews, recall scenarios from your experiences that illustrate how you have performed or behaved on the job. Write out examples that demonstrate good performance. Also, be ready to describe how you have handled difficult situations. Students with little work experience should focus on class projects and group situations that illustrate their task performance and interpersonal behavior.

Behavioral Question Response Model. These four steps provide a good model for your answers to behavioral questions:

1. Describe the situation.

2. Explain the actions you took.

3. Describe the outcomes.

4. Summarize what you learned from the experience.

   Example: Describe an accomplishment that demonstrates your initiative.

   Suggested Answer: "While I was working part-time as a computer lab technician for Seattle Technology College, our department received several complaints about service response time. I set a personal goal of answering all troubleshooting calls within 90 minutes. I recorded the exact response time for each call and maintained the 90-minute response time goal for one full semester. I was awarded the Customer Service Certificate for this performance."

Whenever possible, give positive examples that demonstrate measurable achievements. Or, when describing a less positive experience, emphasize what actions you took to correct weaknesses or poor

performance. By giving specific examples, you establish credibility and believability that can translate into a job offer. Some additional examples of behavioral interview questions are listed below.

▲ Tell me specifically about a time when you worked under great stress.

▲ Describe an experience when you dealt with an angry customer or coworker.

▲ Give me an example of your ability to adapt to change.

▲ Tell me about a time when you were forced to make an unpopular decision.

Character Questions

Character questions are asked to learn about your personal attributes, such as integrity, personality, attitudes, and motivation.

1. **How would you describe yourself?**

   Suggested Answer: Emphasize your strongest personal attributes, and focus on those that are relevant to your target job. Review your capabilities and accomplishments. Appropriate responses include these:

   "I'm punctual and dependable. At my current job, I haven't been late or missed one day in the last two years." "I get along well with others; in fact, I've been chosen by my coworkers to represent them in our company's monthly staff meetings." Give specific examples of your strengths. Don't just say "I'm a hard worker" or "I'm dependable"; give concrete examples. Other leads include "I learn quickly," "I like solving problems; for example. . . ," "I like contributing to a team," and "I like managing people."

2. **What rewards do you look for in your career?**

   Suggested Answer: Don't stress monetary rewards. Emphasize your desire to improve your skills, to make a valuable contribution to the field, and to become better educated. These answers show initiative, interest, and

> *"Each experience through which we pass operates ultimately for our good."*
> Raymond Holliwell

professionalism. You can also mention that you expect an income that matches your performance.

3. **What accomplishment are you most proud of, particularly as it relates to your field?**

   Suggested Answer: Relate an accomplishment that demonstrates special effort and initiative—perhaps one that surpassed normal requirements. For example, at your last job, you recognized the need to improve communications within the organization. To identify the causes of miscommunications, you designed a questionnaire that was completed by representatives of every department. Management initiated the changes suggested, and communications improved in the areas identified.

   Another Example: You purchased a computer with earnings from your part-time job and used the equipment to start your own business preparing term papers, resumes, and other items for students and instructors from your school and community. The earnings paid for 80 percent of your school costs.

4. **Do you work well under pressure?**

   Suggested Answer: You may be tempted to answer with a simple yes or no, but don't. Yes and no answers reveal nothing specific about you. Don't miss any opportunity to sell yourself.

   Be honest in your answer. If you prefer to work at a well-defined job in an organized, calm atmosphere (rather than one that involves constant decision making and pressure), say so. Otherwise, you may end up in a job that is a constant source of tension. If you enjoy the challenge of pressure, either in decision making or in dealing with people, make this clear.

   Keep in mind that a large company may have more than one working environment. For instance, an administrative support job in the customer relations department would likely involve more interactive pressure with the public than a support job in the data processing department would.

Stress Questions

Stress questions are asked to determine how you perform under pressure (controlled and composed or nervous and unsettled). They are also used to find out whether you are good at making decisions, solving problems, and thinking under stress.

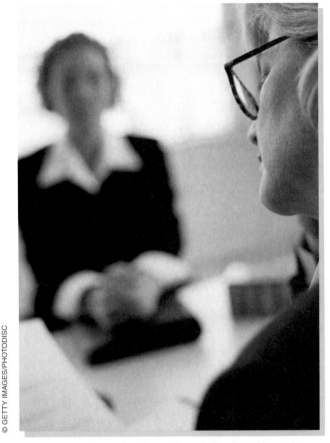

© GETTY IMAGES/PHOTODISC

Answer difficult questions honestly and directly. Address the employer's needs and concerns.

Some questions may be aimed at clarifying issues the interviewer perceives as possible problems, such as being overqualified or underqualified, having physical limitations, and lacking dependability (if your resume shows many different jobs).

Preparing Answers to Stress Questions. Prepare to answer any stress questions that are based on your resume or personal circumstances. Look at a stress question as an opportunity to prove that a situation is not a problem as it relates to your ability to do the job. Career Action 14-2 will help you prepare by having you write out responses to possible stress questions. Rehearse your responses. Either tape-record yourself giving the question(s) and prepared response(s) or ask a member of your support network to help you role-play the interview. Revise your responses based on the feedback you receive.

Success Tip

Prepare for stress questions by practicing your responses. Keep your cool, breathe deeply, use positive self-talk, and take time to think. Demonstrate stress-management skills by thinking the questions through and remaining composed.

Remaining Cool Under Stress. Keep your cool. Remain focused; take three to five calming deep breaths; and tell yourself, "I can do this." If you are asked a question that you are totally unprepared for, don't just ramble through an answer. Use the "that's a good question, let me think about that for a minute" technique. This can buy you time to prepare a well-thought-out response. Your goal is to demonstrate that you can handle stress—that you don't just react but instead think through the situation and remain composed.

1. **Why do you think you are the best candidate for this job?**

   Suggested Answer: Prepare for this one. It might also be phrased "Why should I hire you?" Ask the interviewer to highlight the important objectives and challenges of the job. Then explain how you can handle them. Focus on how you can benefit the employer, citing examples of increasing productivity, saving money, increasing sales, and so on. Summarize your accomplishments, skills, and experience that are pertinent to the job. Then ask, "How does that fit your requirements?" This shifts the focus from you to the interviewer, helping reduce stress for you. The key is to get the interviewer involved in developing your answer. This buys you time to develop an appropriate response.

> *"Adopting the right attitude can convert a negative stress into a positive one."*
>
> Hans Selye

2. **Why do you want to leave your current job?**

   Suggested Answer: This question will likely be posed to determine whether you have a problem with your current job. Accentuate the positive—you are seeking a new challenge, you have mastered your present job and are seeking advancement, you want to work for a company with stability, and so on. If you do have a problem with your current job, avoid discussing it. If you think you must discuss it, describe the situation briefly and unemotionally. Then return the interview to a positive tone, explaining that you think this organization would provide a good opportunity for career growth.

3. **Why have you held so many jobs?**

   Suggested Answer: Naturally, employers are impressed by a work history that implies stability and dependability. Often people have valid reasons for holding numerous jobs. Some jobs are seasonal (agriculture, landscaping, and recreation), some jobs involve frequent relocation (engineering and construction), and some jobs are profoundly affected by the general economy. You may have held a variety of summer jobs while completing your education. Capitalize on this; it shows initiative and provides you with broad working experience.

   You may also have accompanied your spouse, who was required to relocate frequently. If you did, in fact, change jobs frequently, mention that previously you wanted to obtain a broad base of experience but that now your goal is to apply this experience to long-term employment and the development of a career.

4. **What is your greatest weakness?**

   Suggested Answer: "My weakest area is accounting (unless you are applying for an accounting position!), so I'm taking a beginning accounting course at the college. It's going well, and I plan to take the advanced course next semester." The objective is to acknowledge a weakness and to explain your plan for improving it. Choose a weakness that is low on the employer's list of required skills and that you are currently taking steps to improve (through practice, education, planning, and so on).

5. **Have you ever been fired from a job?**

   Suggested Answer: If you have been fired, use terms such as *laid off, terminated,* or *employment ended;* they sound less negative. Be honest about the reason for your termination. Briefly describe the situation. Explain what you learned from the experience and how you could have handled the situation differently. Take responsibility for past mistakes, but end your response on a positive note.

   If you have been laid off for a reason that implies no fault of your own (such as downsizing, a loss of company business, or a lagging economy), remember that this is not the same as being fired. Therefore, you do not need to mention this in your answer to question 5. If quitting a job was your own decision, remember to use more positive language, such as "I left" or "I decided to leave."

6. **Does your current employer know you are planning to leave?**

   Suggested Answer: If your current employer is aware of this fact, say so. If not—and especially if you depend on your current income—make this clear. Say that you prefer your current employer not be informed of your job search until a firm job offer is made and that you will give at least two weeks' notice before leaving. (This demonstrates good ethics and a sense of responsibility—both pluses for you!)

Some questions are not purposely posed to be stressful, but they may be stressful to you. For instance, if the interviewer asks, "Does your employer know you are planning to leave?" and the answer is "yes," because your spouse is being transferred, the question will not be stressful to you. If, however, your reason for leaving is that you can no longer tolerate working for your current employer, the question will probably be stressful.

The following Personal Best feature provides guidelines for handling inappropriate or illegal questions effectively. Review this information carefully, and consider how you can apply it in an interview should the need arise.

PERSONAL**BEST**

Handling Inappropriate Questions

The interview is going along well, and then it happens: "Are you considering having children?" or "How long has your family been in this country?"

On the surface, questions such as these seem innocent enough. Yet the structure and format of the questions may be illegal or, at the very least, inappropriate. Questions that focus on age, gender, race, marital status, children, criminal record, national origin, religion, or disability are inappropriate in a job interview because they can be used as a basis for discrimination.

So you've just been hit with an inappropriate question. What do you do? How do you respond?

If you complain about a question being illegal or unfair and refuse to answer it, you probably won't be offered the job. You certainly have the right to refuse, but first weigh the situation. Is it worth jeopardizing the job over this question? Or, does the interviewer appear so offensive that you don't want to work for the organization anyway?

The most effective approach is to answer the question in a polite, honest manner. Don't offer detailed personal information. Instead, steer the conversation back to your ability to meet the employer's expectations, as in the following example:

Interviewer: Do you have children?

Applicant: Yes, and I'm thorough in arranging dependable child care. It pays off; I've never had to miss a day of work or school for child care purposes (emphasizing planning and management skills).

Anticipate the stress of inappropriate questions. Prepare and practice appropriate responses. This gives you the edge in demonstrating your ability to handle stressful situations calmly and skillfully—just the behavior employers want.

Plan Now: Your Questions Count!

Making the interview an effective two-way communication is important. Prepare to ask three to five well-chosen and appropriate questions. A prospective employer will respect what you inspect, not what you expect. Outline questions that will help you learn more about the employer and the position, as well as questions that show your initiative and preparation.

Don't ask all your questions at the end of the interview. Interject them naturally at appropriate intervals throughout the meeting. Keep your questions positive. Avoid asking any that could elicit a negative reaction from the interviewer. Also, avoid discussing salary until a job offer is made (see Chapter 15).

Good Questions to Ask

Asking appropriate questions demonstrates interest and confidence, showcases your knowledge, and gives you an active role in the interview. Study the following sample questions carefully; then write your own questions as part of Career Action 14-2.

1. **Do you have a training program for this position? If so, would you describe it?** This demonstrates interest in the job and a desire to perform it well.

2. **Would you describe the duties and tasks of this position in a typical workday?** The answer to this question will help you better understand the scope of the job. It may be just what you want, or you may learn that it's not the type of work you are seeking. The information you receive will be important to you in considering a job offer.

3. **May I have a copy of the written job description?** Getting a job description can help you tie your qualifications to those required for the job.

4. **Will the responsibilities of this position expand with time and experience on the job?** Could good performance in this job lead to opportunities for career growth? Answers to these questions will help you determine whether this is a dead-end job or if employee career growth is encouraged.

© GETTY IMAGES/PHOTODISC

Asking an employer if training for the position is available will demonstrate your interest in performing the job well.

5. **Could you tell me about the people with whom I would be working?** To whom would I report, and who would be my peers and subordinates? How will I be evaluated? The answers can help you evaluate company structure and how you might fit into the organization.

6. **Do you require any more information about my qualifications or experience?** This gives you an opportunity to clear up any misunderstanding or lack of information. It also gives you another chance to run your 60-Second Commercial, once again emphasizing just how well qualified you are.

7. **When will you be making your hiring decision?** May I call you if I have additional questions? These types of questions help you judge when to follow up and will keep the door open for further communication.

Success Tip

Prepare and ask appropriate questions; this demonstrates interest, confidence, and intelligence.

Turnoff Questions to Avoid

Following are some questions that are most disliked by employers. Do not ask them; they will make you sound uninformed and diminish your likability.

1. **What does this company do?** You should have done your research well enough to know exactly what the company does. Asking this question will make you appear uninformed and unqualified. Employers are not looking for employees who know nothing about their business!

2. **How much sick leave and vacation time will I get?** Do not ask this question during a first interview. Although employee benefits are important, asking specifically about vacation time or sick leave projects a negative attitude. You should ask this question before making a final decision about a job offer, however.

Employers understand the importance of major benefits to prospective employees.

3. **Will I have an office?** This suggests that you care more about where you will work than about what you will do.

4. **What time do I have to be at work in the morning? How long do you give for lunch?** These questions sound immature and do not project an enthusiastic interest in the work!

5. **How long do I have to work before I am eligible for a raise?** This question tells the employer that you are more interested in the salary than the job.

> **Complete Career Action 14-1**

CAREER ACTION 14-1

Use the Internet to Search for Interview Question-and-Answer Tips

Directions: Use the Internet to search for additional useful tips on interview questions and answers. Summarize the key points or print the relevant articles that you find. File your research in your Career Management Files Binder.

Use the following web sites and your favorite search engines to find tips on interview questions and answers (links can be found on the *Your Career: How to Make It Happen* web site at http://levitt.swlearning.com). If you want to know more about handling inappropriate questions, include this topic in your search.

▲ Net-Temps
  (Click on "Jobseekers" and "Interviewing.")

▲ The Riley Guide
  (Click on "Network, Interview, & Negotiate"; then click on "Interviewing," and select appropriate articles to read.)

▲ Indiana University Bloomington Libraries
  (Perform a search for "interview questions.")

▲ Virginia Tech Career Services
  (Click on "Job Search"; then click on "Interviewing.")

▲ JobWeb

Apply Q-and-A Savvy Strategies

The following strategies for interview question-and-answer sessions are well received by employers.

▲ **Be enthusiastic.** Enthusiasm is a quality that employers look for when hiring.

▲ **Pause to think before you reply.** If you're uncomfortable with a question, go back to the familiar. Stress your assets. Use a "thinking pause" to buy time to answer the question well. One of the following phrases can be used:

"Could we return to this question? I'd like to think about it for a moment."

"That's a good question" or "Let me see. . ." (This works if you need only a little extra time.)

▲ **Be candid and honest.** Be realistic when expressing your preferences and dislikes. You won't be happy in a job that isn't a good fit.

▲ **Do not use canned responses.** Tailor your answers to fit your goals, objectives, and personality, as well as the goals and needs of the employer.

▲ **Be concise.** Keep your responses to the point, but avoid being curt or too brief.

▲ **Answer in complete sentences, and speak correctly.** Speak in complete sentences. Avoid using slang, profanity, incorrect grammar, or repetitive terms. Speak clearly.

▲ **Be positive.** Positive thinking promotes positive behavior and speech, a positive image, positive responses, and a positive atmosphere. It also projects enthusiasm, self-confidence, and initiative.

▲ **Fill in the gaps.** If you sense that the interviewer thinks you have an area of weakness, communicate how you plan to eliminate the weakness or round out your qualifications—perhaps by completing research or coursework in the area.

Complete Career Action 14-2

CHECKLIST

NAVIGATING INTERVIEW QUESTIONS AND ANSWERS

Check each of the actions you are currently taking to increase your career success:

○ Focusing on proof by example; responding persuasively to questions about your abilities; and citing examples of applying your abilities in work, school, and other activities

○ Preparing and rehearsing responses to typical interview questions

○ Anticipating the stress of inappropriate interview questions and practicing careful responses

○ Preparing and practicing responses to stress questions; staying cool, breathing deeply, using positive self-talk, and taking time to think; and demonstrating stress-management skills—thinking the questions through and remaining composed

○ Preparing and asking appropriate questions

○ Avoiding asking questions that diminish your likability, including questions that are too direct, questions that your research should have answered, and questions that make you appear immature or uncommitted to the job

CRITICAL THINKING QUESTIONS

1. What should your main objectives be during the question-and-answer portion of an interview?

2. Why is it important for an applicant to pose some questions during an interview?

3. What specific types of questions do you most need to prepare for to be ready for your interviews? List two examples, and include the answers you plan to give.

4. How should you handle an illegal or inappropriate question from an interviewer?

For convenient access to valuable career resources, activities, and job information links, visit the companion web site for this text: *http://levitt.swlearning.com*

CAREER ACTION WORKSHEET 14-2

Question-and-Answer Planning Sheet

General Information Questions

1. Why do you want this job?

   _____

   _____

   _____

2. What type of work do you enjoy doing the most?

   _____

   _____

   _____

3. What are your strongest skills?

   _____

   _____

   _____

4. What are your long-term career goals, and how do you plan to achieve them?

   _____

   _____

   _____

5. Are you a team player? Give examples.

   _____

   _____

   _____

6. Do you have a geographical preference? Are you willing to relocate?

   _____

   _____

   _____

Continued on next page >>>

CAREER ACTION WORKSHEET **14-2 (continued)**

7. Under what management style do you work most productively?

_____

_____

_____

8. What is important to you in a company? What do you look for in an organization?

_____

_____

_____

Behavioral and Character Questions

1. What have you accomplished that demonstrates your initiative?

_____

_____

_____

2. How do you deal with an angry customer or coworker? Describe an experience you've had.

_____

_____

_____

3. How are you able to adapt to change? Give an example.

_____

_____

_____

4. How would you describe yourself?

_____

_____

_____

Continued on next page >>>

CAREER ACTION WORKSHEET **14-2 (continued)**

5. What rewards do you look for in your career?

_____

_____

_____

6. What accomplishment are you most proud of, particularly as it relates to your field?

_____

_____

_____

7. Do you work well under pressure? Give an example.

_____

_____

_____

8. What do you think are the most important characteristics and abilities a person must possess to be successful? How do you rate yourself in those areas?

_____

_____

_____

Stress Questions

1. Why do you think you are the best candidate for this job? Why should I hire you?

_____

_____

_____

2. Why do you want to leave your current job?

_____

_____

_____

Continued on next page >>>

CAREER ACTION WORKSHEET 14-2 (continued)

3. Why have you held so many jobs?

_____

_____

_____

4. What is your greatest weakness?

_____

_____

_____

5. Have you ever been fired from a job?

_____

_____

_____

6. Does your current employer know you are planning to leave?

_____

_____

_____

7. What kinds of decisions are the most difficult for you?

_____

_____

_____

Questions and Topics to Avoid

1. Why should you avoid asking "What does this company do?"

_____

_____

_____

Continued on next page >>>

CAREER ACTION WORKSHEET 14-2

2. Should you ask about sick leave and vacation time? Why or why not?

_____

_____

_____

3. Why shouldn't you ask "How long do I have to work before I qualify for a raise?"

_____

_____

_____

4. Why should you avoid asking "Will I have an office?"

_____

_____

_____

5. Based on your outside research or reading, what other questions do interviewers dislike being asked by applicants?

_____

_____

_____

Q-and-A Savvy Strategies

Review the "Apply Q-and-A Savvy Strategies" section in this chapter. List the strategies that are most applicable to your job search. Add any others you identified through your Internet research.

_____

_____

_____

Your Questions

Review the sample questions in the section called "Plan Now: Your Questions Count!" In your own words, write the questions you want to ask during your interviews, and save them in your Career Management Files Binder. If necessary, ask for help from a member of your support system. Add questions that are pertinent to your job search and goals.

_____

_____

_____

ACE EMPLOYMENT TESTS AND NEGOTIATIONS

In this chapter, you will:

- Use the Internet to research current salary information for your field.

- Identify the employment testing procedures used and the compensation packages offered in your field for the type of job you are seeking.

- Summarize guidelines for negotiating the compensation package you are offered.

- Summarize how to deal effectively with job offers.

> *"Our computerized preemployment tests help determine the marketability of each applicant. If the applicant does well on the assessment tests, we are more likely to place him or her in a position that requires more skills and pays better."*
>
> Jennifer Evans
> Branch Manager
> Kelly Services

Chapter 15 presents strategies to help you perform successfully when preparing for and taking different types of preemployment tests, including drug screening and background checks. The chapter also presents important guidelines for you to follow when researching salary and benefits information; negotiating a fair compensation package; and evaluating, rejecting, or accepting job offers.

Ace Employment Tests

Doing your homework is a sure way to improve your educational test scores, and it also helps you succeed in employment tests. As part of your research, find out if the prospective employer requires preemployment testing. Many employers don't use preemployment testing, but you may apply to one that does. If a test is involved, find out whether it's a written, oral, combination, or computerized test. Does it test technical knowledge, skills, manual dexterity, personality, special abilities, or other job-related capabilities? Try to find out what will be tested and how.

Well in advance of asking for an interview, contact the employer, speak with a human resources staff person or the office manager, and ask the person to describe any testing procedures used.

The Personality Test

The personality test is the one exception to the "do your homework" rule. Because this type of test is usually designed to determine whether your personal and behavioral preferences are well matched to the work involved, advance study doesn't apply. Technically, there are no wrong answers in these tests. Most personality tests measure your solitary or social tendencies, relative need for stability, preference for efficiency or creativity, style of goal achievement (flexible or fixed), and tendency to accept others' ideas or stick to your own. Answer all questions honestly. If your personality doesn't match the job, you won't be happy in it. For links to some sample personality tests, visit the *Your Career* web site at http://levitt.swlearning.com.

The Skills Test

If you will be taking a skills test, start to review, practice, and improve your skills today. No matter how good your skills are, you can improve them with practice, which increases your employability. Another benefit of polishing your skills is that you'll be able to start your new job with more confidence. Stop

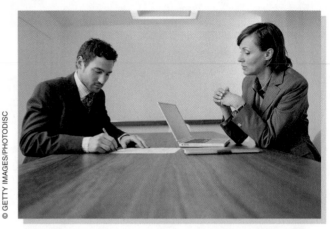

Employers' testing requirements vary. You may be asked to take a simple skills test or a more detailed technical test.

preparing one or two days before you take a skills test, however. Cramming until the last minute increases anxiety and often results in lower performance.

The Technical Test

If you will be required to take an oral or written test for a professional position, try to get some samples of the technical questions that may be asked. Resources for learning about the types of questions are the employer's human resources department, other employees in the company, people who have taken the test, and people who have taken similar tests in your field. Libraries and bookstores also have sample tests.

If you can find sample questions or even general topics that will be covered in the technical test, write out answers to the questions. The important thing is to be as complete as possible in your answers. The purpose of a technical test is to find out how much you know about the subject.

The Computerized Preemployment Test

The computerized preemployment test is useful for large applicant screenings because it saves time and other expenses. The test may be general in content, or it may be a skills or personality test.

Typically, you take this test at the employer's site or at an employment agency. You also may be asked to log on to an employer's web site and take the test online. You receive instructions on how to use the computerized test program and are given a specific amount of time to complete it. The results are usually scored electronically and generated in a report. They are then analyzed by human resources personnel. The best advice for performing well on a computerized preemployment test is to do your best; don't try to outwit the test. Also, avoid using absolutes such as *never* and *always*. These words can signal an extreme personality or lying. If it is a skills test, practicing ahead of time can help improve your score.

> *"In the book of life's questions, the answers are not in the back."*
>
> Charles Schulz

Taking Employment Tests

Employment testing may be an important factor in an employer's hiring decision. Follow these guidelines to perform at your best:

▲ Eat properly before the test, and be well rested. A sluggish body and brain can diminish your test performance.

▲ Do some physical exercise or yoga (or a similar activity) before the test to improve your circulation and your ability to relax and concentrate.

▲ Arrive 10 to 15 minutes early to avoid feeling rushed or tense.

▲ Most firms provide more than enough time to complete a test, so don't rush into poor performance. Ask exactly how much time is allotted for the test, however.

▲ Before beginning, read the test carefully to clarify the instructions and to determine how many points are assigned to each question. If you run short on time, answer the questions that are assigned the largest number of points. If the points aren't indicated, ask the person monitoring the test how the questions are weighted.

▲ Ask whether points will be deducted for questions you don't answer. If so, answer every question. If not, don't spend a lot of time on questions you can't answer easily. (Save those for last!)

▲ Always clarify any directions or questions you don't understand before you start the test.

▲ Many tests are objective, often including multiple choice questions. In true-false questions, extreme statements are frequently false (for example, choices that contain the words *all, never,* or *always*). Moderate statements are often true.

▲ Double-check to make certain you haven't missed any questions. Also, your first response is usually the correct one, so don't change answers unless you're sure you made a careless mistake.

▲ On general math tests, expect some simple addition, subtraction, multiplication, division, fraction, percentage, and decimal problems. Many math tests also include word problems.

▲ Advanced math tests will be geared to your field (engineering and statistical analysis, for instance). Consult others who have taken similar tests to determine what you should review. Educational and working experience are your primary preparation for advanced math tests.

▲ Oral tests or boards are generally given for applicants with advanced college degrees and for senior management/supervisory positions. They test an applicant's technical knowledge. Ask a colleague and/or an instructor in your field to meet with you to review the important technical aspects of your field. Review and study major principles beforehand, and use the meeting to summarize them.

Prepare for Drug Screening and Background Checks

Drug screening and background checks are common preemployment requirements. Be prepared for the possibility that you will be asked to take a drug test or authorize a background check before being hired. An employer can refuse to hire you if you refuse the test or background check.

Drug Screening

Take drug screening seriously. Applicants who test positively for drug use or who admit to using illegal drugs may be screened out of the job immediately. Never give flippant answers to questions about drug use. They could be interpreted negatively.

Policies for drug screening vary considerably from one employer to another. As part of your employer research, find out what the drug screening procedures and requirements are. Check with employers directly and with people who work for them. Schools' career services counselors often have information about drug testing procedures and may be familiar with those of local employers. To protect yourself, before you are tested, report to the employer any prescription or over-the-counter drugs you are taking. Some can result in a false-positive test.

Background Checks

A background check is a consumer report that employers use to screen potential employees. In addition to confirming your education and work history, employers may request a consumer report from a credit reporting bureau to check your social security number, credit payment record, driving record, or criminal history. This type of background check is particularly common for jobs that require government security clearance, but it may be used for any job.

Before employers can get your consumer report, they must have your written consent, however. You always have the option of withdrawing your application if there is information you do not want to disclose. The best way to prepare for a background check is to be truthful on all employment forms, maintain good credit, know what your references are going to say about you, and obtain copies of personnel files from past employers. If necessary, get a copy of your own credit report from a credit bureau, and dispute any incorrect information. Web links to these bureaus can be found on the *Your Career* web site at http://levitt.swlearning.com.

Research Salary and Benefits Ahead of Time

To optimize your ability to negotiate for the best possible salary and benefits, you must become as knowledgeable as possible about the going salary ranges and the types of benefits being offered in your field. You significantly reduce your salary and benefits bargaining power if you omit this research step.

> ### Success Tip
>
> Postpone any discussion of salary until you receive a job offer. This is your strongest bargaining strategy because the employer will already be convinced that you are the person for the job.

The Compensation Package

Salary is not the only important factor you should consider when assessing the value of a job. The complete compensation package includes salary, potential for earnings growth, and all other benefits. All of these are important. Base your compensation considerations on the following:

▲ The trends in your field (based on research)

▲ Your worth (the value you can offer the employer)

▲ What benefits are most important to you: health/life insurance, retirement programs, flextime, dependent care, reimbursement for education or training, and so on

Research Compensation Trends in Your Field

Research the going rate. Increase your chances of being offered the best compensation package by including this topic in your employer and industry research. Talk with leaders in your field, people who hold positions that are similar to your target job, and area placement specialists. Also search the Internet for salary and benefits information.

Some employers provide printed job descriptions that include a fixed salary listing, while others offer salary information on their web sites. A job notice may include a salary range, or the salary may be open. Often you can find the range or approximate salary for a position from the employer's human resources department. In some cases, however, employers don't give out this information. They may give you only the bottom of the range—rarely the top figure. Having a general idea of the range is better than having no idea. Your school's career services office can help you research salary and benefits packages through local contacts and publications such as the

Job Choices journal—an excellent publication by the National Association of Colleges and Employers.

If the salary is fixed, as may occur in some union or government jobs, you must decide whether it's acceptable to you. Research salary and benefits information online. Check the web sites of associations in your career field, and use search engines.

If the salary is negotiable, try for a salary at the top of the range. (You can agree to accept a salary that is lower than the top level, but if you offer to take the lowest end of the range first, that's probably what you'll get.) Study the following section, "Negotiate for Top Salary and Benefits," and prepare to bargain your way up the pay scale.

> **Complete Career Action 15-1**

CAREER ACTION 15-1

Use the Internet to Research Current Salary Information

Part 1 Directions: Visit one of the two web sites listed below. (All links for this assignment can be found on the *Your Career: How to Make It Happen* web site at http://levitt.swlearning .com.) Using the site's salary calculator, compute the cost-of-living differences between two cities in which you would consider working. Print the results.

1. Salary.com

2. Homefair.com

Part 2 Directions: Visit the *Occupational Outlook Handbook* online, and complete the following steps.

1. Select the title of your occupational cluster.

2. Choose the title of your field (and a subtitle if necessary), and then click on "Earnings."

3. Print or summarize in writing the wage ranges listed for the occupation.

Note: For additional salary information, check out the valuable "Salary Info" section at the JobStar web site.

File all of your research in your Career Management Files Binder.

Negotiate for Top Salary and Benefits

To obtain the strongest bargaining position, try to postpone any discussion of compensation until you receive a job offer. Bringing up the topic of compensation too soon could shift the focus away from your qualifications and cost you the job. Concentrate on what the employer will gain (your skills, experience, personal strengths, and so on) before focusing on the price (your compensation). Review and apply the following strategies:

▲ **Whenever possible, let the interviewer bring up the topic of salary and benefits.**

▲ **Do not accept a job offer without discussing the salary and benefits.** You can bring up the topic by asking, "What salary range do you have in mind for the job?"

▲ **Aim for a salary that equals the peak of your qualifications.** The higher you start, the higher the offer is likely to be. State your requirement in a range (upper twenties, mid thirties), making it broad enough to negotiate. Don't specify a low end; if you do, the employer will likely select it.

> *"We make a living by what we get, but we make a life by what we give."*
>
> Winston Churchill

▲ **If the interviewer asks what salary you want, a good response is "What figure or range is the company planning to pay?"** This gives you a starting point for negotiation. If it's higher than you expected, you help yourself by not stating a lower figure first. If it's lower, you now have a place to begin negotiations.

▲ **If the interviewer presses you for your salary requirement, refer to your research.** "The national average for a person with my experience, education, and training is $_____. Considering the cost-of-living factors here, I would expect a salary in the range of _____."

▲ **If the interviewer brings up the subject of salary too early in the interview** (before you adequately cover your qualifications), delay the topic by saying,

"Actually, the position itself is more important to me than the salary. Could we discuss the position a little more?"

▲ **While discussing salary, return to your assets.** Review all the benefits and qualifications you have to offer the company.

▲ **Once you state your salary range, do not back down,** particularly if you think it is equal to your qualifications. Base your range on careful research. The employer will respect your confidence in the quality and worth of your work.

▲ **Do not discuss any other sources of income, and do not whine about your expenses.** Stay focused on the negotiation.

▲ **Discuss the fringe benefits** (insurance coverage, pension plans, paid vacations, and so on) during the discussion of salary.

▲ **Ask about the criteria used to determine compensation increases and the frequency of salary reviews.** If benefits and salary increases are good, they can offset a somewhat lower starting salary.

▲ **If the salary offer is made in a letter and the salary is too low, arrange an appointment to discuss it right away.** Bargaining power is far greater in person than it is by letter or telephone.

▲ **If the salary isn't acceptable, state the salary you would accept,** and close by reaffirming your interest in the company and the job. If the interviewer says, "I'll have to think about your requirements," wait one week; then call back. You may receive a higher or compromise offer. If the interviewer gives you a flat "no," express regret that you were unable to work out a compromise. Restate your interest in the job and organization; then send a follow-up thank-you letter within two days. This could swing the decision in your favor.

Complete Career Action 15-2

CAREER ACTION 15-2

Employment Test/Salary and Benefits Planning Sheet

Directions: This outside assignment will help you succeed in employment tests and in negotiating effectively for fair salary and benefits. Complete Parts 1, 2, and 3 of Career Action Worksheet 15-2, which is provided on the Learner's CD and on page 269 of this text.

File your completed worksheet in your Career Management Files Binder.

Evaluate and Negotiate Job Offers

Before accepting a job offer, you must be sure it meets your career planning needs and goals. The following guidelines will help you assess job offers wisely.

Evaluate a Job Offer

Because the decision to accept or reject a job offer affects your lifetime career plans, consider this important decision carefully. Include the following factors in your evaluation of a job offer:

▲ **The job itself:** Is the scope acceptable? Is the work interesting to you? Will you work in teams or alone?

▲ **The organization and personnel:** Do you feel comfortable with the organizational structure and the people you have met?

▲ **The salary and benefits:** Does the salary match your education and abilities, and is it comparable with that of the competition? Does the potential for increases exist?

▲ **Career development opportunities:** Will you have adequate opportunities for professional growth (through training, continuing education, and experience)?

▲ **The values and philosophies of management:** Are they compatible with your own?

▲ **Expense considerations:** What expenses are required for relocation, housing, living costs, and so on?

▲ **How the job meets your goals:** Consider carefully how the job fits into your long-term career goals.

▲ **The job market:** Are jobs in your field plentiful or in short supply?

A job offer may be made by telephone, by letter, or in person. If the offer is made by letter, you have more time to think it over carefully and less emotionally than you do if it's made by telephone or in person. You may want to discuss the job offer conditions with a member of your support system, a family member, a career specialist, or all of these people. Respond to the offer quickly so you don't jeopardize it in any way.

If the offer is made by telephone or in the interviewer's office, request time to think it over. Occasionally, interviewers will offer to increase the salary or benefits if that appears to be your main concern regarding the job offer. This is particularly true if they are convinced that you are the right person for the job and they don't want to interview any other applicants. If this happens, more power to you! Even if this doesn't happen, though, it's still in your best interest to take at least one day to consider the advantages and disadvantages of the job offer.

Important: Make certain that waiting one day won't be an imposition. Doing so will help you avoid returning the next day to accept the offer and finding that someone else has the job! Be sure you understand all the conditions of the job before you decide whether or not to accept it.

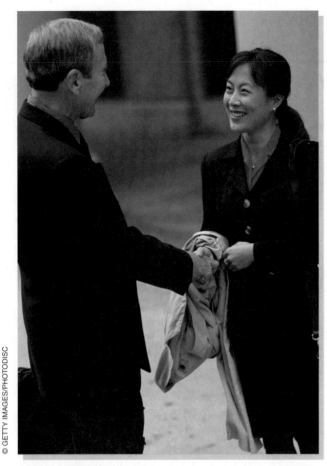

© GETTY IMAGES/PHOTODISC

When accepting a job offer, express your enthusiasm for and interest in the job.

If you have absolutely no doubts or objections concerning the job offer, accept the offer on the spot with enthusiasm. This will reinforce the employer's confidence in your suitability for the job.

Success Tip

Consider all aspects of a job offer (the job and company, compensation, growth opportunities, and expense considerations). Before accepting, negotiate to improve any areas of concern and to provide the best career opportunity for yourself.

PERSONAL BEST

Negotiation Skills

You negotiate for things every day with employers, family members, businesses—with many people you encounter. You may negotiate for a higher salary, better service, or a solution to a disagreement with a coworker. Regardless of the situation, these strategies by author and consultant Barbara Braham will help you handle negotiations more effectively:

▲ **Know yourself.** How do you feel about negotiation? Do you dread it? If so, you may give in too quickly or give away too much. Or, do you want to win, no matter what the cost? If so, you may become adversarial and damage the relationship.

▲ **Think, think, think. Know what you want.** Anticipate what the other party wants. Also try to anticipate what the other party thinks you want.

▲ **Build trust.** Without trust, you'll have manipulation and suspicion masquerading as communication. Be trustworthy. Tell the truth.

▲ **Listen.** Pay attention to what's being said, as well as to nonverbal messages, facial expressions, and voice inflections.

▲ **Know your BATNA.** BATNA stands for Best Alternative to a Negotiated Agreement. Before you begin a negotiation, know what your options are. Can you walk away from the deal? What other choices do you have? What are the pros and cons of each choice? Don't stop there; also consider the BATNA of the other party.

▲ **Know what a win is.** What is your best-case scenario? What is your worst-case scenario? If you can reach an agreement within this range, that's a win! Don't drop below your bottom line. You'll feel bad about yourself and the deal later.

Source: "Negotiation Tips," Barbara Braham web site (the link can be found on the *Your Career: How to Make It Happen* web site).

Accept the Offer Professionally

If you accept the job offer verbally, follow up immediately in writing, summarizing your understanding of the conditions of the offer and stating the position title, starting date, salary, and other pertinent items. (Your employer may do the same, but this helps ensure mutual agreement regarding all the conditions of the offer.)

Contact other organizations with which you have interviewed, and tell them that you have accepted a job. You may deal with these people in your new job, or you may want to contact them in the future regarding employment.

Contact the people who served as references or helped with your job search to tell them about your new job and to thank them for their help. People you thank are more likely to help in the future when you seek a new position or advancement in your career.

Reject the Offer Professionally

If you decide that this is not the job for you, notify the employer by telephone first, if possible. Then politely decline the offer in a letter, thank the employer for the job offer, and wish the employer future success.

Consider How Economics May Influence Your Decision

Your final decision may be influenced by economics—the need to earn a living. If the offer meets most of your requirements but is not a perfectly logical career step, your decision still could be to accept the job. If so, take the job with a determination to excel. It is an opportunity for you to establish your reputation—all while taking home a regular salary. Accept the challenge, and view it as preparation for the next step in your career development.

> **Complete Career Action 15-3**

CAREER ACTION 15-3

Planning for Dealing with Job Offers

Directions: Using Career Action Worksheet 15-3 on your Learner's CD or a separate sheet of paper, provide answers to the following items. File your answers in your Career Management Files Binder.

1. List every factor you should consider when evaluating a job offer. Be thorough in your answer. You may want to discuss this with a member of your support system network, a placement counselor, or both. Include the factors that are specific to your personal job search, as well as general factors.

2. Explain how you can best respond to a job offer made in person:

    a. If you think you want the job

    b. If you are certain you want the job

    c. If you do not want the job

3. How can you best respond to a job offer made by telephone?

4. List the follow-up steps you should take when accepting a job offer.

5. How should you professionally reject a job offer?

6. If economic conditions require you to accept a job that is not exactly what you are aiming for, how can you best approach the new job? What are the benefits of doing so?

CHECKLIST

ACING EMPLOYMENT TESTS AND NEGOTIATIONS

Check each of the actions you are currently taking to increase your career success:

○ Researching to learn what types of tests are given by target employers, practicing beforehand to sharpen your performance in skills tests, and studying concepts for technical tests

○ Taking drug screening seriously, finding out what drug screening procedures are used, and reporting your use of any prescription or over-the-counter drugs to avoid a false-positive result

○ Preparing for background checks by maintaining good credit, being truthful on resumes and applications, and obtaining copies of your credit reports and personnel records

○ Postponing any discussion of salary until after you have received a job offer

○ Considering all aspects of a job offer—the job and company, the compensation package (salary and benefits), growth opportunities, and so on—and negotiating to improve any areas of concern before accepting a job offer

CRITICAL THINKING QUESTIONS

1. What specific strategies for acing employment tests apply to your job search campaign?

2. Is it more advantageous for the applicant or the interviewer to bring up the subject of salary first? Why?

3. What is an appropriate response for you to give when an interviewer asks what salary you are looking for?

4. Base your answers to these questions on your salary research: (a) What is the entry-level salary for the job you are seeking? (b) What salary range do you plan to seek in your job search? On what do you base it?

For convenient access to valuable career resources, activities, and job information links, visit the companion web site for this text: *http://levitt.swlearning.com*

CAREER ACTION WORKSHEET 15-2

Employment Test/Salary and Benefits Planning Sheet

Directions: Contact two employers in your field to learn about the employment testing, salary ranges, and benefits they offer for the type of job you are seeking. Ask your contacts the following questions.

Part 1: Employment Testing Questions

1. Do you require prospective employees to take employment tests?

   _____

   _____

2. What kinds of tests are given (personality, skills, technical, computerized, other)?

   _____

   _____

3. Would you please describe the tests (written, oral, skills, computerized, other)?

   _____

   _____

4. What types of questions are in the tests (multiple choice, true/false, fill in the blank, essay, other)?

   _____

   _____

5. Would you please explain how the tests apply to the job itself?

   _____

   _____

   _____

6. Could a person study for the tests? If so, would you recommend specific methods of study and resources?

   _____

   _____

   _____

7. Do you perform background checks or require prospective employees to take drug tests? If so, what is the procedure?

   _____

   _____

   _____

Continued on next page >>>

CAREER ACTION WORKSHEET **15-2 (continued)**

Part 2: Negotiating Salary and Benefits

1. Does this position have a fixed salary or a salary range?

   _____

2. If the salary is fixed, would you tell me the amount?

   _____

3. If the salary is in a range, would you tell me the range?

   _____

4. Is the salary negotiable?

   _____

   _____

5. What criteria are used for determining the salary for this position?

   _____

   _____

   _____

6. Are salary raises awarded for excellent job performance? If so, what criteria are used in this process?

   _____

   _____

   _____

7. What is included in the typical complete compensation package (benefits)?

   _____

   _____

   _____

Part 3: Summary of Strategies for Negotiating Compensation

Directions: Review the strategies under the heading "Negotiate for Top Salary and Benefits" on page 264. Use a separate sheet of paper to summarize, in your own words, the tactics you plan to use when negotiating a compensation package (salary and benefits). List any additional tips you have found in your Internet or other research.

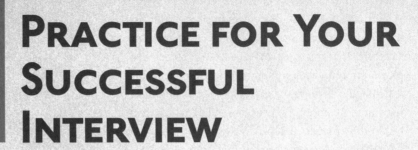

PRACTICE FOR YOUR SUCCESSFUL INTERVIEW

In this chapter, you will:

- Review the techniques for successful interviewing and arrange a practice interview with a member of your support network.

- Arrange a dress-rehearsal interview with an employer in your field.

- Evaluate your practice and dress-rehearsal interviews.

"The interview questions I ask are designed to reveal traits and life priorities. Asking questions like, 'When and why did you decide to become a teacher?' gives insight into an applicant's motivation and commitment to the profession. I also like to ask potential employees what they hope to contribute to our organization. I always pose one last question: 'What would you like me to know about you that we have not discussed?'"

Susan Carter, Principal
Fairfax Elementary
Mariemont City Schools

Chapter 16 provides vital interview rehearsal activities, including a practice interview with a member of your support network and a dress-rehearsal interview with an employer in your field. These activities will sharpen your interviewing skills, boost your confidence, and increase your competitive advantage through carefully planned interview practices. The payoff could be just the job you are looking for!

Gain a Competitive Advantage Through Interview Practice

Users of *Your Career: How to Make It Happen* emphasize that the practice interviews improve their actual interview performance by as much as 100 percent! They say that this valuable practice enhances their preparation, increases their self-confidence, improves the image of competence they project, and reduces their anxiety about the process—all of which improve their performance in actual interviews! Gain these valuable advantages yourself by doing practice interviews.

Review Interview Techniques

To prepare for your practice interviews, review Chapter 11, "Interview Like a Pro." Prepare for and perform in a practice interview as though it were the real thing. A summary of key points for effective interviewing follows.

Prepare for the Interview

To ensure the best results from your practice interviews, prepare first.

▲ **Take the time to look your best.** Eat well and be rested, immaculately groomed, and appropriately dressed. Appearance has a strong impact on interviewers. Make it positive.

▲ **Strengthen your performance with positive behaviors.** Review the information in Chapter 1 on positive self-talk, positive expectations, visualization, and so on.

▲ **Review the Career Action assignments in Chapters 2, 3, 9, and 11.** Focus on your capabilities, accomplishments, 60-Second Commercial, resume, and specific qualifications for your job target.

▲ **Assemble your Interview Marketing Kit** (see Chapter 11), and take it with you.

▲ **Allow travel time.** Arrive a few minutes early. If you're not certain how to get to your interview location, consider driving to the interview site the day before your meeting.

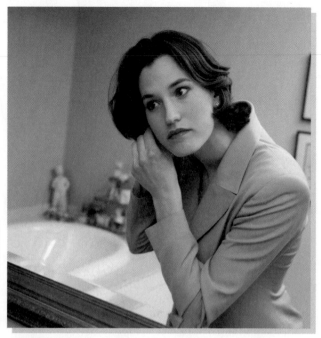

For all interviews—practice or real—make time to look your best. A positive appearance is essential!

Success Tip

To improve your actual interview performance and confidence, schedule and participate seriously in practice interviews.

Apply Interview Success Strategies

To polish your performance, follow these successful interview techniques covered in Chapter 11:

▲ **Remember: There is no "time out" from the moment you enter the building until you leave.** Maintain good posture, project energy and enthusiasm, and think good thoughts. Smile!

▲ **Use the interviewer's name in your greeting.** Identify yourself and the position for which you are applying.

▲ **Be likable and relaxed.** Be courteous and friendly, and show interest in the position.

▲ **Use positive body language and voice tone throughout the interview.**

▲ **Stress your qualifications** and your interest in benefiting the company and advancing yourself.

▲ **Ask a few appropriate questions.**

▲ **Remain calm if asked a stress question.** Allow yourself time to plan an effective answer.

▲ **Close the interview skillfully.** Use the "clincher." Ask the interviewer to summarize the most important qualifications for the job; then stress your related abilities.

> *"The thing always happens that you really believe in; and the belief in the thing makes it happen."*
>
> Frank Lloyd Wright

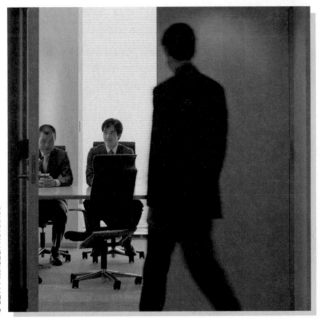

To get the most benefit from your practice interview, prepare for it as though it were real.

© GETTY IMAGES/PHOTODISC

Schedule a Practice Interview

Schedule a practice interview with a member of your support network (a friend, a family member, or an acquaintance), preferably someone experienced in interviewing who knows you personally. Ask one or two others to observe the practice interview, and get their recommendations for improving your performance.

If possible, arrange to have your practice interview videotaped. This will be the most valuable performance feedback you can get—a firsthand review.

Complete Career Action 16-1

Follow Guidelines for Practice Interviews

The following interview guidelines will help you perform successfully in your practice interview.

▲ **Prepare and take your Interview Marketing Kit** (directions in Chapter 11). Practice showcasing relevant items from your portfolio at appropriate points in your practice interview.

▲ **Dress as you would for an actual interview;** you will be rated on your appearance.

CAREER ACTION 16-1

Arrange Your Own Practice Interview

Directions: Schedule a practice interview with your support network members (one interviewer and one or two observers). Use the sample questions in Chapter 14 as a guide for your practice session. You can make a copy of them for the "interviewer" and add any stress questions (or others) you want to rehearse. Encourage the interviewer to expand on the questions, if possible, tailoring them to your job target to give you relevant interview practice. If possible, arrange to have the practice interview videotaped.

▲ **Provide your interviewer with your cover letter, resume, and employment application.**

▲ **Review the Interview Critique Form** on page 280 of this chapter to become familiar with the areas that will be evaluated. The form is designed to give you an overview of your interview skills.

▲ **Give the interviewer and observers copies of the Interview Critique Form to evaluate your performance.**

▲ **Send a thank-you letter to everyone who helps you.**

Success Tip

Ask your support system interviewer to evaluate your practice interview by using the Interview Critique Form.

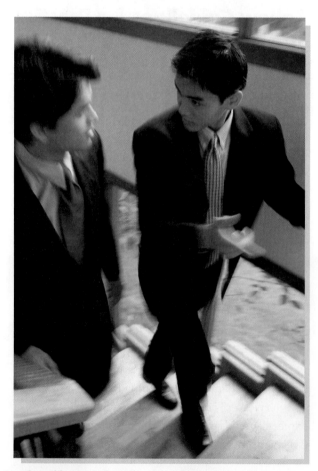

Meeting with an employer for a practice interview also provides an opportunity to learn more about the organization.

PERSONAL **BEST**

Practice Interviewing With an Employer in Your Field

Some people receive job offers as a result of practice interviews with employers. Others obtain leads that result in jobs. Everyone gains necessary interview experience, which is why practice interviewing is so important.

Prepare now to participate in a dress-rehearsal interview with an employer in your field. This is your chance to practice and get feedback that will strengthen your performance in actual interviews. Follow the guidelines below to schedule and participate in this type of important rehearsal:

▲ Make an appointment for a dress-rehearsal interview. Explain that it is a course assignment and that you would appreciate the employer's help in completing it. Say that you would like the interview to be as realistic as possible.

▲ Ask if it would be possible to get an employment application form. If so, pick it up ahead of time, complete it carefully, and take it with you (along with your resume and cover letter) to the dress rehearsal.

▲ Verify the address and other details about the meeting, and thank your contact for agreeing to help you with the assignment.

▲ Take your Interview Marketing Kit, and use it appropriately.

▲ Also take a copy of the Interview Critique Form for the interviewer to use (Career Action Worksheet 16-2, p. 280).

▲ Remember that any job offer should come spontaneously from the employer. Asking directly for a job contradicts your request for help in practicing your interviewing skills. If your contact makes an offer or provides leads or suggestions, however, follow up immediately if you are interested.

Have Interviewers Fill Out the Critique Form

Make copies of the Interview Critique Form found at the end of this chapter. Give them to the interviewers and observers of your practice interviews. After each practice interview, ask the interviewer(s) to use the form to evaluate your performance, identify your strengths and weaknesses, and make suggestions for improvement. Correct your areas of weakness now—before you have an actual interview.

Complete Career Action 16-2

Success Tip

Summarize thoroughly what you learn from your practice and dress-rehearsal interviews. Send thank-you letters to everyone who helps.

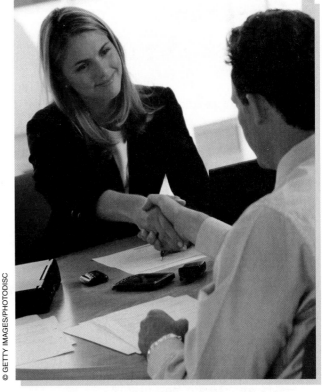

© GETTY IMAGES/PHOTODISC

Take your dress-rehearsal interview seriously. It can help you polish your interview skills and may result in job leads!

CAREER ACTION 16-2

Participate in a Dress-Rehearsal Interview and Evaluate Your Performance

Directions: Contact an employer in your career field, and ask for help with a course assignment. Ask the employer to conduct a practice interview with you and to complete a copy of the Interview Critique Form.

1. Dress appropriately.

2. Take a copy of the Interview Critique Form (provided on page 280) with you, and ask the interviewer to evaluate your performance by completing the form during or after the interview.

3. After the dress-rehearsal interview, evaluate your own performance; complete a copy of the Interview Follow-up and Evaluation Form (provided on page 277).

4. Within two days of your dress rehearsal, send a follow-up thank-you letter to the person who gave you the practice interview.

5. File your Interview Critique Form and Interview Follow-up and Evaluation Form in your Career Management Files Binder.

CHECKLIST

PRACTICING TO SUCCEED IN YOUR INTERVIEW

Check each of the actions you are currently taking to increase your career success:

○ Scheduling practice interviews to improve your actual interview performance and confidence

○ Preparing for a practice interview as though it were real, participating seriously, and applying interview success strategies

○ Asking interviewers to evaluate your practice and dress-rehearsal interviews by using the Interview Critique Form

○ Summarizing thoroughly what you have learned from your practice and dress-rehearsal interviews

○ Sending thank-you letters to those who helped with your practice interviews

CRITICAL THINKING QUESTIONS

1. How, specifically, do you use the success strategies described in Chapter 1 (visualization, positive self-talk, affirmation statements, goal setting, and proactive and assertive behavior) in preparing for and participating in a practice interview? Which of these strategies do you find the most useful?

2. Why is it important to prepare for and perform in a practice interview as though it were the real thing?

3. Whom should you ask to participate in your practice interviews?

4. Summarize any job search/career management advice or job lead information you received from the interviewer during your dress-rehearsal interview. What specific follow-up action do you plan to take with regard to this information?

 For convenient access to valuable career resources, activities, and job information links, visit the companion web site for this text: *http://levitt.swlearning.com*

CAREER ACTION WORKSHEET 16-2

Interview Follow-up and Evaluation Form

Note: Duplicate and use this form for follow-up after every practice and real interview.

Directions: Record a summary of the interview as soon as possible to avoid forgetting important details. Supply the general information about the employer and the interviewer(s). Answer the questions as completely as possible.

Name of Organization: _____

Date of Interview: _____

Name(s) and Title(s) of Interviewer(s): _____

_____

_____

Address: _____

Telephone: _____ Fax: _____

E-mail Address: _____

Summary Activities and Questions

1. On a separate sheet of paper, write every question you can remember being asked during the interview. Take your time, and be thorough. Do this before answering any of the following questions.

2. Based on the knowledge you gained in your interview and research, which of your qualifications would be the greatest assets in this job? Which of these qualifications should be reinforced with the prospective employer in your follow-up?

_____

_____

3. List any questions you think you answered inadequately. Then write out the best possible answer to each question. Use additional paper if necessary.

_____

_____

_____

_____

_____

Continued on next page >>>

CAREER ACTION WORKSHEET 16-2 (continued)

4. Did you forget to provide important information that demonstrates your qualifications for the job? Explain in detail.

_____

_____

_____

5. What questions did you intend to ask but either forgot or didn't have a chance to ask? Write them out now.

_____

_____

_____

6. How could you have presented yourself more effectively (appearance, body language, verbal communication, enthusiasm, describing your qualifications, and so on)?

_____

_____

_____

7. In what area(s) do you think you performed the best in your interview? Why?

_____

_____

_____

_____

8. In what area(s) do you think you performed poorly? What steps can you take to improve in these areas?

_____

_____

_____

9. Describe information you learned about the interviewer that may be helpful in establishing greater rapport in the future (philosophy, current working projects or objectives, personal interests or hobbies, mutual interests, goals, and so on).

_____

_____

_____

Continued on next page >>>

CAREER ACTION WORKSHEET **16-2 (continued)**

10. Is there any point of confusion that needs to be clarified for the employer? Explain.

_____

_____

_____

_____

_____

_____

11. Are you scheduled for another interview with the organization? If so, record the date, time, place, and name(s) of the interviewer(s).

_____

_____

_____

12. Record any other activities you offered to follow up on or were specifically asked to follow up on by the interviewer (for example, provide references, transcripts, certificates, or examples of work).

_____

_____

_____

_____

_____

_____

13. How does the interviewer prefer you follow up (by telephone, by letter, in person)?

_____

_____

_____

14. By what date did the interviewer indicate the hiring decision would be made?

_____

_____

_____

Continued on next page >>>

CAREER ACTION WORKSHEET 16-2 (continued)

Interview Critique Form

Name of Interviewee: _____ Date: _____

Position Applied For: _____

Directions: Circle the appropriate rating of the interviewee (Excellent, Very Good, Good, or Needs Improvement) for each item listed below.

1. **Documentation** (Application for employment, resume, cover letter)

   Excellent   Very Good   Good   Needs Improvement

2. **Attitude** (Interested in position, self-confident, likable, pleasant tone of voice, smiling)

   Excellent   Very Good   Good   Needs Improvement

3. **Appearance** (Generally neat and tidy, appropriately dressed, alert, good hygiene)

   Excellent   Very Good   Good   Needs Improvement

4. **Job Qualifications** (Education, skills, and experience suitable for position; good personal attributes; human relations capability; dependable; punctual; industrious)

   Excellent   Very Good   Good   Needs Improvement

5. **Verbal Communication** (Speaks clearly with positive tone, uses proper English, avoids slang or repetitive words, emphasizes assets, is courteous, uses name of the interviewer)

   Excellent   Very Good   Good   Needs Improvement

6. **Nonverbal Communication** (Positive body language, good eye contact, does not fidget)

   Excellent   Very Good   Good   Needs Improvement

7. **Listening** (Does not interrupt or respond too quickly; asks to have a question repeated, if necessary; takes time to think through important questions; calmly endures silence)

   Excellent   Very Good   Good   Needs Improvement

8. **Enthusiasm** (Demonstrates interest/energy through verbal and nonverbal communication)

   Excellent   Very Good   Good   Needs Improvement

Comments: On a separate sheet of paper, please summarize any other observations you made during the interview. (Note any favorable behavior, and provide suggestions for improvement where necessary.)

INTERVIEW AND FOLLOW UP

In this chapter, you will:

- Review a summary of successful interview techniques.

- Use the Internet to search for additional information on interview follow-up that could be useful to you.

- Prepare an outline for a follow-up telephone call that you can use after interviews.

- Compose a simple follow-up thank-you message that you can use in addition to the follow-up telephone call.

- Prepare an outline of a formal follow-up letter that you can use after interviews instead of a telephone call.

"If you have not received feedback from a company that you interviewed with, don't hesitate to call. Persistence is often the key to furthering your career. Although I do not expect a follow-up call or letter after an interview, I am always pleased and favorably impressed when I do get one; it makes the candidate stand out from the rest."

Linda Stryker
Human Resources Manager
Square D/Groupe Schneider

Previous Career Action assignments (performing employer research, practicing interviewing, and applying the nine success strategies outlined in Chapter 1) have prepared you to succeed in your interviews. Chapter 17 highlights important points for succeeding in your interviews and outlines interview follow-up actions you can take to tip the hiring decision in your favor.

Interview Game Strategies

To prepare for a successful interview, review the strategies covered earlier in this text. Begin by reviewing all of Chapter 11, "Interview Like a Pro." Pay particular attention to Career Action 11-3, 60-Second Commercial; Career Action 11-4, Summary of Core Areas of Successful Interviewing; Career Action 11-5, Summary of Fine Points for Interview Success; and the chapter's summaries of interview techniques. Also review Career Action 14-2, Create a Question-and-Answer Planning Sheet, and your research on salary negotiations and the related suggestions presented in Chapter 15.

If you are asked to interview, the employer is interested in *you!* To connect most positively throughout your interview, focus on four areas:

▲ Be likable.

▲ Emphasize your qualifications.

▲ Show enthusiasm and interest.

▲ Use positive body language and voice qualities.

> *"Opportunity does not knock, it presents itself when you beat down the door."*
>
> Kyle Chandler

Good Follow-up Moves

Interview follow-up can increase your chances of getting the job by 30 percent or more because many applicants don't bother to do it! Interviewers see follow-up by a job seeker as a proactive step that shows initiative and interest. When you follow up, you take action to evaluate your performance in interviews, you remind prospective employers of your qualifications for and interest in the job, and you encourage a speedy hiring decision (to hire you, of course).

Good follow-up reinforces your qualifications and helps you stand out favorably from the competition. Be patient during this stage of the job search. The hiring process often takes longer than the employer expects.

The key in follow-up is action. The steps include:

▲ Writing an evaluation of your interview performance.

▲ Sending a follow-up message to the interviewer by telephone, letter, or e-mail or through a personal visit.

Evaluate Your Interview Immediately

Within one hour of every interview (or at the earliest possible time), summarize and evaluate your interview performance in writing. Do this for interviews that go well and for those that go poorly. This is the best way to learn from the experiences, to improve your performance, and to plan your successful follow-up strategies. Ask yourself the following questions:

▲ What positive impressions did I make? What negative impressions might I have left with the interviewer? Why did I make these impressions?

▲ Was there anything I should have said but didn't?

▲ What other questions would I have liked to ask? What other questions should I have asked?

▲ What questions would I have answered differently? How would I have answered those questions differently?

▲ How did I feel about the interview immediately after it concluded? How do I feel about the interview now?

Plan Your Follow-up Strategies

After each interview, complete an Interview Follow-up and Evaluation Form (Chapter 16, page 277). Circle in red any notes that require follow-up (information you need to clarify or reinforce with the employer, questions you want answered, areas of weak performance and suggestions for improving them, and specific actions you need to take).

© GETTY IMAGES/PHOTODISC

A follow-up call, letter, or e-mail tells the prospective employer that you are interested in the job.

Make your follow-up message brief and polished. Include only the most important questions or information.

Time Your Call. Make your follow-up call within two days of your interview, while your name and the interview are still fresh in the interviewer's mind. Contact employers on days other than those at the beginning or end of the week; Mondays and Fridays are the busiest business days. Just before lunch and just before closing are usually inconvenient times as well. Guidelines for a successful follow-up telephone call are outlined in the Personal Best feature on page 285.

Send a Brief Thank-You Note Too. Even if you make your initial follow-up by telephone, you should send a brief thank-you letter or e-mail message within 48 hours of your interview to be sure your message is received during the decision-making stage. (The body of a thank-you e-mail is similar to that of a thank-you letter.)

You should write a thank-you note to every person who interviewed you. The letters can be basically the same, but try to vary each one in case the recipients compare notes. If you've already made a telephone call, do not restate your qualifications in this message; just thank the interviewer, with no strings attached! Send a thank-you note even if you're sure the job is not for you.

The thank-you letter brings your name before the interviewer in a favorable light one more time, reinforcing your name in his or her mind. It also provides a positive written record of you in the employer's files. Review the brief thank-you letter shown in Figure 17-1 on page 286.

Determine what method of follow-up is most appropriate. If, during your interview, you remembered to ask the interviewer how he or she wanted you to follow up, the decision has been made for you. If you forgot to ask this question, send a follow-up letter rather than make a telephone call. If you sent your cover letter and resume to the prospective employer through e-mail, you may choose to follow up your interview with an e-mail message. If the interviewer approves of follow-up telephone calls, use that method. A telephone call is more personal and lively and gives you quicker feedback. If you call, you should also follow up with a letter or an e-mail because it provides a permanent reminder of you!

Outline Your Follow-up Message. Regardless of the method you choose for follow-up, outline the message first, and include these topics:

1. List any questions you need to ask.

2. Summarize pertinent information you omitted or covered inadequately in your interview.

3. State specifically how the organization could benefit by hiring you (a brief rerun of or an excerpt from your 60-Second Commercial).

Success Tip

Draft a brief follow-up letter or e-mail message that you can send after making a follow-up telephone call.

Send a More Complete Follow-up Letter When No Call Is Made or to Add Information. If the interviewer prefers that you follow up in writing or if you think your interview performance was weak in any area and follow-up is important to getting hired, send a more complete follow-up letter. This letter should include the following:

1. A reference to your interview and the position you are seeking

2. Clarification of any pertinent information omitted during your interview

3. A brief version of your 60-Second Commercial

4. A thank-you for the interviewer's time

5. A statement of enthusiasm for the job

6. Encouragement of a speedy hiring decision

Review Figure 17-2 on page 287 to see how these items are presented in a sample letter.

NOTE: The follow-up letter provides a permanent written record of your qualifications and professional courtesy. The employer can review it any time, making it an effective way to keep your "commercial" running!

Complete Career Action 17-1

CAREER ACTION 17-1

Search the Internet for Interview Follow-up Tips

Directions: Search the Internet for additional tips on interview follow-up that could be useful to you. When you have finished this activity, store your research in your Career Management Files Binder.

When using search engines, try the following search strings: *interview follow-up letters, interview thank-you letters,* and/or *interview follow-up.* Summarize key points that you find useful, or print relevant articles.

Suggested Web Sites:

▲ MonsterTRAK

▲ CareerLab
(Click on "Cover Letter Library." These are excellent models. Then click on "Say 'Thank You' with Class," and browse through the many samples provided.)

▲ Virginia Tech Career Services
(Click on "Students" to go to the Career Services page.)

▲ The Riley Guide
(Click on "Network, Interview, & Negotiate"; then click on "Interviewing.")

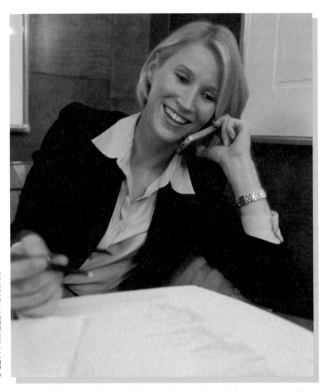

© GETTY IMAGES/PHOTODISC

A prospective employer will consider a favorable recommendation from someone he or she knows and trusts.

Success Tip

Draft a longer follow-up letter to add information or to use when no call is made.

Connect with Your Support Network Again. If a member of your support network is influential with your prospective employer, contact him or her to ask for additional support. A friendly follow-up call from this person to the employer could tip the scales in your favor.

An alternative to the follow-up call by a network member is a letter of recommendation sent to the employer from one or more people who can confirm your qualifications. Some employers routinely request letters of recommendation from former employers, managers, or supervisors of applicants. Arranging to have such letters sent on your own demonstrates initiative—another benefit for you!

PERSONAL**BEST**

Making a Successful Follow-up Telephone Call

If your interviewer approves of follow-up calls, you can set yourself apart from the competition with a well-timed, well-prepared telephone call.

▲ **Demonstrate courtesy.** "Do you have a moment?"

▲ **Begin with a greeting and self-introduction.** "Hello, Ms. Delgado. This is Gregory Tambascio."

▲ **Identify the position for which you interviewed and the date of your interview.** "I want to thank you for meeting with me yesterday to discuss the Data Processing Systems Analyst I position."

▲ **Provide important information you omitted.** "After reviewing our meeting, I realized I hadn't mentioned some pertinent information regarding my (education, work experience, qualifications, certification, other)." Concisely give the specifics.

▲ **Reemphasize your qualifications.** If necessary, give a short, targeted version of your 60-Second Commercial, emphasizing exactly how your qualifications can benefit the employer.

▲ **If necessary, ask questions to clarify any points that were not covered adequately.** This information may include a clearer description of the job responsibilities or clarification of work relationships.

▲ **Thank the interviewer, express your interest, and encourage a speedy hiring decision.** "Thank you again for the interview. I look forward to learning of your hiring decision soon. I believe we could benefit each other, and I'd be pleased to be a part of Mississippi Central Power Company."

2440 Observatory Boulevard
Apartment 34
Los Angeles, CA 90063
July 2, 20—

Ms. Stephanie Nolan
Manager, Auditing Staff
Nolan Henry O'Leary Public Accountants
1410 Granada Avenue, 7th Floor
San Francisco, CA 94115

Dear Ms. Nolan:

Thank you for the opportunity to interview for the position of Staff Auditor I with you and your team. Your invitation to join the first hour of the weekly staff meeting made me feel especially welcome—and sent me to the library to brush up on the finer points of the state's tax credit program for employers who train welfare recipients!

I would enjoy being part of your team and look forward to your hiring decision. Please call me any time this week at 213-555-0128.

Sincerely,

Russell Thistlethwaite

Russell Thistlethwaite

Figure 17-1: Sample of a Brief Thank-You Letter

3493 Huntington Heights
Denver, CO 80202
August 23, 20—

Mr. Frederick J. Gray Wolf
Normandy Copiers, Inc.
3500 Main Street
Boulder, CO 80302-8715

Dear Mr. Gray Wolf:

The enthusiasm you shared this afternoon for the customer-centered philosophy behind the new Normandy Print Center is contagious! I know from experience how satisfying it is to break new ground and to achieve results that exceed all expectations. The Normandy management system sounds unique, innovative, and challenging.

During our meeting, we discussed how I could contribute to your marketing plan, but we didn't have time to talk about store operations. While I managed the parts and service operations of Renaissance Business Systems, our team achieved and maintained a production efficiency rate that consistently placed us in the top 5 percent of the 160 shops nationwide. Sales of maintenance contracts increased every year I was in charge, and we had the lowest return rate for products of all the centers.

Thank you for talking with me about the new opportunities at Normandy. Normandy Copiers, Inc., will be a great success in Boulder, and I would like to contribute to that success. As we agreed, I will call you next Thursday, but you can reach me before that at 303-555-0171.

Sincerely,

Francesca Elena Valdez

Francesca Elena Valdez

Figure 17-2: Sample of a More Complete Follow-up Letter

Waiting-Game Strategies

Waiting to hear about a hiring decision is frustrating. Your best strategy is action!

Evaluate Your Performance and Identify Follow-up Activities

After you complete your follow-up telephone call and letter, review your notes on the Interview Follow-up and Evaluation Form (Chapter 16, page 277). Concentrate on the positive aspects of your evaluation to keep your self-image positive. Check to be certain you have completed all the follow-up activities you circled in red.

> *"Many of life's failures are people who did not realize how close they were to success when they gave up."*
>
> Thomas A. Edison

| Complete Career Action 17-2 |

Call Back If You Don't Hear about the Decision

Refer to the last question on the Interview Follow-up and Evaluation Form: By what date did the interviewer indicate the hiring decision would be made? Call if you don't receive notice of the hiring decision by the date the interviewer gave you.

The following approach doesn't pressure the interviewer:

"Hello, Ms. Delgado. This is Gregory Tambascio. You indicated during our meeting that you expected to make a hiring decision by July 30. I might have missed your call if you tried to get in touch with me."

This technique helps you with the waiting game by giving you current information about the hiring status. Your demonstration of interest and initiative could also persuade the employer to hire you. It happens!

Remember the saying about the squeaky wheel getting the grease? Continue following up, especially if the employer has asked you to. Just be careful not to go overboard and annoy or bother the employer. You'll seem desperate for the job.

Success Tip

After each interview, evaluate your performance and identify ways to improve. List all the necessary follow-up activities, and complete them.

CAREER ACTION 17-2

Follow-up Telephone Call and Letter or E-mail

Directions: Use Career Action Worksheet 17-2 on your Learner's CD or on page 290 to complete the follow-up telephone call and letter or e-mail activities for this assignment. File your worksheet and final documents in your Career Management Files Binder.

CHECKLIST

INTERVIEWING AND FOLLOWING UP SUCCESSFULLY

Check each of the actions you are currently taking to increase your career success:

○ Reviewing interview success strategies: Career Action 11-3, 60-Second Commercial, and Career Action 14-2, Create a Question-and-Answer Planning Sheet

○ Preparing a written script for a follow-up telephone call; if necessary, including questions not asked or information omitted in the interview

○ Drafting a brief follow-up message to send after making a follow-up telephone call

○ Drafting a longer follow-up letter to add important information or to use when no call is made

○ After each interview, completing an Interview Follow-up and Evaluation Form, taking steps to improve areas of weak performance, and completing all necessary follow-up activities

CRITICAL THINKING QUESTIONS

1. What is included in a good interview follow-up?

2. What are the important topics applicants should include in their follow-up communication (telephone call, letter, or e-mail)?

3. What follow-up is required after your dress-rehearsal interview (Career Action 16-2)?

4. What strategies should you use if you are waiting to hear about a hiring decision?

 For convenient access to valuable career resources, activities, and job information links, visit the companion web site for this text: *http://levitt.swlearning.com*

Career Action Worksheet 17-2

Follow-up Telephone Call and Letter or E-mail

Part 1: Follow-up Telephone Call

Directions: Prepare a draft of a telephone call you can make as a follow-up to an interview. Refer to the Personal Best feature on page 285 to review the items you should include in your telephone call. Practice making the call in a role-play situation with a member of your support system.

_____

_____

_____

_____

_____

Part 2: Brief Follow-up Thank-You Message

Directions: Write a brief follow-up thank-you message to use after you have made your follow-up telephone call. This message may be sent conventionally by mail service or electronically, depending on the type of position or company you interviewed with or the type of initial contact you had with the prospective employer (for example, high-tech company and/or resume and cover letter were submitted electronically).

_____

_____

_____

_____

_____

Part 3: Complete Follow-up Thank-You Letter

Directions: Draft a letter that you could use as a follow-up to an interview instead of a telephone call.

1. Write an appropriate greeting and a reminder of the position you interviewed for.

2. Include any pertinent information you omitted during your interview.

3. Summarize your job qualifications briefly with the short version of your 60-Second Commercial.

4. Express your interest in the job and your appreciation for the interview.

PREPARE YOUR NEXT MOVE IF YOU DON'T GET THE JOB

In this chapter, you will:

- Determine how to deal effectively with rejection in your job search.

- Evaluate your job search performance and identify methods of improving it.

"When things do not go the way you want them to go, it's time to ask yourself: What didn't work in the interview? What questions were you struggling with? What do you need to change? Ask people for honest feedback. Sometimes we need to check that the impressions we gave to others were what we intended."

Roxanne Pellegrino
Educational Services Manager
Philadelphia Job Corps

Getting a good job often requires more than one interview; it may take several tries before you land the job you want. Getting a rejection notice is not a great ego booster, but it's not a reason to stop your job search campaign, either. Think of it as a learning experience, and continue with your job search activities. Chapter 18 highlights practical strategies for recharging your motivation, reversing a rejection notice, and trying new angles to land a top job.

Counter Rejection With Success Strategies

To counter natural feelings of rejection, the best approach is taking immediate positive action.

▲ Maintain a positive attitude.

▲ Evaluate your performance and your self-marketing package.

▲ Connect with your network for support, and rework your contacts.

▲ Plan your next job search steps, and follow through.

Taking a short breather helps you renew your energy and enthusiasm. Allow yourself one day—but no longer—to do something you enjoy and to relax. And don't use rejection as an excuse for giving up. Simply regroup and rework your action plans!

Apply the Nine Success Strategies

Reread Chapter 1, focusing on the success strategies that project competence and strengthen self-esteem. Visualize yourself performing successfully in your next interview and on your new job. Also, make a conscious effort to think and act positively and to use positive self-talk and affirmation statements.

Review your self-analysis forms from Chapters 2 and 3 (your talents, skills, qualifications, special accomplishments, and personal attributes). Also review your 60-Second Commercial. Remind yourself of your skills and positive accomplishments.

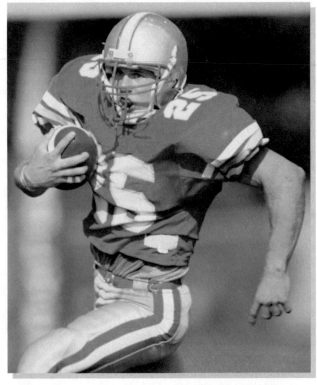

© GETTY IMAGES/PHOTODISC

Don't let a job rejection get you down. Use the tactics athletes use: Analyze your performance, visualize succeeding, and move on.

Persevere for Success

Winners in all fields agree: Perseverance is a major factor in their success. When they meet an obstacle, they find a way around it. Setbacks are not failures; you only fail when you quit trying.

No one can be right for every job. The right person for a job doesn't always get it. The best prepared and the most determined person often does, however. While you may be responsible in part for an initial rejection, you have the power to correct the situation and win the job offer. With belief in yourself, you can still succeed.

Is "No" Always the Final Answer?

Many job applicants have turned a first rejection into a job offer through effective follow-up. Sometimes interviewers get an inaccurate first impression of an

---

Success Tip

After a job rejection, use positive thinking, action, visualization, goal setting, and self-talk to recharge your motivation, fine-tune your job search campaign, and improve your performance in future interviews.

applicant. You can revise that impression through follow-up; consider the following techniques:

▲ **Call and clarify.** Place a timely call to provide missing information, to correct misinformation, to clarify your qualifications, or to restate your interest. Doing so can turn a rejection into employment.

▲ **Call and request a short follow-up meeting.** Explain that you have additional information, portfolio examples, or some other item you think the interviewer should consider before making a hiring decision. Ask for just 10 or 15 minutes to make your case. Do your homework and prepare a telephone script before you call. Make the call organized and concise. Speak with energy and enthusiasm.

Success Tip

Ask the interviewer to evaluate your performance. You need to base your rejection response on facts, not on assumptions; the information you receive can help you identify areas that need improvement.

Get an Evaluation of Your Interview Performance

After receiving a rejection notice, if you're not sure where you fell short, call the interviewer and ask for an honest evaluation. If you are aware of the perceived short-coming, though, prepare a strong written clarification you can refer to while making your rejection follow-up call. Here is a way of asking an interviewer for an evaluation:

> *"If opportunity doesn't knock, build a door."*
> Milton Berle

"Hello, Ms. Nguyen. This is Aaron Goldman. I received your letter stating that I had not been selected for the job, and I appreciate the prompt notification. Could you tell me which areas of my preparation and qualifications need to be strengthened, and could you suggest methods of improving in these areas?"

The interviewer may try to evade your question. Some employers are reluctant to offer specific opinions and are justifiably cautious about disgruntled applicants suing for unfair hiring practices. Even if you don't get concrete help, express your thanks.

Prepare and Respond. If the interviewer is willing to evaluate your performance and make suggestions for improvement, listen carefully and take notes. Accept the concerns the interviewer or company representative conveys to you. Their validity is irrelevant. The important point is that the concerns represent problem areas in the interviewer's perception of you. Devise ways to overcome each negative perception.

If you are prepared to do so, briefly clarify your qualifications or clear up any misunderstanding during the telephone call. Use a friendly tone, and do not react defensively. Remember: You asked for the opinion.

If you need more time to respond, after your call, write out an effective response to the concerns identified by the interviewer. Then write, call, or visit in person to present your new information. A letter can become a permanent part of your application file and can be reviewed more than once, perhaps by someone else in the organization who decides that you do have the required qualifications.

Set Up Another Meeting. If the interviewer seems receptive, explain that you didn't convey your qualifications as completely as you had planned and suggest that you meet once more to review them. Handled well, this approach demonstrates confidence, competence, and assertiveness.

Ask for Referrals. If you reach a point where no further action would get you the job, ask for referrals.

"Thank you again for your time, Ms. Nguyen. I have one more question. Could you recommend another department or organization I can contact to discuss employment possibilities?"

Offer Additional Positive Information

Make a call or send a letter to provide additional positive information about yourself and/or to clarify your qualifications. The purposes of this communication are:

▲ To provide added positive information.

▲ To confirm your enthusiasm for and interest in the job.

▲ To convince the interviewer that you are qualified for the job.

Prepare a telephone script or letter, and review it with a member of your support network before proceeding.

Success Tip

Prepare and deliver a response to a rejection notice. Provide additional information about yourself or portfolio samples. This follow-up may reverse the rejection.

Ask for a referral to another department within the organization. This department may have a position that better matches your skills and qualifications.

Reverse a Job Rejection: A True Case

The following case illustrates how well-planned follow-up can reverse a job rejection. Steve was graduating in engineering from a private university. He applied to several companies, but his first choice was Silar Corporation.

His resume, cover letter, and application for employment got him an interview. He thought the interview was successful because he felt comfortable with the interviewer and solidly demonstrated how his qualifications fit the needs at Silar. He was encouraged by the positive feedback he received from the interviewer.

Steve was shocked when he received a cordial letter of rejection a week later. The letter emphasized that his 3.2 grade point average didn't meet that of the competition. Many applicants would have accepted the rejection as final proof that this particular job wasn't within their reach. Not so with Steve.

He discussed the subject with his professors and other members of his support network and decided a follow-up telephone call would be appropriate. Steve had not made it clear during his interview that he had worked full-time while earning his university degree. In addition, his performance was below average in the first year while he clarified his degree objective and learned to develop good study habits. This is typical of many students. Because his grades were excellent the last three years, Steve thought an appeal to Silar based on his demonstrated improvement and achievement was in order.

Review Steve's Success

Steve called the department manager with whom he interviewed at Silar Corporation. He said that he had received the rejection letter but believed additional circumstances should be considered. He explained that he had worked full-time during his four years in college and that he didn't clearly identify his degree or career objectives until the latter part of his first

294

year. After the first year, with clear goals in mind, his academic performance was excellent, including a 3.8 grade point average in his engineering major.

Three days later, Steve received a call from the department manager offering him a job! The manager explained that Steve's initiative and belief in his qualifications convinced him and his colleagues that Steve had the qualities they were seeking.

Model Your Success

Steve's technique (or a variation of it) has been used by thousands of applicants, and the results have been remarkably successful. You may have a perfectly valid reason for clarifying your qualifications to an interviewer after receiving a rejection notice. It takes courage and determination, but the possible reward for your effort is the successful conclusion of your job search. If you receive a rejection notice, you have nothing to lose and everything to gain by trying this tactic.

Word your rejection response carefully. Ask for help from a member of your support network who has strong communication skills. Work with this person to develop your rejection response using the guidelines in the Personal Best feature on this page.

Consider Another Position in Another Department

If your rejection response doesn't land you this job, ask whether another position would be more suitable for you. Emphasize your enthusiasm for working for the employer, and ask whether you are more qualified to fill another position. This strategy encourages the interviewer to give you more consideration and can land you a "hidden job." If another position isn't available, ask for a referral to another employer. Employers are impressed by applicants who demonstrate initiative and confidence. If you project confidence and competence, you greatly increase your chances of convincing others of your potential.

PERSONAL**BEST**

Responding to Rejection

No one enjoys getting "no" for an answer. But your response to a rejection can turn a potential negative into a positive for your job search.

To respond to a rejection notice:

▲ Describe in writing the shortcomings the interviewer perceived that resulted in your rejection.

▲ Summarize any misunderstandings you think contributed to your rejection.

▲ Summarize important information you omitted during the application or interview process.

▲ Draft your rejection response, clarifying any misunderstandings, adding information you omitted, and expanding on your qualifications and work experience.

▲ Make your response positive, active, and pleasant. Don't dwell on negatives.

▲ Review and practice the content of your response with a member of your network.

Making this extra effort provides further proof of your initiative and interest in the job. This can be the factor that convinces the interviewer to choose you over another candidate.

Success Tip

Ask for referrals to other departments or organizations. Such leads often uncover new employment possibilities!

Don't Be Afraid to Reapply

If you don't get a job with your preferred employer now, don't give up. Even if you take another job for a while, opportunities can develop later. If an opening comes up in the future, you have the advantage of being known by the employer because a known applicant saves valuable time in recruiting a new employee. Besides, you never know how close to being hired you were. You might be at the top of the list the next time an opening occurs. Keeping your name in front of the employer can put you first in line for the next opening. One way you can do this is by calling the interviewer every couple of months just to check in. Keep the phone call brief and polite. Your purpose is to keep your name at the top of the list of applicants. Consider the following true story.

Mercedes applied to a large, well-known corporation for a job as an administrative assistant in the human resources department. The department manager interviewed her. She knew she did well in the interview, but she didn't get the job because someone was promoted from within (a common practice).

A month later, the manufacturing department manager found Mercedes's file and interview rating sheet in the human resources department. He noted that the manager had decided not to hire her, despite excellent qualifications, because her personality was "too strong for the human resources department." The manufacturing department manager decided immediately that someone who was "too strong for the human resources department" was exactly what he needed in the manufacturing area. Result: The manufacturing department manager interviewed Mercedes and hired her at a higher salary than she would have been offered for the first position. Five years later, she was promoted to a supervisory position with a salary 125 percent higher than her starting salary.

> *"To keep a lamp burning, we have to keep putting oil in it."*
>
> Mother Teresa

Be Persistent

Be persistent in pursuing your preferred job. Stay focused on your goal, and consider all the factors that may affect the status of the position for which you have applied.

Business conditions change daily and may include expansion, new product development, new government regulations, mergers and takeovers, and so on. Any one of these conditions could affect the status of your target job. They can result in the creation of new jobs; the modification of existing jobs; or, in some cases, the elimination of jobs. Carefully consider how changes in business conditions may present new opportunities to you as a job seeker.

Many organizations and businesses keep applications in their active file for a specific period of time (usually six months). After that time, an application will not be considered for new job openings. Therefore, if you are interested in a position with a particular company, find out the organization's policy for keeping applications active. You may need to call a prospective employer periodically to keep your application active and to remind the organization that you're interested in new job openings.

Success Tip

Don't be afraid to reapply. You could be first on the backup list; employers save time and money hiring candidates from this list. Continue to check back to keep your name recognition high.

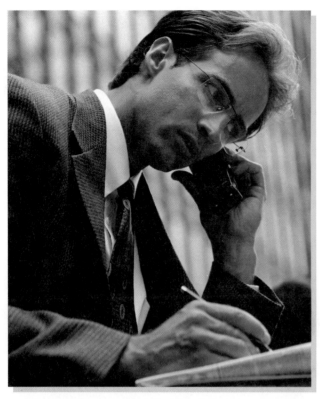

© GETTY IMAGES/PHOTODISC

Business conditions change daily. Such changes may represent new job opportunities for you.

Follow Up on Your Job Search Performance Evaluation

The keys to your success are preparation and positive thinking. Remember: You must plan and organize to succeed. Ask yourself these practical questions. Then take action to strengthen your job search effectiveness.

▲ Have I overlooked any skills, training, or competencies that support my job target?

▲ Have I checked with my support network members to find out whether they have any new job leads?

▲ Could my resume be improved or tailored to a new job target? How could it be improved? Who could do a good job of helping me with it?

▲ Should I make additional telephone calls/personal visits or write additional letters to prospective employers?

▲ Could my cover letters be improved? How could they be strengthened?

▲ Have I followed up on every interview with telephone calls, messages, and personal visits? Have I followed up on the cover letters and resumes I sent and on all job leads?

▲ Have I done thorough research on my current job leads— enough to talk intelligently and persuasively about how I would fit in with the organization?

▲ Have I tried every possible job source?

▲ Should I reapply with any employers? When?

▲ Did I do a thorough job of interview follow-up?

▲ Have I scheduled my job search on my daily and weekly calendars?

Career Action 18-1 will help you outline practical actions you can take to strengthen your job search effectiveness.

> **Complete Career Action 18-1**

CAREER ACTION 18-1

Action Plans for Improving Your Job Search Campaign

Directions: Access Career Action Worksheet 18-1 on your Learner's CD or on page 299 of this text. Complete the form, and take the follow-up actions required to improve your job search effectiveness. File your completed action plans in your Career Management Files Binder.

CHECKLIST

RECHARGING YOUR JOB SEARCH CAMPAIGN

Check each of the actions you are currently taking to increase your career success:

○ Using positive thinking, action, visualization, goal setting, and self-talk to recharge your motivation and to improve your job search campaign

○ Asking each interviewer to evaluate your performance so that any areas that need improvement can be identified

○ Preparing and delivering a response to a rejection notice; providing additional information or portfolio samples and clarifying qualifications or misunderstandings as needed

○ Asking for referrals to other departments or organizations

○ Reapplying at a later date; calling back periodically to check the organization's hiring status

CRITICAL THINKING QUESTIONS

1. After a rejection, how should you approach your continuation of the job search?

2. Should you abandon your efforts to obtain a job with a particular prospective employer if, following your interview, you are notified that you were not selected for the position? Why or why not?

3. What can you gain from seeking an evaluation of your interview performance from an interviewer who rejected you?

4. If all your efforts fail to result in a job offer, what last request should you make of an interviewer?

 For convenient access to valuable career resources, activities, and job information links, visit the companion web site for this text: *http://levitt.swlearning.com*

CAREER ACTION WORKSHEET 18-1

Action Plans for Improving Your Job Search Campaign

Directions: Review your complete job search campaign thoroughly. Answer each of the following questions in detail. Where necessary, include specific action plans you will take to improve your job search effectiveness. Check off each item as you complete the related actions.

1. After reviewing my self-analysis activities in the Career Actions from Chapters 2 and 3, have I overlooked anything important that supports my job target? (List the items, and describe any needed research or improvement.)

    _____

    _____

    _____

2. Have I checked with my support network members to find out whether they have any new job leads? (List them here, and follow up immediately.)

    _____

    _____

    _____

3. Could my resume be improved or tailored to a new job target? How could it be improved? Who could do a good job of helping me with it?

    _____

    _____

    _____

4. Should I make additional telephone calls/personal visits or write additional letters to prospective employers? (List detailed actions on a separate sheet of paper, and begin following up today. Don't put these actions off.)

    _____

    _____

    _____

5. Could my cover letters be improved? How could they be strengthened?

    _____

    _____

    _____

Continued on next page >>>

CAREER ACTION WORKSHEET 18-1 (continued)

6. Have I followed up on every interview with telephone calls, messages, and personal visits? Have I followed up on the cover letters and resumes I sent and on all job leads? (List any follow-up needed in these areas.)

_____

_____

_____

7. Have I done thorough research on my current job leads—enough to talk intelligently and persuasively about how I would fit in with the organization? (List any research that must be completed.)

_____

_____

_____

8. Have I tried every possible job source? (Refer to the list of suggested job sources in Chapter 6. List any you could use now.)

_____

_____

_____

9. Should I reapply with any employers? When?

_____

_____

_____

10. Review Chapter 17. Did I do a thorough job of interview follow-up? (Make note of any follow-up activity you omitted that might have improved your chance of being selected.)

_____

_____

_____

11. Have I scheduled my job search on my daily and weekly calendars? If not, do it now!

_____

_____

_____

YOU'RE HIRED!
TAKE CHARGE
OF YOUR CAREER

In this chapter, you will:

- Review guidelines for adjusting successfully to a new job.

- Learn strategies for achieving peak performance in a new job.

- Evaluate your previous or current performance in a job, in volunteer work, or in another responsible activity.

- Learn techniques for managing change and being adaptable.

 Search the Internet for job and career success tips.

- Research your industry for tips on job success, promotion, and making a job change.

"While learning the essentials of a new position, also pay particular attention to those people around you who have contributed much to the organization. Glean knowledge and perspective from them. Watch how they approach new assignments. Observe how they handle tough situations. The more you learn about 'your' company, the bigger asset you become!"

R. E. Keiter
Manager
Wilson Associates

Chapter 19 presents guidelines for adjusting to and succeeding in a new job. Techniques are included for developing successful interpersonal skills, achieving top work efficiency, quickly mastering new responsibilities, and learning how to prepare for a successful job performance evaluation. The importance of taking responsibility for achieving a high quality and quantity of work and for being adaptable to change is also emphasized. Once you master your job and are performing at your peak, you will likely be interested in working toward career development and advancement opportunities. This chapter also provides clear guidelines for earning a promotion and achieving career growth.

Adjust to Your New Job

All workers who start new jobs have one challenge in common: adjusting to the job. This adjustment includes learning to perform specific job functions, learning how the job relates to the business as a whole, learning to work with others (superiors, team members or coworkers, and customers), and understanding the formal and informal chain of organizational command. Mastering all these elements requires time and effort on your part and training assistance from your employer.

Don't expect to achieve top efficiency overnight. It doesn't happen. Experiencing some anxiety while trying to learn so much new information and so many new procedures is normal. Maintaining enthusiasm, an eagerness to learn, and a positive attitude will help you adjust successfully.

> "As for the future, your task is not to foresee, but to enable it."
>
> Antoine de Saint-Exupery

Expect that adjusting to your new job will take some time. Be alert, listen, and stay positive. Look, speak, and act professionally.

Starting a new job is an important personal and professional step that helps shape your lifetime career. Successful careers are developed through planning and determination to succeed. You will achieve peak success by being persistent and by accumulating skills, knowledge, and experience.

Your employer will want you to succeed, and your coworkers will help you get off to a good start. The following techniques will help you adjust to a new job and achieve a successful lifetime career.

Project a Positive Attitude: The Most Important Success Factor

Employers hire and promote employees who have positive attitudes and demonstrate enthusiasm. Employees who demonstrate a defensive, negative, or disinterested attitude are not promoted and may eventually be terminated. Two employees with equal job skills but vastly different attitudes will develop widely different career paths. The one with a strong, positive attitude will progress steadily, while the one with a negative attitude will stagnate.

Approach new tasks, colleagues, and superiors with the attitude that you will do your best and that you expect the best from them, while being patient with their constraints. People most often live up to the expectations others have of them.

Project a Positive, Professional, and Competent Image

People perceive the image you project as a reflection of the quality of work you do. Your image projects from three sources: your inner confidence, your outward appearance, and your verbal and nonverbal communication. Review and practice the tips on self-esteem, appearance, and communication skills from Chapters 1 and 11. Maintain the professional appearance you had in your job interviews, but dress appropriately for your job duties and organization.

If you project an unsure attitude through your speech, appearance, and actions, you will be perceived as a tentative, unsure worker—even if your work is excellent. Purposely think, speak, dress, and act positively. This projects career-building confidence and competence.

Projecting a positive, professional, and competent image gives you a competitive edge. For example, if you make an error, your professional image may influence people to view the error as a part of learning rather than a sign of incompetence. Successful people act positively, practicing the nine success strategies presented in Chapter 1 until they become habits.

Emulate the habits of successful people. Think of yourself, see yourself, groom yourself, and talk about yourself as a winner.

Develop and Practice Good Interpersonal Skills: Be a Team Player

Job success depends largely on the ability to work well with others. Studies repeatedly verify that job failure is most frequently the result of poor interpersonal (behavior and attitude) skills—not lack of skill.

Be a Team Player. Get along well with and assist others, show interest in their work, and work efficiently alone or with others. Team players are promoted first.

Be Tactful. The world's most successful people have these qualities in common: They are tactful, diplomatic, courteous, and helpful in dealing with other people.

Treat People the Way You Want to Be Treated. Help others accomplish their assignments, compliment them on work well done, critique their work tactfully only when necessary, and listen to what they have to say. This behavior encourages others to treat you the same way.

When you need help with a project or are in line for a promotion, your reputation for working well with others will more likely be rewarded. Treat all people (your employer, your peers, the custodian) with respect.

Success Tip

Focus on three goals to help you adjust successfully to a new job: Keep a positive attitude; project a professional, competent image; and be a good team player.

Get Off to a Successful Start

When you're hired, your employer expects you to have the basic knowledge and skills needed to do the job. You acquired these through your education and prior work experience. The challenge now is to apply them to the best of your ability in performing your job.

> *"The only certain means of success is to render more and better service than is expected of you, no matter what your task may be."*
>
> Og Mandino

Be a good learner, and expand your abilities. You will be expected to become a productive employee within a reasonable training period. You can improve the quality and speed of your learning and performance by applying the following techniques for mastering a new job.

Learn About Your Company

It is important to learn as much as you can about your company or employer and its leaders. Read the annual report if the company has one. (Many are online at the Securities and Exchange Commission web site and are available through employers' investor relations or human resources departments. Your manager might also have one.) Read your company's web site thoroughly and/or visit your local library to research the company's history and news stories.

In addition to learning about your employer, learn about its industry and main competitors. Research the competitors' products or services, their strengths and weaknesses, and why customers might buy them instead of your company's offerings.

Talk to long-time employees about their experience and recollections. Knowing the employer's history can help you understand its culture.

Embrace your employer's values and goals. Most places of business have a mission statement, goals, and values. For example, a value might be social responsibility. Get involved in community activities, especially in company-sponsored events. Many employers sponsor volunteer or community service activities and organizations. Participation provides many benefits, including expanding your network of contacts, developing leadership skills, and demonstrating your support for the employer's goals and related activities.

Pay Attention to Your Job Orientation

Your employer is responsible for informing you of your job duties and for providing an orientation to the work procedures. You should also be told about work hours, parking requirements, and related information. Learn what the rules are, and follow them. Ask for copies of policies and procedures that pertain to your job and workplace.

Your employer should explain when and how your performance will be evaluated. To help focus your efforts and achieve the best possible performance evaluation, find out immediately *exactly how and when your job performance will be evaluated.* If your employer overlooks any of this orientation or job evaluation information, request the information yourself.

Be Smart About Compensation and Benefits

Take the time to learn about employee benefits, and take full advantage of those that can save you money.

> *"Never be afraid to try something new. Remember: Amateurs built the Ark; professionals built the Titanic."*
>
> Anonymous

Enroll in benefit programs at the start of your employment, and update your benefit selections during your company's annual benefit enrollment period.

In addition to insurance programs, many employers offer flexible spending accounts that allow you to set aside pre-tax income to pay for medical expenses and dependent care. Such accounts can lower the amount of your income that is subject to tax. Some employers also offer such accounts for using mass transit, for paying parking fees, and so on. If your new position doesn't have all the benefits you hoped for, you may need to make alternative plans for health and disability insurance. These are available through professional organizations, credit unions, auto clubs, alumni groups, etc.

Plan for Retirement Now

It's never too early to start saving for retirement, so take advantage of any savings plans that your employer offers. Many large companies offer tax-deferred savings plans—known as 401(k) or 403(b) plans—and will contribute to your retirement savings if you participate in the company-sponsored plan through payroll deductions. Because you save your own money *and* contributions from your employer, this is one of the best ways to save for retirement.

Depending on your savings plan, the amount you put aside can reduce your taxable income, the gains aren't taxed until you retire, and you may draw from the plan to pay for your education or purchase a home. Also, seek investment and retirement savings advice from a financial planner or an investment banker who can help you establish your own individual retirement account (IRA), if needed.

Be Aware and Alert

Observe carefully the way work flows through your department, and be a good listener. This will help you adjust more quickly. Others appreciate good listeners and not having to repeat information. Also, pay attention to subtle attitudes and unstated policies that influence work operations.

Learn the Organizational Culture

Every organization has a unique personality and culture. To enhance your success, develop organizational savvy. Learn and adhere to the culture's values, including the expected work ethic and social norms. For example, are social activities in and out of the workplace the norm? Will you be considered aloof if you don't participate? Pay attention. Not all cultural norms are spelled out. You will discover them through observation.

Use a Question-and-Answer Notebook

As you learn each aspect of your job, use a notebook or an electronic organizer to record all your questions and the instructions you receive. Ask your supervisor and coworkers what times are best for discussing your questions (to avoid annoying them with poorly timed interruptions). Maintaining your notebook is important for several reasons:

▲ You will improve your efficiency by clarifying information that hasn't been explained fully.

▲ You won't have to repeat your questions.

▲ Your supervisor will appreciate your efficiency.

Remembering every detail required to master a new set of job tasks is impossible. A notebook provides a quick review and a reminder of tasks and procedures.

Success Tip

To enhance your success in a new job, pay attention and listen well. Stay alert to subtle and unstated policies, cultural norms, and work ethics. Take notes, so you will be able to clarify information and instructions.

Be Dependable, Punctual, and Industrious

Be professional, hardworking, and accurate in performing your job. This sets a positive example for your coworkers. Employers value and look for these qualities when retaining and promoting people.

Maintain an Excellent Attendance Record.

Absenteeism causes work inefficiency, disruption of workflow, and lower productivity. It also places stress on workers who must cover for the absent employee, causing resentment and frustration. If you must be absent because of a severe illness, a serious emergency, or an unavoidable problem, let your employer know as soon as possible. Chronic absenteeism is not tolerated by employers and is an eventual ticket out the door. *Abuse* is the key problem. Patterns of questionable excuses raise questions in the employer's mind.

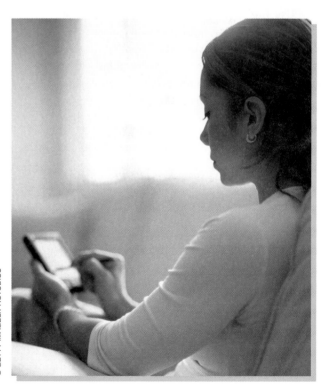

© GETTY IMAGES/PHOTODISC

Use time management and personal organization tools to keep track of your activities.

PERSONAL**BEST**

Managing Your Time

Managing your time effectively is one of the keys to becoming an efficient worker. Follow these time management tips to increase your productivity:

Be on Time. Be at your desk ready to work on time (or a little early) every day. Being on time gives you an edge of preparedness and an unhurried mind-set that improves work performance.

Determine Priorities and Plan Your Work Around Them. Ask your coworkers and supervisor what tasks are most vital to the successful operation of your department. Prioritize your work based on their answers. Do your most important daily tasks first to avoid overlooking vital tasks during rush work periods. Reassess your priorities as new tasks are assigned, and review these with your team or supervisor periodically.

Use Time Management Tools: Calendars and Job-Tracking Forms. Keep your work calendar current, coordinate it with your work team, and check it daily. Keep a reminder notebook of tasks to be completed. Prepare a daily to-do list, recording the tasks in order of importance. Do your best each day to complete as many tasks on your list as possible. Move any incomplete tasks to the next day's to-do list.

Develop Good Time Management Habits. To attain maximum efficiency, group all similar tasks and complete them in one block of time. This focuses your attention and task performance rather than fragmenting it. For example, schedule one block of time to prepare documents and another to place phone calls.

Keep Your Work Area Well Organized. If your work area is well organized, you can locate and use resources efficiently; this increases productivity, decreases frustration, and enhances your professional image.

Be Punctual and Dependable. Be on time for work at the start of the day and after breaks or mealtimes. Be punctual for meetings. Those who make an effort to be punctual will not appreciate your being late. Be on time! Being on time also means finishing projects and assignments when they are due.

Demonstrate Initiative. Personal initiative is a major factor affecting your promotability. After you've finished your assigned duties, *don't sit and wait for more work to be assigned.* Find an appropriate task to perform on your own, notify your supervisor that you are ready for another assignment, or ask how you can help someone else. Think creatively about better ways to do your job. Then research and plan how to implement your ideas. If a coworker is overloaded, offer to help.

Focus on People As Well As Job Duties

The way you relate to the people in your work will influence your career success as much as the quality of your job performance—no matter how skilled or educated you are. Make time for your coworkers, supervisors, employer, clients, and/or customers. Be courteous and helpful.

Get to Know Your Coworkers. Make an effort to spend time with your coworkers during breaks and mealtimes. Network with others, and get to know them. Be friendly and approachable. Don't let yourself become a loner; it won't enhance your career success.

Be Aware of Organizational Politics. Every organization has formal and informal politics, which are affected by changes in personnel. Learn who is respected—or even feared—in your place of employment. These people often influence office politics greatly and are usually powerful within the organization. Learn to deal with them successfully.

Note, however, that first impressions are not always accurate. Take time to observe and learn the office politics. Avoid affiliating closely with any individual or group that is not reputable and in harmony with your philosophy and the employer's.

Be a Good Communicator

Good communication skills are important for career success. Effective verbal communication, listening, and written communication can improve your productivity and enhance your interactions with coworkers and managers.

Use Excellent Phone Manners. Phone manners are important, especially in a customer-service economy. Greet callers pleasantly and promptly, listen carefully, and answer their questions patiently and thoroughly. Check your voice-mail messages frequently, and leave very brief, specific, and clear messages for others. Return calls promptly.

Listen Actively. Active listening can be a powerful tool for gaining information and solving problems. In a conversation, give the other person your full attention. Focus on what is being said, look directly at the other person, and never interrupt. Ask questions to show the other person that you want to understand. A good rule of thumb is to listen twice as much as you talk!

Recognize Communication Styles. Even in the same culture, people have different communication styles. This means that they process information differently, approach problems differently, want information given to them differently, and socialize differently. A key to success in any organization is learning the different styles of the people you deal with (especially customers and managers) and adapting your style accordingly. This ability can be a key step in resolving disputes and avoiding conflicts in the workplace.

Use Strategies for Effective Writing. In most careers, you can count on writing being used frequently in your daily business. To make a good impression, your e-mails, memos, letters, and reports must be professional, precise, and error free! Follow the "4 C's" of effective writing. Make certain all your written correspondence is complete, concise, correct, and clear. Always use a businesslike tone, and proofread your work. Never use slang or inappropriate humor in business writing.

For important workplace documents, follow the steps of the writing process to achieve your best work and make writing tasks seem less overwhelming.

1. **Pre-write.** Identify your audience, purpose, and main topics. Generate ideas by brainstorming and making lists.

2. **Draft.** Start creating a rough draft by writing out your ideas in sentence form—on paper or on the computer.

3. **Revise.** Improve your draft by reorganizing paragraphs, adding details, and making your sentences more precise.

4. **Edit and Proofread.** Review your work and check your facts. Correct all spelling and grammar errors. If possible, have someone else review your work, too.

5. **Present and Publish.** Present your final work in a professional, properly formatted document.

Use E-mail Appropriately. E-mail has become one of the most popular forms of workplace communication and should follow the rules of effective business writing. Make e-mail messages businesslike and brief, and always include informative subject lines. E-mail should not be used to handle serious issues or difficult problems that are best resolved in person. Remember: E-mail is not private and can be monitored by employers, so don't use it to send sensitive or personal information, to convey information that you would not want to be shared, or to send jokes or other non-work-related messages.

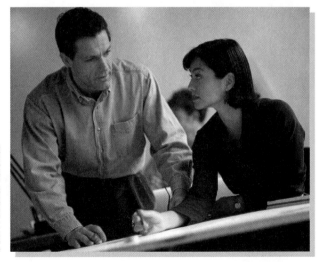

© GETTY IMAGES/PHOTODISC

Learn to be an effective communicator in face-to-face, telephone, and written communications. This will improve your productivity and enhance your interactions with coworkers and managers.

Manage Yourself

Learn to deal with difficult people, control your emotions, and manage stress and conflict. Maintain a good fitness program and a healthy life balance. Also, manage your family and transportation needs; anticipate and prevent problems. Many excellent classes, books, CDs, DVDs, videos, and web sites are available on all of these subjects.

Build a Network

Actively build a network of people who are willing to help you understand how to work most efficiently and effectively in the organization. Whenever possible, reciprocate by helping people in your network. Become involved in one or more professional, trade, or technical associations to expand your resources and networking opportunities.

Seek Feedback and Accept Criticism

Actively asking for feedback from your supervisor demonstrates initiative and professionalism. Periodically ask your supervisor directly if your

Periodically seek feedback from your supervisor, and learn to accept criticism professionally. Consider criticism an opportunity for improvement.

performance is meeting his or her expectations or if you need to improve. Ask for specific recommendations for improvement where necessary.

Because you are human, you will make an occasional mistake. Gasp! The challenge is to learn from your mistakes and accept criticism maturely. When you work for someone else, you agree to perform according to that person's standards. Because your employer pays your salary, he or she has the right to criticize your performance or behavior if it doesn't meet established standards.

If the criticism is deserved, don't deny fault. Don't react defensively or blame others. Accept the criticism professionally, and make improvements. To learn from your mistakes, request suggestions for improvement from the person who criticizes you. If you don't think the criticism is justified, tactfully present evidence that supports your opinion.

If your employer or supervisor continually criticizes you unfairly, particularly in front of others, request a meeting to discuss the reason for this behavior. If the criticism continues even though you make the recommended improvements, consider seeking a position in another department or looking for a new employer.

Make Your Supervisor Look Good, and Be Supportive

Find out what your supervisor needs to meet goals and excel, and do what you can to provide it. Regularly using your initiative to meet your supervisor's needs is a career booster!

In return for offering you a job and salary, the employer expects your support. Speak well of the firm and its personnel, products, and services. Speaking negatively about an organization harms the employer's reputation and may result in your being fired. If you're unhappy and see no way to gain satisfaction, move on.

Demonstrate Maturity

Be responsible for your actions. Perform at your best level, and expect the same from those you supervise. Be aware of your strengths and weaknesses. Capitalize on your strengths, and make efforts to improve your areas of weakness. Be self-reliant and self-disciplined. Maintain stable emotions in the workplace, leaving your personal problems at home. Show your maturity by thinking like a manager, acting like a leader, and being an example to others.

Know your customers. Understand that you have two types of customers, internal and external. Internal customers are the people or groups that use your service or depend on you to help get their jobs done. For instance, a programming group is a customer of the training department that provides computer classes. Every group is a customer of human resources to provide employees who are qualified to fill open positions. Get to know your internal customers, what their needs are, and how they depend on you or your group, and then go out of your way to provide great service.

Don't be afraid to take risks or to fail. Although success is rewarded, no one is perfect. Take appropriate, measured risks when needed, and always have a back-up plan for when things don't go as you intended. Learn from your mistakes, and don't repeat them.

Take initiative. Become proactive—especially in providing service to your customers. Don't wait until your customers present a problem to offer a suggestion that could improve their business. Ask questions to improve your knowledge; then take the opportunity to make suggestions.

Set goals. Establish realistic yet challenging goals and deadlines for your work. Manage your time carefully, and have a plan for meeting your goals.

Offer feedback. Take advantage of opportunities to give feedback to your employer, such as through on-line employee surveys and continuous improvement teams and task forces. Don't complain or criticize. Instead, offer creative yet practical suggestions for improving procedures, saving money, and exploring better ways of doing things.

Prepare for Your Job Performance Evaluation

Learn how and when you will be evaluated on your job performance so you know where to focus your efforts to achieve a good evaluation. This will also help you avoid overlooking an area considered important by your employer. You need to know how heavily the employer weighs each performance area so you can concentrate on the important ones. If you don't receive this information during orientation, ask your supervisor to explain the process.

> *"Perpetual optimism is a force multiplier."*
>
> Colin Powell

If your employer uses an informal method of job evaluation, ask what is considered good job performance and what criteria are used in determining promotions or raises. This will provide guidelines for your successful performance. As you become more knowledgeable about your job, show initiative. Set your own goals and deadlines for performance improvement and growth.

Many employers schedule annual, biannual, or quarterly meetings to review their employees' job performances in writing, orally, or both. Usually, the purpose of these evaluations is to identify the strengths and weaknesses of the employees and to establish short- and long-term goals for the employer and employee. A sample job performance rating form that is representative of those used by many organizations is shown in Career Action Worksheet 19-1.

Complete Career Action 19-1

CAREER ACTION 19-1

Job Performance Evaluation

Directions: Access Career Action Worksheet 19-1 on your Learner's CD or turn to page 316 to complete the Job Performance Evaluation form. If you have never held a paid job, evaluate yourself on volunteer work, internship work, or another significant activity in which you were responsible for carrying out assigned tasks and for working with, organizing, or directing others. File your evaluation in your Career Management Files Binder.

Success Tip

To succeed in your job, manage yourself professionally. Be efficient and dependable, focus on people, and prepare for your performance evaluation.

Succeed in Today's Changing Workplace

As emphasized in Chapter 4, today's technology and increasing workplace competition are escalating the pace of work and changing the way work is performed. Employers need employees who are flexible, adaptable to change, and able to work independently when making decisions and solving problems. Competition requires increased efficiency.

Meet Your Employer's Quality Needs

Employers expect each worker to take responsibility for achieving maximum productivity while continuously looking for ways to improve quality. To meet your employer's expectations and achieve peak career success:

▲ Produce top-quality work.

▲ Produce the highest possible quantity of work.

▲ Be alert for problems, and take action to prevent or solve them.

▲ Contribute efficiently and effectively as a team member.

Be Flexible and Manage Change

In addition to quality performance, focus on developing and improving your ability to be flexible and adapt to change.

Be Flexible. Expect differences (some major) between the way your employer conducts business and the methods you learned in school or on another job. While schools often teach theories, employers interpret and apply theories and techniques (often developing their own) to accomplish specific work goals and tasks. Changing technology makes some textbook theories obsolete. Personalities also influence work methods. For example, an outgoing person will typically use different methods from those used by a shy person.

A process that may seem inefficient to you or may be different from the method used in your previous job may serve a valuable organizational purpose that is not immediately apparent to you. Projecting a know-it-all attitude to your supervisor or others is a sure way to alienate yourself, perhaps permanently. If you think a technique could be improved, request a meeting with your supervisor to clarify the reasons for

Stay Up-to-Date

Continually update your skills and knowledge through education and training. We are living in an economy that is increasingly based on knowledge and service and less on manufacturing and goods. In the late 1990s, for example, enormous wealth was created by *ideas*—many of which were applied to software and processes that increased productivity.

Innovation (new ways of doing things) was the key. Just as companies invested in new factories and machines during the Industrial Age, investment in employees with knowledge and information is the key in today's Information Age. That is why it's important for you to invest money and time in your ongoing training, education, and learning.

Complete Career Action 19-2

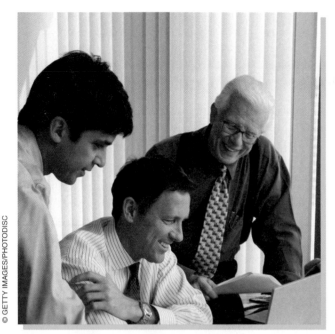

Maintain an open, flexible atttitude toward change. Employers value employees who are adaptable to new work processes, tools, and equipment.

using it. Asking thoughtful questions is a good strategy for opening the discussion.

There is a right time, place, and method for presenting your ideas or suggestions to your supervisor. Learn by observing how others present theirs. If the clarificaiton by your supervisor still doesn't convince you that a technique is the most effective option, explain the theory or technique you have learned or devised, offering it as a suggestion for consideration. Do not try to bulldoze your idea through, however.

Adapt to Change. Rapid technological, global economic, and other changes require continual changes in work processes, tools, and equipment. You must be flexible in evaluating the need for or adapting to changes in procedures, equipment use, and so on. Office automation affects the way business is conducted and the way work is performed. Keep an open, flexible attitude toward change. Don't make yourself obsolete through stubborn resistance; you may miss an open door to a career development opportunity.

Manage Your Career Development/Advancement

Once you believe you've mastered your job responsibilities, you've overcome areas of weakness in your performance, and your employer is satisfied with your performance and understanding of the job, focus on managing your career development and seeking growth or advancement opportunities. You may want to work toward a new career goal—a lateral move or a promotion, for example.

Be Willing to Take on New Responsibilities

Find out what new responsibilities are included in any new growth opportunities or position you seek. Outline the required action steps; pursue them with an expectation of success; and be willing to accept, learn, and carry out all new duties. Get any training you need to perform at the levels required.

CAREER ACTION 19-2

Use the Internet to Search for Current Job and Career Success Tips

Directions: Search the Internet for articles related to the topics presented in Chapter 19 (adjusting to and succeeding in a new job, succeeding in today's changing workplace, and pursuing a new career goal). Use any of the sites listed below or others you identify (links can be found on the *Your Career: How to Make It Happen* web site at http://levitt.swlearning.com). Write a summary of at least two articles that are useful to you, and file them in your Career Management Files Binder.

▲ CareerJournal.com

▲ JobWeb

▲ Quintessential Careers

Some keywords to use in your search include *career advancement, promotion, time management, performance evaluation, adapt to change,* and *mentor/mentoring.*

Earn Your Advancement or Promotion

Keep in mind that you don't *get* a promotion or advancement opportunity; you *earn* it! When you know you're adequately prepared for advancement, start demonstrating your qualifications for it. The following guidelines will help you achieve this goal:

▲ **Maintain and update your career portfolio.** Continually add to the career portfolio you've developed through the exercises in this text. This is your collection of documents and other items that provide evidence and examples of your work accomplishments, certifications, skills, qualifications, and more. Throughout your career, add records of all your work-related achievements, including samples of exemplary work; letters of recognition for a job well done; and other documents that support your good job performance, achievements, and related activities.

> *"The secret of getting ahead is getting started. The secret of getting started is breaking your complex overwhelming tasks into small manageble tasks and then starting on the first one."*
>
> Mark Twain

▲ **Seek a mentor.** A mentor is someone inside or outside your organization who can advise and coach you—someone who is respected and knowledgeable in your field. Seek advice from mentors who are experienced in the areas you need to improve. Don't limit yourself to just one mentor. Look for people who are sensitive to your concerns, who help you learn new skills, and/or who take time to explain organizational dynamics. Keep your relationship with a mentor professional. A true mentor will develop an interest in you, make you aware of useful resources, and arrange opportunities for you to meet key people and grow professionally. Strive to meet your mentors' expectations for your performance.

▲ **Develop expertise.** Identify your greatest working strengths and interests, and build on them. Take advantage of all training in these areas. Become known for your special expertise. This will help focus your career in a direction that best suits you and will expand your career opportunities.

312

▲ **Be professional.** Think, act, speak, and dress professionally. If you want a promotion, act as though you already fit the part.

▲ **Expand your knowledge and skills.** Keep current in your job and industry knowledge (trends, technology, and improved methods of job performance). Correct any deficiencies immediately through reading, involvement in professional groups, training, and education. Submit reports of what you have learned to your supervisor.

▲ **Do high-quality work.** Do the best possible job, and achieve the highest possible quantity and quality of work.

▲ **Increase your organizational awareness.** Learn all phases of the organization, its goals, and how each job is designed to meet the overall goals.

▲ **Increase your visibility.** Get involved in organizational committees and cross-team projects in which you can excel. Show extra initiative, and demonstrate leadership. Develop your speaking abilities.

▲ **Use subtle self-promotion techniques.** Sometimes it's not enough to perform well; you must also make your superiors aware of your achievements—without bragging. Focus on your experience, not on yourself. Whenever you talk with coworkers and managers, be positive and enthusiastic about your job and your projects. Speak with confidence about your experience and accomplishments, but avoid making too many "I" statements.

▲ **Seek a promotion.** Once you've accomplished most of the items in this list, tell your supervisor you're interested in progressing and learning more. Demonstrate your ability to handle additional responsibility.

Think Like a Free Agent

Career-long employment with one company is no longer the norm; in fact, today's workers can expect to change jobs about 10 times during the course of their careers! According to some experts, the average length of a job today is 3.7 years. An employer and an employee are partners in a contract that has to work for *both* parties. Every job may be temporary, so you must keep an open mind, stay networked, and constantly be prepared to take the next step in your career.

Consider a portfolio career—a career made up of a variety of complementary activities that capitalize on your strengths and provide you with an acceptable level of income. These activities may include full-time work, part-time work, a temporary or contract work arrangement, a hobby that turns into a home-based business, or any combination of these.

In this scenario, you must keep your ears open for new opportunities, network constantly, read frequently, work to acquire new skills, stay organized, and use your resume as a sales tool to highlight your relevant skills and successes—not just your jobs.

Complete Career Action 19-3

Success Tip

To succeed in today's workplace, be a high-quality, top producer and a problem solver; adapt to and manage change; and be flexible.

© GETTY IMAGES/PHOTODISC

Increase your visibility. Get involved in organizational committees and cross-team projects, and develop your speaking abilities.

CAREER ACTION 19-3

Research Your Industry for Tips on Job Success, Promotion, and Making a Job Change

Directions: Access Career Action Worksheet 19-3 on your Learner's CD, use the questionnaire provided on page 319, or design your own custom questionnaire to complete this assignment. Survey knowledgeable people in your field, and record their answers on the form. File your forms and research in your Career Management Files Binder.

Success Tip

To achieve new career goals, take on new challenges, broaden your skills and knowledge, seek a mentor, keep your career portfolio current, network, and increase your visibility.

Maintain Your Network and Career Management Files

Once you're employed, send a thank-you note to all the members of your network who helped you or expressed interest in your job search. Tell them about your new position. You want to keep in touch with your contacts for the next time you're ready to pursue a career goal. Realize that networking is not a job search activity to be discontinued once you get a job. To achieve the greatest levels of career success, continual networking is a must.

Remember: Staying networked all the time pays off! When you need important information or the time comes to seek a new job, you'll be leagues ahead of the competition that doesn't stay networked.

Keep your Career Management Files Binder current; don't abandon it. You've done a great deal of work in the exercises in *Your Career: How to Make It Happen*. Remember that this information will be useful throughout your entire career. Save your work (this book, the written assignments, and your computer files); you'll be glad you did!

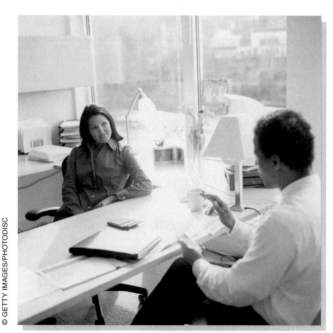

Continual networking is a must for achieving the greatest levels of career success.

CHECKLIST

SUCCEEDING ON THE JOB

Check each of the actions you are currently taking to increase your career success:

○ Focusing on three goals to help you adjust successfully to a new job: keeping a positive attitude; projecting a professional, competent image; and being a good team player

○ Learning about the company and culture, working efficiently, being dependable, focusing on people, and preparing for evaluation

○ Being a good communicator, managing yourself, building a network, and demonstrating maturity

○ Being a high-quality, top producer; being a problem solver; learning to adapt to and manage change; and being flexible

○ Taking on new challenges, broadening your skills and knowledge, seeking a mentor, developing expertise, keeping your portfolio current, networking, and increasing your visibility

○ Keeping your job search network active and maintaining your Career Management Files Binder to use in future career development activities

CRITICAL THINKING QUESTIONS

1. What is the most common cause of job failure?

2. How can you most effectively learn a new job? Name five things you can do to help yourself master a new job.

3. Why is it important to know how your performance will be evaluated?

4. Why is it essential to adapt to change, and how can you demonstrate adaptability?

5. Once you have mastered a new job, what specific actions can you take to increase your professional development and make yourself promotable? List additional training or coursework you could take to increase your knowledge and skills. Identify growth-oriented responsibilities you would be interested in pursuing. List other actions you could take to prepare for a promotion and increase your visibility.

 For convenient access to valuable career resources, activities, and job information links, visit the companion web site for this text: *http://levitt.swlearning.com*

CAREER ACTION WORKSHEET 19-1

Job Performance Evaluation

Directions: Rate your job performance in your current or past work experience, in volunteer or internship work, or in another significant task-oriented activity. In the space to the left of each Performance or Behavioral Category, place the rating code you think most appropriately represents your performance (O = Outstanding, V = Very good, G = Good, A = Acceptable, U = Unacceptable). On the line below each item, give one or two examples of your performance. Then go back and circle the items you rated acceptable or unacceptable; make these your targets for improvement.

Rating Code   **Performance or Behavioral Category**

_____   **ABILITY TO ACQUIRE AND USE INFORMATION AND FOLLOW INSTRUCTIONS**
(Uses initiative in acquiring, interpreting, and following instructions and using references)

List specific examples: _____
_____
_____

_____   **INTERPERSONAL SKILLS** (Is tactful, understanding, and efficient when dealing with people)

List specific examples: _____
_____

_____   **BASIC SKILLS** (Is proficient in reading, writing, mathematics, listening, and verbal and nonverbal communication)

List specific examples: _____
_____

_____   **JOB SKILLS** (Demonstrates command of required knowledge and skills)

List specific examples: _____
_____
_____

_____   **THINKING/PROBLEM-SOLVING SKILLS** (Generates new ideas, makes decisions, solves problems, and reasons logically)

List specific examples: _____
_____
_____

Continued on next page >>>

CAREER ACTION WORKSHEET 19-1 (continued)

_____ **ABILITY TO COOPERATE WITH OTHERS** (Works well with team members and under supervision, exercises leadership, and works well with people of diverse backgrounds)

List specific examples: _____

_____

_____

_____ **QUANTITY OF WORK** (Does required amount of work)

List specific examples: _____

_____

_____ **QUALITY OF WORK** (Does neat, accurate, complete, and efficient work)

List specific examples: _____

_____

_____ **GOOD WORK HABITS** (Maintains good attendance and punctuality, is dependable, and follows safety/work procedures)

List specific examples: _____

_____

_____

_____ **ATTITUDE** (Demonstrates enthusiasm, interest, and motivation)

List specific examples: _____

_____

_____ **TECHNOLOGY** (Works well with technology–tools, computers, and procedures)

List specific examples: _____

_____

_____ **PERSONAL QUALITIES** (Demonstrates responsibility, initiative, self-confidence, integrity, and honesty; practices good self-management; sets and maintains goals; exhibits self-motivation; and is cooperative)

List specific examples: _____

_____

_____

Continued on next page >>>

CAREER ACTION WORKSHEET **19-1 (continued)**

Overall Evaluation of Performance and Behavior

Directions: Review the rating code (Outstanding, Very good, Good, Acceptable, or Unacceptable) you placed next to each category of your Job Performance Evaluation on the previous pages. Place a check mark below next to the rating you recorded the most frequently.

_____ Outstanding   _____ Very good   _____ Good

_____ Acceptable   _____ Unacceptable

Employee's Short-Term Goals: (List your short-term job or career goals here.)

_____

_____

Employee's Long-Term Goals: (List your long-term job or career goals here.)

_____

_____

_____

Suggestions for Improving Performance or Behavior: (List the steps you can take to improve your work performance or behavior.)

_____

_____

_____

General Comments Regarding Employee's Job Performance: (Add any other appropriate comments to describe the quality of your work performance.)

_____

_____

Signature of Supervisor: (This is where your job supervisor would sign your performance evaluation.)

_____

Signature of Employee: (This is where you would sign the performance evaluation.)

_____

Date: _____

CAREER ACTION WORKSHEET 19-3

Research Your Industry for Tips on Job Success, Promotion, and Making a Job Change

Directions: Arrange meetings with knowledgeable people in your field to learn the following: (a) how the job performance of employees is evaluated, (b) what techniques help ensure success on the job, (c) how employees can earn promotions, and (d) what methods are recommended for making a job change. Use the following questionnaire, adding pertinent questions that are relevant to your field. If you prefer, you can design and use your own questionnaire. Try to obtain sample job performance evaluations.

1. What advice would you give a new employee (in a position similar to the one you are seeking) to help him or her adjust quickly to the job, the company, and the people the employee would interact with?

   _____

   _____

   _____

   _____

2. What are the most important things to learn about your company when starting employment there?

   _____

   _____

   _____

   _____

3. What advice would you give a new employee to help ensure the highest degree of job success?

   _____

   _____

   _____

   _____

4. How does communication affect productivity and success on the job in your company?

   _____

   _____

   _____

   _____

Continued on next page >>>

CAREER ACTION WORKSHEET **19-3 (continued)**

5. Does your organization encourage risk taking? In what ways?

_____

_____

_____

_____

6. What criteria do you use to evaluate the performance of an employee? Do you have a job performance evaluation form I could review?

_____

_____

_____

_____

7. What advice would you offer employees to help them increase their visibility?

_____

_____

_____

_____

8. How can an employee earn a promotion here?

_____

_____

_____

_____

9. If an employee must leave your company, what steps do you prefer the employee take? How much notice do you expect? Do you prefer that the employee help train the replacement? Do you expect a letter of resignation?

_____

_____

_____

_____

MAKE SUCCESSFUL JOB AND CAREER CHANGES

In this chapter, you will:

- Focus on lifelong learning.

- Learn the difference between a job and a career and identify issues to consider when changing jobs or careers.

- Learn how to resign from a job professionally.

- Identify factors to consider when relocating.

 Use the Internet to research relocation and salary information.

- Learn how to survive being laid off or fired.

"In today's business environment, career changes are inevitable. If you cannot find a suitable career opportunity in your field, give serious consideration to alternatives. Use your experience to expand a company's target market, placing yourself in a key position. In other words, if you can't find it, create it!"

Jerry Solomon
President
Engineered Environments, Inc.

This chapter defines the difference between a job and a career and presents strategies for determining whether you want to consider changing your job or career. People rarely spend their entire lives working in the same positions for the same employers at the same locations. This chapter also explains the importance of lifelong learning in achieving career success. In addition, Chapter 20 provides guidelines for considering a job change or a career change. Methods are also presented for relocating successfully and for coping with being laid off or fired from a position.

Know the Difference Between a Job and a Career

A job involves performing a designated set of responsibilities and duties for a specific employer. A career encompasses a family of jobs. Your career is your life's work. Thus, *high school history teacher for Washington High School* is a job, and *teaching* is a career. Similarly, *sportswear clerk for After Five Stores* is a job, and *retail sales* is a career.

Many people don't understand the difference between a job and a career. As a result, they spend a great deal of time and money changing careers when they only need to change jobs. In other cases, people change jobs repeatedly and continue to be dissatisfied because they're not in the right careers.

Most people change jobs at least eight times during their working lives. With changes in technology and in people's values and interests, it's also common for people to change careers at least once during their lifetimes. If you realize that your current employment situation is no longer satisfying, first consider whether the dissatisfaction is with your career or with your specific job.

If you're unhappy with your supervisor but enjoy your work, for example, you may need to change jobs. This doesn't mean you need to change careers. If you don't enjoy the type of work you do, however, you may want to consider a career change.

Success Tip

Before you change your job or career, analyze whether your discontent is from your specific job or from your career choice. Don't change your career just because you don't like your supervisor, and don't keep changing jobs when you really aren't well suited for your career.

PERSONAL BEST

Be a Lifelong Learner

Rapidly changing technology and a global economy have created a fast-changing world. Jobs and careers are changing dramatically. To have a successful career and to distinguish yourself from the pack, you must update your current skills and add new skills quickly and continuously. In short, you must make learning a lifelong pursuit. You need to develop and sustain the habit of continuing your education to avoid being left behind.

You can become a lifelong learner by:

▲ Participating in workshops and training programs.

▲ Taking college- or graduate-level courses.

▲ Subscribing to journals and other print or online news and information related to your field.

▲ Joining professional associations related to your career.

Distance learning programs offered on the Internet make lifelong learning opportunities more accessible than ever. Online instructional services such as extremelearning.com, Thomson NETg, University of Phoenix Online, and Element K can help you find continuing education courses related to business and management, college studies, technology, training, graduate studies, and more. Links to these services can be found on the *Your Career: How to Make It Happen* web site at http://levitt.swlearning.com.

To ensure your continuous and future employability, make sure you have the skills required to meet the demands of the changing workforce. To remain a viable employee in the twenty-first century, you must make lifelong learning a part of your career management plans.

Complete Career Action 20-1

CAREER ACTION 20-1

Lifelong Learning Considerations

Part A Directions: Identify a career for which new training has become necessary for a person to remain employable. Explain the reason for the change, and describe the type of education or training required to meet the changing need.

Part B Directions: Think about the career you're planning to pursue. List at least two likely changes or situations in this career field that will require further education or training.

File your research in your Career Management Files Binder.

Know When You Should Change Jobs

You may want to consider a job change if:

▲ Your current employer can't offer you job growth or advancement.

▲ A poor economy requires layoffs, or an entire class of jobs is being shipped overseas in an offshoring trend.

▲ You want to move to a new location.

▲ Your department is dissolved.

▲ Your philosophy and values conflict with those of your current employer.

▲ You want a new challenge.

Never Quit a Job before You Have a New One

If possible, complete your job change while you are still employed. Because being employed is current proof that you do a job satisfactorily, you're considered more employable when you're currently employed. As a mountain-climbing instructor says to students, "Never let loose of your support before you have hold of another one."

Don't Rush into a Job Change without Adequate Planning

Give any change of job serious thought and planning. You'll regret a hasty decision to take a new job if it turns out to be worse than your current one. A job may look good, but without proper research, you could find yourself in a situation that is as bad as or worse than your current one. Evaluate your current job by asking yourself, "Is there room for advancement to a higher position, or are other important opportunities available?" If the answer is no and you will not be happy staying in the same position, you have strong grounds for considering a new employer. If the answer is yes, there may be advantages to staying with your current employer.

Know the Advantages of Staying with Your Current Employer

Seeking advancement or growth with your current employer can offer many advantages, including the following:

▲ Staying is less risky because you are already established and don't need to repeat the process of adjusting to new surroundings and people.

▲ Your reputation for job stability is better if you stay rather than move frequently from one employer to another.

▲ In outsourcing and offshoring situations, some employers recognize the value of keeping their best employees. They may offer you retraining opportunities and help you transition out of a vulnerable position.

▲ You won't lose accumulated benefits, such as vacation time, retirement, and profit sharing.

▲ If your current job offers important benefits such as excellent health care coverage and life insurance, it can be risky to give them up. With today's rising cost of benefits, some employers are finding it too expensive to offer extensive coverage. When considering a job change, always consider benefits in conjunction with rewards and compensation.

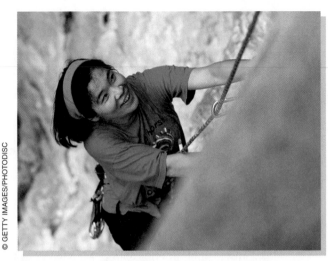

© GETTY IMAGES/PHOTODISC

Never let loose of your support before you have hold of another.

▲ A job change may result in quicker advancement than you could achieve by seeking a promotion within your current organization.

▲ You gain knowledge, broaden your experience, and increase your support network, expanding your career growth opportunities.

▲ You start with a clean slate as you develop your reputation for good job performance.

Success Tip

Change to a new job after carefully considering the advantages and disadvantages of staying in your current one. Avoid quitting your current position until you have obtained a new one.

Know What You Can Gain by Changing Employers

Changing employers can also offer many advantages, including the following:

▲ You increase your job interest by becoming involved with new challenges, surroundings, and people.

Know When You Should Change Careers

If, after thorough consideration, you decide that you aren't happy in your work and a change to another job within the same field would not bring satisfaction, you may want to consider a career change. Ask yourself the following questions:

▲ **Have I changed positions several times only to find that I'm still unhappy?** Repeated changes of employment that don't improve your job satisfaction may indicate a career problem, not a job problem.

▲ **Are my problems the result of personality or philosophical conflicts with my supervisor or fellow employees?** If so, it's more likely that you need a new employer rather than a new career. The exception occurs when the types of people usually found in your career field, regardless of the organization, don't fit your personality or philosophy.

▲ **Am I unhappy with the work environment?** If you don't like to work constantly at a desk, for example, decide whether this is common to your career field or only to your job. Would you prefer outdoor work? You may want to look at other careers if your career doesn't provide the opportunity for the type of work you desire. Is your problem with the work environment common to the career or only to some jobs within the career field?

▲ **Am I constrained in expressing my values?** Again, is this a function of your job or your career?

▲ **Is my position interesting?** What are your interests? Are you unable to satisfy them in your career or just in your current job?

▲ **Am I frustrated that I'm not using my skills and abilities?** Is this a job-related or career-related problem?

Even if you determine that your unhappiness is related to your career rather than your current job, you still have to weigh the pros and cons of making a career change. Rarely can you just jump into another career without making sacrifices, such as taking a lower salary. You need to evaluate the advantages and disadvantages and whether you're gaining more than you're losing.

> *"An investment in knowledge pays the best interest."*
>
> Benjamin Franklin

Success Tip

Change to a new career if you determine that your unhappiness is related to your career (not just to your current job) and that an alternative career is realistically available and will meet your needs.

Reassess

First, determine what alternative careers fit your interests and abilities. Study the options to decide which alternative you would prefer. Apply the strategies presented in Chapters 2 and 3. Then, after you have selected an alternative career, find out what additional education or training you need, how long it takes to prepare for the field, and what it will cost. Also determine whether the education or training is available nearby and whether you can get the necessary skills while continuing your current job or if you need to return to school and/or relocate.

Be Realistic

What are the job opportunities in the new field? Are the jobs in a desirable location, and will the pay meet your requirements? Be aware that when you change careers, you often have to start over at the entry-level salary.

What kind of risk taker are you? Are you willing to give up the security of your current position and career and take a chance? Do you expect to be significantly more satisfied in the new career? In the final analysis, decide whether the probable advantages of a new opportunity sufficiently outweigh the disadvantages and whether you are willing to assume any risk involved.

You must also be prepared to discuss your decision persuasively with prospective employers who may question whether you will be happy with such a career change. It is important to convey to employers that you have considered and planned for this change carefully and that you believe the advantages outweigh the disadvantages.

Complete Career Action 20-2

CAREER ACTION 20-2

Plan for Career Development Alternatives

Directions: Consider your career development. Then access Career Action Worksheet 20-2 on your Learner's CD to complete the following tasks.

1. List the name of your current target career; then list three jobs you might hold within that career field.

2. List two issues you would need to consider if you were evaluating a career change. List two issues you would need to consider if you were evaluating a job change.

3. File your work in your Career Management Files Binder.

Resign Professionally

Resigning professionally is good career insurance. Make every effort to leave your current employer with good feelings; do not leave in anger or with hostility, no matter how dissatisfied you might be. Throughout your career, references from your past employers will be requested each time you seek a new job. For this important reason, you should leave a job gracefully, pleasantly, and professionally.

Follow these guidelines to ensure that your resignation is accompanied by feelings of goodwill and a willingness by your employer to provide a good reference for you.

▲ Find out how your current employer typically reacts when learning that someone is looking for a new position. Does your employer become upset and fire that person or try to make it difficult for him or her to find new employment? Does your employer respond positively by offering to support the person in finding new employment? Or, even better, does your employer provide positive inducements (such as pay raises or promotions) to keep the person within the organization? If this is the case, you need to consider whether you're willing to accept a pay increase or promotion and stay.

▲ If your current employer responds positively to people leaving, it's advantageous to discuss your plans immediately. The employer may provide you with references, helpful suggestions, or even a better opportunity where you are.

▲ If your current employer resents losing employees and even fires those who seek other opportunities, do not give notice that you are planning to leave until you have another firm offer. You don't want to jeopardize your current position. Remember: You are more employable when you are currently employed.

▲ Do your current job to the best of your ability through your last day on the job. You're most likely to be remembered by how well you performed at the end of your employment. This can greatly influence the quality of future references from your current employer.

▲ Update your career portfolio before you leave. If appropriate, request letters of recommendation from your supervisors. Assemble samples of your work and documentation of your achievements that are pertinent and exemplary.

▲ Plan for an orderly and efficient transition of your responsibilities to the person taking your place. If asked to help train your replacement, be as thorough as possible, taking care to explain your duties clearly and completely. Where appropriate, provide written instructions to help your replacement carry out the duties of your position.

▲ Give your employer at least two weeks' written notice before you leave your current job. This is common courtesy and important in maintaining good standing with your employer. Giving less notice is considered unprofessional. You should submit a formal letter of resignation. An appropriate sample is shown in Figure 20-1.

Success Tip

Resign professionally. Your future could depend on it!

Complete Career Action 20-3

Know When You Should Consider Relocating

Sometimes deciding to relocate is easy. You may not have commitments keeping you in your current location, the job in the new location offers such great benefits that you can't afford to turn it down, or you just prefer to live elsewhere. On the other hand, the reasons you can't relocate may be compelling and require you to make a difficult decision. You may need to weigh several important factors to decide whether relocation is best. The most important issues are personal or family considerations and the impact on your career goals.

Affecting Loved Ones

The impact of relocation on your loved ones generally is the most difficult factor affecting a relocation decision. Your spouse or partner may have an excellent career position that would be lost if you relocated. You may have aging parents who need you to remain nearby. You must weigh the advantages of relocation against the possible negative effects it would have on your spouse, children, or other important people in your life.

Good communication with those who would be most affected by your decision to relocate is important. If you're married and your spouse works, you need to discuss openly the advantages and disadvantages of moving for each of your careers. If you have children, you should consider how they feel about moving, the quality of schools in the new area, and the availability of other resources that are important to your family in the new community.

Considering Your Values and Interests

Another important task in considering relocation is determining whether your values and interests are being met in your current location. For example, if you're living in Florida but love to snow ski and have an opportunity to live in Denver, clearly you can list one advantage of moving to Colorado.

To help make the best decision, write a list of the pros and cons of all aspects of relocation.

CAREER ACTION 20-3

Write a Letter of Resignation

Directions: Review Figure 20-1 on page 328. Then prepare a letter of resignation for a position you currently hold or have held. File your completed letter in your Career Management Files Binder.

March 9, 20—

Mr. George Diallo
Henson-Standlin Company
1414 Cromwell Avenue
Memphis, TN 38115

Dear Mr. Diallo:

This letter is to serve as notice that I will be leaving the Henson-Standlin
Company on March 31. I have taken a position as a service manager with
Gantry and Sons in Salem, Oregon.

I have truly enjoyed working for Henson-Standlin and view my employment
here as a valuable experience and an opportunity for professional development. Thank you for your guidance and assistance during the past three
years; I sincerely appreciate it.

Best wishes to you for continued success.

Sincerely,

Kelli Sullivan

Kelli Sullivan

Figure 20-1: Sample Letter of Resignation

Affording Relocation

The other main personal consideration is economic. What will relocation cost? Don't just look at the cost of a moving van. Expenses include utility connections and other start-up costs required to move into new living quarters. If you are offered a job in another location, what portion, if any, of these costs will your employer cover? Also research the differences in living costs.

The costs of housing, transportation, utilities, food, taxes (state, local, sales), insurance, and other portions of your budget may vary greatly from place to place. The Internet is a valuable source of information on this topic.

Get copies of the local newspapers from all the communities you are considering. Review grocery advertisements, classified listings for houses and apartments, and other indications of costs in the areas. The classified listings of many newspapers are also available on the Internet. Use your support network to identify individuals you can contact who may be familiar with the locations.

The following web sites can help you make important relocation decisions (links can be found on the *Your Career* web site):

▲ **JobStar** links to some general and specialized surveys. Click on "Salary Info."

▲ **Homefair.com** provides a cost-of-living calculator, comparisons of areas' crime rates, a moving cost calculator, and other relocation tools.

▲ **Monstermoving.com** provides a wide variety of relocation information and online tools.

▲ **Homestore.com** offers an "Apartments & Rentals" link for information on rental costs in various locations and tips for evaluating specific rental properties.

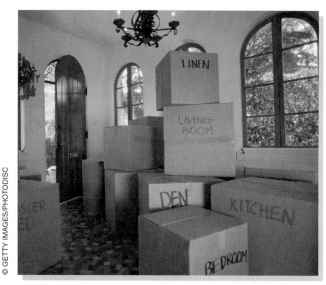

© GETTY IMAGES/PHOTODISC

Use the Internet and area newspapers to find helpful relocation information.

Success Tip

When making a relocation decision, consider the impact on your career goals, the impact on your loved ones, your values and interests, and the costs involved.

Affecting Your Career Goals

Another important area of concern is the impact of a relocation on your career goals. Will the move provide opportunities to gain valuable experience and advancement that are not currently available? How will the move look on your resume if, later on, you look for another new position? Is education or training that would provide added benefits available at the new location (but not where you are now)? Will you be exposed to new people who can help your career growth? Review your career plans. Will relocating better help you realize your goals?

Your decision whether or not to relocate will depend on your personal goals, needs, and circumstances. Base your relocation decision on thoughtful and careful consideration.

Use Relocation to Grow, Not to Start Over

Assume that you have decided to relocate. What can you do to make the move as smooth and as positive an experience as possible? How can you ensure that you will continue to move forward in your career?

Moving companies often provide free pamphlets that describe the steps you need to consider, as well as handy checklists. Check the Internet and your library for information on moving. Some important career-related issues are discussed below to help you get off to a good start in a new location.

See How Research Pays Off

Learn as much as you can about your new community before you move. If you belong to professional associations, find out whether they have chapters in the new community and arrange to transfer your member-ships. If an association has a web site, check it for links to local chapters. This will help you get professionally involved immediately and expand your support network to your new location. Subscribe to a newspaper to become familiar with your new area. Most communities have web sites that provide comprehensive information on the area. Enter the name of your new community in a search engine to learn all you can about the location before you move.

Complete Career Action 20-4

Success Tip

Make your relocation smooth and positive by researching the new community prior to your move, and build a new support network immediately upon your arrival.

CAREER ACTION 20-4

Use the Internet to Research Other Work Locations

Directions: Visit the web sites listed below to learn more about a community you might consider relocating to. (Links can be found on the *Your Career: How to Make It Happen* web site.) Use Career Action Worksheet 20-4 on your Learner's CD or a separate sheet of paper to prepare a written report summarizing your answers to the following questions. File your findings in your Career Management Files Binder.

1. How does the climate/weather of the new area compare with the climate/weather where you live now?

2. What kinds of recreational and cultural opportunities are available in the new area?

3. Is information on educational opportunities provided?

4. What cost-of-living information is provided?

5. What medical facilities are available in the new area?

DataMasters

Salary.com

USA CityLink

Monstermoving.com

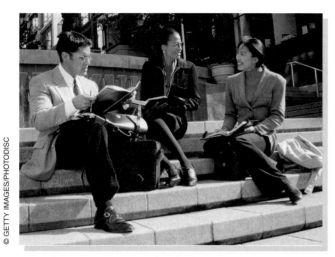

Expand your support network to include people in your new community.

Build a Support Network Branch

When you arrive in your new community, work at establishing a broad support group. Get involved in the community. Volunteer to work for a charity or an organization that fits your interests. This is an excellent way to become involved in the community and to expand your support network. You also have the opportunity to learn new skills or enhance old ones through volunteer work. Make this effort as soon as possible to speed the process of meeting new people, making new friends, and developing a healthy social network.

Know What to Do If You Lose Your Job

For many reasons, you may find yourself unemployed. Rapidly changing technology, economic downturns, and corporate mergers are a few of the reasons you may be laid off. Many people face this at some point during their careers.

Sometimes employees are fired. Firing may be the result of a personality conflict, office politics, a lack of skills, a poor attitude, absenteeism, or other unpleasant circumstances. You may never actually be fired, but it does happen. Regardless of the fairness of the situation, the results are the same: unemployment and the need to find a new job.

If you receive the proverbial pink slip as a result of being either laid off or fired, heed the following do's and don'ts:

▲ **Do** try to have a calm and nonthreatening conversation with your supervisor to clarify the reason for your termination if you don't already know it. Ask your supervisor for advice and support. Find out whether the organization offers outplacement assistance. By responding to your termination professionally, you can limit or eliminate a negative reference. You may even receive a positive reference and assistance in finding another job.

▲ **Do** give yourself a day or two—but no longer—to reflect on what happened and to put it into perspective. Begin to think about a positive future.

▲ **Do** review all of Chapter 1. Consider how you can apply the nine success strategies to strengthen your job search and career planning activities. Focus on positive self-talk, visualization, effective goal setting, proactive action planning, and assertiveness. This will energize your job search campaign.

▲ **Do** reestablish and rebuild your personal support system. You need it now more than ever.

▲ **Do** connect with and add to your network. Begin contacting people and asking them to refer you to several others to get a strong network established again. Repeat the process you used to obtain your last position.

▲ **Do** review this text, all the information you developed and stored in your Career Management Files Binder and your

> *"When one door closes, another door opens; but we so often look so long and so regretfully upon the closed door, that we do not see the ones which open for us."*
>
> Alexander Graham Bell

Learner's CD. Update your resume, and begin the job-hunting process anew. Carefully consider whether you need a new job or a career change.

▲ **Don't** make things worse by verbally (or physically) attacking your supervisor or anyone else before leaving. Prospective employers are likely to contact your previous employers for references. Do not add to your problems.

▲ **Don't** begin applying for jobs the same day you get the bad news. You won't be in the right frame of mind to make good decisions or to present a confident and positive image to a potential employer.

Dealing with a Layoff or Downsizing

In the case of permanent layoffs or downsizing, the employer usually gives some advance notice. *Before* the actual layoff occurs is the time to reapply the job-seeking skills presented in earlier chapters of this book. Acting quickly is critically important because being employed is one factor that makes getting hired easier.

Use the term *laid off* rather than *fired* in your responses during job interviews; *laid off* has a less negative connotation than *fired*. Discuss the situation as briefly and as positively as possible. Avoid making negative statements about your former employer. Instead, emphasize the positive things you have learned from the experience that will make you a valuable employee.

Surviving Being Fired

There is life after being fired! Should this misfortune be your fate, take heart in knowing that literally hundreds of thousands of people who lost their jobs

> *"A sense of purpose generates action and movement in the direction of dreams and goals. Set your sights on what you want in your career and then make it happen. Now, what are you waiting for?"*
>
> Joan C. Borgatti, R.N., M.Ed.
> Editorial Director,
> NursingSpectrum.com

sometime in their past are now happily and successfully employed. You can successfully survive a job loss if you focus on looking for new opportunities. Also keep the following pointers in mind:

▲ **Do** analyze objectively what you learned from the experience. What did you gain from the work experience? What can you improve or avoid in future situations to make yourself a good employee for someone else?

▲ **Don't** blame others and don't dwell on how unfairly you were treated or on all the injustices your former employer committed against you and other employees.

▲ **Do** remember that many people have been fired and have gone on to enjoy highly successful careers. Remind yourself that this is the beginning of new opportunities, not the end of the world.

Using Your Career Management Files Binder and Your Learner's CD to Speed Up Your Job Search

Keep this book and your Career Management Files Binder containing all your completed assignments. They provide a solid foundation that will make your next job search easier and more efficient. Update and revise your job search documents as necessary. This will help you greatly during the process of finding a new job—after a layoff or by your own choice. Immediately reactivate and rebuild your network groups. Start by contacting people with whom you are close. Ask each of them to provide you with the names of two other people you can contact to expand your network.

Complete Career Action 20-5

CAREER ACTION 20-5

Review Your Proactive Success Action Plan

In Chapter 1, Career Action 1-5, you accessed the *Your Career: How to Make It Happen* web site and completed the Proactive Success Action Plan form. You completed the form by identifying a goal that was most important to you at the time. In addition, you identified success strategies from Chapter 1 that you could use to accomplish the goal you identified. You then filed your completed Proactive Success Action Plan form in your Career Management Files Binder.

Directions: Retrieve and review your Proactive Success Action Plan. Review it carefully, and then note exactly what progress you have made on the plan since you first wrote it. If you applied the strategies you outlined on the form, you should have made some clear progress. Update your plan as needed, and re-file it in your binder. Keep in mind the importance of using the nine success strategies throughout your career to reach your fullest potential!

Success Tip

When making a job change, build a network of contacts, follow your Proactive Success Action Plan, apply the success strategies (especially positive thinking!), and refer to your tools (your Career Management Files Binder and this book). You can make it happen!

Conclusion

The average American makes a minimum of eight job changes in a lifetime. (Some career changes are included in this number.) All the work you have done in this book to assess and document your experience, education, interests, goals, objectives, and capabilities and to develop resumes, cover letters, and other career management documents will be useful to you now and in the future. This experience will give you a decided competitive edge throughout your career. As you progress in your career throughout your life, continue to set your sights on what you want and then make it happen. You have all the tools—now go out and do it!

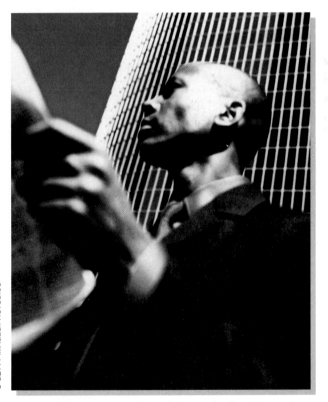

© GETTY IMAGES/PHOTODISC

Set your sights on your goals, and then make them happen!

CHECKLIST

MAKING SUCCESSFUL JOB AND CAREER CHANGES

Check each of the actions you are currently taking to increase your career success:

○ Staying on the cutting edge of the workforce by continuing your education

○ Before changing jobs or careers, determining whether your discontent is job-based or career-based

○ Considering the pros and cons of staying in your current job before making a change; not quitting until after you have secured another job

○ Changing to a new career if it's realistically available and meets your needs

○ Resigning professionally from your current job

○ In relocating, considering the impact on your loved ones, the impact on your career goals, your values and interests, and the costs involved

○ In relocating, researching the new community before moving and building a new support network immediately upon arriving

CRITICAL THINKING QUESTIONS

1. Why has lifelong learning become crucial to career success?

2. What are at least two benefits you can gain by changing employers when seeking a job change?

3. Under what circumstances should you consider changing careers?

4. What actions should you take to resign professionally from a job?

 For convenient access to valuable career resources, activities, and job information links, visit the companion web site for this text: *http://levitt.swlearning.com*

Appendices

SAMPLE BUSINESS LETTER AND E-MAIL FORMATS

To project professionalism in your job search and career development written communications, use appropriate business formats. Listed below are guidelines for formatting a business letter and an e-mail message. Illustrations of these document formats follow the guidelines.

Business Letter Format (see model on page 338):
Use the following guidelines to format your business letters correctly:

1. Prepare standard business letters on 8 1/2- by 11-inch letterhead. If you don't have your own letterhead stationery (not expected for an individual) use a high-quality bond stationery.

2. Use the block style letter format illustrated on the following page. General guidelines for the placement of the letter parts are indicated on the illustration. A few specific tips are emphasized below.

3. Place the return address and date based on the length of the letter.

   For an average-length letter, begin the return address at the left margin at approximately the 2-inch top margin point. If the letter is long, place this section higher on the page to achieve a more balanced placement. Place the date directly under the return address and at the left margin.

4. Key a double space (two hard returns) between the salutation and the body of the letter, between each paragraph, and between the last line of the body of the letter and the complimentary close.

5. Key four hard returns between the complimentary close and the name of the sender.

E-mail Message Format (see model on page 339):
Follow the guidelines below to format an e-mail message correctly:

1. **Format:** Use a heading similar to that of a standard business memo. Include the To, From, Date, and Subject information to communicate clearly and quickly. Most e-mail programs contain a form at the top of the message screen for filling in this information.

2. **Case:** Use the standard mix of upper- and lowercase letters. (Using all caps is like SHOUTING ON THE NETWORK!) Entire messages in all capital letters are also extremely hard to read.

3. **Brief but complete:** Keep e-mail messages short and focused on one subject, but be sure to include all information necessary for the recipient to take appropriate action and to reach you.

4. **Professional:** As with hard-copy documents, your professional reputation is reflected in e-mail:

   a. Plan and organize the message.

   b. Prepare a draft, proofread, and revise.

   c. Be courteous.

   d. Use correct spelling and grammar.

1008 North Lindsey Avenue   (Begin writer's address at left margin at
Boise, ID 83706   approximately the 2-inch top margin point.
January 25, 20—   Starting line varies based on letter length.)
     (Date)

(4 line spaces, 3 blank lines)

Mr. Benito Suarez   (Letter address at left margin)
1235 Lake Hazel
Boise, ID 83709

(Always 2 line spaces, 1 blank line)

Dear Mr. Suarez: (Salutation)

(Always 2 line spaces, 1 blank line)

**** ***** **** * **** ** **** *** ** *** ** **** *** **** ***** *** ****** (Body of letter)
**** * ***. ********* ****** * ******* ***** *** ***** *** * ****** *** **** *
***** ** *** ** **** ********* **** ** **********.

(All lines start at left margin.)   (Always 2 line spaces, 1 blank line)

**** **** **** **** *** * *** **** ** **** ** *** ********* ***. * **** ** **** *****
***** **** *** * *****.

(Always 2 line spaces, 1 blank line)

****** ***** **** ** * ***** *** **** **** *** **** *** ***** *** *** * ****** *** ** *
******. **** ** * ********* *** ******** ******** ** *** ********. ** **** *** ***
**************** **** **** ******* *** **** *********.

(Always 2 line spaces, 1 blank line)

Sincerely,   (Complimentary close at left margin)

(4 returns)

Ashley Curie (Sender's written signature here)

Ashley Curie   (Keyed name of sender at left margin)

Business Letter Format

From: Joe Ming   *(E-Mail heading,*
Date: Friday, May 8, 20— 1:57 PM   *usually a form fill-in)*
To: Cheryl Yordy, MacroTech Corporation
Subject: Confirmation of Meeting, May 12, 20—   *(Include a subject.)*

This message is a confirmation of *** * ****** ******* **** ***** ** ******* *** *****
* ** ******* ****** ******** ** ******** **** ****** **** ****** **** *** ****** ****
*** ******** *** ***** ***** ** ***** ****** **** ****.   *(Body of message)*

** **** ******* **** ** ***** ****** *** ***** **** **** **** **** **** *** ** ** *** *** **** **
******* **** ** ***** ****** ***.

* **** *** **** **** *** * *** ***** *** ******** *** **** *** ** **** ***** **** * **** ***
*************.

Contact Information:
Joe Ming
E-mail address: ming@provider.net
Web site: www.jming.com
Fax number: 707-555-0180
Telephone: 707-555-0181
Mailing address: 8200 Whitney Avenue, Vacaville, CA 95688

E-mail Message Format

CAREER MANAGEMENT AND MARKETING TOOLS

Three important career management and marketing tools are recommended to help you reach your full career potential: (1) a Career Management Files Binder, (2) a career portfolio, and (3) an Interview Marketing Kit. These tools are discussed in various chapters throughout this text and are further summarized below as a convenient reference.

Career Management Tool 1: Career Management Files

In using this textbook, you will develop information and documents you can use throughout your life to help achieve each new job and career goal. This material will consist of information you record in your Career Actions as well as drafts of job search documents you create in these assignments, such as your resume, cover letter, networking lists, and more. Altogether this valuable career data will form your Career Management File. This data provides the essential base of career information you will need throughout your career. This information will also be in a format that is easy to retrieve and update any time you seek a new position in your career.

Compiling Your Career Management Files

1. **Organize Your Data—Create a Career Management Files Binder.** Set up a system for collecting, organizing, and updating your career information. You will need most of this data whenever you seek a new job, an advancement, or a new career. Use a ring binder to serve as your Career Management Files Binder. Include 20 divider tabs, labeled Chapter 1 through Chapter 20.

2. **File Completed Career Actions.** Place all completed Career Action forms or other written assignments (such as your resume, cover letter, and other career documents you develop) behind the corresponding chapter tab in your Career Management Files Binder. You can also use tabs with topic labels, such as "network list," "references," "resume," "cover letter," and so on.

IMPORTANT: Look for this icon appearing with selected Career Actions:

 Career Management Files Binder. This icon indicates that the completed assignment should be printed and stored in your Career Management Files Binder.

3. **Use Your Learner's CD or the Career Action Forms in Your Text.** Most of the Career Action Worksheets in the text are also available on your Learner's CD. Use the electronic version of these forms on the CD whenever possible (although you can use the paper forms included in your textbook). The new Learner's CD increases the convenience of preparing Career Action Worksheets because the forms are interactive Word files you fill out using the keyboard.

IMPORTANT: Look for this icon appearing with selected Career Action Instructions:

 This icon indicates that the information you record for the Career Action can be accessed and prepared using your Learner's CD.

4. **Back Up Your Career Action Work:** Save your completed Career Action forms from your Learner's CD as well as the other career documents you create in this course (resume, cover and other letters, reference sheet, and so on) onto your hard drive or network drive. Much of this information will be valuable to you throughout your career for use in revising and updating your career documents and reference data. Also back up your files on a CD or other storage media.

File your Learner's CD and backup CD along with the printouts of your assignments in your Career Management Files Binder. In this way, you will be creating an electronic "Career-to-Go" of data you can take with you and easily update or revise any time you seek a promotion or a job or career change.

Career Management Tool 2: Career Portfolio

The Career Portfolio is an organized master collection of items demonstrating job-specific skills and work qualifications. Some examples of appropriate portfolio items include your resume; an official copy of your transcript(s); exemplary samples of your work, such as business writing, graphic arts samples, and printed samples from software presentations; evidence of sophisticated computer usage, such as desktop publishing and web site creation; awards and commendations; work performance evaluations; and letters of reference.

Portfolio samples can be from paid or volunteer work, internships, cooperative education, clubs, community activities, and more. A comprehensive list of appropriate items and ideas for building your portfolio is included under the heading "Sample Portfolio Items," which appears in the next column.

Note: You will likely want to file original documents, such as school transcripts, in your Career Management Files Binder and include copies of these documents in your Career Portfolio. This way you will retain a clean master and still have a copy for demonstration during interviews.

Identifying Items for Your Portfolio

Begin by identifying your skills and experiences that relate directly to your job target. Then consider carefully what you have done or accomplished that best demonstrates those qualifications. For example, if you are seeking an accounting job, include your transcripts listing appropriate course work; a CD containing samples of budgets you developed or accounts receivable or accounts payable reports you prepared; a letter of recommendation from an employer for bookkeeping or accounting work you performed; and so on. See a comprehensive list of ideas for portfolio items under the heading, "Sample Portfolio Items," which appears below.

Assembling Your Portfolio

For a traditional portfolio, use a professional-looking three-ring binder that holds 8 1/2- by 11-inch pages. File and categorize all of your portfolio documents behind tabbed sections in the binder. Use sheet protectors, CD inserts, and other accessories to display and protect your portfolio items. Larger portfolios (17 by 22 inches) are appropriate for art designers, journalists, advertising specialists, and technical writers to store and categorize oversized documents and credentials.

Sample Portfolio Items

Examples of portfolio components include:

▲ Paper documents.

▲ CDs containing text-based documents.

▲ Multimedia CDs or DVDs containing sound or video clips and other presentation content.

▲ Video- or audiotapes.

▲ Pictures/photographs.

▲ Other items that can be used to demonstrate your qualifications.

To aid in assembling your portfolio, review the following list of suggested components, but don't limit yourself to these. Use your imagination and strive for a close match with your target job.

To Demonstrate Work Experience, Work Performance, and Credentials

▲ **Resume:** Include error-free copies of your resume printed on quality paper. This should be the first item in your portfolio.
  Also, include in your portfolio a CD that contains your scannable print resume and your electronic resume for employers who prefer those formats. Place the media in a protective jacket or case.

▲ **Employer or Internship Performance Reviews:** Include copies of all favorable reviews.

▲ **Licenses:** Include for professions requiring a license to work in the field.

▲ **List of References:** Include a listing of references' names, addresses, and phone numbers and their association to you. Past employers, direct supervisors, and instructors are all good references.

▲ **Letters of Recommendation/Commendation:** Include these letters since they speak for themselves.

Education, Training, Degrees, and Certificates

▲ **Diploma/Degree:** Place a copy of your diploma(s) or degree(s) in your portfolio; place originals in your Career Management Files Binder.

▲ **Transcripts:** If your academic performance was good, keep copies of your transcripts in your portfolio to demonstrate this strength. Place your original transcripts in your Career Management Files Binder.

▲ **Certificates:** Include professional certification (CPA, CPS, CET, PE, teaching certificates, and so on) since this is evidence of life-long learning. Certificates of completion for continuing education, specialized training, workshops, seminars, and so on, are important because they, too, demonstrate career development.

▲ **Awards:** Include awards showing perfect attendance on the job and in school; academic accomplishments; or employee of the month, quarter, or year. Awards are proof of outstanding accomplishments and are of interest to employers.

Samples of Work, Use of Technology and Information

▲ **Design Work:** Include computer or manual drawings in the field of drafting to prove technical ability in mechanical, architectural, structural, or electrical designs. Include computer-aided drafting design (CAD) examples where appropriate. Interior design work as it pertains to decorators can also be demonstrated through drawings, photographs, and videotapes.

▲ **Artwork:** Include samples of sketches, drawings, and paintings; photographs or video footage; or computer-generated items in your career portfolio.

▲ **Writing Samples:** Showcase your best work if you are an author, an editor, or a reporter. Include samples of technical writing, reports, articles, business plans, instructional or training materials, institutional improvement plans, proposals, written

content for web sites, and mission statements you have composed. The ability to communicate is important to employers.

▲ **Software-Generated Documents:** Include your best examples from school if you're preparing to graduate and lack related job experience. Provide such items as electronic spreadsheets, database documents, newsletters, or presentation documents. If you have on-the-job work experience, include relevant copies of your actual work.

▲ **Publicity/Press Coverage:** Include articles highlighting your work, volunteer, community, or professional activities or other special accomplishments. Sources for these are school, employers, or professional publications such as newsletters, newspapers, journals, magazines, and so on. Use printed and online resources.

Other

▲ **Examples of Community Service:** Include any materials that demonstrate active involvement in community service.

▲ **Forms of Identification:** Place front and back photocopies of a valid driver's license, social security card, or photo ID in your portfolio for easy retrieval. Many employers request at least two forms of identification to process your application.

▲ **Proof of Citizenship.** Include copies of your birth certificate, passport, visas, and/or immigration forms. These documents can be used to show you are eligible to work.

Web E-Portfolio

For some career industries, a career portfolio developed as a web document is appropriate. This is called an e-portfolio or web portfolio, which contains documents formatted for display on the Internet. Virtually everything you could assemble in a standard portfolio (described above) can be formatted as pages of a web portfolio. If you develop a web resume or personal web site, you can include a link to your web portfolio. Use your favorite search engine to find samples of web portfolios and articles on web portfolios that may provide useful ideas for you. Enter the search string *web portfolio* to initiate your search. You can also include web addresses for your web site and web portfolio in your cover letter and on your resume and business card.

Career Management Tool 3: Interview Marketing Kit

The Interview Marketing Kit is a professional-looking folder containing items from the master Career Portfolio. You select the items from your master portfolio to meet the specific needs of each employer. In other words, your Interview Marketing Kit should be tailored and assembled using Career Portfolio items selected specifically for each interview. During interviews, you can extract appropriate portfolio items from your Kit that demonstrate your qualifications. This tangible evidence of abilities often gives candidates a winning edge in competing for a job. Choose items that match the needs of the specific target employer. After your interview, you can refile the items in your master Career Portfolio.

The kit should also contain an "Interview Survival Pack." These are supplies that can bail you out of a situation that could diminish your confidence and performance. They include rescue items such as a comb, a toothbrush, breath freshener, and a spare tie for a man or an extra pair of nylons for a woman.

Selecting Portfolio Items to Place in Interview Marketing Kit

Before each interview, select items from your Career Portfolio that best pertain to this specific job target. Don't use every item in your primary Career Portfolio for every interview. Place the items you select in your Interview Marketing Kit. Arrange the portfolio items in your Interview Marketing Kit in the order that best demonstrates how your abilities relate specifically to the employer's needs. Examples of appropriate items for your Interview Marketing Kit are as follows:

1. Items from your Career Portfolio that best support the needs of the organization with which you are interviewing:

   ▲ Job-related samples of your work, if applicable (from your work, educational, or training experience)

   ▲ Required certificates, licenses, transcripts, or other related documents

   ▲ Forms of identification

   ▲ Spare copies of your resume

   ▲ Letters of recommendation

   ▲ List of references appropriate for the job

2. Your 60-Second Commercial summarizing your qualifications for the job (see Chapter 11)

3. A list of pertinent questions you can ask during the interview (see Chapter 14)

Note: Review items 2 and 3 just before your interview. Don't read from them during the interview.

Using Portfolio Items During Your Interview

Ask if the interviewer would like to see samples from your portfolio before displaying anything. Even if the interviewer prefers not to review them, having portfolio items conveys that you are professional and organized. During the interview, you may still have an opportunity to offer a portfolio sample if the topic suggests it. Employers typically ask questions about your resume. At this point, you can use your portfolio items to support your responses. Do not misrepresent yourself in the portfolio items; the work must be your own. Be prepared to reproduce the work if requested to do so.

To make a good first impression and to capture the interviewer's attention, refer to one of your most impressive accomplishments first. Provide evidence of the accomplishment with an appropriate portfolio item. Save another exceptional item for the end of your interview to leave a memorable final impression.

Have a friend conduct a mock interview with you, and practice referring to your portfolio items at key points during the questioning process. This will prepare you to make a smooth delivery during your actual interviews.

REFERENCE READING

Job Search and Career Management

Bolles, Richard N. *What Color Is Your Parachute 2005?* Berkeley, CA: Ten Speed Press, 2004.

Cook, Marshall J. *Time Management: Proven Techniques for Making the Most of Your Valuable Time.* Holbrook, MA: Adams Media Corporation, 1998.

Criscito, Pat. *e-Resumes: A Guide to Successful Online Job Hunting.* Hauppague, NY: Barron's Educational Series, Inc., 2004.

Decker, Bert. *Speaking With Bold Assurance: How to Become a Persuasive Communicator.* Nashville, TN: Broadman and Holman Publishers, 2001.

Dikel, Margaret Riley. *Guide to Internet Job Searching, 2004-2005.* New York: McGraw-Hill, 2004.

Dixon, Pam. *Job Searching Online for Dummies.* New York: Hungry Minds, Inc., 2002.

Ferrara, Thomas. *Job Seeker Secrets: Making the Internet Work for You.* Cincinnati, OH: Thomson South-Western, 2003.

Ireland, Susan. *The Complete Idiot's Guide to the Perfect Resume.* Royersford, PA: Alpha, 2003.

Job Choices. Bethelem, PA: National Association of Colleges and Employers 2005. (Annual publication, usually available at college career centers.)

Johnson, Spencer and Kenneth H. Blanchard. *Who Moved My Cheese? An Amazing Way to Deal With Change in Your Work and in Your Life.* New York: Putnam Pub Group, 1998.

Kelly, Robert E. *How to Be a Star at Work: Nine Breakthrough Strategies You Need to Succeed.* New York: Random House, 1999.

Kennedy, Joyce Lain. *Job Interviews for Dummies.* New York: Hungry Minds, Inc., 2000.

Kennedy, Joyce Lain. *Resumes for Dummies.* New York: Wiley Publishing, Inc., 2003.

Krannich, Caryl. *Interview for Success: A Practical Guide to Increasing Job Interviews, Offers, and Salaries.* Manassas Park, VA: Impact Publications, 2002.

Parker, Yana. *Damn Good Resume Guide, Fourth Edition.* Berkeley, CA: Ten Speed Press, 2002.

Tracy, Brian and Campbell Fraser. *TurboCoach: A Powerful System for Achieving Breakthrough Career Success.* New York: American Management Association, 2005.

Wahlstrom, Carl and Brian Williams. *College to Careers: Your Road to Personal Success.* Cincinnati, OH: Thomson South-Western, 2004.

White, Aggie. *Interview Styles and Strategies, The Professional Development Series.* Cincinnati, OH: Thomson South-Western, 2003.

Yate, Martin. *Cover Letters That Knock 'Em Dead.* Holbrook, MA: Adams, Inc., 2004.

Yate, Martin. *Knock 'Em Dead 2005: The Ultimate Job Seeker's Guide.* Holbrook, MA: Adams, Inc., 2004.

Personal Motivation, Communication, and Assertiveness

Alberti, Robert E. and Michael L. Emmons. *Your Perfect Right.* San Luis Obispo, CA: Impact Publishers, 2001.

Baer, Jean. *How to Be an Assertive (Not Aggressive) Woman in Life, in Love, & on the Job: The Total Guide to Self-Assertiveness.* New York: NAL Ford-Dutton, 1991.

Bennett, Carole. *Business Etiquette and Protocol, The Professional Development Series.* Cincinnati, OH: Thomson South-Western, 2001.

Booher, Dianna. *E Writing: 21st Century Tools for Effective Communication.* New York: Pocket Books, 2001.

Booher, Dianna. *Speak With Confidence: Powerful Presentations That Inform, Inspire and Persuade.* New York: McGraw-Hill, 2002.

Briles, Judith and John Maling. *The Confidence Factor: Cosmic Gooses Lay Golden Eggs.* New York: Mile High Press, 2001.

Brown, Patricia. *Electronic Presentations, 10-Hour Series.* Cincinnati, OH: Thomson South-Western, 2001.

Buckingham, Marcus and Curt Coffman. *First, Break All the Rules: What the World's Greatest Managers Do Differently.* New York: Simon & Schuster, 1999.

Buckingham, Marcus and Donald O. Clifton. *Now, Discover Your Strengths.* New York: Simon & Schuster, 2001.

Burnell, Ivan. *The Power of Positive Doing—12 Strategies for Taking Control of Your Life.* Center Ossipee, NH: IPD Publishing, 1999.

Carnegie, Dale. *How to Win Friends and Influence People.* New York: Simon & Schuster, 1998.

Cooper, Ann. *Professional Image, The Professional Development Series.* Cincinnati, OH: Thomson South-Western, 2003.

Covey, Stephen R. *The 7 Habits of Highly Effective People: Powerful Lessons in Personal Change.* New York: Simon & Schuster, 2004.

Covey, Stephen R. *The 8th Habit: From Effectiveness to Greatness.* New York: Free Press, 2004.

Downing, Skip. *On Course: Strategies for Creating Success in College and in Life.* Wilmington, MA: Houghton Mifflin Company, 2004.

Frankl, Viktor. *Man's Search for Meaning.* Boston, MA: Beacon Press, 2000.

Goldsmith, Joan and Kenneth Cloke. *Resolving Conflicts at Work.* San Francisco, CA: Jossey-Bass, 2000.

Goleman, Daniel. *Emotional Intelligence: Why It Can Matter More Than IQ.* New York: Bantam Dell Publishing, 10th Anniversary Edition, 2005.

Goleman, Daniel. *Working with Emotional Intelligence.* New York: Bantam Dell Publishing, 2000.

Gordon, Douglas, Career Solutions Training Group. *Self-Management and Goal Setting, Quick Skills Series.* Cincinnati, OH: Thomson South-Western, 2000.

Gray, John. *How to Get What You Want and Want What You Have.* New York: HarperCollins, 2000.

Heim, Pat, Susan Murphy, and Susan Golant. *In the Company of Women: Turning Workplace Conflict into Powerful Alliances.* New York: J.P. Tarcher, 2001.

Hill, Napoleon. *Think and Grow Rich.* San Francisco, CA: Wilshire Publishing, 1999.

Knight, Sue. *NLP at Work.* Naperville, IL: Nicholas Brealey Publishing, 2002.

Leech, Thomas. *How to Prepare, Stage, and Deliver Winning Presentations.* New York: AMACOM, 2004.

Levitt, Julie G. and Jeff Craig. *Power Tools for Business Writing.* Cincinnati, OH: Thomson South-Western, 2006.

Peale, Norman Vincent. *The Power of Positive Thinking.* New York: Random House, 1996.

Peters, Thomas. *In Search of Excellence: Lessons From America's Best-Run Companies.* New York: HarperCollins, 2004.

Phelps, Stanlee and Nancy Austin. *The Assertive Woman.* San Luis Obispo, CA: Impact Publishers, 2002.

Robbins, Anthony. *Unlimited Power: The New Science of Personal Achievement.* New York: Simon & Schuster, 1997.

Rokes, Beverly. Career Solutions Training Group. *Advancing Your Career, Quick Skills Series.* Cincinnati, OH: Thomson South-Western, 2002.

Rokes, Beverly. Career Solutions Training Group. *What Your Employer Expects, Quick Skills Series.* Cincinnati, OH: Thomson South-Western, 2002.

Rozakis, Laurie. *The Complete Idiot's Guide to Public Speaking.* New York: Alpha Books, 1999.

Siegel, Bernie. *Prescriptions for Living.* New York: HarperCollins, 1999.

Tracy, Brian. *Focal Point: A Proven System to Simplify Your Life, Double Your Productivity, and Achieve All Your Goals.* New York: AMACOM, 2004.

Waitley, Denis. *The Psychology of Winning.* Niles, IL: Nightingale-Conant, 2005. (Audio CD and MP3 download)

Ziglar, Zig. *See You At the Top.* El Toro, CA: Pelican Publishing Co., 2000.

401(k) or 403(b) plans   tax-deferred savings plans offered by many large companies

A

active close   a cover letter closing in which you say that you will call to request a meeting or an interview

affirmation statements   positive self-statements or reminders to help achieve goals; positive messages that motivate your subconscious to work for you

aggressive body language   body language that appears brash and overbearing and sends offensive messages that convey hostility, pushiness, intimidation, and a domineering attitude

assertive behavior   behavior that promotes equality and a healthy balance in human relationships (includes standing up for your rights; expressing yourself honestly, courteously, and comfortably; and observing and respecting the rights of others)

assertive body language   body language that is relaxed, open, and confident; it agrees with and supports your words and conveys competence, self-assurance, caring, and credibility

attitude   the essence of your personality

B

baby boomers   the 76 million people born between 1946 and 1964

background check   a consumer report that employers use to screen potential employees

behavioral interview   structured interview in which the interviewer asks questions aimed at getting the applicant to provide specific examples of how he or she has successfully used the skills required for the target job

behavioral questions   interview questions that probe the applicant's specific past performance and behaviors; based on the premise that past performance is the best predictor of future behavior

board or panel interview   structured interview performed by more than one interviewer at the same time

business etiquette   expected professional behavior in business; based on courtesy and cultural norms

C

campus interviews   prearranged screening interviews given by organizations to graduating students in such fields as engineering, electronics, business management, legal, accounting, computer information systems, and marketing

career   a family of jobs; your life's work

career goal setting   recording clear objectives and the actions required to achieve them

career information surveys   meetings you arrange to obtain general career information and advice from prospective employers or from employees who hold jobs that are similar to your job target

career portfolio   an organized collection of relevant examples of skills and achievements that can be presented during an interview as tangible proof of your qualifications

character questions   interview questions that are asked to learn about the applicant's personal attributes, such as integrity, personality, attitudes, and motivation

code of ethics   a set of principles—written or unwritten—that guides your behavior

comparison-list style cover letter style that highlights a job seeker's qualifications in a two-column, side-by-side comparison of the employer's requirements and the job seeker's experience; also called a T-letter

compensation package the salary, potential for earnings growth, and all other benefits that come with a job

computer-assisted interview screening interview in which the applicant answers computerized multiple-choice, true/false, and/or essay questions at a computer workstation

computerized preemployment test preemployment test that is performed on a computer; may be general in content or a skills or personality test; often used for large applicant screenings

confidentiality agreement type of agreement that states that a company's representatives will not disclose or use clients' or suppliers' business information except for the legitimate purposes detailed in the agreement; also known as a nondisclosure agreement

Continuous Quality Improvement (CQI) quality assurance program adopted by companies to achieve International Organization for Standardization (ISO) certification; also known as Total Quality Management (TQM)

corporate ladder (or multilevel) interviews interview process involving several steps that is sometimes used by large organizations; the first step is a screening interview with the human resources department, the second step is an interview with a divisional manager or department head, and the third and possibly fourth steps are more specific interviews with employees who are closely related to the job opening

D

direct-mail job search mailing cover letters with requests for interviews along with your resume to prospective employers

E

electronic resume an ASCII text resume designed to be delivered via e-mail or an online e-form; must be completely stripped of word processing codes and is, therefore, a plain-looking document

ethics the moral principles that determine the rightness or wrongness of particular acts or activities

external customers customers who contribute to the success of companies by purchasing the final products and services

extranet a company's or an organization's private, closed computer network that is expanded to include customers, suppliers, and partners outside the company or organization

F

firewall a network security system that uses a special combination of hardware and software to restrict the types of information that can enter or exit the network, thereby protecting the computers on the network

follow up to take action to evaluate your performance in interviews, to remind prospective employers of your qualifications for and interest in the job, and to encourage a speedy hiring decision

G

gatekeeper the person who stands between you and an employer; may be an administrative support person, a receptionist, a supervisor, or a human resources staff member

general information questions interview questions that are asked to obtain factual information about the applicant; usually address the applicant's skills, education, work experience, and so on

groupware applications such as e-mail, team areas on web sites, and newsgroups; one of the three types of technologies used in an extranet

H

hidden job market   jobs that are not advertised

I

innovation   new ways of doing things

internal customers   employees who build on the work of coworkers and depend on receiving quality work to complete their own jobs successfully

Internet computer-assisted interview   screening interview in which the applicant answers computerized multiple-choice, true/false, and/or essay questions via the Internet

Internet video interview   interview that is performed over the Web using two-way video; cameras are attached to computers at two separate locations

internship   a period of supervised training in a workplace

intranet   a private, closed computer network used for internal communications to protect business information from competitive spying or sabotage

J

job   an occupation that involves performing a designated set of responsibilities and duties for a specific employer

job club   a group of job seekers who meet regularly to share experiences and advice, set goals, and offer encouragement; also known as a networking or job search club

job objective   a statement of your employment goal; a section in a resume

Job Qualifications Profile   a document that describes your abilities and experience and explains how they relate to your job target

job references   individuals who can and will vouch for your capabilities, skills, and suitability for a job; typically people who have been your instructors and coaches in school or your supervisors or coworkers in volunteer and paid work environments

job search package   resume, cover letter, and employment application

job-specific skills   the technical abilities that relate specifically to a particular job

K

keywords   specific words and phrases that represent the qualifications a company has instructed resume-search software to look for

M

mentor   someone inside or outside your organization who can advise and coach you; someone who is respected and knowledgeable in your field

N

networking   the process of developing relationships with people who can assist with job search strategies and in finding strong job leads

networking letter   a letter you send to a job search network member that explains your job search goals and requests specific help with the process

networks   systems of computer and communications technology that are used to link resources, making it easy for people to find, send, and receive information

nondisclosure agreement   type of agreement that states that a company's representatives will not disclose or use clients' or suppliers' business information except for the legitimate purposes detailed in the agreement; also known as a confidentiality agreement

nonverbal communication   body language

O

offshoring   the shipping of jobs overseas, where labor is cheaper

P

passive body language   body language that looks nonenergetic and diminishes your credibility by conveying insecurity, weakness, anxiety, and a lack of self-assurance and competence

passive close   a cover letter closing in which you request that the reader call you

personality test   preemployment test designed to determine whether your personal and behavioral preferences are well matched to the work involved in the job

portfolio   a collection of documents and other items that demonstrate your skills, abilities, achievements, experience, and training

portfolio career   a career made up of a variety of complementary activities that focus on your strengths and provide you with an acceptable level of monetary compensation

positive behavior   purposely acting with energy and enthusiasm

positive self-talk   purposely giving yourself positive reinforcement, motivation, and recognition

positive thinking   making a conscious effort to think with an optimistic attitude and anticipate positive outcomes

positive visualization   purposely forming a mental picture of your successful performance and recalling the image frequently

print resume   a word-processed resume designed to be visually appealing; to be delivered as an e-mail attachment, by mail, in person, or by fax; and to be scanned clearly into a database by computer software

proactive approach   a career-boosting approach to dealing with challenges that focuses on problem solution and positive action

R

reactive approach   a detrimental approach to dealing with challenges that focuses on problem avoidance and negative personal reactions

references   individuals who can and will vouch for your capabilities, skills, and suitability for a job; typically people who have been your instructors and coaches in school or your supervisors or coworkers in volunteer and paid work environments

resume   a short document that details your qualifications for a particular job or job target

S

screening interview   a preliminary interview conducted by a member of a company's human resources staff; performed to verify the information in the applicant's cover letter, resume, and application, as well as to get a sense of the applicant's personality

self-esteem   belief in your abilities and your worth

sexual harassment   type of discrimination that occurs when one person makes continued and unwelcome sexual advances toward, requests sexual favors from, and displays other verbal or physical conduct of a sexual nature toward another person against the person's wishes

skills test   preemployment test that evaluates your specific job-related skills

stress interview   type of interview that is designed to test the applicant's behavior, logic, and emotional control under pressure

stress questions   interview questions that are asked to determine how you perform under pressure and to find out whether you are good at making decisions, solving problems, and thinking under stress

structured interview   formal approach to interviewing that typically involves a planned pattern of questioning and sometimes the recording of the applicant's responses on a checklist or an interview rating form; the focus is on obtaining factual information

support system   the group of people who can motivate, advise, and encourage you during your job search and throughout your career

T

task-oriented interview   interview in which the applicant is asked to demonstrate his or her skills by performing specific tasks

team interview   structured interview that may be given by a group of three to five employees; each employee interviews the applicant separately

technical test   preemployment test designed to determine how much you know about a particular subject

telecommuters   individuals who work in virtual corporations or offices; also known as teleworkers or virtual employees

telephone interview   screening interview performed over the telephone

telework   the use of computers and telecommunications to change the accepted geography of work

teleworkers   individuals who work in virtual corporations or offices; also known as telecommuters or virtual employees

"tell me about yourself" interview   type of interview in which the interviewer takes a few minutes to build rapport with the applicant and then says, "Tell me about yourself."

T-letter   cover letter style that highlights a job seeker's qualifications in a two-column, side-by-side comparison of the employer's requirements and the job seeker's experience; also called comparison-list style

Total Quality Management (TQM)   quality assurance program adopted by companies to achieve International Organization for Standardization (ISO) certification; also known as Continuous Quality Improvement (CQI)

transferable competencies   abilities that can be applied in more than one work environment

U

unstructured interview   informal approach to interviewing that is generally taken by people who are not professionally trained in interviewing, especially owners and managers of small organizations

V

value   according to *Webster's New World Dictionary*, "that which is desirable or worthy of esteem for its own sake; the social principles, goals, or standards held or accepted by an individual"

virtual employees   individuals who work in virtual corporations or offices; also known as teleworkers or telecommuters

W

web resume   a resume that is formatted in HTML so it can be posted on the Internet as a web document; looks like an attractive print resume but can contain more sophisticated graphics